As God is my Witness

The Presbyterian Kirk The Covenanters & The Ulster Scots

By

Brian J. Orr

Published 2002 by

HERITAGE BOOKS, INC.
1540E Pointer Ridge Place, Bowie, Maryland 20716
1-800-398-7709
www.heritagebooks.com

ISBN 0-7884-2114-X

DEDICATION

FOR MY GRANDSONS

IAIN AND CIARAN

THAT THEY MAY KNOW THEIR ANCESTRY

TABLE OF CONTENTS

PART II - THE PEOPLE OF THE COVENANT

APPENDICES

Maps and Photographs

Maps

Photographs

Preface and Acknowledgements

By far the greater part of the primary sources for the history and biographies of the Covenanters now reside in the National Archives and the National Library of Scotland, or regional museums and in quite rare antiquarian books and papers in private collections. The early books and pamphlets were written mainly by ministers of the Kirk. And, as was the practice in the eighteenth and nineteenth centuries, they contain much biblical cross-reference. Pertinent and effective though the comments are to families brought up with 'the taking of the book' and twice daily family prayers, the colourful use of language can also make reading hard going. My aim therefore, has been to distil the essential history of the Reformation, the Presbyterian Kirk and the Covenanters along with the known facts of individuals, and present them for the interested reader who may not be so familiar with their Bible.

I should say that I have not in any way sought to make this book a definitive statement of the times or of the Covenanters, and not every person, nor detail of every debate or skirmish is necessarily dealt with. The English Civil Wars, the Irish Rebellion of 1641 and the subsequent war and Cromwell's campaign in Ireland, for example, are major events in their own right and outside the scope of this work save for a few highlights. The biographies in Part II are each a separate story about one of the men or women of the Covenant, including the Marquis of Montrose and Archbishop Sharp who later transferred their allegiance. In Part III, I have included a short history of the migration of the Scottish peoples, mainly Presbyterians, who went to Ulster in the Plantation period to escape persecution. From these hardy people stem the Ulster Scot migrants to America.

A substantial time line has been provided to help the reader place events in context and of itself is a precis of the history of the Scottish Reformation. The bibliography is in four broad categories to indicate further reading depending whether the interest is about the people, the history, Ireland or antiquarian resources. The appendices reproduce in part some of the text of documents central to the Presbyterian way and their persecution that are not easily come by. An appendix lists over 1,000 of the known martyrs and their untimely end; and others list the surnames of Scottish families and early ministers of the Kirk in Ireland, some of whom migrated with their congregation to America or fathered dynasties that did.

My thanks to Sandy Pittendreigh of the Dumfries and Galloway Family History Society who has allowed some of his excellent photographs to be used and Bill Blain in Waterdown, Ontario for his assistance in researching the Margaret Wilson statue. I sincerely hope that, as a whole, the book presents itself as a good read for all who are interested in their Scottish ancestry.

Brian J. Orr

Part I
History of the Covenanters

I. An Overview of the Seventeenth Century

The history and changes that occurred in Scotland and subsequently in Ireland through the seventeenth and eighteenth centuries are often highly charged by one word - Covenanters. So, who were they and why were they so influential?

It is easy to say that they were the Presbyterians who signed the "National Covenant" to uphold the Presbyterian religion in 1638, and the "Solemn League and Covenant" of 1643. But it isn't as simple as that - it was their stand for political and religious liberty and above all the rights of God on earth, that led to almost a century of persecution, and widespread migration to Ireland and then to the American colonies. Very importantly for the Scottish Nation, the Reformation brought an end to 500 years of French (Catholic) influence in Scotland.

The Presbyterian beliefs and demands contributed also to a close alliance with Protestant England, the union of the Protestant thrones of Scotland and England in 1603; the usurpation of Oliver Cromwell; the oppression of Charles II; the invitation to the Protestant William of Orange and Mary II (nephew and daughter respectively of the deposed King James II) to take the throne in 1689; and the Act of Union in 1707 joining the countries together politically.

Statue of John Knox
Courtesy of A. Pittendreigh

It is also necessary to understand what Presbyterianism is since it is not just another religion. A Presbyter was an elder, a senior member of the congregation, in the early Christian church. The name is also used for priest. In the Presbyterian denomination he is a member of the Presbytery, which is an official court of the district composed of pastors and elders. Therein lies the clue and fundamental issue to understand when Covenanter is mentioned. Presbyterianism, like any creed, is a way of life, but with a specific organisation set apart from the State. It recognises the government of each church by its elders with the churches associated in local presbyteries; represented in provincial Synods and in a General Assembly which is the highest court of appeal. This structure is that of the Scriptures which was closely and literally interpreted by 'The Covenanters' who were believers in a strict form of Presbyterianism. As witnesses for the rights of God and Christ as head of the Church, they opposed the rule by Bishops (Episcopacy) and the rule of the Church by the state (Erastianism), which were both absolute anathema to Presbyterians. Johannes Vos in *The Scottish Covenanters* succintly explains that

> *Their basic principle was not political, nor humanitarian but theocratic. They found the rights of God revealed in Scripture and they wished these to be practically recognised and respected in every sphere of life, including the State and the Church.*

The story of the Reformation in Scotland begins with the decline of the monasteries as they became less concerned with spiritual matters and more with the economics of land tenure and the material benefits the rents and tithes provided. The office of Bishop was frequently filled by political appointees from whom the monks, friars and nuns took their lead. It did not help matters that even the King took advantage of the system to ensure that his illegitimate children were cared for by such appointments - James I of Scotland, for example, had his eleven year old son created Archbishop of St. Andrews, securing for him the incomes that flowed to the post. The real needs of the populace at large was for true, local, pastoral care which neither the State nor Church was delivering.

The Protestant Reformation had begun in Europe with the work of Martin Luther (1483-1546), who on All Soul's Day, 31 October 1517 posted his ninety-five Theses on the church doors at Wittenberg, Germany. Another great influence was John Calvin (1509-1564) a French theologian who pursued a great moral reformation in Europe, especially in Geneva. The central theme of their beliefs was that of predestination - everything that happens is the will of God. It accepts the concept of eternal salvation and with it also eternal damnation. However, Calvin brought with it improved organisation and an encouragement for education. His was a harsh, but logical, creed that had enormous influence in Europe and later in the emerging America through the Presbyterian migrants.

The banner of Reformation in Scotland was taken up by John Knox (1515-1572), who, after a colourful early life (he was a French galley slave for a while), brought the Calvinist beliefs to Scotland in 1558. Knox was soon a leading light and a clever politician who came to an understanding with the Protestant Queen Elizabeth I of England that gained for himself and his friends the direction of their affairs. Knox was undoubtedly intolerant of some things and almost recklessly outspoken, while some regarded him as a fanatic for his defiant stance. But this was his strength that was used to devastating effect against the Romanism of the day. He was zealous in his pursuit of his beliefs and a powerful influence in moulding the religious and educational life of Scotland. He left to posterity his *Confession of Faith* (1560), *The First Book of Discipline* (1561), a new liturgy *The Book of Common Order* (1564) and a translation of Calvin's *Catechism*.

The reign of James VI in Scotland (1567-1625) saw a long struggle between the Presbyterians and the king who pursued his agenda to reintroduce bishops, ceremony, and himself as Head of the Church of Scotland. After Knox's death, the mantle of reform fell upon Andrew Melville (1545 - 1622), who held even more stringent views than Knox and he proposed a new system of church courts and synods. Underpinning this was the continued demand that all the old church properties, tithes and lands should be handed over to the new Protestant - Presbyterian Church who would use it to fund Poor Relief and education. The Crown's response in 1584 was to reaffirm the king as Head of the Church and the bishops as the tools for its management.

There was some relaxation in 1592 with the return of presbyteries and suspension of the role of the bishops. The King's agenda received a boost when, in 1603, he succeeded to the throne of England and removed his court to Westminster. Surrounded by sycophantic courtiers, and acknowledged as Head of the Church of England, he pursued his policy by stealth. In 1610, the administrative role of the bishop was reintroduced with more generous provision of funds for the church in the parish. Melville and his supporters continued to preach and circulate manuscripts and books illegally and gathered the support and admiration of the common people.

It was the accession of Charles I in 1625 that was a catalyst for yet more change and Civil War. Charles particularly threatened to take back the churches' rights to property and tithes, which greatly alarmed the holders of former church lands in Scotland. Charles was also a stubborn and extravagant man under the influence of his wife, Henrietta Maria, a French, Catholic, princess. Two of his ministers who featured very large in dealings with the Presbyterians and the Covenanters in particular were Thomas Wentworth, later created the Earl of Strafford, and Lord Deputy in Ireland, who was a zealous persecutor in Ulster; and, William Laud, Archbishop of Canterbury,

Statue of Andrew Melville
Courtesy of A. Pittendreigh

the senior prelate in the kingdom. Laud sought to impose on the Scots a new prayer book and the reintroduction of the mass and other Catholic practices in 1637. The King's decision to force the use of the Canons and Lauds Liturgy were both the cause and pretext for revolt in Scotland.

At Greyfriars Kirk in Edinburgh, representatives of the Scottish peoples gathered on 28 February 1638 to sign a "National Covenant." This restated the struggle against "popery" and declared their resistance to change in worship not previously approved by free assemblies and parliament; and pledged the signatories to defend their religion against all comers. It was not in fact anti government, nor did it refer to the bishops, but King Charles over reacted and regarded them as rebels. He assembled an army but relented and allowed the first General Assembly in twenty years to be convened at which the Assembly abolished the bishops. He rejected the decision, and once again, the army was mobilised while the vast majority of Scots united behind the Presbyterian cause.

In 1640, the Covenanting army, under Alexander Leslie, marched into northern England and occupied the city of Newcastle in Northumberland from which most of England's coal supplies were sent south. Charles I desperately sought to retain his throne, calling, dismissing and recalling Parliament several times in his desperation to obtain money to fund his enterprises. However, the Puritan opposition in Parliament, led by John Pym, were growing tired of Charles' autocratic and undemocratic ways and began to demand proper representation and the observance of Parliament's will in exchange for limited funds. This was the beginning of parliamentary democracy and the end of the Divine Right of Kings. In 1641 the English Parliament presented Charles with a "Grand Remonstrance" which listed the acts of oppression and tyranny for which he had been responsible in the past sixteen years. He attempted to arrest some Members of Parliament but failed and in January 1642 he left London.

In 1643, in return for a promise to give military help to English rebels, the Covenanters entered into a "Solemn League and Covenant" with the English Parliamentarians which would have enforced Presbyterianism as the faith in England, Wales and Ireland. The Covenant was endorsed by the Kirk in Scotland, but not in England. At last it seemed to the Covenanters that their goal was in sight but joy was relatively short lived as there were further bloody battles at Marston Moor (1644) and Naseby (1645) before King Charles was finally defeated.

After the King's execution in 1649, the Scots immediately proclaimed his son, Charles II, King of Scotland. The conditions required him to accept Presbyterianism and the Covenants, which he signed in June 1649. This was unacceptable to Cromwell and there followed a bloody battle at Dunbar on 3 September 1650 where he showed no mercy, exiling survivors to Plantations in America and Ireland. King Charles II was nevertheless crowned at Scone on 1 January 1651 but subsequent resistance by the royalist supporters was finally crushed by Cromwell at the battle of Worcester on 3 September 1651. From then, until 1660, the Covenanters were again suppressed, albeit by a more tolerant regime that allowed the Presbyterians and other non-conformist faiths to hold their meetings peaceably.

The return of Charles II from exile in 1660 began a period of revenge as he persecuted those who did not accept the Book of Common Prayer. The summoning of a new Parliament in 1661 saw, within days, a resolution (17 May 1661) that the Covenant should be publicly burnt and a Bill that declared the "Solemn League and Covenant" illegal (30 May 1661). In Scotland the Act of Uniformity in 1662 was mirrored by an Act of Proclamation in 1662, which banished all ministers who did not have a bishop's licence. Over 300 ministers were ejected from their manses in Scotland while in England the most accurate figure is 1909 ejected of whom about 170 later conformed to episcopacy. In Ireland about 64 ministers were ejected.

There were also fines imposed for non-attendance at church, which were collected by military force. The use of force in Scotland led to armed resistance with more bloodshed and eventually "The Killing Time" of 1684-5.

The Covenanter army, led by Colonel James Wallace, was defeated in a skirmish at Rullion Green near Edinburgh on 28 November 1666 by the King's troops, under the command of General Sir Thomas Dalziel of The Binns. Some fifty Covenanters and two Irish ministers were killed and over 100 prisoners taken and some executed as an example to others. The tale is told that the bodies of the dead were left where they lay and were scavenged for their clothes, boots, swords and personal effects and bodies stripped naked. It was the women who came out from Edinburgh and wound the bodies in cloths for burial.

A poignant place to be on a quiet summer eve is alongside the memorial raised to Rev. John Crookshank and Rev. Andrew McCormack and the Covenanters who died that day. This stands in a small railed enclosure on the edge of a pine plantation behind which are the rolling Pentland Hills into which the survivors fled, some to live and fight again, others to die of their wounds alone in the bogs and moors.

The Lowlands was under military rule by 1670 with troops billeted among the people. In the same year, an act was passed that sought to make the holding of conventicles impossible by requiring religious meetings to be held in parish churches. It also required the taking of an oath concerning conventicles, which turned neighbours and friends against one another. Failure to provide information was punishable by fine, imprisonment or banishment. Children had to be baptised within thirty days and parents had to produce the certificate on demand or be fined one quarter of their annual income. Rewards were offered for the capture of conventicle preachers and if the preacher was killed in the arrest then the-would be captor was promised freedom from prosecution. Further legislation in

1676 was the issue of Letters of Intercommuning. This was a legal device used for about 100 people who had failed to appear before the Privy Council when summoned. The letters had the effect of barring communication with these persons, and made it a crime punishable by death to associate with them or to provide shelter, food or to provide any kind of help whatsoever.

James Sharp, Archbishop of St Andrews was assassinated in 1679 and the Covenanters had modest military success against General John Graham of Claverhouse at Drumclog. But the Covenanter army of over 5,000 men was defeated at Bothwell Brig, near Glasgow, by the Duke of Monmouth on 22 June 1679 with 400 left dead and 1,100 taken prisoner. Two ministers were hanged and other prisoners were executed. The mass of the prisoners were placed under guard in a high walled and open yard adjacent to the Greyfriars Kirk, scene of the 1638 signing of the National Covenant. The prisoners were held for five months during which time they were brutally treated and many died from exposure. Those prisoners, who gave a bond and an undertaking never to take arms against the King, were released, while some 257 were sentenced to transportation to the West Indies. However, their ship - the "*Crown*," of London, sank in bad weather off of Deerness, Orkney with the hapless prisoners locked and chained below decks. Only forty-six are known to have survived. It is ironical that in the Greyfriars graveyard near by the open prison yard is the mausoleum of Sir George MacKenzie of Rosehaugh, who as King's Advocate for Scotland had prosecuted the Covenanters and was known as "Bluidy MacKenzie."

The effect of persecution was reflected in substantial migration of Scots to Ulster minded to settle there if land was available. It was estimated that about 30,000 went to Ulster between 1660 and 1690 and the numbers increased following bad harvests with an estimated 10,000 in 1692 alone. These migrants mostly entered Ulster via Londonderry and settled in the west of the province.

Ironically, the Scottish administration noted their concern at the exodus fearing that some heritors (landlords) would be left without tenants.

Despite defeats and severe penalties, the Covenanters continued to resist, led by such ministers as Donald Cargill and Richard Cameron, and were known as "Society Men" and "The Cameronians." Richard Cameron was killed in the summer of 1680 at Ayrsmoss but not before publishing a "Declaration at Sanquhar" calling for the removal of Charles II and effectively declaring war against the royalist government. The strongest and most extreme forms of Covenanting were to be found in Ayrshire and the southwest in Dumfries and Galloway where dissenting ministers became field preachers to large congregations. Their resistance took the form of guerrilla tactics which included having armed members of the congregation at open-air meetings or "conventicles." They were harassed by the government who were suspicious of treason, and by heavy-handed military and judicial reprisals.

After April 1681 harassment increased when a further proclamation was issued against conventicles requiring landlords to report the holding of them to the sheriff. Yet more stringent and Draconian legislation against the Covenanters appeared, this time making the giving or taking an oath or writing in defence of the National Covenant and the Solemn League and Covenant acts of treason and punishable as such. The death penalty was imposed for just attending a conventicle and private family worship with more than five non-family members present was treason. The horrors of "The Killing Time," when over a hundred Presbyterians were executed for their faith, lasted through 1684-5.

It was no better when James II took the throne in 1685 and his open support for the mass and appointments of Catholics to positions of power confirmed the worst fears of the Protestants in England and Scotland. However, other forces in England led to the call to William of Orange and Mary to take the Crown. In Ireland the Battle of the Boyne in 1690 finally assured the Protestant succession in Britain. Although the religious oppression had ended the strict Covenanters did not join the Revolutionary Church of Scotland but remained outside it as Praying Societies until 1743 when they became the Reformed Presbytery.

II. The Kirk and its impact on the people

The Covenanters were the staunchest supporters of Presbyterianism, the radicals of their day, who followed to a varying degree the very strict rules of John Calvin in Geneva, John Knox and Andrew Melville in Scotland. Although having the external appearance of cohesiveness, there were nevertheless internal contentions that reflected their belief that the congregation should be free to manage its own affairs according to their particular wants and needs. This gave rise to a range of reactions to the changes brought about by the Reformation in Scotland, which varied from a staid and resigned acceptance to vehement and vociferous opposition with breakaway pastors and congregations such as the "Cameronians."

So far as the general populace was concerned, they were not much bothered with the mechanics and politics of management by Presbyteries and Synods and a General Assembly. They listened to their minister and heeded his advice and instruction, but interference with the style of their worship by James VI and other autocratic Stuart kings riled them immensely. The changes imposed on them from 1625, when Charles I came to the throne, were much more visible and the populace responded accordingly. There was resentment of his policies while increased taxation of the burgesses filtered down to all levels that until then had been mainly concerned with their day-today existence. There were also periods when the Kirk took a firmer hold on society such as with a growth of Puritanism and the stricter Presbyterianism of Andrew Melville.

The "First Book of Discipline", produced by John Knox in 1560, made the Kirk the focus for the Presbyterians in which the elected senior members - the Elders, and the minister held great sway. It was through the "Kirk Session" - the local church court, that the day-to-day life of the congregation was overseen. Conceptually the Kirk session was responsible at local level for matters of conscience and religion but in practice ranged across almost everything. Amidst the turmoil, the Presbyterian way sought to bring social discipline and extended to drunkenness, excesses of all kinds whether drink or style of dress, fornication, oppression of the poor such as excessive taxation; deception in matters of buying and selling goods; and lewd behaviour.

The Presbyterian way also looked to help "the deserving poor" - the victims of old age and misfortune; the sick, the elderly, the widow and the fatherless but it was strongly opposed to helping the able bodied idle and beggars. With this social conscience came the ambitious proposal for a national education scheme, which would educate the young and provide a teacher in every church. Free education for the poor and the general requirement of education would, in time, be reflected in the relative literacy of migrants which would lead them to better jobs, and the ethos that a good education was important.

There was not a movement to Presbyterianism overnight, and isolated pockets of Catholicism, or other 'unacceptable practices', lingered on, especially in the Highlands and amongst the nobility. Another group outside the compass of the Kirk was the able-bodied vagrants, tinkers, traveling musicians and the like who owed loyalty to no one. Otherwise in the Lowlands of Scotland, the people generally became regular churchgoers and adherents to the rule of the Kirk. In some cases there

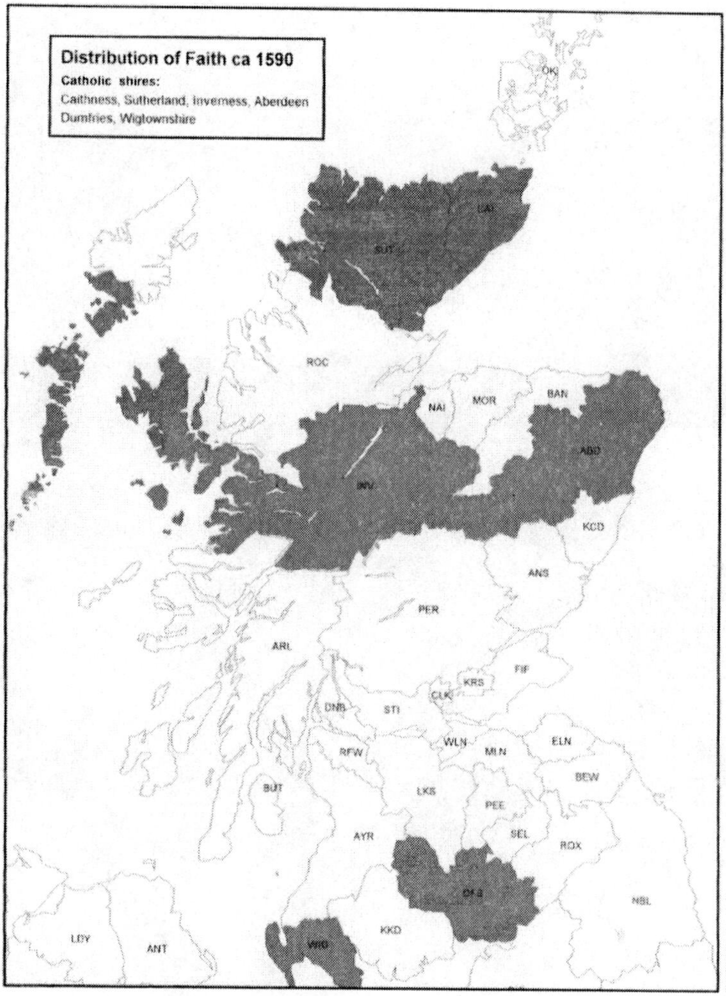
Distribution of Faith ca 1590
Catholic shires:
Caithness, Sutherland, Invemess, Aberdeen
Dumfries, Wigtownshire
SUT
ROC
NAI
MOR
BAN
ABD
INV
KCD
ANS
PER
ARL
FIF
KRS
CLK
DNB
STI
WLN
MLN
ELN
BEW
BUT
LKS
PEE
SEL
AYR
ROX
NBL
KKD
LDY
ANT

were pious burgesses and lairds whose sons entered the ministry. This involvement of the burgesses, who were often the local magistrates, enabled an early attack on moral delinquents, absentees from church and disrespectful behaviour.

The main offence heard by the kirk session seems to have been adultery and fornication. The penalty for adultery was to stand, dressed in sackcloth, bare headed and bare feet at the kirk door, then to sit on the stool of repentance in front of the congregation for perhaps six months or longer and be publicly reprimanded by the minister. Sometimes the punishment included fines and whipping. Few resisted, as under a law of 1581, the adulterer who refused the kirk's punishment could be put to death. Fornication, lewd behaviour, and prostitution were often punished by banishment from the town after the men forced to make public penance and the women by ducking in the foulest water available. Misbehaviour in the countryside was often not detected until pregnancy was obvious when much effort was put into identifying the father and compelling marriage. There was, too, several weeks of doing penance for the guilty couple.

Andrew Melville (1545-1622) was responsible for the "Second Book of Discipline" which is the basis of kirk management today. In the period 1574 to 1612, Puritanism and a zealous Presbyterianism that Melville advocated gained a foothold that punished a wide range of alleged excesses. These included attacks on Christmas and traditional holidays, such as Midsummer Eve, pilgrimages, dancing, carol singing, merrymaking at weddings, and wakes; and failing to work on Christmas Day were all subject of condemnation. In 1579 a law was passed banning Sunday travel, bodily recreation and drinking. The rules were relaxed for a while but a second and more intense phase of Puritanism appeared after 1638, with a renewed vigour, that was subsequently endorsed by Oliver Cromwell. In 1656 the ultimate law was passed that forbade frequenting taverns, dancing, listening to profane music, washing, brewing ale, baking bread, travelling or conduct any business on a Sunday. This, for example, led to punishment of children for playing on a Sunday, and a public warning about carrying water, sweeping the house or clearing ashes from the fireplace. In Glasgow there were paid spies to report lapses by the congregation.

So far as schooling was concerned, there was already a system of education and three universities in Scotland before the days of the Covenanters, but, this was available to those who could afford it, or depended on ministers who also acted as schoolmaster in the parish. There were thriving grammar schools in some burghs as well as monastic and singing schools attached to cathedrals and collegiate churches. Stirling, for example, in 1557 had a grammar school that rivalled the Glasgow College in classical languages and taught Latin, Greek and Hebrew. It also had schools for 'bairns' under six years of age who were taught to read and write. There were similar extensive classes available in schools in Aberdeen and Dunbar.

John Knox's "First Book of Discipline" was a declaration of policy and aims, which included the responsibilities of the community to maintain and improve the moral and social attitudes of the people. The plan for education was extensive and became a powerful force for the future of Scotland and its thousands of migrants to the far corners of the British Empire. In the Lowlands progress was quite good and at the turn of the sixteenth century there is evidence that parishes were competing to hire the best teachers they could afford. There was an element of kudos in having a school that taught Latin and it became a matter of status and self respect. But at local level money was the inherent problem. Suprisingly the local ministers managed remarkably well given the lack of resources, and seemed to be able to get additional male and female teachers when needed.

It was not until 1616 that an act was passed commanding that every parish should have a school, if circumstances allowed. The 1616 law was important because it introduced the principle that payment of the schoolmaster's stipend was not to be the sole responsibility of the parents, but was the responsibility of the parishioners as a whole. This meant everybody contributed, whether or not they had children of school age and whether or not they would benefit from the schooling. An act of 1633 added the clause that a 'stent' or local tax, should be levied on land according to its value and was to be paid by heritors and tenants for the maintenance of the school. The new clause was discretionary but a system of local rates or taxes had been born and would last for three hundred and sixty years.

Parliament again intervened in 1646 when it specifically ordered that parishes were to provide 'a commodious house'; and to pay a minimum stipend to the teacher of not less than 100 merks and not more than 200 merks a year (a merk was the equivalent of 13s.4d sterling, about 66.7 pence or one dollar US at today's values) The earlier laws, which were loosely worded and discretionary, were replaced by this mandatory requirement. Hand in hand with the statutory requirements there also existed a system akin to 'school governors' and parishes would take pride in the quality of both their schoolmaster and the teaching that was given In many case there were specific rules laid down as to when and how schooling was conducted, even specifying that between 11 a.m. and noon each day should be reserved for writing practice.

An ongoing issue that involved education was the effort to break the hold of the Gaelic language, its law and culture. James VI had ordered the planting of Lowlanders in the Highlands in 1598. He later ordered the Highland chieftains to send their sons south and be educated so that they might break the old and barbarous ways and obey the King's law. It was a slow process but by the 1670s some 70 percent of the Highland and Western Isles parishes had schools and were gaining ground on the 90 percent found in the Lowlands.

In the seventeenth century, school started at the age of five and was meant to continue for five years before the child might pass to a higher school or university depending on ability. The peasant child might leave by age eight to help the family by working, particularly during the harvest. The school day often started at 6 a.m. in summer and lasted between eight and twelve hours with breaks of an hour for breakfast and lunch. The teaching varied with the ability of the schoolmaster, but always focused on "godliness and good manners" Everyone learnt to read and write and many schools taught Latin to the more able student. In the burgh schools they taught arithmetic. Compulsory attendance at church with the teacher was common and the children would be required to discuss the sermon and its meaning on the Monday.

Some schools set nightly homework such as learning by heart some portion of the Lords Prayer, the Commands and Graces or Catechism which would be repeated to the teacher the following morning. With this grounding from an early age it is little wonder that as adults they were aware of the Bible and the issues which arose with the Covenants, Episcopacy and Erastianism. It also meant for some that they had been sufficiently educated to argue their case before the prelates in the oppressive Court of High Commission.

The Restoration of Charles II saw some easing of the rules for schools and teachers because the 1646 law was among those rescinded, but this lasted only to about 1690, when the General Assembly made a determined attempt to return to stringent controls. However, over time the repressive rules were adhered to less and less and were only kept by the Seceding churches that had broken away from the Church of Scotland. In the South of Scotland, strict observance of the Sabbath continued well into the eighteenth century.

The General Assembly of 1700 sought improvements in education when the Synods of Ayr and Glasgow were invited to give their views on state education and how it might be improved. Long before the modern pundits discovered the issues, the review identified that emphasis was needed firstly, on teaching the children what was useful and would help them to a chosen occupation. Secondly that teaching should be attractive and agreeable. These tenets were implemented during the eighteenth century.

Overall, the ideals postulated by Knox failed, but there were the indelible marks of the Kirk, which helped create a pious Protestant country and set new moral standards. By 1780 Scotland had developed an educational system in advance of anything in Europe at the time with consequent impact on its culture and the important ability to help maximise the talents of its people. Some might say that the long affair with Presbyterianism also gave rise to the dour, serious minded Scottish character. What it clearly did was to create a respect for sobriety and industry and inculcate the people with positive attitudes and a sense of purpose - values for which they were much admired in the new lands across the sea.

III. Tales of the Covenanters

The heartland of Covenanter resistance was in the south west of Scotland. It was here that the likes of Richard Cameron, James Renwick and Alexander Peden preached to open-air congregations or "conventicles" that numbered thousands and where many bloody reprisals were made by the military. It is of these people, and in this land, that the dramatic and allegorical tales of sudden and violent death or instances of Divine intervention that saved the persecuted Covenanters are set. They make fascinating reading and it is easy to see how in the days of yore an air of mystery surrounded many events and how mystical powers were attributed to some preachers such as Alexander Peden. Two publications that tell of the troubles and tribulations are *Traditions of the Covenanters* by the Rev. Robert Simpson (1867) and *Men of the Covenant*, by the Rev. Alexander Smellie (1903)

The southwest of Scotland is a large area bounded by water on three sides: in the north by the River Clyde; on the west by the Firth of Clyde and the North Channel of the Irish Sea; and along the south west boundary by the Solway Firth. The area is rich in history and there are several ways of describing the geographical regions, which from the River Clyde south are Renfrewshire, Lanarkshire, Ayrshire, and along the Solway Firth-Wigtownshire, the Stewartry of Kirkcudbrightshire (which together are frequently referred to as Galloway) and Dumfrieshire. The coastline is cut by many creeks and inlets with fishing villages on the shore. Some of the larger towns had wharves and quays from which local produce, especially cattle and tough Galloway ponies where exported. The Isle of Arran, and the long promonitory of Kintyre shelters the west coast, while the hills of Ulster just over twenty miles away can be seen on a fine day. Inland beyond the fertile coastal plain there are rolling hills; deep ravines and large expanses of moor and bog which in the seventeenth century was not easily accessible. Towns as we know them were also very few with most of the population living in rural areas. The villages were often just a cluster of cottages at the head of a valley or where bridle paths crossed, or around a blacksmith's shop or corn mill alongside a stream. Farms were often isolated buildings on the edge of the moors or hidden in the depths of a valley. There were few roads which were maintained and travel was by foot or horse along narrow bridle paths that followed the contours of the land. The pack horse was the main method of carrying goods. Even today Dumfries and Galloway is not a landscape for hiking without the proper dress and stout hiking boots. It is a land which has its own sub climate because of the surrounding seas, where swirling mists can descend without warning and cause disorientation; squally showers can turn to hail, sleet and snow within minutes - not the conditions to be caught out in the open unprepared.

In these beautiful but sometimes harsh surroundings the shepherds were the masters of travel and knew of the best sites where conventicles, the illegal open air prayer meetings, could be held in relative safety. It was here that resistance to the government was centred after the Act of Uniformity in 1662, reintroduced the rule of the church by bishops. Daniel Defoe, author of *Robinson Crusoe,* was witness to a conventicle in Nithdale in which an audience of some 7,000 was ranged round the hillside to listen to a preacher. They had come fifteen miles or more to hear the sermons that lasted for almost seven hours before setting

Typical location for a house, a sheltered spot by clear running water

A Covenanter's Farm House
Biggar Museum

Covenanter Bedroom
Biggar Museum

Covenanter at his desk
Biggar Museum

off on the long walk home. Some conventicles would include the Communion service and might extend over a weekend.

After the publication by Richard Cameron and supporters of the "Declaration of Sanquhar" in 1680, which openly sought the removal of King Charles, the military actions against the Covenanters hardened. The main detractors were John Graham of Claverhouse, later Viscount Dundee, who operated from his castle at Stranraer and Sir Robert Grierson of Lag. There were at least eighty summary executions that were witnessed in 1684 - 1685 and more that were not seen. Others were hung without trial such as William Johnston, John Milroy and George Walker for simply being Covenanters. The last of the Covenanter preachers to be martyred, was James Renwick who was executed in February 1688, not long before the last of the Stuart Kings, James II of England (VII of Scotland) was forced to vacate the throne.

The worst and most brutish incident is that of a young woman, Margaret Wilson of Wigtown, aged eighteen, and Margaret MacLachlan, aged sixty-three, who were tied to stakes in the sea and executed by drowning. Many of the incidents involving the Covenanters of southwest Scotland have passed into folk lore and make fascinating reading as well as being a social history of the late seventeenth century. The following description of a trooper bent upon a search of a home although in flowery language by today's standards, conveys the fear that the soldiers engendered:

No sight was more appalling to the helpless peasantry than that of a gruff looking, swearing trooper, roughly clad, sunk to the knees in large boots, with a grisly helmet on his head, a coarse cloak hanging from his shoulders and a huge cumbrous scabbard rattling on his heels. These for the most part were men of blood, who rioted in human sufferings, and to whom the wailings of humanity were merriment.

The Babe of Tweedhope-foot and John Hunter.

The tale is told of a man named Welsh, commonly called "The Babe of Tweedhope-foot." How he got this name is not too clear other than the location of his farm, but he was a man of very great bodily strength and perhaps, as big men often are, he was a gentle man. He was a Covenanter and his home was often a shelter for conventicling ministers but, because of this, he was also earmarked for regular visits by the troopers. Having heard that Colonel James Douglas, a zealous persecutor, was in the area, he and a friend, John Hunter, resolved to conceal themselves above the remote Water of Annan They were, however, pursued and likely to be overtaken so they headed for a spot known as "Straught Steep". This is a very steep hillside, which the dragoons would be unable to ride on horseback. The pursuers began to shoot at the two men and John Hunter was struck by a ball,

He fell among the stones over which he was scrambling, and his life's blood oozed forth upon the rocks, where he expired. This good man, who was suddenly taken away by a violent death, had no time afforded him to pray, or to compose his mind, before his immediate entrance into eternity, but then he was habitually prepared ... in the expectation of a hasty summons into the other world, he was always ready for his departure. Be ye also ready; for in such an hour as ye think not the Son of man cometh.

The Babe, meanwhile, fearing the worst for his companion, raced on heading for a place called Carterhope. Arriving at his destination unobserved the Babe sat down exhausted by the fireside to await the arrival of his pursuers who would surely search there. They duly arrived and "entered in their usual uproarious manner" and ignored the figure in the fireside chair since they had no detail of their quarry. The mistress of the house, however, fearing discovery approached the Babe dozing in front of the fire, and gave him a heavy blow between the shoulder blades. Chiding him for his sloth and for cowering in front of the fire, she drove him out of the house to "get on with his proper business." The Babe took the hint and left the house while the soldiers looked on. He later remarked, "that the kindest cuff he ever received was from the gudewife of Carterhope."

The "Straught Steep" is a slope at the end of a blind valley, which was also known as the Corrie of Annan. Today it is called "The Devil's Beef Tub" and is not far from the border town of Moffat. In the valley bottom can be seen a stone pen or corral which was probably used in the sixteenth century by the Johnstones to hide cattle from their predatory raids, it was also known as "The Marquis of Annandale's Beef Stand." Prisoners from Prince Charlie's army were marched this way in 1746 when one of the men escaped by rolling down the steep hill into a thick mist. Sir Walter Scott borrowed the incident to use in his story *Redgauntlet.*

John Hunter is buried in the peaceful and idyllic surrounds of the kirk at Tweedsmuir. Overlooking the Devil's Beef Tub, at the side of the road, a monument records his untimely death

On the hillside opposite
John Hunter
Covenanter
was shot
by
Douglas's dragoons
in 1685

His grave is in
Tweedsmuir Kirkyard.

Frazer of Dalquhairn

Tales vary between those of Divine deliverance from pursuers to exploits of the ministers and personal bravery of the people shielding them knowing that if found, they would probably be killed. One Covenanter of renown, John Frazer of Holm of Dalquhairn, in the parish of Carsphairn was safely delivered from arrest on a number of occasions. Whether by good fortune, slackness or sympathy on part of the searchers or indeed some Divine power cannot be determined, but he was a Covenanter who got away more than once.

One incident happened when he was necessarily supervising some work on his farm and he was unable to make an escape in full view of oncoming soldiers. He ran inside the house, into a small closet and concealed himself in a bed stored there. With great presence of mind, a domestic servant quickly piled some wet turfs on the fire, which in those days was in the centre of the kitchen, and filled the place with "dense blue smoke which rolled its lazy volumes from the floor to the roof." Despite the smoky atmosphere, a soldier found Frazer and demanded that he sing a profane song to prove he was not a Covenanter, but Frazer responded with the words of a hymn. For reasons unknown, the soldier warned Frazer to be careful of his words else he would be mistaken for a non-conformist and left him, the soldier saying nothing to others in the search party.

On another occasion, he was trapped in his house and surrounded by troops. In desperation he climbed through a window to land at the feet of a soldier where the following conversation is said to have taken place:

I am in your power, said Frazer.

Yes, replied the trooper. *But I feel, somehow or other, as if I am not inclined or present to use that power; no one is witness to this interview - run to that covert, and hide yourself; do not flee to the hill, for your flight might perchance be seen; and though you were as light of foot as a roe, our fleet horses will outrun you.*

Frazer was often an exile from his home and occasionally returned when judged safe to do so. He was finally captured while sitting down to dinner with his family and quickly taken prisoner. But the soldiers then helped themselves to the meal and consumed copious amounts of home made beer. Meanwhile Frazer had been placed in the barn trussed up ready for transfer to prison. He managed to stand up and shuffle into a dark corner to await his fate. Providence again intervened with the drunken soldiers climbing on their horses and riding off without him. Frazer, accompanied now by his wife who feared the revenge of the troops when they realised what they had done, returned to living in the caves where they remained until

the welcome news of the Revolution sounded, like the silver trumpet of a hallowed jubilee, through the length and breadth of a wasted land. The happy tidings that the arm of the oppressor was broken, and that the children of tribulation were now to walk forth out of the furnace, reached the dreary caves in the wilderness.

This wonderful use of language to paint a glowing picture of events is symptomatic of a bygone age but even so it conveys the essential truth of great persecution for having a particular belief. Sadly persecution appears in every age of man and it is hoped that the oppressed can always be as fortunate as John Frazer and his wife Marion Howatson, and enjoy Divine intervention in their time of trouble.

The Testimony of Thomas Harkness, Andrew Clark and Samuel McEwan

The raid at Enterkin Pass is a famous event in Covenanter lore which took place in June 1684. A party of Claverhouse's troopers, who were escorting prisoners from Dumfries to Edinburgh, were ambushed and the prisoners rescued. The ambush took place at a spot called Glenvalentine on the pass where there were several deaths and most, if not all the prisoners were released. Claverhouse was greatly annoyed, possibly taking it as a personal affront that it was his men who had been ambushed. Be that as it may, he personally ran a number of the participants to ground and arrested them. Included in those he captured was James "Long Gun" Harkness, the organiser of the rescue, who later escaped from custody along with twenty-five fellow prisoners from the Cannongate Tolbooth in Edinburgh. James continued in his Covenanting ways and lived a long life. However, his brother Thomas "White Hose" Harkness was also taken and suffered the penalty prescribed by law.

Following the ambush orders were issued for the male population of Nithsdale over the age of fifteen to assemble in stated locations and intensive searches took place. It was next ordered that the curates in the dozen or so parishes next to Enterkin should announce that all over fifteen assemble at New Delgarno to swear on oath as to their involvement. An enormous crowd assembled on the due date and the authorities could not cope so they directed attendance at further local meetings. Attendance at these meetings was enforced with imprisonment for those failing to attend, or to have troopers quartered on them. This went on for six weeks to the great discomfort of the populace.

Gravestone of James "Long Gun" Harkness

Thomas Harkness of Locharben, Andrew Clark of Leadhill and Samuel McEwan of Glencairn were seized by Claverhouse as they were sleeping in the fields.

They were so fast asleep that the soldiers had to rouse them; and when they opened their eyes, and saw their enemies standing over them, like ravenous beasts ready to pounce on their prey, they attempted to flee, but in vain

They were taken to Edinburgh "arriving about one of the clock, and that same day they were sentenced and executed by five of the clock." Though the men had little time to live they nevertheless managed to write a joint testimony to the truth for which they were about to suffer. Their testimony is given in *The Traditions of the Covenanters* as follows:

The joint testimony of Thomas Harkness, Andrew Clark. and Samuel M'Ewan, from the Tolbooth of Edinburgh, August 5 [1684]

Dear friends and relations whatsomever, we think fit to acquaint you, that we bless the Lord that ever we were ordained to give a publick testimony, who are so great sinners. Blessed be he that we were born to bear witness for him, and blessed be the Lord Jesus Christ that ordained the Gospel and the truths of it, which he sealed with his own blood; and many a worthy Christian gone before us hath sealed them. We were questioned for not owning the king's authority. We answered, that we owned all authority that is allowed by the written Word of God, sealed by Christ's blood. Now, our dear friends, we entreat you to stand to the truth, and especially all ye that are our own relations, and all that love and wait for the coming of Christ. He will come and not tarry, and reward every one according to their deeds in the body. We bless the Lord that we are not a whit discouraged, but content to lay down our life with cheerfulness, and boldness, and courage; and if we had a hundred lives, we would willingly quit with them all for the truth of Christ. Good news! Christ is no worse than he promised. Now we take our leave of all our friends and acquaintances, and declare we are heartily content with our lot, and that he hath brought us hither to witness for him and his truth. We leave our testimony against. Popery, and all other false doctrine that is not according to the Scriptures of the Old and New Testaments, which is the only Word of God.

Dear friends, be valiant for God; for he is as good as his promise. Him that overcometh he will make a pillar in his temple. Our time is short, and we have little to spare, having got our sentence at one of the clock this afternoon, and are to die at five this day; and so we will say no more, but farewell all friends and relations, and welcome heaven, and Christ, and the cross for Christ's sake.

THOMAS HARKNESS.
ANDREW CLARK.
SAMUEL M'EWAN.

The Rev. Robert Simpson sums up this event, pointing out that the peace and evenness of mind which the men displayed, proves that the experience of the truth on the heart is a reality, and that faith of the Gospel is capable of sustaining the soul in the most trying and appalling circumstances. And he ends

O how precious is that Gospel which supports the soul amid all the cares, and anxieties, and tribulations of life, and at last, in death, soothes the heart into a sweet and holy serenity - which enables the believer to triumph even in the moment of dissolution.

There are many tales told of these dreadful times and the Covenanters of Nithsdale were possibly among the most persecuted.

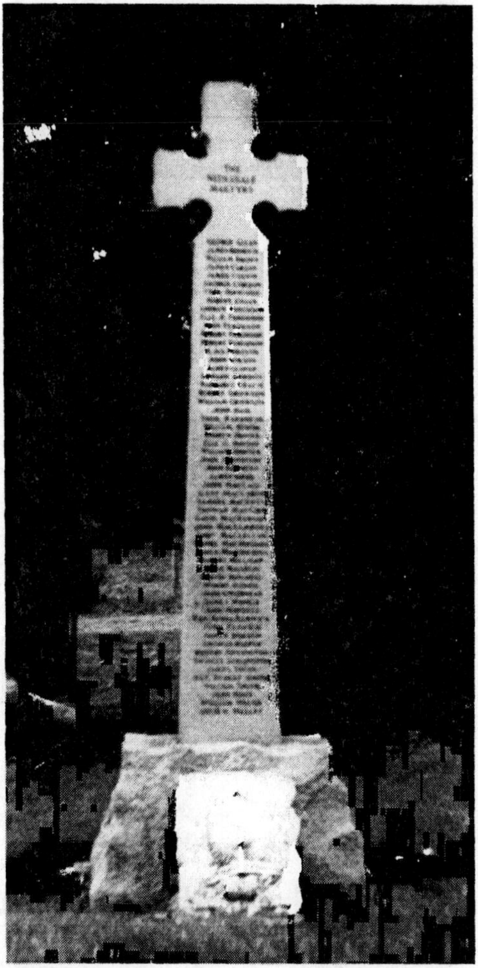

Nithsdale Cross, Martyrs of Nithsdale
Dalgarnoch

The 'Nithsdale Cross' in the old kirkyard of Dalgarnock is a memorial to fifty-seven known local people who died for their faith.

Nearby the Cross lie many of the Harkness family, including James, who died of old age on 6 December 1723, in his seventy-second year. His memorial reads:

Here lyes the body of James
Harkness in Locherben who
died 6th Dec 1723 aged 72 yea's
Belo this stone this dust doth ly
who indured 28 years
persecution by tirrany
Did him persue with echo and cry
Through many a lonesome place
At last by Clavers he was tane
Sentenced for to dy;
But God, who for his soul took car
did him from prison bring
Because no other Cause they had
but that he cUld not give up
with Christ,his Glorious king,
and swear alligence to that beast
the duke of york, i mean,
In Spite of all there hellish rage
a naturel death he died
in full asurance of his rest
with Christ eternaly.

IV. What's in a Name? Presbyterian, Covenanter, Seceder, Mountain Men; Burghers and Anti Burghers, Old Lights, New Lights, Subscribing, Non Subscribing

In our wanderings through Scottish history and the origins of the Ulster Scots we come across references to Presbyterians, Covenanters, Seceders, Burghers and Anti Burghers; Mountain Men, Old Lights, New Lights, Subscribing and Non Subscribing churches. Here, for the benefit of the casual enquirer, is an outline of what they were.

Lets us begin with the basics - a covenant is defined as a mutual agreement between two or more people to do or refrain from doing certain things. Importantly, everybody in the covenant is consulted and agrees with the final terms. The Presbyterian belief was that they, as individuals, had a covenant with God and expected that their religion and arrangements concerning it would be the subject of mutual agreement or covenant according to the Scriptures.

The splinter groups that arose were due to internal disagreements about interpretations of faith or as a response to ongoing external pressures from the government of the day. These groups remained Presbyterian in structure, but clung to their particular belief. There were very many changes in the make up of Presbyterianism from its beginnings with John Knox in 1560 even into the twentieth century.

Presbyterians

Presbyterians are adherents of that faith which has at its heart the Disciplines evolved from the teachings of John Calvin (1509-1564) and John Knox (1515-1572). It recognises, as in the Scriptures, the government of each church by its Session consisting of elders and the minister. The churches were associated in local presbyteries; represented in provincial synods and in a General Assembly, which was the highest court of appeal. They believed that they had a covenant between themselves and God and were particularly opposed to the rule by the bishops (Episcopacy) who had no place in their scheme of things and the interference and claim of supremacy by the state (Erastianism). Above all the Presbyterians believed and were concerned to implement the rights of God in both religion and government. Most of their persecution for over a century was associated with their objections to Episcopacy and Erastianism which the succesive Stuart Kings sought to impose by force.

Covenanters

The Covenanters were those Presbyterians with a concern for a strict faith and its management. They were signatories or adherents to the "National Covenant" of 28 February 1638, which was a response to the King's attempts to change the style of worship of the Church which had not been previously approved (covenanted) by free assemblies and parliament. In August 1643 the Covenanters signed the "Solemn League and Covenant," which was a political treaty with the English Parliamentary party. Under this covenant the agreement was to impose Presbyterianism in England, Wales and Ireland. In return for this, the Covenanters agreed to support the English Parliamentarians against King Charles I in the Civil War that had broken out.

When King Charles II returned from exile in 1660, the rule of the bishops (Episcopacy) was imposed on Scotland and a very tough line taken against any dissenters. Many people did not conform - especially in the southwestern shires of Ayrshire, Dumfries and Galloway. These Presbyterians, followers of a strict form of their religion espoused by Richard Cameron, were bloodily persecuted, especially after an armed revolt and battle at Bothwell Brig on 22 June 1679. Despite the Revolutionary Settlement in 1688 and the establishment of Presbyterianism as the approved religion, many of these Covenanters declined to join the Church of Scotland because they objected to the Erastianism, the bishops, and to William and Mary as heads of state. This remnant of about seven thousand people formed themselves into Praying Societies which in 1743 became the Reformed Presbytery.

New Light, Old Light

The Kirk was already divided into dissenting groups such as the Covenanters or Cameronians, when it faced a damaging theological challenge from within its own ranks. There arose in the universities a movement towards "moderatism" in which the gospel was reduced to a series of moral rules. Led by the eloquent Francis Hutcheson, son of the Rev. John Hutcheson of Armagh, he and his followers sapped the foundations of the evangelical Presbyterian Church. In Ireland the Belfast Society ventured similar debates. Some ministers became more concerned with culture than salvation and dismissed their heritage. Thus there came yet another split between the parties, the Old Light who were orthodox and rejected moderatism, and the moderate New Light movement who held a softer line - that every man must be allowed to hold only what his conscience was persuaded as right and should not be bound by any rule of faith or conduct.

A second secession in 1752 saw another group - the Relief Church, come into being. The two groups of New Lights, who accepted the principle of moderate change, eventually joined together in 1820 as the United Secession Church. The two groups of Old Lights finally joined together as the United Original Seceders in 1842.

Seceders

Presbyterianism became the Established Church in Scotland by law in 1690, but there were still those such as the Societies, who would not accept the settlement because it did not acknowledge the supreme sovereignty of Christ the King, nor was it a "covenanted" settlement. Within the main body of the Church of Scotland there were a series of doctrinal issues that would further divide them. In 1712 the Patronage Act reintroduced patronage as the means of appointing ministers, thus repealing the earlier agreement of 1689 and taking away from the congregation its cherished right to choose its own minister, There was also a trend towards liberalisation as Scotland turned more towards England for its political lead, and with it renewed theological conflict.

Opposition to moderate moves was resisted with orthodoxy, subscription of the Confession of Faith and adherence to the National Covenant. In 1732 the Rev Ebenezer Erskine preached against patronage and was admonished by the General Assembly. He and three others, Rev. W. Wilson, Rev. Alexander Moncrieff and Rev. James Fisher signed a protest and were suspended from office. They left the Church and on 5 December 1733 constituted themselves into the Associate Presbytery. These Seceders and their Secession Church eventually became the Reformed Presbyterian Church.

Burghers and Anti Burghers

In 1733 the patronage issue finally caused dissenting congregations to form the Secession Church. The Associate Presbytery, into which the Seceders formed themselves, grew rapidly to form an Associate Synod with some twenty pastors. But the reintroduction of patronage and the taking of an oath created another split in this already divided group. On this occasion it was over the requirement to take an oath when elected to serve on town councils in Scottish burghs that they would support "the true religion presently professed within the realm and authorised by the laws thereof." There was no imposition of this specific oath in Ireland who anyway already had the Test Act of 1704 that effected local official appointments. The oath was exacted by the authorities in Edinburgh, Glasgow and Perth but the strict Seceders protested about it at the 1745 Synod meeting as they felt that they could not take an oath which approved the Establishment they had left. Those prepared to tolerate this weakening in principle, which they considered as directed at Popery, were called the Burghers; those against the change were the Anti Burghers. Thus in 1747, another split took place.

The issues in Ireland

The Kirk in Ireland broadly followed Scotland in the theological debates as its ministers were trained there. There were the same debates over the Covenants of 1638 and 1643 and the acceptance or rejection of assorted oaths. Despite the arrival of a Protestant King in William III, there were still matters of conscience that troubled the Presbyterians in Ireland. The Test Act of 1704, added further to their woes as it excluded them from virtually all forms of office.

But a cloud on the horizon came with the formation of the 'Belfast Society' in 1705. This was a group of younger ministers led by Rev. John Abernethy of Antrim. The Society discussed new approaches to religion, to issues of conscience, and of doctrine. This gave rise to the New Light - Old Light controversy in Ireland that rumbled on for some years and ended in the Subscribing and Non Subscribing division of the Kirk.

The "Mountain Men"

There were followers of Richard Cameron who became known as the "Mountain Men" or "hill folk" after the wandering preachers who held conventicles in the hills and dales of southwest Scotland. In Ireland a few families were found around Carrickfergus who maintained the rigid principles of the Scottish Cameronians, refusing to join in communion with other Presbyterian groups. The church of the "Mountain Men" was at Kellswater, to which the congregation would travel from as far away as Carrickfergus, a distance of fourteen miles. The early ministers were William Martin (1760-72), William Gibson (1787-97) and William Stavely (1800-25).

Seceders in Ireland

A concomitant of the Seceder movement was the desire of those seceding ministers and congregations for a return to the stricter ways of the Kirk. They objected to the growing laxness in doctrine and the trend towards greater earthly rewards for ministers. A result was an increasing demand for new congregations often spread over quite large rural areas. In 1728 the Synod of Ulster refused to allow a new congregation in Clenanees, about 6 miles from Aughnacloy. In 1753 it was ordered that a minister would not be ordained to any charge which did not promise a stipend of £40 a year. Later this was increased to a minimum of £50 stipend. In this environment the Seceding congregations in fact grew in number and sought ministers from the Associate Presbytery. They continued with visiting ministers from Scotland until the first minister, Isaac Patton, was ordained at Lylehill on 9 July 1746. His charge included Lisburn and Belfast and he received much support from the populace who yearned for the old style Gospel message.

Subscribing, Non Subscribing

The cause for more division in the Kirk was objection to the requirement to subscribe to the Westminster Confession because, it was argued, no man should be required to declare his belief in any creed or confession drawn up by man. This belief led to further splits in the congregations and in 1829 three Presbyteries - Armagh, Bangor and Templepatrick left the Synod of Ulster and formed the Remonstrant Synod of Ulster. In 1910 the Remonstrant Synod and the Presbytery of Antrim formed the Non Subscribing Presbyterian Church of Ireland.

Whatever the shade of Presbyterianism the Ulster Scots followed, each and every one of them was the son or daughter of the Kirk's upbringing, The traditions and values of the Covenanters, with its high moral purpose, its disciplines, and the ethos of education for all from an early age, prepared them for the challenge of the new frontiers across the seas.

V. The Covenanter Ships -"Eaglewing," "Crown," and "Henry & Francis"

The flow of Scottish migrants to the Province of Ulster was significant in the Plantation of Ireland (1610-30), most of who came in search of land and religious freedom. However, in a short space of twenty years there was a change in the relationships with the government in Dublin, particularly when Thomas Wentworth, later Earl of Strafford, became the Lord Deputy in Ireland (1633). At the same time in England Archbishop William Laud brought back the rule of the bishops and many Catholic practices to the established church.

The Scots had tried hard to fit in at the start but friction was continuing in Scotland with resentment to the religious policies of James I and his successor, Charles I. There was also the fervour of evangelical groups, especially the Covenanters, that added friction to the Presbyterian communities in both Scotland and Ulster and the thoughts of a few turned to the possibility of joining the exodus to Massachusetts. Whether the impetus came from Scotland, where as early as 1630, there had been discussions, or from Ulster is uncertain.

However, a group of the Planters and Presbyterian ministers John Livingston and Robert Blair among them, agreed in 1634 to seek information from the Massachusetts settlers about the prospect of acquiring land and the freedoms they desired. Letters were sent to John

Winthrop, the governor, and seemingly encouraging replies were received as some Planter families prepared to emigrate.

The Eaglewing

Into the scenario came John Winthrop, the son of the Governor, who had been at Trinity College, Dublin in 1622-1623. He returned to England in 1635 to purchase live stock to be sent to the colony and is known to have visited Scotland where he had contact with Provost John Stewart in Ayr, Rev. David Dickson in Irvine and James Murray in Edinburgh. In Ulster, one of his contacts was the affluent settler, Sir John Clotworthy. The Clotworthy family had prospered under James I and, amongst other things, had been granted the license to sell wine and spirits in most of County Antrim and County Down. It is likely that their wealth supported the planned emigration. Sir John wrote to Wentworth that a ship was being built and that he was anxious that the emigrant party should get under way as soon as possible as he feared action would be taken to prevent future emigration. The ship was the "*Eaglewing,*" its name coming from Exodus Ch 19 v 4:

Ye have seen what I did to the Egyptians, and how I bare you on eagles wings and brought you unto myself.

The building of the ship got under way at the small village of Groomsport on the shore of Belfast Lough and it was not until the autumn of 1636 before it was ready. At 150 tons the "*Eaglewing*" was barely big enough for the 140 passengers who had gathered together to face the dangers of the seas in this small craft. Although stoutly built, the "*Eaglewing*" was untried in the rough seas that it was to encounter following the departure from Carrickfergus on 9 September 1636. Difficult winds drove the ship into Loch Ryan almost before it had cleared the harbour, but at length they set sail once more. John Livingston, minister at Killinchy, who had been at the heart of the emigration plans, was to say afterwards that the ship was three or four hundred leagues from Ireland when it was hit by turbulent seas and a hurricane that broke the ships rudder; heavy seas broke over the vessel and poured down into the cabins and the hold. The rudder was repaired, but the ministers and the passengers aboard held a meeting and concluded that it was God's will that they should return to Ireland. On 3 November, the ship arrived back in Belfast Lough.

The Scottish passengers returned home and the Ulster Scots, having previously sold their possessions, sought with difficulty to pick up the threads of their former life. There was no further attempt to make the trip to New England. The embarrassment of failure was felt by the ministers, no doubt, and they were subject of some scathing criticism - "their faith not being answerable to their zeal," as the Bishop of Derry wrote to the arch persecutor Archbishop Laud.

The failure of the expedition did, however, have a good side as it meant that these strong willed Scots were able to bring their influence to bear in subsequent events in Scotland. Amongst these were John Livingston and Robert Blair, a minister of Calvinist leanings at Bangor, who was responsible for a revival of the Presbyterian Church in County Antrim and County Down. They and others, such as Robert Cunningham minister of Holywood, were forced to flee to Scotland to escape the persecution of Wentworth. From their new homes in Scotland these staunch supporters of Presbyterianism were present to add their respected voices to the issues that led to the National Covenant of 1638.

There was a sweet revenge in many ways as Sir John Clotworthy was to play a part in the impeachment of Wentworth, Earl of Strafford, who was subsequently executed at the Tower of London in 1641.

The Crown

The second of the Covenanting ships in this trilogy was the "*Crown*" which had prisoners on board most of whom met a watery grave. In Scotland there was increasing dissent and Covenanting fervour was bloodily persecuted for another fifty years after the failure of the expedition on the *Eaglewing.* There was increased persecution of ministers from 1660, the Pentland Rising in 1666 and the first armed resistance and a modest victory for the Covenanters at Drumclog on 1 June 1679. On a wave of euphoria and, paradoxically, of internal dissent, the Covenanters were routed at the Battle of Bothwell Brig on 22 June 1679. About 1100 prisoners were taken and incarcerated in a make shift, open air prison next to the Greyfriars Kirk in Edinburgh. After some five months those who were prepared to take an oath and give a bond for their future good behaviour were allowed to go home. Most of the common prisoners were discharged on 14 August when an Act of Indemnity was proclaimed. But by an Order of the Privy Council on 4 July "Ministers, Heritors, and Ringleaders" were to be prosecuted and banished to the plantations.

Within the Greyfriars Prison there was a hardcore of prisoners who objected on grounds of conscience to giving a bond, which would, they believed, have indicated that the battle was wrong. Their ringleader was a Robert Garnock, a 'Stirling hammerman' or blacksmith, who ironically was not actually at Bothwell Brig. He had led an itinerant life roaming round the Lowlands, sometimes in Edinburgh, other times in Stirling where he had refused to attend a muster and was ordered to be arrested. His downfall was to attend a conventicle at Fintry on 8 May 1679 where there had been a skirmish with shots exchanged and the military were on the alert. He had returned to Stirling in the evening, was detained by soldiers and cast into the common prison. Here he was mixed in with the worst and vilest offenders of Edinburgh and Leith and although a reasonably strong man from his blacksmithing, he was nearly killed by a drunken murderer. Perhaps with a sigh of relief he and about a hundred other prisoners were later transferred to Greyfriars Kirkyard possibly with the intention of transporting them with the Boswell Brig prisoners.

Garnock was bitterly opposed to the bonds and he was encouraged in his stand by the more extreme ministers, including John Blackader who wrote to him from his prison on the Bass Rock. Within the prison he repeatedly refused to give a bond and his vehement objections and criticism were greatly resented by the other prisoners. He was it seems, a marked man and troublemaker whom the authorities clearly wanted to be rid of and he was moved to the Tolbooth prison. After a great deal of harrassment there he was arraigned before the courts and convicted of declining the King's authority. He and five others were executed at the Gallows Lea, between Edinburgh and Leith, on 10 October 1679. He was not to know of the watery grave that may have awaited him had he remained in the Greyfriars Prison. Of the remaining prisoners, 257 of the erstwhile ringleaders and ministers were sentenced to transporation to the West Indies or Virginia as white slaves.

William Paterson a merchant in Edinburgh contracted with Provost Milns, the Laird of Barnton, to transport the prisoners to the West Indies or Virginia. He engaged Thomas Teddico, the captain of the *Crown* (sometimes called *The Crown of London,* where the ship was registered). The normal route to the Atlantic and the open seas was round the northern tip of Scotland but it was not the easiest of voyages in summer conditions let alone in a stormy winter. The vessel set sail on 27 November 1679, but within days, was forced by bad weather into the Orkney port of Deersound, where, despite local advice, she set out once more into the deep swells of the Atlantic Ocean. The ship had hardly cleared land when she struck rocks and was wrecked at Scarva Taing about a mile west of Mull Head near Deerness.

It is said that the captain was a heartless and cruel man who did not care whether the prisoners lived or died and, despite the pleas of the frightened prisoners, he ordered the hatches to be chained. The crew escaped by cutting down a mast and using it as a bridge to the shore, but prisoners who tried to do the same were forced back into the foaming sea. Thus it was on 10 December 1679, that 211 Covenanters were consigned to a watery grave A mere forty-six Covenanters survived the wreck only to be transported later, although there is the possibility that up to nine may have escaped.

There is very little by way of contemporaneous records about the event although a local Notary Public in Kirkwall, Thomas Brown, made a brief not in his diary, cited by W. M. Bryce in *The Flodden Wall*

The 10th of Decr, 1679, being Wedinsday, at 9 in ye evening or yrabout, the vessell or ship callit ye Croun, qrin was 250 or yrby of ye Quhiggs takin at Bothwall Brigs to have bein sent to Verginy, parochted at or neirby ye Moull head of Deirnes.

An imposing granite memorial some forty feet high was paid for by public subscriptions and stands on some elevated ground at Deerness. Money left over was used to place a small marble obelisk in front of St Mungo's cathedral. The main memorial reads:

For Christ, His Crown and Covenant.
Erected
by
public subscription
Aug 1888
to
the memory of
200 Covenanters
who were taken prisoners
at Bothwell Bridge and
sentenced to transportation
for life, but who perished by
shipwreck near this spot,
on 10th December 1679.

The Henry & Francis

It was the practice to commit dissenters, particularly those who refused to take an Oath of Allegiance, to be imprisoned, but there were so many that a policy evolved whereby Covenanters could migrate to the American colonies. If, however, they were convicted, they were sent as slaves. A Scottish laird, by the name of Scott, was allowed to select a party of about 100 prisoners to take with him to New Jersey. He was required to land the party in America before September 1686. To this purpose, Scott chartered a 350-ton ship, armed with twenty cannon, called the "*Henry and Francis,*" captained by Richard Hutton.

There were other emigrants who were required to pay £5 passage money, but they could alternatively be indentured servants for four years after which they would receive twenty-five acres of land. The ship set sail on 5 September 1685 from Leith and made landfall at Perth Amboy, New Jersey, in December. It was a traumatic journey with the ship suffering leaks, shortages of food and water, as well as fever. Of the 125 that set out, some thirty-one of their number died, including Scott and his wife. During the voyage the son in law of Scott, called Johnstone, had urged the prisoners to accept a four-year servitude so that the costs of the venture could be recovered, which the prisoners resisted. The ship's master wanted to sail for Jamaica or Virginia since a better price would be obtained in either place for the prisoners. Perhaps it was Divine Providence intervening for these Covenanters, but a change of wind forced the ship into New Jersey as originally planned.

Although Johnstone sought to recover costs in the courts, which could have resulted in the imprisonment or slavery of the emigrants, they were cleared of charges because they had not come voluntarily, nor had they entered into any agreements. Thus this party was scattered throughout Pennsylvania, New York and Connecticut succeeding where their earlier compatriots had failed.

Greyfriars Kirk from the lower graveyard

VI. Greyfriars's Kirk and The National Covenant

Greyfriars Kirk takes its name from the Order of the Grey Friars, founded in 1209 by St Frances of Assisi who also founded the Poor Clares for women in 1212. Their name came from the colour of the long wool tunic with a hood or cowl that they wore A group of the friars came to Edinburgh in the reign of James I (ruled 1406-1437) and were well known for their charitable deeds. Living in great poverty often sleeping rough in church doorways or other shelter, they were respected by all in the town. In Edinburgh they were given a modest building at the bottom of what is now Greyfriars Kirkyard where they also had a small garden where they grew herbs used to make into medicine.

The Order was held in high esteem by the nobles and the Grey Friars were in the wedding procession of James IV and Margaret Tudor in 1503. At the start of the Reformation both the Grey and Black friars were attacked by John Knox and they were forced out of the city. Their buildings were among those the mob attacked and it was razed to the ground. The following year, 1561, the Edinburgh Town Council realised that they were running out of space for burials and approached Mary, Queen of Scots, for the use of the lower end of Greyfriars yard. This was granted. The Council decided in 1601 that a new church was needed and authorised the use of stone from the razed convent of the Sisters of Siena. After some problems obtaining timber from Scandinavia the new church of Greyfriars was dedicated on Christmas Day 1620.

For a church of great renown Greyfriars is actually quite plain and sparsely furnished. It would have been almost cavernous when first used as it was practice for the congregation to bring their own stools Fixed pews had yet to appear. Other customs were that men wore their hats during the sermon but a penitent on the Stool of Repentance was bareheaded. The wearing of a hat was a useful indication to late arrivals that the sermon had started. There was no organ until the nineteenth century and psalms were led by the minister or precentor and these gradually reduced in number to about a favourite dozen which were known by heart by the congregation. These were sung with the congregation seated

The church building has a chequered history since it was first used in 1620. It served as a cavalry barracks for Cromwell's soldiers between 1650 and 1653 and had to be refurbished before it could be used again for services. Subsequent discussions by the Edinburgh Council were in favour of an ornamental spire, but this did not take place. On 7 May 1718 a huge explosion blew the end of the chutch away; this was due to the town's supply of gunpowder that was stored in the tower, igniting. The usable bays were soon bricked off and it was decided to build a new church adoining the existing building. This was completed in 1722 and was paid for by a local tax on beer. The consequence was a fairly unique situation with two churches under one roof. A more modern tragedy was a furious fire on 19 January 1845 that virtually destroyed the Old Greyfriars and much of the furniture of the New Greyfriars. The repairs took a while as a new timber roof was added but Old Greyfriars was back in use by 1857. The two congregations came together in 1928 and in 1938 the dividing wall was removed, ending two hundred and twenty years of separate prayer.

Copy of the National Covenant, 1638
St. Giles Church, Edinburgh

The National Covenant 1638

The Greyfriars's Kirk is dear to the memory of the Covenanters and the Reformation of the church in Scotland because it was within the Kirk itself that "The National Covenant" was first read and signed on Wednesday, 28 February 1638. Archibald Johnston of Warriston, later Lord Warriston, and Rev. Alexander Henderson drafted the document. The Covenant was in three parts - first, a reproduction of the Confession of King James VI (later James I of England) of 1581 (see Appendix 4); second, a detailed list of the Acts of Parliament which confirmed Presbyterianism and condemned Popery; and, third, a protest about the changes in worship. These included an attempt to force Episcopal reforms on the nation; a ban on extempore prayer; a ban on meetings of the General Assembly; the furnishings of churches were specified and a specific liturgy was ordered to be used (see Appendix 5).

Paramount in the objections was the decree that worshippers must use a revised Book of Prayer, introduced in 1637. This had given rise to a celebrated event at the nearby St. Giles Cathedral on Sunday 23 July 1637, when a woman by the name of Janet Geddes objected to its use. She allegedly threw her small stool at the Dean of the church saying, "Fause loon! Dost thou say Mass at my lug?" Her stool is on display in the Museum of Scotland and the spot from which she threw it is marked by a plate in the floor which reads:

> *Constant oral tradition affirms that near this spot a brave Scotswoman Janet Geddes on 23 July 1637 struck the first blow in the great struggle for freedom of conscience which after a conflict of half a century ended in the establishment of civil and religious liberty.*

Plate recording the spot from which Jenny Geddes threw her stool at the Dean of St. Giles Church, Edinburgh

The signing of the National Covenant was certainly a momentous occasion and took place in the centre of the Kirk alongside the pulpit. A description of the event is quoted in *The Greyfriars Story - A Celebration* by Padi Mathieson (1990).

after it had been read over publicly and a long speech had been made by the Lord Loudoun in commendation thereof, Mr. Alexander Henderson seconded him with a prayer, and then all fell to swear and subscribe, some of the nobility leading the way. The first was John Gordon, Earl of Sutherland, and the next was Sir Andrew Murray, Lord Balvard, minister at Ebdy in Fife: two noblemen who, out of zeal to their profession thought it a happiness to be amongst the first subscribers and swearers to the Covenant. All who were present at Edinburgh at that meeting in the month of February, subscribed and swore to the Covenant before they went from thence; and at their parting, ministers, and noblemen, and gentlemen, who were well affected to the cause, carried copies thereof along with them, or caused

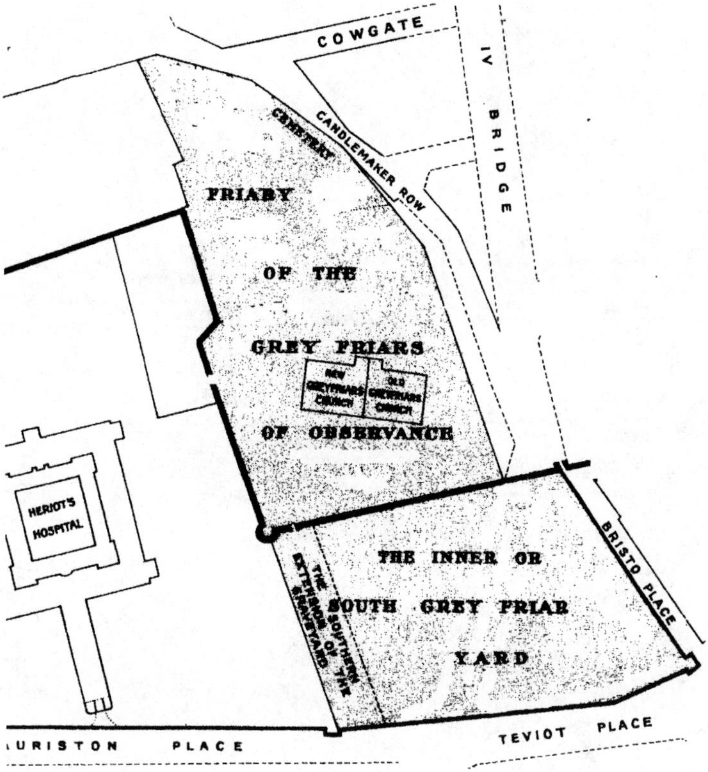

Plan of the Original Greyfriars Kirk Yard

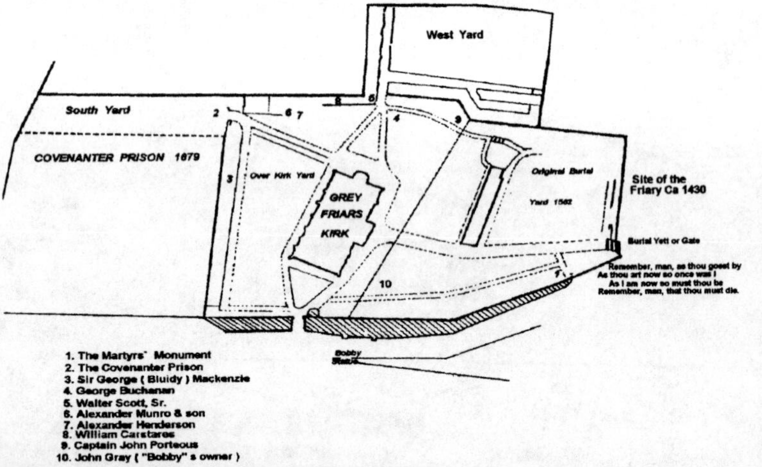
West Yard
South Yard
COVENANTER PRISON 1679
Over Kirk Yard
GREY
FRIARS
KIRK
Original Burial
Yard 1562
Site of the
Friary Ca 1430
Burial Yett or Gate
Remember, man, as thou goest by
As thou art now so once was I
As I am now so must thou be
Remember, man, that thou must die.
Bobby
Statue
1. The Martyrs' Monument
2. The Covenanter Prison
3. Sir George (Bluidy) Mackenzie
4. George Buchanan
5. Walter Scott, Sr.
6. Alexander Munro & son
7. Alexander Henderson
8. William Carstares
9. Captain John Porteous
10. John Gray ("Bobby" s owner)

Plan of the current Greyfriars Kirk Yard

them to be written out after their return to their several parishes and counties of Scotland.

Time has added the embellishment, including a painting by Sir William Allan ca. 1840, that the Covenant was taken outside for signature by the common people gathered there, but truth is that the flat gravestones did not then exist and it was not taken outside. The following day it was taken to the Tailor's Hall in the Cowgate where burghers and ministers signed and on subsequent days it was taken to other churches for signature. There were, however, many copies made which were sent to the principal towns of Scotland and to Ireland where local people were able to sign. The original is thought to be that in the Huntley House Museum, but Greyfriars has its own 'original' copy in pride of place in the Kirk Session room.

The Greyfriars Kirk again became the focus of the Covenanters, when their army was crushed at the battle of Bothwell Brig (near Glasgow) on 22 June 1679. About 1100 prisoners were taken and imprisoned in Greyfriars Kirk Yard - since called the Covenanter Prison. At the time the space was called the Inner Greyfriar Yard and consisted of about three acres of grassland surrounded by high walls. Only a small portion of the yard is visible today because of building in the intervening years. Here they were held in the open with little food for up to five months. Some signed a bond and were released, but a hard core of over 300 remained. Five were hanged in reprisal for the murder of Archbishop Sharp despite their having nothing to do with it. Some prisoners were moved to the

Tolbooth prison and the balance of 257 was sentenced to slavery in the Colonies. These were shipped aboard the ill fated "*Crown*" in which 211 of them met a watery grave. The survivors were later transported to America.

The "Martyr's Memorial" stands within the Greyfriars Kirk Yard. It commemorates some 18,000 Covenanters who died for their faith. The source for this often quoted figure is *The Scots Worthies* by John Howie of Lochgoin,

Of these 1700 were shipped to the plantations, besides 750 who were banished to the northern islands, of whom 200 were wilfully murdered. Those who suffered by imprisonment, confinement, and other cruelties of this nature were computed at or about 3,600, including 800 who were outlawed, and 55 who were sentenced to be executed when apprehended. Those killed in several skirmishes or on surprise, and those who died of their wounds on such occasions, were reckoned to be 680. Those who went into voluntary banishment to other countries were calculated at 7,000. About 498 were murdered in cold blood, without process of law, besides 362 who were by form of law executed. The number of those who perished through cold, hunger and other distresses, contracted in their flight to the mountains, and who sometimes even when on the point of death were murdered by the bloody soldiers, cannot well be calculated, but will certainly make up the number above specified.

The grand total may well be in excess of 30,000 since Howie does not take into account the thousands of Covenanter soldiers who died in battles, of which over

12,000 died in the Montrose campaigns of 1644 and 1645, with more at Dunbar in 1650 and Worcester in 1651.

The memorial itself poignantly marks the area where the remains of those executed in the nearby Grassmarket are buried. It is said that the executed should not lie in hallowed ground but the gravediggers at the time are thought to have ensured the martyrs were properly buried away from the common thieves and murderers. The inscription reads:

Halt passenger take heed what thou dost see
This tomb doth shew for what some men did die
Here lies interr'd the dust of these who stood
Gainst perjury resisting unto blood
Adhering to the Covenants and Laws
Establishing the same which was the Cause
Then their lives were sacrificed unto the Lust
Or Prelatist's abjur'd though here their dust
Lies mix with murders and other crew
Whom justice did justly to death pursue
But as for this in them no cause was found
Worthy of death but only they were found
Constant and steadfast zealous witnessing
For the prerogatives of CHRIST their king
Which truths were feared by famous Guthrie's head
And all along to Mr. Renwick's blood
They did endure the wrath of enemies
Reproaches torments deaths and injuries
But yet they're these who from such troubles came
And now triumph in glory with the LAMB

From May 27th 1661 that the noble Marquess of Argyle suffered to the seventeenth of Febr 1688 that Mr. James Renwick suffr'd were executed at Edinburgh about an hundred of Noblemen Gentlemen Ministers & others noble martyrs for JESUS CHRIST. The most part of them lies here.

This Tomb was erected anno 1706.

Ironically, near the "Prison" stands the mausoleum of Sir George MacKenzie, who as King's Advocate, was responsible for the zealous prosecution of the Covenanters and gained for himself the title "Bluidy" MacKenzie Nearby also stands the memorial of Rev. Alexander Henderson who was attacked even in death, by soldiers sent to deface the stone, and at which they fired their rifles.

VII. The Bishops' Wars and Wars of the Three Kingdoms 1639 - 1646

The best-known events of the Covenanters tend to be the pivotal National Covenant (1638), the Solemn League and Covenant (1643) and the horrors of "The Killing Time" (1684-5). But in between there were other events of significance, which should not be overlooked. Not least of these were "The Bishops' Wars" and the ongoing interference of the three countries - England, Ireland and Scotland, in one another's affairs that became the Wars of the Three Kingdoms.

In the course of 1639 and 1640, Charles I clashed twice with his Scottish subjects in the Bishops' Wars - so called because of the resistance by the Presbyterians to the rule by bishops (episcopacy). But there was also in a short space of time the rebellion of the Catholic Irish (and Old English settlers from Norman times) in October 1641 for which a Scot's army went to Ireland in 1642. Meanwhile, Civil War erupted in England in August 1642 in which the Covenanters' Army became embroiled after the signing of the Solemn League and Covenant in 1643. If that wasn't enough, an Irish force under Alastair McColl landed in Argyll in 1644 and joined up with the royalist forces under the Marquis of Montrose. Thus Scotland was involved in wars on three fronts for three different reasons - the Covenanters for religion; the political objectives for a

Greater Britain; and the private ambitions of the Marquess of Argyll to acquire the Lordship of the Isles.

The Bishops' Wars

Following the National Covenant of 1638, there was a wave of euphoria that surged through the Presbyterian leaders resulting in dreams of extending "the royal prerogative of King Jesus through all the earth." For the King there was significant dangers as not only were the Covenanters challenging his authority in Scotland, it also stimulated the Puritan movement in England. The Bishops' Wars were almost non-events with little real fighting at national level, but was an excuse for feuding between local families in the northeast and west of Scotland.

The First Bishops' War began in March 1639 and lasted for about five weeks during which there was skirmishing in Invernesshire. Under Montrose (at this juncture a Covenanter) and Alexander Leslie, Aberdeen was taken by Covenanting forces marching under flags bearing the legend "For Religion, the Covenant and the Country." The rank and file wore a blue scarf across their chests and under the left arm - called "the Covenanter's ribbon." The Earl of Huntley was seized and taken to Edinburgh, but the first serious blood to flow occurred on 10 May in the "Trot of Turriff" which was a victory for the royalists followed by their recapturing Aberdeen. However, the Covenanters forces under Montrose and Leslie chased them out again within the month.

In the south, the Covenanters took control of the strong castles of Dumbarton and Edinburgh and by May they had some 20,000 men in arms. On 9 May Leslie was commissioned to command it "for defence of the Covenant, for religion, crown and country." King Charles meanwhile was approaching with an army of about 21,000 and had issued a proclamation at Newcastle offering representation in Parliament and requiring the Scots to withdraw ten

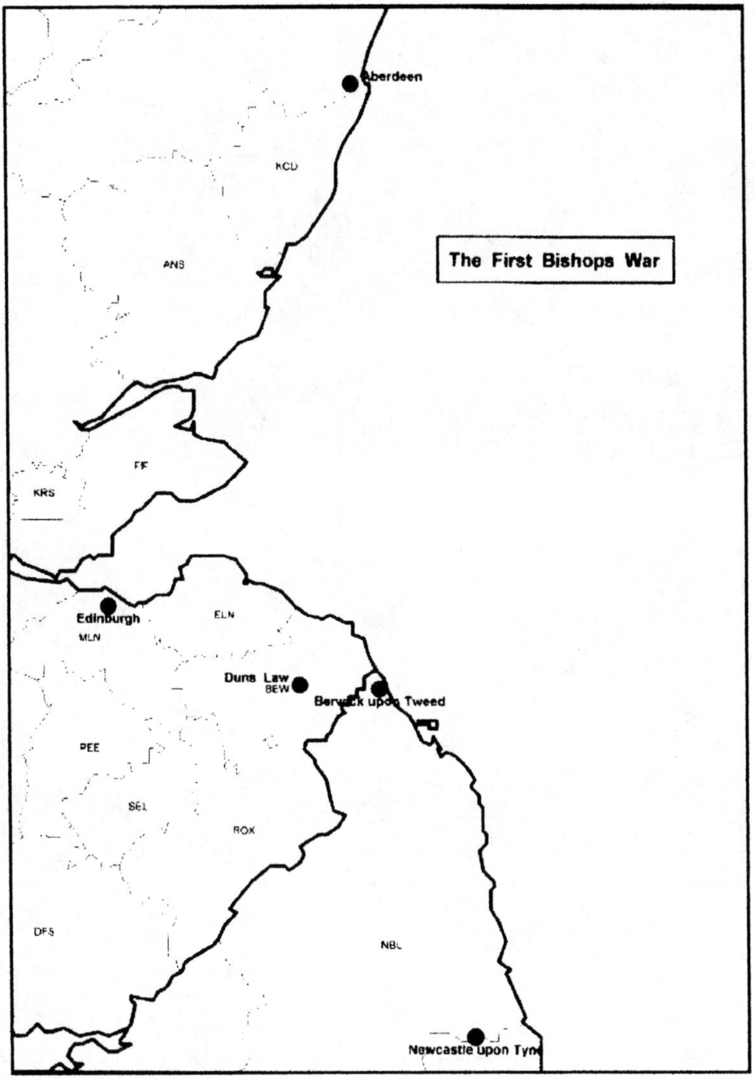

The First Bishops War
Aberdeen
KCD
ANS
FIF
KRS
Edinburgh
MLN
ELN
Duns Law
BEW
Berwick upon Tweed
PEE
SEL
ROX
DFS
NBL
Newcastle upon Tyn

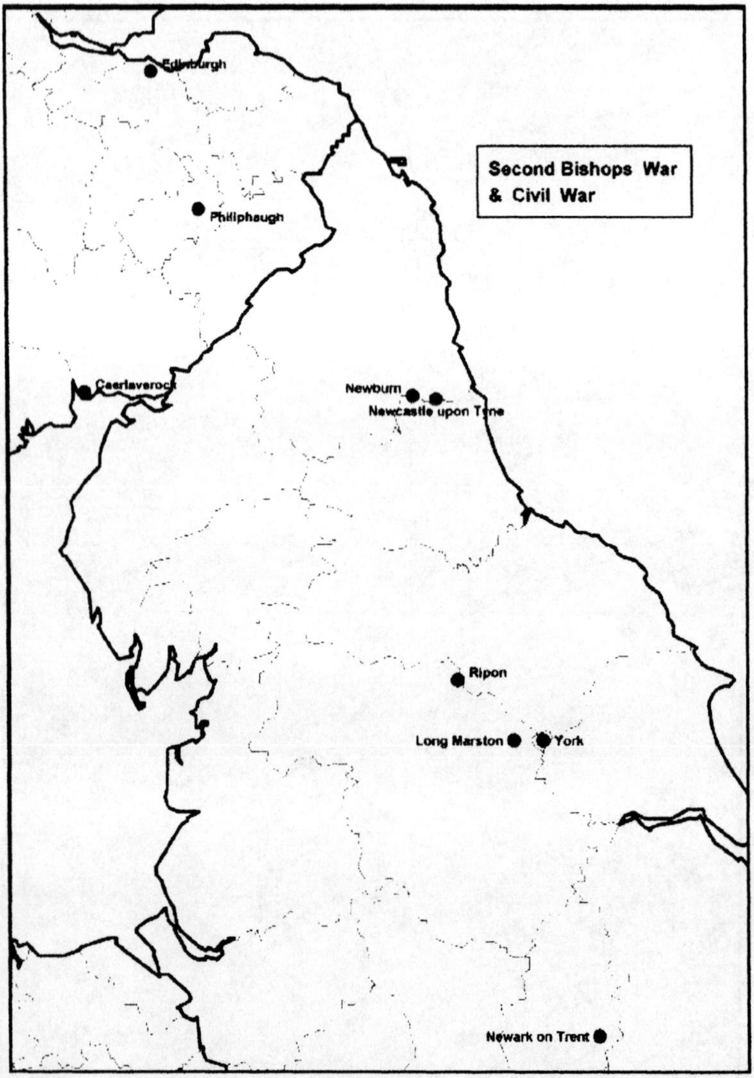

Second Bishops War & Civil War
Edinburgh
Philiphaugh
Caerlaverock
Newburn
Newcastle upon Tyne
Ripon
Long Marston
York
Newark on Trent

miles from the border. Leslie and his troops camped at Duns Law twelve miles away. The main battle proposed by Charles never developed, instead there was a low key stand off at Duns Law in the Borders on 5 June 1639 followed by the Treaty of Birks (Berwick) thirteen days later. The Covenanters withdrew with Charles's undertaking to accept civil and ecclesiastical control by the Parliaments and Assemblies respectively, ringing in their ears.

The treaty was at best a convenient breathing space, but was rejected by the General Assembly and The Estates. In August 1640, the Covenanting army made a pre-emptive strike and pushed the Royalist forces back to the River Tyne, defeated it at the battle of Newburn on 28 August and entered the city of Newcastle on the 30th. Although some pockets of resistance remained for a while - Caerlaverock Castle and Edinburgh held out till September, hostilities ceased with the Treaty of Ripon on 26 October 1640.

It is of note that that the leading dissenting nobles - Loudon, Eglinton and Rothes led regiments in the First Bishops' War and many feudal nobles regained their status of old as warlords. Their troops also included a backbone of professional officers and sergeants - Alexander Leslie was a field marshal in the Swedish Army. Many of the regiments also had their own ministers with them such that over a third of the ministers of the Kirk served in the dozen or so armies of the Covenant conveying the message of it being a holy war. But, there was also an element of settling old scores, with Archibald Campbell, the eighth Earl and first Marquis of Argyll, engaged in a private war in the Braes of Mar, Atholl, Angus and Rannoch before he moved on to secure Dumbarton Castle against a threat from Ireland.

The Bishops' Wars did not, however, bring a feeling of security to any of the combatants. In Scotland there was a move for political change and significantly no representation was given the Covenanters on the newly formed executive - "The Committee of Estates." The English Parliamentarians were fearful of the price the Scots might ask for their support whether in terms of money or religion. The Marquis of Argyll had his own agenda and saw the prospect of further war between himself and the MacDonalds, both Scots and Irish, which had centred on Kintyre and the islands of Colonsay and Islay in 1639.

Meanwhile in England

While Scotland was engaged in the Bishops' Wars there was growing resistance to the autocratic ways of King Charles I who used the English Parliament merely as a source of funds for his policies. The English Civil Wars fell into two distinct phases 1642-6 and 1648-9, while the Irish war was bubbling away from 1641-9 when Cromwell descended upon them.

The outbreak of the First Civil war saw the distinction between the royalist 'Cavaliers' from the Spanish caballero meaning knight or horseman, who were reasoned to be royalists, and feudal gentry who supported absolute power, and were favourably inclined to a quasi Catholic religion. The Parliamentarians were identified as 'Roundheads' from the close-cropped hairstyle of the Puritans, and had the support of the City of London Guilds - the source of funds that the king so often turned to. But these stereotypes do not really fit as the populace was divided across all issues. It is probably true, however, that few Catholics belonged to the Parliamentary party and not many Puritans belonged to the royalist party.

Oliver Cromwell

Oliver Cromwell was born in Huntingdon in 1599 and was educated at Cambridge University from 23 April 1616, but he left when his father died 24 June 1617. It is likely that he studied law at Lincoln's Inn, as had his father. At the age of twenty-one he married Elizabeth Bourchier at St Giles Church, Cripplegate, London on 22 August 1620. She was the daughter of Sir James Bourchier of Tower Hill, who was a fur and leather dealer. She bore Cromwell eight children. At one point he was disposed to migrate to America but his fortune changed greatly in 1636 when an uncle, Sir Thomas Steward, left him a very substantial estate in the cathedral town of Ely. His efforts on behalf of the local people earned him the nickname of 'Lord of the Fens' (the wetlands of Cambridgeshire).

He became the Member of Parliament for Huntingdon in 1628 and for Cambridge in 1641. He appears to have suffered a period of troubled conscience before he became a committed Christian and Puritan about 1638. It is from this time that he showed tremendous will power and sense of purpose that was his trademark. He knew what he wanted and spared no one and least of all himself, until his objectives were secure. He served in the army when civil war broke out and soon distinguished himself as a natural leader and brave soldier. At Edge Hill in 1642 he rallied the Parliamentary troops following a royalist cavalry charge. Again he was distinguished at Marston Moor in 1644 where he is quoted as saying "God made them as stubble to our swords." At Naseby on 14 June 1645 the New Model Army was again victorious and a month later the royal forces in the West of England were routed at Langport in Somerset. By 1646 King Charles was at the end of his tether and placed himself into Scottish hands.

Dissension in the Scottish ranks.

There was dissension in the Scottish ranks, as James Graham, fifth Earl and first Marquis of Montrose, had formed the "Cumbernauld Bond." This was a pledge with other nobles to promote the public aims of the Covenant. It came about because they were concerned by the politics of Argyll and his pursuit of self-interests. Montrose also had second thoughts about the National League and Covenant, objecting to the pledge under cover of religion, to wrest the regal authority from the King. Whether this was so, or pique at not being made the commander of the armies, or more likely that his arch enemy Argyll had pride of place among the Covenanters. Whatever the reason he took up arms for the King. So 1644 also saw the direct intervention of the Irish soldiers in Scotland. Led by Alastair MacDonald, son to Coll the left-handed of Colonsay (ousted by the Campbells from Colonsay), and a MacDonald of Dunnyveg, he was close kin to the Earl of Antrim. With him came some 1,000 clansmen with families and cattle, who landed at Ardnamurchan on the west coast of Scotland and joined up with Montrose at Blair Atholl.

There followed a golden year for Montrose and his band, with victory at Tippermuir near Perth (1644). At the Bridge of Dee, his troops saw off the best the Covenanters could offer and sacked Aberdeen with three days of pillage, rape and murder. Argyll himself managed to escape, only to be thrashed again at Inverlochy (1645) Further successes followed at Auldearn, near Nairn Alford, and at Kilsyth on the Borders, where he swept the Covenanter army down the hill to have Scotland at his feet.

With the government and Argyll fled into England, Montrose made peace with the local noblemen and burghs. However, fate and the self-interest of his supporters deserted him with his Gordon soldiers leaving in a huff, and the Irish left to go and settle some more old scores with the Campbells. Thus weakened, his luck ran out at Philiphaugh (1645) where, lacking good intelligence, he was routed by David Leslie and the Covenanter Army. Montrose fled to exile on the Continent, to return over four years later in support of Charles II, but ended upon the gallows in Edinburgh.

The Scots in England

The initial reaction of the Covenanters to the English First Civil War (1642-1646) was to try and keep out of it. However, in August 1643, the English parliament appealed to the new and political Committee of Estates for military help. Within days Alexander Henderson produced a draft of the Solemn League and Covenant. Three months later a Scottish Army of the Covenant, under Alexander Leslie (now Earl of Leven), crossed the Border and was met with resistance at Newcastle, which they bypassed. Attacking York, they were able to play a significant part in the royalist defeat at Marston Moor in July 1644. Returning to Newcastle the Covenanters besieged the city, which finally surrendered in October.

Meanwhile, the alliance with the English Parliamentarians was under strain with the Scots complaining that the promised monies for the army were much delayed, its needs were not being met and the hope of religious uniformity was fading. The English Parliamentarians saw Scottish forces being withdrawn to meet Montrose and feared another deal with King Charles. Elsewhere, Leven turned to towards Newark - the last surviving stronghold in the Midlands that Charles held. The siege began in November 1645 and was still in progress on 5 May 1646, when Charles made his way to surrender to the Scottish Army.

The English First Civil War was at an end leaving the hard line Covenanters, once again, in charge of Scotland. King Charles, meanwhile, was taken to Newcastle where he was held prisoner, much to his disgust. On 24 July the Propositions, the final ultimatum of the Solemn League and Covenant, were put to the King. These required him to accept the Covenant, establish religious uniformity in Scotland and England, yield his partisan supporters and surrender control of the militia for twenty years. Charles was as stubborn as ever and declined the terms offered.

The Scots wanted to get out of the alliance and to withdraw their army, but the English Parliamentarians resolved that they could do as they wished with the King while he remained on English territory. This placed the Scots in a quandary, as they either had to give up "their" King or face the might of the Independent's army - the New Model Army of Cromwell. Practical considerations eventually held the day with the Scots accepting £400,000 in full discharge of their claim for arrears of pay, etc. On 3 February 1647, half the due payment was made and on the same day, Charles was handed over to Parliament's Commissioners. Here ended the Solemn League and Covenant.

In England a split was developing between the Parliamentarians and the Independents led by Oliver Cromwell. With his New Model Army (so called because they were trained in and adopted the latest Swedish military skills) he set them to organise the public peace and liberties and in 1647 it entered London. The mainly local disturbances in 1648 led to the Second Civil War. These rebellions were quickly dealt with but the country was then hit by a terrible harvest, bread prices soared and the army was unpaid. Scotland meanwhile was unhappy with the New Model Army on its doorstep. The army had no oath or Covenant, and allowed toleration of all religions, which troubled the Scottish Presbyterians. This led to yet more intrigue, a split in the Covenanter ranks and the 'Engagement' with King Charles. It would end with the Union of three countries and the Protectorate under Oliver Cromwell.

VIII. Engagers and Resolutioners vs. Whigs, Protesters and Remonstrants

After King Charles surrendered to the Scottish Army at Newark in May 1646, the first Civil War was at an end. The Covenanters retreated with their prize to Newcastle where King Charles remained a hostage of the Scots for some nine months, refusing to take the Solemn League and Covenant, which would have committed him to a Presbyterian settlement in all three kingdoms. Eventually the English Parliament paid £200,000, half of the arrears of pay, and the Scottish army marched out of Newcastle leaving Charles to his fate. The kidnapping of King Charles at Holdenby by soldiers under the command of Cornet Joyce of the New Model Army in June 1647, created yet another crisis for the Covenanters, which would see them entering into an agreement to provide military aid to King Charles in exchange for an assortment of watered down promises and commitments. Meanwhile the fanatics in the New Model Army denounced Charles as responsible for the recent bloodshed in the wars and voices were raised demanding his life. In November 1647 Charles escaped to Carisbrook Castle on the Isle of Wight off of the south coast of England, and convenient for a dash to France if necessary. The next few years would see one of the most varied and variable periods in Scottish politics.

The Engagement

The dichotomy for the Scots was their general acceptance of a King, as long as he did not interfere with religion. So it was that royalists, led by the Duke of Hamilton, met with the King on the Isle of Wight in December 1647. Here they drew up a secret treaty in which Hamilton and his party agreed to raise an army in Scotland to assist the King to regain his throne in England. For their help, the King promised to allow the Solemn League and Covenant to be approved by the English Parliament and to support a form of Presbyterian government for three years after which an assembly of divines and twenty commissioners appointed by the king should meet and determine the future nature of church government. This treaty was known as "The Engagement" and the Duke of Hamilton and his party were known as the "Engagers." Had knowledge of the agreement got out there would have been an immediate invasion of Scotland, so the document was wrapped in lead and buried in the gardens of Carisbrook Castle.

It was no surprise, however, that when the details of "the Engagement" became known there was widespread dissension among the Covenanters. The Commission of the General Assembly met and a statement was issued declaring the arrangements to be sinful and in breach of Covenant vows. But the royalists were in control of the Parliament at this time and the Covenanters' objections were disregarded. Now more than at any previous time, Robert Burn's lament: described the misfortunes to follow.

The Solemn League and Covenant
Now brings a smile, now brings a tear;
But sacred Feedom, too, was theirs -
If thou'rt a slave, indulge thy sneer.

The Scottish Parliament started down a dangerous path by passing an act that required all subjects to sign a bond supporting "the Engagement." But the General Assembly, which met in July 1648, promptly rejected the legislation and warned all members of the Church of Scotland of the unlawful nature of the treaty. They also censured ministers who supported the Engagement. A letter was sent to the King warning him that the concessions were not enough and urged him to accept the Covenant so they could support him. As to be expected the resistance to the treaty was at its strongest in the southwest of Scotland. Generally the smaller land owners and tenants, artisans, the professional classes and the poor strongly opposed the treaty and held out for full implementation of the Solemn League and Covenant, including Presbyterianism in England.

The alliance with the Parliamentarians in England rapidly dissolved and so, once again, there was a demand for military conscription. However, ten years of discord, the batterings by Montrose and a dreadful year of the plague, let alone a treaty which they did not support, had its consequences among the populace. Enough was enough and large areas of the country simply refused to join the new army, many fled to Ireland and others banded together to resist the conscription. The districts of Clydesdale, Kyle and Cunningham for the first time associated themselves with Fife in supporting the Covenanters. Representatives assembled at Mauchline Muir in armed protest on 12 June 1648 but were disorganised and dispersed with some bloodshed by the military. But it set the tone for the relationships with the south and west of Scotland for the next forty years.

At length the new army was mustered and set out to fight the royal fight. This time the Duke of Hamilton led them, ten years previous he had sought to close the Glasgow Assembly. They were, however, but a third of the hoped for 30,000, and mostly raw recruits hardly able to sit on a horse when at the trot, with no cannon and poorly trained. On 8 July 1648 they crossed the border and entered Carlisle where Hamilton hoped to find English royalists and Scots veterans from Ireland. His progress south was slow over heavy roads and with insufficient transport and a month later was outside Preston in Lancashire. The English response was slow in coming but devastating in its effect when, on 17 August Cromwell's army inflicted heavy losses, finally destroying the Scots at Uttoxeter on 25 August.

The Protester Whigs

The news of the Engagers' lost causes at Preston and Uttoxeter had a dramatic effect on their opposition, which included those from the Mauchline Moor incident. By 28 August the Covenanters were marching on Edinburgh. On this occasion they had leadership by the Earls of Loudon, Eglinton and Cassillis - all from Ayrshire, the support of the Earl of Argyll and the sympathetic support of the two army leaders - the Earl of Leven and David Leslie. The march was called "The Whiggamore Raid" and entered Edinburgh on 5 September to overturn the Engager government that showed little resistance. Fleeing to Stirling the government surrendered after three weeks and on 26 September the Earl of Argyll took the initiative to communicate with Cromwell.

Some would say that there was a clerical tyranny set to rule Scotland. Cromwell entered Edinburgh on 4 October 1648 and left three days later reasonably satisfied with arrangements that would deal rigorously with the Engagers and secure the position of the Protesters as the Whigs (after Whiggamore) were also called. A new Parliament was convened in January 1649 with Argyll and the Kirk in prominence, with only sixteen peers in it - all supporters of the die hard Covenanters. To this end, all supporters of the Engagement were prevented from representation and were followed by legislation that would bar them from offices of trust. - the "Act of Classes for purging the Judicatories and other places of public trust." came into being on 23 January 1649. On 30 January 1649, King Charles I was beheaded in London.

King Charles II

The execution of a Scottish King by the English proved too much for even the radical Covenanters. The Scottish Parliament reacted by declaring the Crown Prince as King Charles II of England, Scotland and Ireland conditional on him accepting the National Covenant and the Solemn League and Covenant. After much prolonged negotiations, King Charles II went to Scotland on 23 June 1650, and became for all practical purposes the prisoner of the Covenanters. But, his aspirations to become King of England were severely dented by Cromwell's army mounting a pre-emptive strike at the battle of Dunbar 3 September 1650. Here a numerically superior, but demoralised and purged, Scottish army was vanquished and, once again, Cromwell seized Edinburgh.

The ruling Covenanter organisations were the Committee of Estates and Commission of the Kirk, both of which moved to Stirling and then Perth where they prepared for further resistance to Cromwell. It would make for a question in a modern day quiz to ask what happened next - to which the inevitable answer is they again disagreed with one another. Meanwhile, two events took place. Early in October 1650, Charles made a desperate dash for freedom - known as "the Start," but was brought back to Perth within a few days. And on 22 October the die hard Covenanters met at Dumfries and produced a document or "Remonstrance" demanding the King's full compliance with both Covenants. They also attributed the defeat at Dunbar to there being too many Engagers in it and demanded a further purge of the army.

The government, then in Perth, rejected the Remonstrance and a large number of the ministers on the Commission of the Kirk walked out. The remainder passed resolutions repealing the Act of Classes and became known as the "Resolutioners." Yet again, the political situation had polarised into two groups with varying labels - the die hards were variously called Whigs, Protesters, and Remonstrants; and the moderates were called the Engagers and the Resolutioners.

The leaders of the Protestors were some of the most famous Covenanters - the Rev. James Guthrie, Patrick Gillespie, Lord Wariston and Rev. Samuel Rutherford who warned of dangers and called for national repentance. With hindsight it can be said that the Protesters were right and the Resolutioners were wrong to repeal the Act of Classes. Many of the people who now rose to power with the more moderate policy were enemies of the Covenanters and became persecutors of Presbyterians after 1660.

The die hard Covenanters received a further set back when on 1 December 1650 their army was tempted into battle at Hamilton and was badly beaten by a superior English force. This put an end to organised military resistance by the Covenanters, although their grassroots objections to royal authority and episcopacy continued until 1688.

The consequence of the defeat was a surge of support for the King with erstwhile patriots and persons previously excluded by the Act of Classes crawling out from hiding to declare their support. On this groundswell Charles was compromised into signing the two Covenants and also a document that apologised for his father's sins against Scotland and for idolatry of his mother, a Roman Catholic. He would remember these personal insults to his family but at the time political necessity drove him on as he desperately needed a base from which to mount his claim to the English throne. Thus on 1 January 1651 at Scone, Argyll placed the crown on the head of King Charles II.

King Charles II was, however, to have a short reign when at Worcester on 3 September 1651, the Scottish army was destroyed and he fled into nine years of exile. Cromwell meanwhile, mopped up resistance in Scotland

and proceeded to build a chain of forts across the country to keep the nation in order. For the first time there was one authority throughout the Kingdoms and in 1654 a new Union flag was devised. It had four quarters with quarters 1 and 4 containing the red cross of St George, quarter 2 the rampant lion of Scotland and quarter 3 the Irish harp, thus symbolising a British Republic under Oliver Cromwell, Lord Protector.

IX. Cromwell; the Restoration of King Charles II and a return to episcopacy

The supremacy of Cromwell brought Scotland an unaccustomed experience of a general peace. For eight years, the Scots had been demanding ecclesiastical harmony of the English, but in retaliation the Cromwellian regime enforced political cooperation and ecclesiastical tolerance. From this flowed a firm and impartial government that was honest, even handed and efficient. For good measure in an act of considerable magnanimity, the Scots were offered a union with England and representation in the English Parliament.

In January 1652, a group of Commissioners assembled at Dalkeith with the aim of implementing a union. The assembly formally annulled every authority derived from Charles Stuart and summoned the shires and burghs to send representatives to meet with them. Here the representatives were given three propositions:

1. Acceptance of Parliament's "Tender" of union.

2. Acknowledgment of Parliament's authority in Scotland

3. To provide information as to what was considered necessary to bring the union into effect.

The agreement was almost unanimous with twenty-nine out of thirty-one shires accepting the Tender - Ayr and Renfrew dissenting. Of the fifty-eight burghs, fourteen in the southwest of Scotland dissented. The main, and not unexpected, concern of the populace was the proposed treatment of religion.

In England there was a period of friction between Cromwell and the Parliament. The Bill of Union was not passed first time round and Parliament was dissolved. In the following Parliament the Bill did not reach its third reading, which would have made it law. On this occasion, Parliament yielded its power to Cromwell who then issued his Instrument of Government on 16 December 1653, which established "a Commonwealth of England, Scotland and Ireland." "The Ordinance of Union" was passed by the Protector and Council on 12 April 1654, and was proclaimed in Edinburgh on 4 May. The Bill of Union finally received Parliamentary assent and became law on 28 April 1657.

History records a range of denunciations of Cromwell by the Presbyterians. Generally they regarded him as a usurper because he was not the anointed king, although with time, the vehemence of the language has gradually diminished. Objectively, it has to be said that Scotland as a whole derived much benefit from a firm hand on the reins of power. The Union created representation in Parliament; abolished the monarchy and the right of the Estates to assemble; established trade free of customs duty between England and Scotland; abolished vassals and the feudal system and forced a relative peace throughout the land, and finally it ordained the inclusion of the Cross of St. Andrew in the Arms of the Commonwealth in public seals

In May 1655 a separate Council of State for Scotland was set up which had two Scots among its nine members. In addition to ensuring the continuance of the Union and the establishment of good government, the Council was directed to encourage the preaching of the Gospel; encourage the growth of Universities and schools; purge the burghs of disaffected magistrates; administer justice; to approximate the judicial system to that of England; encourage trade and foster the revenue. The burghs were able to elect their magistrates and Justice of the Peace courts were set up.

In the area of religion, the Cromwellian regime favoured the Protesters against the Resolutioners essentially because they had a history of being anti royalist. In a way this helped balance the fact that about 750 of the total 900 ministers in Scotland were Resolutioners. Cromwell had dissolved the General Assembly in 1653, which was not to meet again for the next thirty-seven years. However, the Synods and Presbyteries were allowed to continue their functions. In 1654, Scotland was divided into five provinces to which were appointed 'Provincial Certyfers' who were responsible for appointments of ministers, and control of the manses and stipends. In 1655 the role of the Certifyers was passed to the Presbyteries, on condition that any new minister who was appointed agreed to live peaceably under the Protectorate.

On 3 September 1658 the Lord Protector, Oliver Cromwell, died leaving the reins in the hands of his son, Richard, who was not of his father's calibre. In a short space of time a Parliament was called and then, on 24 April 1659, dissolved. Richard Cromwell stood down and the army was left in power. The demand for parliametary authority and abolition of rule by the sword gathered momentum in England but it was in Scotland that action took place. Here General Monck summoned representatives to Edinburgh and launched his plan to restore a Scottish king and Scotland's independence. They were charged with maintaining order in his absence while he and his army marched to London, arriving in February 1660.

A bizarre incident occured in London where some royalist supporters decided that they wanted to show their hatred for the former Protector and on 29 January 1660 they dug up Cromwell's body. They also dug up the body of Henry Ireton, Cromwell's son-in-law who had died in Ireland in 1652; and that of another Member of Parliament, John Bradshaw who had died in 1659. The bodies were stored overnight in a public house, the Red Lion Inn at Holborn in London. The following day the bodies were hung up on public display at Tyburn exposed to stones and mud thrown by the populace. After about six hours the bodies were cut down and (as for the executed Covenanters) the heads hacked off. It took eight blows to severe Cromwell's head as his body had been embalmed. The heads were taken to the Westminster Hall where they were placed on the railings and remained there till 1684. The bodies are believed to have been thrown into a pit at Tyburn.

Cromwell's head is said to have been blown down during a storm and a sentry picked it up and took it home. The head was subsequently sold by the soldier's daughter to a family in Cambridgeshire who sold it on to an actor named Samuel Russell. It was later displayed for a while and eventually went to Sydney Sussex College at Cambridge University, where it was secretly buried in 1960.

The Restoration of King Charles II

In England the Rump Parliament was restored and the issue of the Union was raised but discussion was not serious. In their fourth session in April, the Parliament voted in favour of restoring the old constitution and Scotland had her independence and its own monarch once more.

Meanwhile the largely Presbyterian Parliament voted for Presbyterianism and adopted the Westminster Confession; printed and distributed the Solemn League and Covenant and prepared a Bill for reorganising the Church on a Presbyterian model. On the 16 March, however, Parliament was dissolved and General Monck took charge assisted by a Council of State. Monck then did and about face turning from purported loyalty to the army and declared he was for the King. The terms proposed by the Council for Charles' return were vetoed by Monck recognising that it was up to Parliament to set any terms and conditions, especially as to those exempted from any general pardon. As a result it was made known to King Charles the policies that Monck considered should be adopted. These were: a general amnesty with few exceptions; to confirm possession of the confiscated property whether obtained by purchase, or a gift, or were Crown or Church lands, or forfeited; to grant liberty of conscience to all his subjects. The King's terms of acceptance were made in his Declaration at Breda on 14 April 1660 (Appendix 14)

In the period leading up to the Restoration, the Presbyterians had charged the Rev. James Sharp of Crail, Fife, leader of the Resolutioners, with the task of preparing the King for his return and, importantly, to ensure that the King would accept the Covenants. But before long Sharp disclosed his true colours and became a turncoat Episcopalian and was made Archbishop of St. Andrews

In Holland the emissaries of England met with Charles to agree the terms of his restoration to the throne. The assumption appears to have been made that the Scots would just tag along with the English agreements. The Declaration at Breda (Appendix 14) clearly states that he is "Charles, by the grace of God, King of England, Scotland, France, and Ireland, defender of the faith, &c." Equally clear is that the assurances that Sharp had been specifically briefed on - "that the Kirk of Scotland may, without interruption or encroachment, enjoy the freedom and privileges of her established judicatures, ratified by the laws of the land." were not stated, which rather left the way open for Charles to do more or less what he pleased.

On 14 May 1660 Charles was, again, proclaimed King in Edinburgh and Scotland set its cap at having another Stuart King despite the antecedent problems that they had brought the Presbyterians. It seems almost naive of the Presbyterians to think that they would be better off under King Charles II, but, Scotland had undergone some twenty-five years without a monarch and a generation had grown up without the stern disciplines of the Covenanters. All they could see around them was a Kirk yet again divided and riddled with dissension. Forgetting the past, the populace greeted the new king with celebrations.

Episcopacy returns

At the time of King Charles's return, Scotland had over 900 parishes divided into sixty-eight Presbyteries and fourteen Synods. Every parish had its minister; every village a school and most families had their family Bible. The ministers subscribed to the Westminster Confession, preached three times a week and catechised once a week The only blot was the dissension by the Whiggamore, Protesters or Remonstrants who rejected Charles in 1650 and deemed him now, as then, as insincere and treacherous.

By this time it was too late to prevent Charles's clamp down on Presbyterianism. The Act Recissory was pushed through Parliament, all legislation since 1633 was declared annulled and the Covenants declared illegal. There was no General Assembly called, while synods and presbyteries were forbidden to meet. The bitterest blow was the King's announcement of his intention to restore the Bishops' rule in the Church of Scotland. There followed the inevitable settling of old scores with the executions of the Marquis of Argyll (27 May 1661), the Rev. James Guthrie (1 June 1661) and Lord Warriston (22 July 1663).

In his appointment of ministers, Charles indicated that he would not have any truck with the Covenanters and clearly favoured the Engagers. Thus Middleton, the hard drinking soldier, was now an Earl and responsible, as Lord High Commissioner, for calling Parliament. He was also Commander in Chief of the army. The Earl of Glencairn was made Chancellor and other royalist supporters were appointed to positions of power - the Earl of Crawford received the Treasury and the Earl of Rothes Presidency of the Council. Last but by no means least, John Maitland, Duke of Lauderdale, a man against Popery and with Presbyterian leanings, was appointed to Secretary of State. Having the King's ear Lauderdale was able to shape policy and was for all practicable purposes the ruler of Scotland for the next twenty-two years.

In Scotland, Middleton saw through some 400 pieces of legislation in the first year, which took over seven hours to proclaim at the Mercat Cross in Edinburgh.

The Mercat Cross, Edinburgh

In June 1662, the "Act of Presentation and Collation," sometimes called Middleton's Act, made the lawful worship by the Presbyterians almost impossible. The Act required ministers who had been appointed by congregations or

Presbyteries since 1649 to be represented by a patron and to re-apply through the bishops in order to continue their ministry. By the summer of 1653, of the 952 ministers in the Church of Scotland, over 300 were "outed," with the west of Scotland being particularly badly hit. The Synod of Dumfries lost more than half of its ministers and those of Glasgow and Ayr lost some two thirds of their ministers rather than they submit to lay patronage and endorsement by the bishops. This precipitate action sowed the seeds for rebellion, especially in the southwest.

Shortly after, in March 1663, Middleton fell from grace and the Scottish Privy Council was restored to authority in Edinburgh where Archbishop Sharp held sway until in the aftermath of the Pentland Rising, Lauderdale intervened in the excesses. The Earl of Rothes, a drunk and debaucher, and son of a former Covenanter became the new Lord High Commissioner

An early act of the Privy Council, under Lauderdale's supervision, was to reintroduce the ancient method (dating from 1367) of appointment of the Lords of the Articles. The original arrangement was to create a representative Committee (of burghers), but was translated to become one where the Bishops chose eight nobles, the nobles chose eight Bishops; the sixteen then chose as many from the combined burgesses and county barons, and finally the Lord High Commissioner added the Officers of State. This very powerful Committee was immediately seeded by Sharp with his chosen Bishops and was seen as a welcome move towards episcopacy by Lauderdale.

Politics aside, the Privy Council was enjoined to counter a growing resistance to the curates who had been appointed to the parishes where the ministers had been "outed." In July 1663 they produced an "Act for Separation and Disobedience to Ecclesiastical Authority," also known as the "Bishops Drag Net," which imposed variable and heavy fines on persons who did not attend their parish church and included the ominous and repressive provision "and such other corporal punishment as they (the Council) shall see fit." When John Welch of Irongray and Gabriel Semple of Kirkpatrick, in the Presbytery of Dumfries, started to preach in the fields, fresh legislation was enacted in the August of 1663, requiring outed ministers to remove themselves and their families twenty miles from their former parish, neither were they to reside within six miles of a cathedral city or three miles from a royal burgh.

The most invidious action was by Archbishop Sharp, who being dissatisfied with Lauderdale's soft approach, sought the King's permission to set up a Court of High Commission to ensure that Acts of Parliament and the Privy Council were "put into vigorous and impartial execution." This Court of High Commission became, at once, the tool for Sharp's persecution of the Presbyterians, although it was also used against Catholics and resembled the Inquisition. The court consisted of nine prelates and thirty-five lay members with a quorum consisting of any five including at least one prelate. It was heavily loaded with bishops and ecclesiastics and would meet in places where the Council could not be readily summoned. Thus this arbitrary court which had no basis in law - "Crail Court" as it was called after the place of Sharp's original ministry - began to use the military strength of Sir James Turner to exact the fines of twenty shillings for non attendance at church; to quarter his soldiers with delinquents until they had paid the fine; and to follow up on complaints and lists of absentees from the curates. This repression continued throughout 1664 when the Court was discharged. However, the unpaid fines were called in and used to fund a force of some 3,000 soldiers, including dragoons, in the southwest of Scotland.

In 1665 war with Holland finally broke out and there was fear that the "Whigs" were in correspondence with them and that money and arms might be forthcoming for an armed rebellion. The fears were not ungrounded for plans were laid for the Dutch to capture Edinburgh, Dumbarton and Stirling Castles. In London the Plague and the Great Fire in September was seen as a sign of Heaven's displeasure with the breaking of the Covenant. To top all, the Scottish Privy Council made attendance at a conventicle an offence, then decided to take up the Indemnity fines, made heritors and landlords responsible for the action of their tenants, and to disarm them all. It was with this wider remit that Sir James Turner and his troopers were sent into Galloway and led to his own capture in the opening days of the Pentland Rising.

X. The Pentland Rising - Rullion Green

The Pentland Rising and the battle of Rullion Green is an important event in Covenanter history because it was the first time the Covenanters had come together as a substantial force to protest about the constraints upon their religion. Pressure had been building on the Covenanter ministers from 1662, when about 300 were ejected from their churches and in 1664, two more rules were introduced which prohibited any ejected ministers living with twenty miles of their former church. Severe penalties were also imposed on parishioners who failed to attend the church services conducted by the curates who had been appointed by the government. The protesters came mainly from the West of Scotland, from Dumfries and Galloway, Ayrshire, and Lanarkshire, where the ministers who had been ejected from their churches continued preaching by holding open-air meetings - "conventicles." To hold such meetings was an offence and many suffered for it, but their flock grew, especially among the peasantry.

The spark to the march on Edinburgh occurred on 13 November 1666, at St. John's Dalry in Kirkcudbrightshire. An elderly man was unable to pay a fine for not attending church and was beaten and threatened with being stripped and placed on a red-hot gridiron by some of Sir James Turner's soldiers. A group of four local Covenanters, led by MacLellan of Barscobe, came to the rescue with drawn pistols and were joined by other villagers who helped disarm the soldiers, with one of them being shot and wounded. The crowd gathered and, reckoning that they would be severely punished if caught, they decided to march on Dumfries. On their way, they repeated their deed in Balmaclellan where they took sixteen soldiers prisoner and killed one. The band of rebels had grown to about 180 by the time they arrived at Dumfries, with about half on horses armed with swords and pistols, and those on foot with pikes, swords, scythes and other implements. Arriving in the morning around breakfast time they found the town lightly defended and the commander of the troops, Sir James Turner, ill in bed, whom they took prisoner. Turner remained with the rebels for the next fortnight during which time attempts were made to convert him to Presbyterianism but without success. He was treated well by the Covenanters and his worst punishment was said to be his dislike for the tedious Grace that was said before and after meals.

The Covenanters found their military leader at Bridge of Doon where the experienced soldier, Colonel James Wallace of Auchens, joined them along with his deputies, Major Learmouth, Captain Andrew Arnot and Captain John Paton of Meadowhead who had fought shoulder to shoulder with Dalziel at Worcester in 1651. Now having some professional leadership, the gathering multitude marched to Ayr They collected further recruits at Mauchline and Lesmahagow, and by the time they had swung round to Lanark they numbered about 1,200. Here on the morning of the 26th November they renewed the Covenant and issued a declaration which stated their regard for the King and his civil rights but questioned the return to episcopacy, the rejection of the Solemn League and Covenant of 1643 and other impositions upon them such as fines and quartering of soldiers on the people. Some signs of disagreement began to show themselves and support wavered with some 200 deciding to return home rather than go on to Edinburgh; the weather at that time did not help with much rain and strong winds making the marching very uncomfortable. On 27 November they reached Colinton about five miles from Edinburgh where messengers from the city advised that the gates were armed with cannon and there was no support for their cause in the city. With this disheartening news it was decided to return to Galloway and some of the group dispersed to make their way home. However, the news of the rebellion had come to the ears of the Privy Council who were greatly surprised by it and ordered an army raised.

On 28 November the Covenanters had turned homewards towards far off Galloway when they were intercepted by General Thomas Dalziel of The Binns, commander in chief in Scotland, a seasoned commander who had seen service in Russia and Poland where he had earnt the label 'The Beast of Muscovy' for his tyranny. His 3,000 professional soldiers met strong resistance from a Covenanter force that now numbered about 900 and had the advantage of the ground. The Covenanters were first assaulted by the horsemen of Dalziel's forces and several charges were repelled. The battle then resorted to sword and hand to hand fighting in which the honours were about even. But by about four o'clock the winter evening was drawing in and sheer weight of numbers eventually crushed the Covenanters. The survivors fled into the Pentland Hills leaving behind two ministers from Ulster and about fifty Covenanters dead on the slopes of Rullion Green. Several of the wounded Covenanters were brought in by country people and others were shot or slain in their flight and were buried in neighbouring kirk yards of Penicuik and Glencorse. The kirk session records of Penicuik lists a payment to a grave digger of 3s 4d for "making westlandmen's graves."

Colonel Wallace survived the battle and went to Holland, leaving a terrible condemnation of the local people who, he said, left the Covenanters unburied for a day and a night and stripped the bodies of their apparel. It was the women of Edinburgh who came and wrapped the bodies with winding sheets and buried them. Even in exile vindictive ministers pursued Wallace and he never returned to his homeland, dying in 1678 among his friends of the Scottish Congregation in Rotterdam.

About eighty Covenanters were taken prisoner and brought to Edinburgh where they were incarcerated in a temporary prison called "Haddocks Hole" which was a small room on the side of St Giles Cathedral. The prisoners had the great misfortune to come before the Privy Council presided over by James Sharp who was in no way inclined to mercy even though they had surrendered on such a promise. Sharp's response was "You were pardoned as soldiers but you are not acquitted as subjects." Twenty prisoners (and another whose death is uncertain) were hanged at the Mercat Cross in Edinburgh and others at various places in the south west of Scotland as a warning to others.

Many of the wounded are believed to have died in the bogs when trying to reach their homelands in the west. One tale is told of a nameless Covenanter dying from his wounds, who reached the home of an Adam Sanderson, a farmer at Blackhill. The wounded man sought relief and wished to be on his way soon realising the danger to his host, but in a parlous state and dying he asked to be buried in sight of his homeland of Ayrshire. The next day he was found dead and Adam Sanderson carried the body to a spot on Black Law and buried him. A tombstone marks the spot from which, on a clear day, Ayrshire can be seen over twenty miles away.

Rullion Green lies about eight miles south of Edinburgh on the slopes of the Pentland Hills and was, as

now, prime sheep country. On the fringe of a small wood perhaps half a mile from the farm house there is a railed enclosure containing a single headstone commemorating the events of 1666. Behind

Rullion Green
Memorial Plate

it lie the colourful rolling hills into which the survivors fled. The inscriptions on the solitary stone read:

Side 1.

"Here
and near to
this place lyes the
Rev. Mr. John crookshank
and Mr. Andrew m'cormick
ministers of the Gospel and
About fifty other true coven-
anted Presbyterians who were
killed in this place in their own
Inocent self defence and def-
ence of the covenanted
work of Reformation By
Thomas Dalzeel of Bins
upon the 28 of november
1666 Rev 12. 11 Erected
September 28, 1738"

Side 2.

"A cloud of witnesses lyes here,
Who for Christ's interest did appear
For to restore true Liberty
Overturned then by Tyrrany
And by Proud Prelats who did rage
Against the Lord's own heritage.
They sacrificed were for the Laws
Of Christ their King, his noble cause,
These heroes fought with great renown,
By falling got the Martyr's Crown."

The Pentland Rising came as a great shock to the Earl of Rothes, the King's Commissioner for Scotland, and his cohort Archbishop James Sharp. The latter had earlier sought the King's permission to bring back the Court of

High Commission to deal with the summary trial and conviction of the troublesome Covenanters. With these absolute powers the persecution of the Presbyterians took a bloody turn. Prisoners from Rullion Green were hauled before the Court and ten of their number hung on 7 December 1666. After death, their right hands were cut off and sent to be nailed to the prison door at Lanark and their severed heads sent to their respective home areas to be exhibited as a warning. Five more were executed on 14 December and six more on 22 December 1666 - a bloody Christmas message indeed for the Covenanters.

Elsewhere, there was a bloody price paid in Ayr. Eight men were sentenced to hang, but the official hangmen from Ayr and nearby Irvine both declined to act. One of the prisoners, Cornelius Anderson, was bribed, made drunk and acted as hangman for the remaining seven. Anderson also acted as hangman at the execution of two more Covenanters in Irvine. In Glasgow four were executed on 19 December 1666, and two in Dumfries on 2 January 1667. For the lucky ones, there was hope of life as the prisons were overflowing and many were transported to slavery in the West Indies and the American colonies.

So it was that the Pentland Rising was put down, but it left a fear in the government because they had seen that the Covenanters were capable of banding together and could be an effective military force. On the other hand, the excesses of retribution by the Earl of Rothes were subject of political pressures and he was replaced in 1667 by John Maitland, Earl of Lauderdale, a more humane man who had some sympathy for the Presbyterians and under whom repression eased for a while.

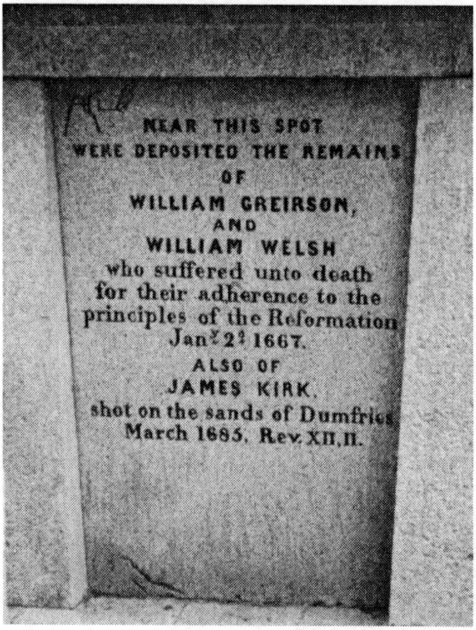
NEAR THIS SPOT
WERE DEPOSITED THE REMAINS
OF
WILLIAM GREIRSON,
AND
WILLIAM WELSH
who suffered unto death
for their adherence to the
principles of the Reformation
Janʸ 2ᵈ 1667.
ALSO OF
JAMES KIRK,
shot on the sands of Dumfries
March 1685. Rev. XII. II.

Dedication
on
Martyr's Monument,
St. Michael's Church,
Dumfries

Martyr's Monument
St. Michael's Church, Dumfries

The Bass Rock prison from the ruins of Tantallon Castle

XI. The Bass Rock and Dunnottar Castle prisons

The history of the Covenanters is one of persecution, execution and imprisonment in a wide variety of local prisons especially in Glasgow, Leith and Edinburgh in the "Tolbooths." After the battle of Boswell Brig there was the infamous incarceration of prisoners in the Greyfriars Kirk yard where many died during the months of imprisonment in the open air without shelter and poorly cared for. There are two particularly desolate places where many of the leaders of the Covenanters were held, these were the Bass Rock and Dunnottar Castle.

The Bass Rock lies about three miles off the North Berwick coast, although it looks closer, and is opposite the ancient castle of Tantallon. Today it is a well-known sea bird sanctuary with a large colony of Gannets, but it has a much darker past as a singularly desolate prison for many of the Covenanter leaders between 1673 and 1687. The island at one time belonged to Sir Andrew Ramsay who sold it to John Lauderdale, Secretary of State for Scotland for £4,000. Lauderdale had it turned into a prison, which was to house thirty-nine Covenanters in extremely tough conditions.

The Bass Rock is itself only about three quarters of a mile in circumference and at its high point 313 feet above sea level. There are sheer cliffs on three sides; on the fourth is a narrow and dangerous landing point. Even on calm days the seas swell and roll round the island with a dangerous tidal flow between it and the mainland - not a place to attempt escape by swimming. On the island, once a retreat for a Welsh monk in the seventh century, there was little shelter until the building of the prison quarters and a Governor's house. In heavy seas the buildings would be awash. Some of the cells had only one small window, which was out of reach of the prisoner who was therefore unable to view the outside. Other cells looked only upon a paved walkway where the soldiers stood guard. There was, too, a dark, dank dungeon - the Black Hole. The severe conditions were alleviated for some of the prisoners who were allowed to walk around the pasture land on top of the Rock where sheep, renowned for their sweet meat, grazed among the wild solan geese and sea birds.

Into the Bass were cast many of the more troublesome Covenanters for periods ranging from a few months to six years including:

William Bell
Robert Bennett of Chesters near Ancrum.
John Blackader
Sir Hugh Campbell of Cessnock
Sir George Campbell of Cessnock
Robert Dick, merchant
John Dickson
James Drummond, chaplain to Marchioness of Argyll.
Alexander Forrester
James Fraser of Brea
Alexander Gordon of Earlston

Thomas Hogg of Kiltearn
Joseph Learmont
John McGilligen of Fodderty
James Mitchell
Alexander Peden
Archibald Riddell
Thomas Ross of Kincardine
Gilbert Rule
Alexander Shields
John Spreul of Glasgow
George Scott of Pitlochie
Robert Trail, the younger.

John C Johnston's *Alexander Peden* throws some interesting light on the prisoners of the Bass Rock. The first to be incarcerated on the Bass was Robert Gillespie who was charged that "he had several times preached, expounded Scripture, and prayed at conventicles." He did not answer the summons and was put to the horn (declared a rebel) and finally brought to the Bass. He was for a while a companion to Alexander Peden who was brought there on 26 June 1673. George Gillespie, son of Robert, was a friend of Ebenezer Erskine who was one of the four ministers who seceded from the church in 1733 and founded the Secession Church. Thomas Ross was a minister who had been convicted of holding a conventicle in Morayshire and was eventually released because of failing health and allowed home to die. Another was James Mitchell charged with shooting at Archbishop Sharp, who was later executed on the perjured evidence of the four judges - Lauderdale, Rothes, Hatton and Sharp. Fraser of Brae was a zealous preacher and imprisoned for his beliefs. He was later released then re arrested for preaching and spent time in Blackness Castle and the Newgate Prison. MacGilligen of Fodderty was another friend of Peden's who was imprisoned for his opposition to prelacy and for taking part in a Communion service. He was one of the ministers who were allowed to walk on the plateau, although he was later placed in close confinement. The last to leave the Bass prison, on 12 May 1687, was John Spreul an apothecary who had been incarcerated for six years.

Dunottar Castle, now a ruin, is about a mile and a half south of Stonehaven and about fifteen miles south of Aberdeen. Built on an outcrop of sandstone that juts out into the sea, it has a rugged beauty and in its day was a fearsome stronghold. It is thought that St. Ninian had been here in the fifth century and William Wallace besieged the castle in 1297 when he burned the English garrison alive in the castle church. Later in 1336 Edward III seized it and held it for a few months and in 1645 it withstood siege by the Marquis of Montrose.

The castle is remembered as the stronghold in which the Scottish Crown Jewels were held for safe custody. The garrison of sixty-nine men with some forty-two guns withstood assault by Cromwell's troops for eight months in 1651. But, the Regalia had been smuggled to safety by lowering them in a basket to a servant woman apparently gathering seaweed on the shore, who took them to the parish church of Kinneff a few miles away where they remained hidden below the floorboards until the Restoration in 1660.

Dunottar's place in Covenanter history is from its use as a prison in 1685 for one hundred and twenty two men and forty-five women. Here they were packed so tight that they could not sit, lean or lie down and many of them died. The incarceration of the Covenanters in Dunnottar stemmed from fears that they might support the rebellion of the 9th Earl of Argyll (son of the Marquis of Argyll executed in 1661) who was expected from Holland with troops, because of this 224 Covenanters from the Tolbooth prisons in Edinburgh were hurried away in May 1685. Of these, some thirty-six men and four women were able to convince the authorities that they were not dangerous and were returned to Edinburgh. Of the remainder, some escaped and others died on their march through Fife and Forfar to their prison in the dungeons of Dunnottar Castle.

Dunnottar Castle
Courtesy of A. Pittendreigh

They were thrown into the "Whigs Vault" which was a room about 55 ft long, 15.1/2 ft wide and 12 ft high with two tiny barred windows. The cell was described as cramped without room to sit down, the floor was ankle deep in mire, and there was little fresh air to breathe. Their keep was rudimentary and they were even forced to pay for water to drink. Forty of the Covenanters were later transferred to a deep dungeon, and some relief was afforded the women who were allotted two rooms.

There was an attempt by twenty-five of the prisoners to escape by descending the steep cliff overhanging the sea, but in their feeble condition fifteen of their number were soon recaptured. Despite their poor condition, the escapees were lashed to low benches and tortured for three hours by placing burning slivers of wood between their fingers. For some this treatment was too much, and they lost fingers or subsequently died from their injuries.

Among those cast into Dunnottar were:

John Fraser
Alexander Dalgleish
William McMillan of Galloway
William Niven
William Hannah of Tundergarth
James Forsyth of Lochmaben
William Campbell of Middlewood, Ayrshire
Robert Goodwin of Glasgow
Quintin Dick of Dalmellington

After the danger of insurrection had passed, the prisoners were released from Dunnottar and thirty men and seven women took the Oath of Allegiance. The remainder, who refused to take the oath, were transported to America.

In Dunnottar Kirk yard there is a simple memorial commemorating those who died in the dungeons of Dunnottar Castle and in an attempted escape:

Here lyes John Stot. James Atchi
son. James Russell & William Bro
un and one whose name wee have
not gotten and two women whose
names also wee know not and two
who perished comeing doune the rock
one whose name was James Watson
the other not known who all died
prisoners in Dunnottar Castle
Anno 1685 for their adherence
to the word of God and Scotland's
Covenanted work of Reformation.
Rev11. Ch 12 Verse

It is thought that the four missing names from the inscription are John Whyte, William Breadie, Mary Gibson and Jean Muffet. Of historical interest is that this stone was created by Robert Paterson, "Old Mortality" of Sir Walter Scott's novel, who met here while the work was being done.

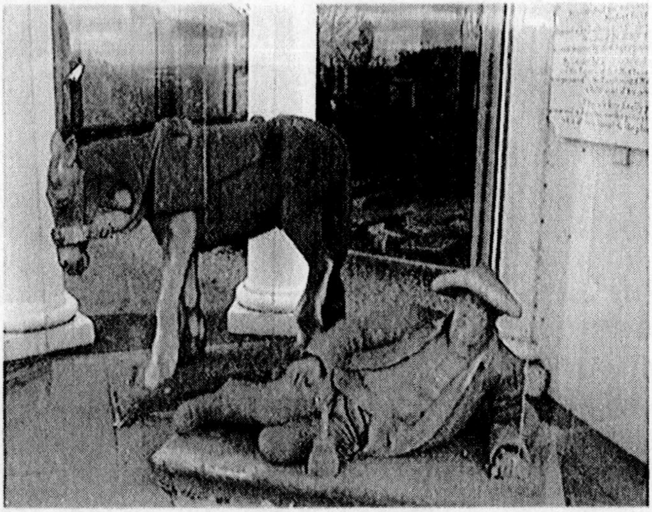

Old Mortality memorial
Dumfries Museum

Sanquhar Tolbooth or prison
Courtesy of A. Pittendreigh

XII. The Sanquhar Declaration - the Cameronians

Sanquhar is a small town in Dumftries, in the south west of Scotland. It is of ancient origin, the name being Celtic and meaning Old Fort. It lies in north Nithsdale and is approximately midway between Dumfries and Kilmarnock. Small though it may be on the map, Sanquhar was the scene for at least six "Declaration at Sanquhar." These were on 22 June 1680, (the Cameron Declaration of armed resistance), 28 May 1685 (the Renwick Declaration witnessing against the Papist James II) and four after the Revolution by parties who were not satisfied by the existing state of things. The four later Declarations were made on 10 August 1692, 6 November 1695, 21 May 1703 and in 1707.

There was, however, a precursor to the Cameron Declaration known as the Queensferry Paper, which was the work of Donald Cargill in collaboration with Richard Cameron. Donald Cargill, born at Rattray in Perthshire in 1619 was at St. Andrews University at the same time as a later oppressor, the Earl of Rothes, but he was of mature years before he was ordained as minister of the Barony church in Glasgow in 1655. He was cast out of his ministry in 1662 and banned from the south side of the River Tay so he turned to private meetings and conventicles to pursue his ministry. He was left for dead at the battle of Bothwell Brig but recovered to collaborate with Richard Cameron over The Queensferry Paper. It was a solemn declaration of faith and disavowed the sinful rulers. It is the strongest of the Covenanter manifestoes, but was never published by the Covenanters themselves. Its disclosure came about because Cargill's companion Henry Hall was taken prisoner at an inn at Queensferry on 3 June 1680. Cargill managed to escape, but Henry Hall was injured and later died. It was when his clothes were searched that the compromising paper was found.

Undaunted by the disclosure of the Queensferry Paper, Cargill continued his work and memorably preached at a gathering at Torwood, near Stirling. When he had completed his sermon from Ezekiel, "Thus saith the Lord God, Remove the diadem and take off the crown," he calmly and formally excommunicated Charles Stuart, King of England; James Duke of York; James Duke of Monmouth; John Duke of Lauderdale; John Duke of Rothes; the Kings Advocate Sir George MacKenzie; and Thomas Dalziel of the Binns. Sadly it was not long before he was seized at Covington Mill where he had rested for the night. He and companions, Walter Smith and James Boig, were hustled away to prison in Edinburgh. On 27 July 1681 he was executed at the Mercat Cross and his head hung on the Netherbow Gate in Edinburgh with his hands poised as if in prayer beneath - the manner reserved for Covenanting ministers.

It was on 22 June 1680 that the townspeople of Sanquhar were astonished to see some twenty horsemen ride up the main street with swords drawn and pistols at the ready. The group halted at the market cross and two dismounted - these were Richard Cameron and his brother Michael. After a psalm was sung, a prayer was offered to the assembled throng, and Michael Cameron read aloud the Sanquhar Declaration. When he was done, the Declaration was nailed to the town cross and the horsemen returned from whence they came. Thus was done an act, which was the seed corn for a free Parliament and an unshackled church.

The Sanquhar Declaration, which is forever associated with the "Cameronians," was published exactly one year after the Battle of Bothwell Brig, and a month prior to Cameron's own death at Ayrs Moss. This Declaration deserves notice, both on account of the prominence given to it at the time by the persecuted Presbyterians, and also because it was used as an excuse for criminal prosecution of those who acknowledged it. "Do you own the Sanquhar Declaration?" was a question to which an answer of "yes" meant they would be subjected to whatever punishment the whim of the judges or the soldiers in the field might see proper to inflict - usually death, often on the spot.

It was regarded as a manifesto of a highly treasonable nature because it disowned King Charles as the lawful king of the realms, and coming so soon after the battle of Bothwell Brig, it was the means of stimulating the persecution of the Covenanters. Moreover, the attention of the government became focused on that part of the country where this Declaration was made public. As a result, the army was the instrument of a merciless persecution and execution of the Covenanters in the south west of Scotland. So many people died for the principles of the Declaration it is worth reproducing it in full. "The Declaration and Testimony of the True Presbyterian, Anti-prelatic, Anti-erastian, persecuted party in Scotland." Published at Sanquhar, June 22, 1680, is quoted from *The Traditions of the Covenanters* by the Rev. Robert Simpson (1867).

It is not amongst the smallest of the Lord's mercies to this poor land, that there have been always some who have given their testimony against every cause of defection that many are guilty of; which is a token for good, that he doth not, as yet, intend to cast us off altogether, but that he will leave a remnant in whom lie will be glorious, if they through his grace, keep themselves clean still, and walk in his way and method as it has been walked in, and owned by him in our predecessors of truly worthy memory; in their carrying on of our noble work of reformation, in the several steps thereof, from Popery, Prelacy, and likewise Erastian supremacy-so much usurped by him who, it is true, so far as we know, is descended from the race of our kings; yet he hath so far debased from what he ought to have been, by his perjury and usurpation in Church matters, and tyranny in matters civil, as is known by the whole land, that we have just reason to account it one of the Lord's great controversies against us, that we have not disowned him, and the men of his practices, whether inferior magistrates or any other, as enemies to our Lord and his crown, and the true Protestant and Presbyterian interest in this land-our Lord's espoused bride and Church. Therefore, although we be for government and governors, such as the Word of God and our covenant allows; yet we, for ourselves, and all that will adhere to us as the representative of the true Presbyterian Kirkand covenanted nation of Scotland, considering the great hazard of lying under such a sin any longer, do, by these presents, disown Charles Stuart, that has been reigning, or rather tyrannizing, as we may say, on the throne of Britain these years bygone, as having any right, title to, or interest in, the said crown of Scotland for government, as forfeited, several years since, by his perjury and breach of covenant both to God and his Kirk, and usurpation of his crown and royal prerogative therein, and many other breaches in matters eccelesiastic and by his tyranny and breach of the very reges regnandi in matters civil. For which reason we declare, that several years since he should have been denuded of being king, ruler, or magistrate, or of having any power to act or to be obeyed as such. As also we' being under the standard of our Lord Jesus Christ, Captain of Salvation, do declare a war with such a tyrant and usurper, and all the men of his practices, as enemies to our Lord Jesus Christ, and his cause and covenants; and against all such as have strengthened him, sided with, or anywise acknowledged him in his tyranny, civil or ecclesiastic; yea, against all such as shall strengthen, side with, or anywise acknowledge any other in like usurpation and tyranny-far more against such as would betray or deliver up our free reformed mother Kirkunto the bondage of Antichrist, the Pope of Rome. And, by this, we homologate that testimony given at Rutherglen, the 29th of May 1679, and all the faithful testimonies of those who have gone before, as also of those who have suffered of late, and we do disclaim that Declaration published at Hamilton, June 1679, chiefly because it takes in the king's interest, which we are several years since loosed from, because of the aforesaid reasons, and others which may, after this, if the Lord will, be published. As also, we disown and by this resent the reception of the Duke of York, that professed Papist, as repugnant to our principles and vows to the Most High God, and as that which is the great, though not alone, just reproach of our Kirk and nation. We also, by this, protest against his succeeding to the crown, and whatever has been done, or any are essaying to do in this land, given to the Lord, in prejudice to our work of reformation. And to conclude, we hope after this, none will blame us for, or offend at, our rewarding those that are against as they have done to us, as the Lord gives opportunity. This is not to exclude any that have declined, if they be willing to give satisfaction according to the degree of their offence.

The "Cameronians" as they became known, refused to take an oath of allegiance to King William III after the religious settlements of 1689 - 1690. They felt that they could not join the newly formed Church of Scotland, even though Presbyterian, because it ignored the Covenants and accepted some State interference in religious matters. The Cameronians accepted the Crown's right to dissolve Assemblies and they even accepted the system of patronage so they were not totally against the King. For sixteen years, the dissenting Covenanters maintained their own Societies for worship and religious correspondence. By I706 there existed in Scotland twenty such Societies, with a membership of roughly 7,000. In 1743 these Societies formed their own Reformed Presbytery, which spread to Ulster and America.

The Church membership increased quite rapidly and was a clear reflection of a desire for a firm Presbyterian Church. In 1810 the Presbytery was divided regionally into a Northern, Eastern, and Southern Presbytery. A year later, these three Presbyteries convened as the first Synod of the Reformed Presbyterian Church of Scotland. In 1810 the Irish and the North American Reformed Presbyterian Churches-offshoots of the Scottish Kirk, were also strong enough to set up their own first Synods.

There was further division among the Cameronians in 1863 over the question of parliamentary franchise when a majority took the view that they should do away with the rule about political dissent which meant abandoning a principle of the Covenant to share responsibility for national sins. The minority set up their own Synod and reiterated that they would not accept political systems, which, in the Synods view, ignored the primary rights of Christ Jesus as King of the world's nations. In 1876 most were reconciled with and joined the Free Church of Scotland.

The final word on the trials of the Covenanters perhaps lies in the stark detail of the inscription on the Martyr's monument in Old Greyfriars Kirk yard which says that between May 1661 and February 1688 that:

were one way or other murdered and destroyed for the same cause about eighteen thousand, of whom were executed at Edinburgh about a hundred of noblemen and gentlemen, ministers and others - noble Martyrs for Jesus Christ. The most of them lie here.

XIII. Execution by Drowning

Execution by drowning was a method specifically prescribed for women Covenanters, although there is an earlier record of a woman drowned for her faith. She was the wife of a Robert Lamb of Perth, he was convicted and hung for having interrupted a friar who was preaching and she was tied in a sack and drowned because she refused to pray to the Virgin Mary during childbirth. Some events that we hear of may be the result of the oral tradition such as that concerning Janet Smith and her grandchild Nanny Nivison who resided near the Frith of Cree. This tale comes from *Tales and Sketches of the Covenanters, a Selection of Narratives* published in 1880. The father of Nanny, John Nivison, was shot on the Galloway Hills and her brother, Thomas, fled to America. However, his ship was wrecked off the Isle of Arran and his return was betrayed to the authorities by a smuggler.

When the soldiers came looking for him, Nanny and her grandmother resolutely refused to tell of Thomas's whereabouts. The women were stripped and tied to stakes at the flood mark and questioned by an officer on a horse as the tide crept in. The grandmother died first, drowned, but Nanny it seems remained steadfast and she too died, "not drowned but chilled to death."

In all the persecution of Presbyterians, one of the most brutish and clearly documented incidents was that of a young woman, Margaret Wilson, aged eighteen with her life before her, and Margaret MacLachlan, aged sixty-three, a widow who had little save her faith. They were tied to stakes in the sea and executed by drowning. Their crime was that they were followers of James Renwick, a Presbyterian preacher and leader of the extremist Covenanters - the Cameronians or Society people. When challenged they had refused to deny their faith or take an "Abjuration Oath" rejecting a Declaration that Renwick had recently distributed in the area.

Renwick took over the mantle of leadership of the Covenanters after the death of Richard Cameron and was responsible for several Declarations in defence of faith and the Covenanters opposition to government. But the one with the greatest impact on his followers was his "Apologetical Declaration and Admonitory Vindication against Intelligencers and Informers" of 28 October 1684. In this Declaration it speaks about the hardships they had suffered; their avowed principles of faith and said that they were not intent on killing anybody whose opinions differed from theirs. But they regarded those who persecuted them - judges, soldiers, informants and 'false witnesses' to be the enemies of God and would deal with them accordingly. The Declaration was posted on church doors and market crosses throughout southwest Scotland.

The Declaration caused considerable alarm within the government and the Privy Council proclaimed a loyalty oath called "The Abjuration Oath." This allowed that any person who refused to swear the oath on demand could be properly put to death in the presence of two witnesses. The wording of the Oath cited in T. Campbell's *Standing Witnesses* was:

I ... doe hereby abhorr, renunce and disoune, in presence of the Almighty God, the pretendit Declaratione of Warr lately affixed at severall paroch churches in so far as it declares a warr against his sacred Majestie and asserts that it is laufull to kill such as serve his Majestie in church, state, army or countrey, or such as act against the authors of the said pretended declaratione now shewne to me. And I doe hereby uteerly renunce and disoune the villanous authors thereof who did (as they call it) statut and ordaine the same, and what is therein mentioned, and I swear I shall never assist the authors of the said pretended declaratione or ther emissaries or adherents in any poynts of punishing, killing and makeing of warr any manner of way as I shall answear to God.

Margaret Wilson was the daughter of Gilbert Wilson, a farmer in Glenvernock, in Dumfries, who was an Episcopalian, but his children, Margaret, aged eighteen, Thomas, aged sixteen and thirteen year old Agnes refused to adopt the creed of their parents and to take the Abjuration Oath. As a result, the children were outlawed, their friends were forbidden to help them and farmers and shepherds were required to pursue them. They were compelled to leave their comfortable home in February 1685 to hide in the caves and moors of the surrounding countryside. While Thomas continued to hide in the hills, the downfall of Margaret and Agnes was to try and find food and warmth in Wigtown. They were recognised, seized and cast into prison in the "Thieves's Hole" amongst the very worst of the criminal society. Here they remained for some six or seven weeks, without any privacy, subject to the rigours and privations of the common felons and banned by law from receiving succour and help from their friends.

In April they were charged with being supporters of the battles at Bothwell Brig and Ayrsmoss; and for refusing to take the Abjuration Oath. It is pertinent that only a few weeks prior to their conviction on 13 April 1685, the Privy Council had ruled that while a man who did not disown James Renwick's Declaration was to be hung, a woman who "had been active in the said courses in a signal manner" was to be drowned in loch or stream or sea. Thus the judge sentenced them to be:

ty'd to palisados fixed in the sand, within the flood mark, and there to stand till the flood overflowed them and drowned them.

Agnes was saved from execution by the intercession of her father who traveled to Edinburgh and made a bond of £100, but there was no timely reprieve for Margaret who steadfastly resisted all attempts to get her to recant her faith and take the detestable Oath. Despite representations and documents allegedly recanting their deeds and a reprieve granted by the Privy Council on 30 April - which was misdirected to Edinburgh, Margaret MacLachlan and Margaret Wilson were led to the sea on 11 May 1685.

It is supposition that perhaps the execution party, led by Sir Robert Grierson of Lag and Major Winram, still hoped the women would yield. The women were tied to stakes some distance apart, Margaret Wilson being nearer to the safety of sandbanks. Perhaps they hoped that the sight of the approaching tide taking Margaret MacLachlan, would make the young girl take the Oath, but it was not to be and both women perished.

Years after, the tale goes, an old man was seen wandering the streets of Wigtown, afflicted by a terrible thirst, and always carrying with him a large jar of water. The local people believed his affliction was a punishment, for he was the Town Officer of Wigtown who, it was alleged, had pushed Margaret Wilson's head under the foam with his halbert, saying "Tak' anither drink, hinny!" thus he was reaping the harvest of his evil doings.

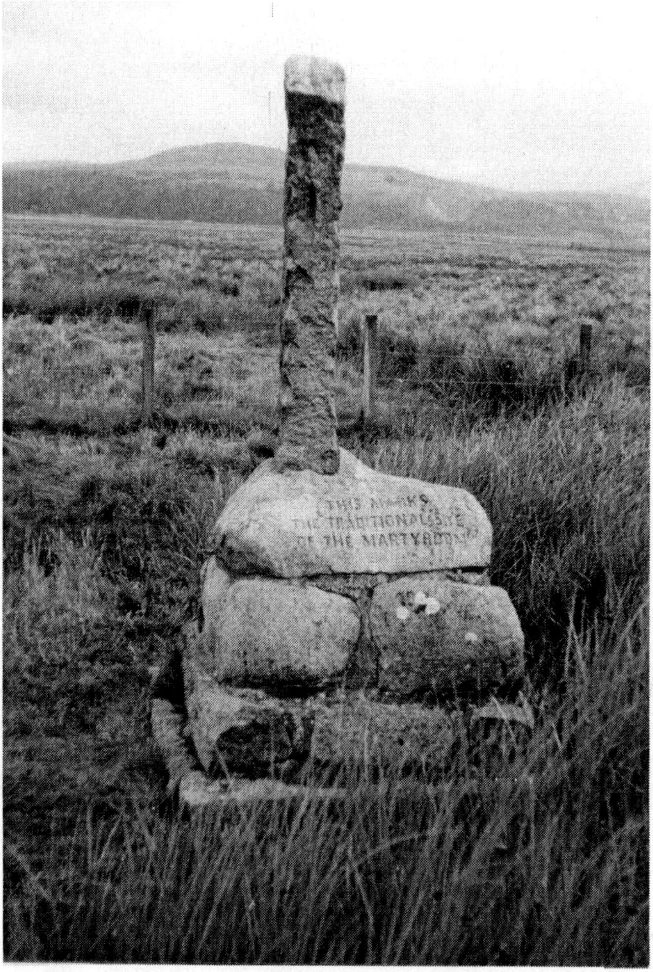

Martyrs Monument
On the Merse at Wigtown

Margaret Wilson's tombstone in Wigtown Churchyard reads:

Here lyes Margrat
Willson Doughter
To Gilbert Willson
In Glenvernoch
Who was drouned
Anno 1685 aged 18.

Let earth and stone still witnes beare
Heir lyes a Virgin Martyre here
Murtherd for ouning Christ supreme
Head of his Church and no more crime
But not abjuring Presrytry
And her not ouning Prelacy
They her condem'd, by unjust law,
Of Heaven nor Hell they stood no aw
Within the sea tyd to a stake
She suffered for Christ Jesus sake.
The actors of this cruel crime
Was Lagg Strachan, Winram and Grhame
Neither young yeares nor yet old age
Could stop the fury of there rage.

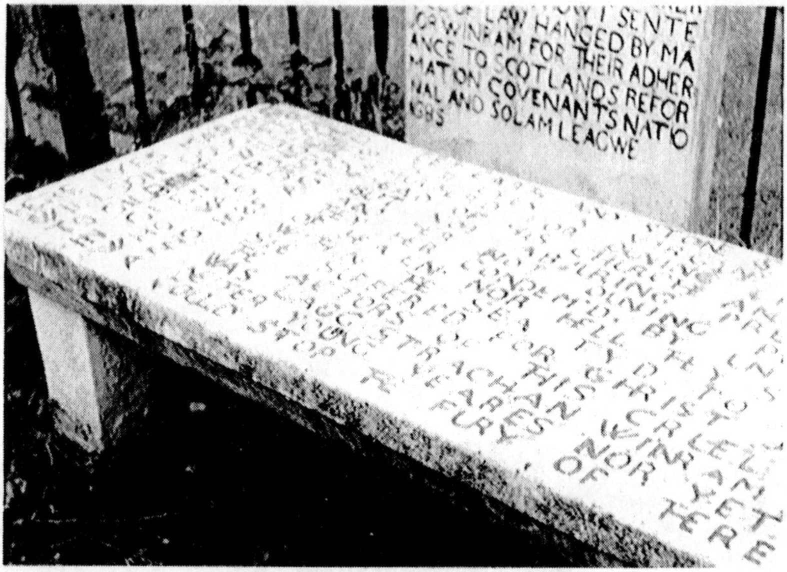

Margaret Wilson's gravestone
Wigtown

Did it really happen?

Research of the Covenanters will reveal some rather odd events and variations on several Covenanter Tales. But even if gilded on occasion by retelling, and particularly where recounted with much biblical quotation and attribution of an individual's dying words, there is always a germ of truth. There are inevitably comments and differences of opinion after such a long time, but there are also the cynical and mocking denials that the events ever took place.

Of the hundreds of deaths that took place, that of the Solway Martyrs, Margaret Wilson and Margaret MacLachlan, is one where positive attempts were made by the Sheriff of Wigtown to deny it took place. The rejection was on the basis that a reprieve had been granted, although he doesn't clarify that the documents were sent to

Martyrs Monument
Windyhill Wigtown

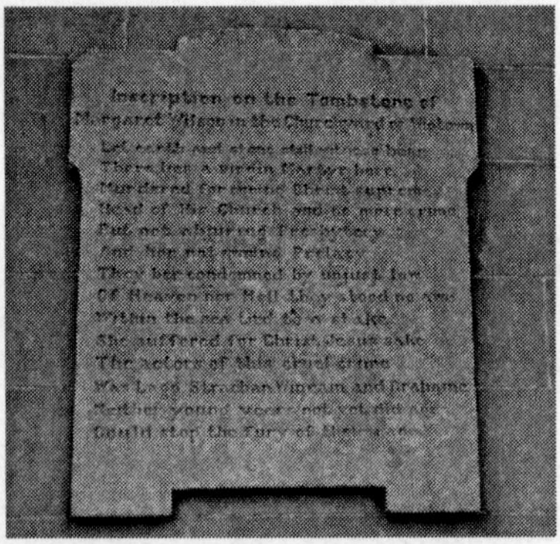

Inscriptions on the Martyrs Monument
Windyhill Wigtown

Edinburgh, not Wigtown. In later years there have been allegations that the event did not occur because the whole of Wigtown would have been present so where were the eyewitness reports; and there were variances in the dying testimony reported (forty years after the event). The author in that case possibly did not know that the Kirk Sessions had been requested by the General Assembly in 1711 to provide testimony "for the record." Here is what was minuted.

The Kirk Session Minutes

The minute books of the Kirk Sessions of Kirkinner and of Penninghame are the root source for what happened at Wigtown in May 1685 being testimony by persons who knew of the events first hand. These extracts are reproduced in *The Martyr Graves of Scotland* by Rev. J. H. Thomson (1906). The minutes were drawn up by order of the General Assembly in order to be forwarded to the Rev. Robert Wodrow for his forthcoming publication, *History of the Sufferings of the Church of Scotland from the Restoration to the Revolution,* first published in 1714.

Kirk Session of Kirkinner, 15 April 1711

"Post preces sederunt, all the members except John McCulloch, William Hanna and John Martin, younger in Airles. Inter alia: - The minister gave in the account of the sufferings of honest Godly people in the late times which was read, and is as follows: Margaret Laughson of known integrity and piety from her youth aged about eighty, widow of John Milliken, Wright in Drumjargan, was in or about the year of God 1685, in her own house, taken off her knees in prayer, and carried immediately to prison and from one prison to another without the benefit of light to read the Scriptures; was barbarously treated by dragoons, who were sent to carry her from Mahirmore to Wigtown; and being

sentenced by Sir Robert Grierson of Lagg to be drowned at the stake within the flood mark just below the town of Wigtown for conventicle keeping and alleged rebellion, was, according to the said sentence, fixed to the stake till the tide made and held down within the water by one of the town officers by his halbert at her throat till she died."

After narrating twelve other cases of suffering, in the forms of banishment, imprisonment, fining, etc., the minute concludes:

"The which particulars aforesaid being read, they partly from credible information, partly from their own personal knowledge, do believe the said information to be matters of fact, and appoint the same to be recorded in their session book ad futuram et memoriam, and the clerk to give extract to the Presbytery of Wigtown according to appointment. Sederunt. Closed with prayer."

Kirk Session of Penninghame 19 February 1711

"Gilbert Wilson of Glenvernock, in Castle Stewart's land, being a man to ane excess conform to the guise of the tymes, and his wife without challenge for her religion, in good condition as to worldly things, with a great stock on a large ground, (fit to be a prey) was harassed by his children who would not conform. They being required to take the test and hear the curates, refused both; were searched for, fled, and lived in the wild mountains, bogs, and caves. Their parents were charged, on the highest peril, that they should neither harbour them, speak to them, supply them, nor see them; and the country people were obliged by the terror of the law to pursue them as well as the soldiers with hue and cry."

"In February 1685, Thomas Wilson, of sixteen years of age, Margaret Wilson of eighteen years, Agnes Wilson of thirteen years, children of the said Gilbert - the said Thomas keeping the mountains; his two sisters Margaret and Agnes went secretly to Wigtown to see some friends,

were there discovered, taken prisoners, and instantly thrust into the thieves hole as the greatest malefactors; whence they were sometimes brought up to the Tolbooth after a considerable tymes imprisonment, where several others were prisoners for the like cause, particularly one Margaret M'Lachlan of Kirkinner parish, a women of sixty three years of age."

"After their imprisonment for some considerable tyme, Mr. David Graham, sheriff, the Laird of Lagg, Major Winram, Captain Strachan, called ane assize, indicted these three women, viz Margaret M'Lachlan; Margaret Wilson, Agnes Wilson, to be guilty of the Rebellion at Bothwell Bridge, Airds Moss, twenty field conventicles, and twenty house conventicles. Yet it was well known that none of these women ever were within twenty miles of Bothwell or Airds Moss; and Agnes Wilson being eight years of age at the time of Airds Moss could not be deep in rebellion then, nor her sister of thirteen years of age and twelve years at Bothwell Bridge its tyme. The assize did sitt and brought them in guilty, and these judges sentenced them "to be tied to palisados fixed in the sand and within the flood mark, and there to stand till the flood overflowed them and drowned them."

They received their sentences without the least discouragement, with a composed smiling countenance, judging it their honour to suffer for Christ's truth, that He alone is king and Head of His Church. Gilbert Wilson foresaid got his youngest daughter, Agnes Wilson, out of prison upon his bond of one hundred pounds sterling to produce her when called for, after the sentence of death past against her; tyme they were in prison no means were unessayed with Margaret Wilson to persuade her to take the oath of abjuration and hear the curates with threatening and flattery, but without any success.

Upon 11 May 1685, these two women, Margaret M'Lachlan and Margaret Wilson, were brought forth to execution. They did put the old woman first into the water, and when the water was overflowing her, they asked

Margaret Wilson what she thought of her in that case? She answered, "What do I see but Christ wrestling there? Think ye that we are sufferers? No, it is Christ in us, for he sends none a warfare on their own charges." Margaret Wilson sang Psalm XXV, from the seventh verse, read the eighth chapter of the Epistle to the Romans, and did pray, and then the water covered her. But before her breath was quite gone, they pulled her up and held her till she could speak, and then asked her if she would pray for the king. She answered that she wished the salvation of all men, but the damnation of none. Some of her relations being on the place cried out, "She is willing to conform," being desirous to save her life at any rate. Upon which Major Winram offered the oath of abjuration to her, either to swear it or return to the waters. She refused it, saying, "I will not, I am one of Christ's children, let me go." And then they returned her into the water, where she finished her warfare, being a virgin martyr of eighteen years of age, suffering death for her refusing to swear the oath of abjuration and hear the curates.

The said Gilbert Wilson was fined for the opinion of his children, harassed with frequent quartering of souldiers upon him, sometimes ane hundredth men at ance who lived at discretion on his goods, and that for several years together; and his frequent attendance in the courts at Wigtown almost every week; at thirteen miles distance for three years tyme; riding to Edinburgh on these accounts, so that his losses could not be reckoned and estimate (without doubt) not within five thousand merks; yet for no principle or action of his own, and died in great poverty lately a few years hence; his wife, a very aged woman, lives upon the charity of friends; his son Thomas lived to bear arms under King William in Flanders and the castle of Edinburgh; but had nothing to enter the grounds which they possessed where he lives to certifie the truth of these things with many others who knew them too well."

The entry is attested:

The Session having considered the above particulars and having certain knowledge of the truth of most part of them from their own sufferings, and eye witness of the foresaid sufferings of others, which several of this Session declares, and from certain information of others in the very tyme and place they were acted in, and many living that have all these things fresh in their memory, except those things concerning Gilbert Milroy - (he was banished, sold as a slave in Jamaica, had returned, and was then an elder in the neighbouring parish of Kirkowan) - the truth whereof they think there is no reason to doubt of; they do attest the same, and order an extract to be given in their name to the Presbytery, to transmit to superior judicatories. Sederunt closed with prayer.

The Rev. J. H. Thomson observes that to the Scottish people who were well acquainted with the trustworthiness and truthfulness of the men who discharge the duties of an elder in their different congregations, it will seem impossible to doubt the veracity of these narratives attested by the respective Sessions, and that, indeed, they bear the marks of truth stamped upon their every line.

The independent view of Daniel Defoe in his *Memoirs of the Church of Scotland* succinctly explains that when the women refused to pray for the King, it was simply because they could not ask a blessing to rest upon a ruler who had broken every pledge he had made when he ascended the throne, and who, in his daily life, was trampling upon the laws of his country as well as those of God.

XIV. The Societies

Throughout the history of the Scottish Church there is a continuing theme of internal dissent over theological issues that centre upon the conscience of the individual. The followers of Richard Cameron and Donald Cargill were of the harder school in which they sought the purest adherence to the Covenants. Their followers were the people who became Society members and would in time become the Reformed Presbyterian Church. Many regarded these dissenters as extremists who supported violence as a way of getting their own way.

It is essential, however, to remember that they believed in the Divine Right of God above all else. These same people would argue, for instance, that the First Amendment to the American Constitution (1791) (Congress must not legislate about religion) alienates God from day to day work, school and play and that, therefore, a God centered faith is needed. It is this sort of debate about principles that drove the separation of the Societies from the mainstream Presbyterian Church in the seventeenth and eighteenth century.

The defeat at Bothwell Brig was a crushing blow to the hopes and aspirations for religious freedom, but spirits were revived when Richard Cameron arrived from Holland early in October 1679. In their charismatic leader and his declaration of war in the Sanquhar Declaration of June 1680, hope sprung anew, yet all was dashed with his death at Ayrsmoss on 22 July 1680. Worse was to follow when Donald Cargill was seized and executed on 27 July 1681. The Cameronians or Cargillites were thus left leaderless and without a preacher who dared to attack the state intervention in church matters and the acceptance by some Presbyterian ministers of the Indulgences.

The Government itself, however, broke the hiatus by introducing the Test Act in 1681 that required every holder of a public office to swear loyalty and acknowledge the supremacy of the King in all things temporal and spiritual. An Act of Succession at the same time put beyond doubt that the Catholic Duke of York would be the next King. The Test Act was applied vigorously by the likes of Claverhouse and his ilk, whether or not the office was a public one. It also served to ruffle the feathers of the surviving groups of the extreme, and geographically wide spread, Covenanters

These remnants formed themselves into "Praying Societies" and held their first convention at Logan House on 15 December 1681. The place for the meeting was selected for its location being central to Muirkirk, Strathaven and Lesmahagow and about six miles or so to each. To the north there was mossy ground and inaccessible to troopers, while to the south was the high Nutberry Hill, from which watchmen could see for miles.

Reasonably secure, therefore, the convention set about preparing a Declaration following the lines of the earlier Sanquhar Declaration of 22 June 1680, which it ratified. They declared that King Charles had forfeited his right to the Crown of Scotland and pointed to six of his misdemeanours - overturning in Parliament the constitution formed by his ancestors; intruding his will on civil and ecclesiastical matters; dissolving parliament whenever his wishes were questioned; assuming supremacy in Church and State; excessive taxation for the sole purpose of maintaining the debauchery and depravity of his court. And, lastly, the Test Act which was intended to "unhinge Protestantism itself."

It was resolved that the Declaration would be made at Lanark on 12 January 1682 and it should be a day of fasting and prayer for all those that stayed at home. On the day the assembled throng heard the proclamation of an "Act and Apologetic Declaration of the true Presbyterians of the Church of Scotland," after which they broke the Cross of Lanark and burnt copies of the Popish statutes of which they disapproved.

The meeting also adopted a proposal that there should be "a general correspondence to run circular through the whole Societies of the nation every fourteen days, or at least once a month." By this means, the intention was that, members were kept abreast of developments at short intervals. It was further resolved that future meetings should be held quarterly. This was carried out in fact as the Societies held no less than forty-one consecutive meetings between 15 December 1681 and 3 January 1691 without interruption despite the efforts of spies and informers.

Another important resolution was that no individual should act in "public matters" without consent of the Society of which he was a member, and no Society should act publicly without the approval of a General meeting. These rules helped the Societies to act in harmony and constrained the hot heads. It also meant that on occasion it enabled the Society movement to step aside from potentially dangerous situations such as any involvement in the shooting of Peter Pearson, the Curate of Carsphairn, by Black James McMichael on 11 December 1684.

The organisation and structures that were set in place soon began to bear fruit with delegates being sent to the Continent and Ulster raising the awareness of the struggle and its continuance. The meetings in the counties were conducted under the supervision of the District Society or Correspondence and every three months commissioners were sent to the General Meeting to which matters of difficulty were sent for debate and resolution. In 1683 there were some eighty societies in existence with about

7,000 members. The organisation of this underground church meant that there was a means to relight the torch of Richard Cameron when the Rev. James Renwick came from Holland in September 1683. The government's response was to become harsher and more vindictive as it ramped up action that culminated in "The Killing Time" of 1684-5.

There is an interesting view by Thorbjorn Campbell in his *Standing Witnesses* that the Killing Time came to an abrupt end when the Earl of Argyll landed in Campbeltown, Kintyre on 20 May and commenced his ill-fated revolt. It is also true that on 28 May 1685 a convention at Blackgannoch adopted resolutions that were proclaimed by James Renwick at Sanquhar - the "Protestation and Apologetical Admonitory Declaration" which gave an undertaking "disclaiming all Sectarians, Malignancy, and any Confederacy therewith." It poses the tantalising question whether there was a trade off by the government with the Societies if they did not involve themselves in support for Argyll - who had not been a particular friend of the Covenanters anyway.

It is appropriate to point out that the Societies were responsible for promulgating the memory of the Martyrs when, at a meeting at Crawfordjohn on 29 October 1701, they resolved to erect suitable monuments over all martyr graves in Scotland. It was in pursuance of this resolution that the Edinburgh authorities commissioned a collective memorial in Greyfriars churchyard overlooking the gallows site in the Grassmarket. Most of the bodies were buried without markers in "The Thieves Hole" - the corner reserved to felons, although it is said that the gravediggers secretly buried the Covenanters in an unpolluted area.

While visiting Ireland the spirit of the Covenant was kept alive by Alexander Peden between 1679 and 1681 and then by James Renwick until his execution in 1688. Here, too, there was separation from both the Established Church of Ireland and the Presbyterian Church and the setting up of Societies, or "Hill Men", who corresponded with the Scottish Societies.

A leading figure was the Rev. David Houston, born in Paisley in 1633, who came to Ulster as a licentiate and preacher with the Route Presbytery in 1661. Often a thorn in the flesh of the Presbytery, Houston was committed to the Scottish Covenants and caused some dissension among the congregations such that he was suspended in February 1672. The suspension was lifted in 1673, possibly in the hope that he would go back to Scotland, but he continued preaching in both Ulster and Scotland until he was deposed in 1687. But, by then he had become recognised by the Scottish Societies and was highly thought of by James Renwick. At his death in 1696, he had done much to establish the Societies in Ulster and sown the seed for Reformed Presbyterian Church that would come from the close ties with the Scottish Societies.

The Revolution, and the accession of William and Mary, saw Presbyterianism established in Scotland, but it was not the form desired by the Societies in either Scotland or Ulster. It ignored the Covenants and seemed to surrender spirituality, with the power to convene and dissolve Assemblies lying with the civil authorities. This led to a continued separation of the Societies from the national church and a sixteen-year period when they had no ministers. The Societies were however, encouraged by the accession of the Rev. John MacMillan, minister ejected from Balmaghie, who joined them in 1706. He was their only minister for thirty-seven years until joined by the Rev. Thomas Nairn who had been expelled from the Associate Presbytery for holding similar views to MacMillan.

Nairn's coming allowed for the formation of the Reformed Presbytery on 1 August 1743 at Braehead by MacMillan, Nairn and ruling Elders. The General Meetings of the Societies continued for several years after the formation of the Presbytery, but the latter took charge of all the ecclesiastical matters. There followed a relatively quite period as the movement consolidated its position.

In 1745, the Covenants were renewed at Auchensaugh and the Sacrament administered at the same time. Between 1744 and 1751 five young men were licensed to preach and ordained. Among these was John Cuthbertson who went to Ulster to help the Societies there before he went to America. He became a founding member of the American Reformed Presbytery, which united with the American Reformed Presbytery in 1782 and in 1858 united with the Associate Synod of North America to become the United Presbyterian Church of North America.

Although the Societies were soon consigned to history, there was further theological dissension to come with the posthumous publication in 1749 of a book entitled, "A Treatise on Justifying Faith" by the Rev. James Fraser who had died in 1698. The debates that followed would divide the Reformed Presbytery in 1753.

Part II
The People of the Covenant

XV. James Graham - First Marquis of Montrose (1612 - 1650)

James Graham, Marquis of Montrose, was born in 1612 and succeeded his father in 1627. He was among the first to sign the National Covenant in Greyfriars Kirk in 1638 and was, for a while, a most diligent servant of the Covenanters. King Charles ignored him for service, but like so many other Scottish Lords, he disapproved of the power that had been given to the bishops. As one of the older noble families, his estates at Braco had been carved from the bishopric of Dunblane and he would have been concerned if there was a move to reclaim Church lands by the new order. However, he sat in the first General Assembly at Glasgow as an Elder and was soon dispatched in July 1639 to bring the people of Aberdeen to heel. In this expedition he was accompanied by Alexander Leslie another great general, a former field marshal in the Swedish Army. Unsuccessful with persuasion, Montrose was to return after outbreak of the First Bishops' War and quickly subdue Aberdeen by force.

Between the Bishops' Wars Montrose was beginning to think that the Covenanting revolt had gone far enough and he was beset by problems of conscience over the National Covenant's requirement of defence of both Kirk and King. Concerned also at the Marquis of Argyll's rampaging and self-interest, he sought out others of like conservative mind to form the "Cumbernauld Bond." But this did not stop him leading the Covenanting Army into England crossing the Tweed in August 1640, trouncing the royalist army at Newburn on 28 August, and entering the city of Newcastle on the 30th. In the ensuing peace after the Treaty of Ripon he corresponded privately with King Charles, but all it got him was a rebuff and the summer of 1641 locked in Edinburgh Castle when the Covenanter leaders, especially the Marquis of Argyll, learnt of his contact.

In the aftermath of the Bishops' Wars and further falling out amongst the Covenanters, King Charles threatened to bring in support from Ireland. This threat was of considerable concern to Argyll whose Clan Campbell had long been at odds with the MacDonalds in the West, but it was not until 1644 that it came to reality. The Scottish politicians blundered badly when they hoped that Montrose would lead their army against the Irish. But Montrose had only objected to the Earl of Antrim leading them; he did not object to serving the King or to the use of Irish soldiers in Scotland. So it was that he changed sides and began a year of startling and often brilliant battles against the Covenanter Armies, and great humiliation for the Marquis of Argyll.

Montrose wished to act with the full authority of the King, but this arrived almost three months too late for him to join in an uprising by Sir John Gordon of Haddo. This attempt failed and Haddo and supporters became the first casualties of systematic execution. In April 1644 Montrose had taken 1,000 men with him and seized Dumfries but had no local support, while the Marquis of Huntley had similarly seized Aberdeen for the King. In the face of the local indifference, Huntley disbanded and retired to his castle, while Montrose pondered the next step as he waited for the promised troops from Ireland to arrive.

In Ireland the Earl of Antrim's army was also delayed waiting for weapons and ammunition to be delivered, but it headed out from Fort of Passage, Waterford, on 27 June 1644. On their way across the Irish Sea, the frigate *Harp,* carrying Alastair McColl and his officers, came across

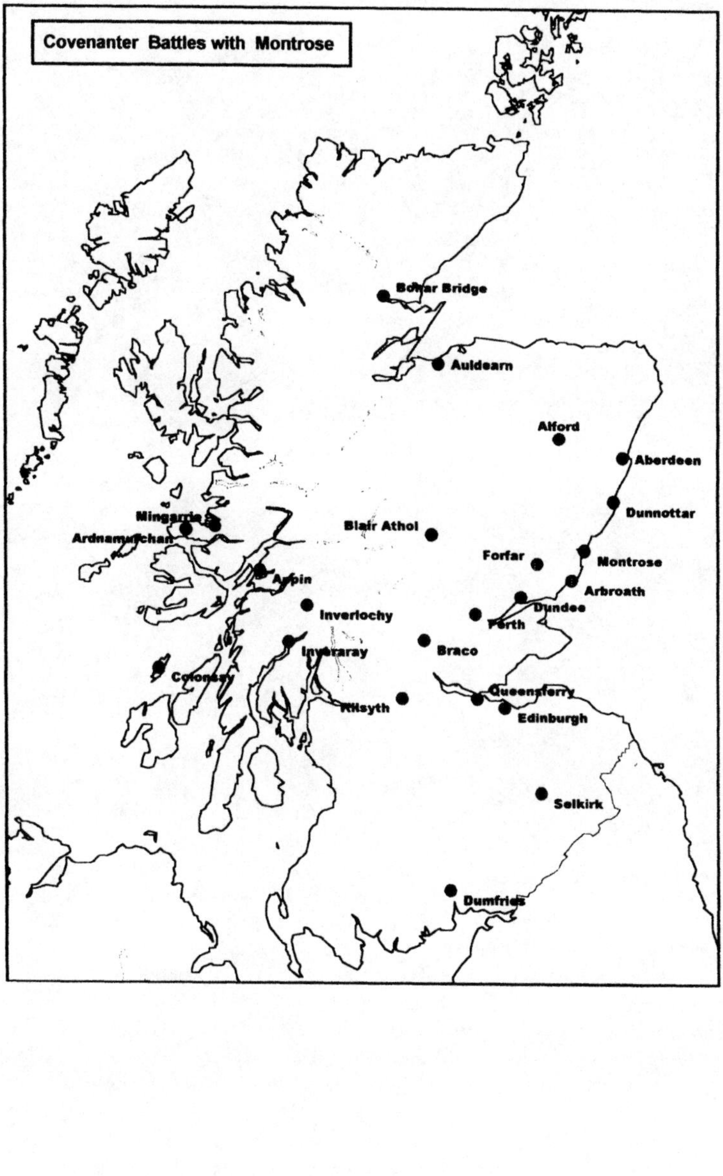
Covenanter Battles with Montrose
Bonar Bridge
Auldearn
Alford
Aberdeen
Dunnottar
Blair Athol
Mingarrie
Ardnamurchan
Forfar
Montrose
Appin
Arbroath
Inverlochy
Dundee
Perth
Inveraray
Braco
Colonsay
Queensferry
Kilsyth
Edinburgh
Selkirk
Dumfries

three vessels, two with food and much needed provisions and the third had some forty Covenanters including three ministers - Rev.s Weir, Watson and Hamilton who were taken hostage.

The Irish force landed at Ardmurchan on the west coast of Scotland on 8 July 1644 and found that the promised help of the Earl of Seaforth had evaporated - he had joined the Covenanters. However, the two Argyll forts of Mingarrie in Ardmurchan and Lochaline in Morven were poorly guarded and were quickly seized. These were to be important staging posts for the Irish forces in the months ahead. McColl then unleashed his ferocious band of about 1200 on northern Argyllshire, the Seaforth lands, and made a punishing attack on the Clan Mackenzie. Arriving at Badenoch, he sent a fiery cross to the Covenanters of Moray commanding them to rise and follow Montrose. History is unclear which band saved which, but Montrose, learning of McColl's arrival in Badenoch, moved out to meet him at Blair Athol leaving the Irishmen to fight their way there. This they did, even though outnumbered and pursued by Argyll with three times the men, and they had even stormed the castle at Blair Athol before Montrose got there.

Tippermuir 1 September 1644

Needing provisions, the combined force of hardened military Irishmen and Montrose's local recruits turned to attack St. Johnstone (Perth). Arriving on the plain of Tippermuir, they were confronted by the Covenanter "Army of God" of 8,000 men, armed with nine cannon and a detachment of cavalry numbering 800.

Montrose placed McColl and his band at the centre, his bowmen under Lord Kilpont to the left and Montrose and his Athol men to the right. Facing them were the Fife and Perthshire militia led by David Wemyss, Lord Elcho. The royalist victory lay in the daredevil charge of the Irish, who having only one round for their muskets, dashed in close, fired their one shot, then reversed their weapons and used them as clubs - an unknown tactic in those days. Then having gained a foothold, the Irishmen resorted to using the skein or short sword, with which they were so adept. The Covenanter cry of "Jesus, and no quarter" was of little use to them as they broke ranks and fled, with over 1,300 of them dead on the battlefield and 800 taken prisoner. Following their victory the royalist army occupied and ransacked Perth for two days.

Aberdeen 13 September 1644

After plundering Perth, the little army of Montrose crossed the River Dee at Crathes, about fifteen miles north of Aberdeen and marched on the city. On 13 September 1644 they found about 3,000 foot soldiers, 500 cavalry and three cannon facing them. Here, too, the Irishmen seemed to be at the heart of things, with Captain John Mortimer adopting another unusual stratagem of mixing foot soldiers within the cavalry and adopting the wild charge upon the Covenanters. Captain Mortimer would later follow Montrose into exile and return in 1650 to fight at Philiphaugh. Elsewhere, Sir William Forbes of Craigievar charged his cavalry at Alastair McColl's troops, who fell apart and let them through, then turned in on them and slaughtered them. The Covenanters had about 800 killed.

After Aberdeen, the victors returned to Blair Athol, where a detachment was sent to the assistance of the Irishmen left at Mingarrie and Lochaline who were under attack from Argyll. On the face of it, Argyll was seeking to save the three Covenanter ministers that had been captured and which would have been readily exchanged for Alastair McColl's father and two brothers that Argyll held captive. He refused to exchange and pursued his attack as the castles were critical to the defence of his lands, but when the relieving Irish troops came near, the assault was abandoned. Arising from this failed siege was the joining to the royalist cause of Clanranald of Lochaber, including all the MacDonnells of Garragach and Keppoch, and the MacDonnells of Glencoe.

Fivy 28 October 1644

Meanwhile Montrose's campaign restarted by marching from Blair Athol towards the lowlands when the armies came across one another at Fivy, west of Montrose, on 28 October 1644. Argyll and his troops had been tracking the movement of Montrose's forces at a respectful distance and had occupied himself by devastating the districts of Lude, Speirglass, Fascally, Don-a Vourd and Ballyheukane, firing the land to Angus and northwards to Dunnottar. His force of 1,000 claymores, 1,500 militiamen and seven troops of cavalry under the Earl of Lothian, came upon Montrose and his troops. Once again it was the Irishmen, this time under Captain Manus O'Cahan, who dislodged Argyll's troops from an important firing position. The Covenanters again turned and fled with many of the cavalry, especially, left dead.

Campbell lands - Inveraray.
December 1644 - January 1645

Montrose returned to Blair Athol to be rejoined by Alastair McColl who had been on a recruitment drive in the northwest. With him were John of Moydart, Captain of Clanranald and 500 men; Keppoch and his men from Lochaber; the Stewarts of Appin; the warriors of Knoidart, Glengarry, Glennenis and Glencoe; Camerons from Lochy and Farquharsons of Braemar. These had all suffered under Argyll's fire and sword attacks and it was resolved that they should similarly retaliate. The Montrose forces were divided into three divisions, one under Montrose, a second led by Alastair McColl and the third under John of Moydart. They descended on the Campbell lands between 13 December 1644 and 29 January 1645 burning homes and raiding for cattle throughout in Glenurchy, Inverawe, Lawers in Breadelbane and then to Auchenbrach in Kintyre. They left 900 Campbell soldiers dead in their wake.

The Marquis of Argyll had been at Inveraray on the shores of Loch Fyne when he heard that Montrose was dashing headlong through the passes of the southern Highlands to attack and loot Castle Campbell at Dollar, in the heartland of Argyll and Clan Campbell. With this news he fled, taking a fishing boat on the loch and to all intents and purposes abandoning his people. Tales vary whether this was cowardice or that he was strongly advised by the ruling Covenanters to save himself - he was no use to them if dead. But it is quite likely that the common people of Argyll felt abandoned by his action and chose not to resist the plundering forces of Montrose.

Inverlochy 2 February 1645

The army went then to Lochaber where they were joined by an advance party of the MacLeans under their chieftain Sir Lachlan MacLean, of Dowart in the Isle of Mull, and about thirty soldiers. Going to Glengarry, where more joined them, Montrose learnt that Argyll and his cousin Sir Duncan Campbell of Auchinbrack, who had been recalled from Ireland, were at Inverlochy. At the other end of the Great Glen the Earl of Seaforth had gathered a force to prevent Montrose from escaping. The 3,000 Campbells gathered at Inverlochy were confidant that they were safe in their remote lands in winter especially, but that did not deter Montrose. He reckoned that the animosity of his forces to the Campbells would be to his advantage and was proved right. He marched his army through the Glen of Albin, along the rugged river valley of the Tarf, over Lochaber Mountains and round the edge of Ben Nevis to do battle in a driving snowstorm on Sunday 2 February 1645.

At Inverlochy, on the Saturday evening, Argyll again set himself aside from his troops, taking to a barge on Loch

Linn from where he dictated his battle orders. Argyll's forces opened fire on the royalists with cannon and muskets shortly after sunrise, but again after the first exchange of muskets the Irish troops advanced rapidly and took Argyll's standard and the standard bearer. The loss of the standard was followed by the army breaking up and there followed a hot pursuit for over nine miles in which hundreds of the Campbell men were slaughtered. Campbell of Auchinbrack was killed, beheaded - helmet and all, by one sweep of Alastair McColl's claymore, with sixteen or seventeen other Campbell chiefs and some lowland chieftains; four more Campbells were taken prisoner at Bearbrick on Loch Awe. In all some forty ranking Campbells were killed and twenty-two lowland chieftains released on giving their oath not to bear arms again; and 1,700 of Argyll's troops were also killed. The military reputation of the Campbells was effectively destroyed by this action and led to Seaforth disbanding his troops and Lord Gordon with his cavalry joining Montrose.

Dundee March 1645

Towards the end of March 1645, Montrose was pursuing the Covenanter General Urry across the river Esk to Dundee, which was a town that had previously resisted Montrose. To the south Covenanter General William Baillie barred his way. With a view to satisfying his men's demand for plunder Montrose allowed the city to be attacked by Alastair McColl and his Antrim soldiers along with troops led by Lord George Gordon, a younger son of the Marquis of Huntley. A formal surrender was being concluded when a message was received that Generals Baillie and Urry, with 3,000 Covenanting foot soldiers and 800 cavalry, were just outside the city. Montrose retired very quickly to Arbroath with his small force of about 700.

The Covenanting generals rested the night at Forfar, thinking that they had Montrose bottled up, and planned to deal with him the following morning. But during the night, Montrose daringly took his army past the Covenanters and escaped via Kerriemuir to South Esk. Learning that more of his troops had escaped, he made a forced march of three days and two nights to escape into the Grampian Mountains.

Auldearn 9 May 1645

The next conflict was 9 May 1645 at the village of Auldearn near Nairn. On this occasion Montrose's forces were outnumbered by the army of Sir John Urry who was assisted by George MacKenzie, the Second Earl of Seaforth; John the thirteenth Earl of Sutherland; and James Ogilvy First Earl of Findlater. With this mixed bag of of about 4,000 regulars, Highlanders and militia Urry attempted to suprise Montrose but musket firing, by soldiers checking that their powder was not damp, alerted the royalists. In this battle the royal standard was entrusted to Alastair McColl and his Irishmen. Montrose with a force of only 1,700 could only allow about 400 troops for the defence of the Standard and instructed McColl to stay within the trenches where they were placed. But in the heat of battle the Irishman could not resist a dash at the enemy and he and his band were instantly surrounded. It required a supreme effort to fight their way back to the trenches. While holding the rearguard, McColl broke his sword and his brother-in-law Davidson of Ardnacross, handed him his, during which, Davidson was mortally wounded. For his impetuosity McColl had seventeen of his officers and veterans wounded but the royal standard was safe. The MacDonalds and the Gordons performed especially well and at the end of the day over 2,000 Covenanters lay dead.

Alford 2 July 1645

On leaving Auldearn, Montrose marched rapidly into Aberdeenshire to overtake a Covenanter army under General Baillie (Baillie of Letham) and Alexander Lindsay, the Earl of Balcarres. This he did at Alford, on the River Don, where Balcarres's horsemen were unable to hold those of Gordon. After the battle some 700 Covenanters lay dead on the field. Montrose suffered losses too, including Lord Gordon of Aboyne, the eldest son of the Marquis of Huntley. General Baillie meanwhile withdrew and made his way to Perth pursued by Montrose's forces. At this juncture there was no serious opposition to the royalists north of the river Tay.

Kilsyth 15 August 1645

Montrose managed to march into the Lowlands with an augmented army of some 5,000 in August much to the consternation of the Covenanters. Thinking that Montrose might be making for Edinburgh, General Baillie and the Marquis of Argyll formed another army of some 7,000 foot soldiers and 1,000 cavalry, which was assembled at the village of Kilsyth. Almost half of the Covenanter forces were made up of raw recruits in the Fife militia. Alastair McColl was again an important factor this time by keeping the impetuous Clans in control who were squabbling over precedence in the battle. This concerned 700 Macleans and 500 Clanranald who had not fought at Alford who wanted honours like the Glengarry had gained previously. On 15 August 1645, yet again, Montrose was victorious, this time pursuing the fleeing Covenanters for fourteen miles and leaving 3,000 dead in his wake. Argyll, this time, fled to Queensferry where he took a boat to Newcastle. Many of the other Covenanter leaders took refuge in Stirling Castle.

Philiphaugh 13 September 1645

Moving on to Glasgow, Montrose and his army were met by a remarkably friendly populace and he sent McColl into Ayrshire, the Covenanter heartland, to negotiate terms with the landowners particularly. This was in the last two weeks of August, during which time most of the Scottish clansmen had returned to their homes with their booty; the Gordons under James, Viscount Aboyne were recalled and McColl who had gone into Argyllshire leaving only 700 of his infantry with Montrose. Thus reduced in number, the denuded forces of Montrose were surprised by David Leslie and the Covenanter forces at Philiphaugh, near Selkirk, on 13 September 1645.

This time the royalist forces were massacred with over 500 of the Irishmen cut to ribbons after they had been offered quarter and had surrendered. There followed a slaughter of the camp followers - boys, cooks and women. 300 Irish women, wives of the soldiers, and many pregnant, were cut up - literally, and unborn babies cut from the womb and cast on the ground with their murdered mothers. The Covenanter ministers compounded this horror and incited all and any retribution on the royalists.

In the period after Philiphaugh and 1 December, many of the Scottish nobility, who had taken part, were rounded up. Any Irish found, or held in prison, were summarily executed by order of the Estates who directed:

This House ordains the Irish prisoners taken at and after Philiphaugh in all the prisons of the kingdom, especially in the prisons of Selkirk, Jedburgh, Glasgow, Dumbarton and Perth, to be executed without any assize or process.

Montrose was forced to flee to the Highlands leaving his forces scattered and massacred. A new force was raised and an attempt made to lay siege to Inverness in the April of 1646 while the Gordons again took the field. But neither was much of a threat to the Covenanters and was easily contained by an army under Major General John Middleton. McColl meanwhile had skirmished with the Campbells at Callander on 13 February 1646 and routed them. While in June the Campbells had revenge on the Lamonts on the Cowal Peninsula and massacred 130 prisoners at Dunoon. The hit and run skirmishing continued for a while but on the Kings command Montrose broke up his forces on 30 July and went to Norway on 3 September. McColl, however, remained in Kintyre. In the summer and early autumn McColl was joined by the Earl of Antrim who tried to raise an army from the clans who resented the Campbells, with the intention of marching into England to release King Charles. In the northeast Huntley and his Gordons seized Banff which they held through the winter

The threat to rescue the King convinced the Covenanters that they had to crush the royalists once and for all and a levy for a New Model Army was raised. Lieutenant General David Leslie and Major General John Middleton led 6,000 foot soldiers and 1,200 horsemen firstly to occupy the Gordon territory in the north east of Scotland where Middleton remained. Leslie headed to Kintyre where his forces routed 1,300 Irish and Highlanders from their camp at Rhunanhaorine Point. In June Dunaverty Castle was captured and 300 prisoners were massacred at the insistence of John Nevay, a Covenanting minister. McColl and some of his original forces with a number of Highlanders managed to escape to Ireland.

Bonar Bridge 27 April 1650

Montrose escaped from the disaster at Philiphaugh into the Highlands and from there he went to Holland and Norway. Still loyal to his King, now Charles II (who was double dealing and negotiating with the Covenanters even while Montrose fought), he had one a last gamble landing in the Orkneys in March 1650 with 1200 continental mercenaries. However, he could gather little help and met with the Covenanter forces under Colonel Strachan at Carbisdale near Bonar Bridge on 27 April. Here the royalist fortunes took a severe battering with some 500 killed, 200 drowned and 250 captured. Montrose himself was seized a week later by Neil Macleod of Assynt at Ardvreck Castle.

Time was short for Montrose, who had been convicted and sentenced in 1644, there was no trial and he was sent to Edinburgh for execution. Come the day of execution, 21 May 1650, it is recorded that he was resplendently dressed in rich scarlet, overlaid with silver lace, white gloves and silken stockings as if going to a wedding. He was hung in the Grassmarket, Edinburgh. After he was dead, his head was severed, as was the custom for alleged traitors, and placed on a spike at the Tolbooth and his limbs were distributed to the four major cities of Scotland for display in places of prominence, Montrose's remains stayed exposed for eleven years until he was finally laid to rest in St. Giles's Church in Edinburgh.

Postscript

Some historians tend to understate the contribution of the Irish troops supplied by the Earl of Antrim. *The Montgomery Manuscripts* tells us that they were not by any means the local militia drummed up for service, or wild hairy men from out of the bogs, but seasoned full time soldiers who had been fighting in Flanders. Moreover, with a proper command structure they were disciplined in battle; they had developed their own novel tactics, which proved very successful; and, were led by a charismatic as well as brave leader in Alastair McColl. Today we might compare them as akin to Commandos or Rangers, who lived off the land, traveled quickly often over rough terrain, who struck decisively at their objective before moving on to the next task. The opportunity to take revenge on their ancient enemy, the Campbells, was undoubtedly the governing factor and also their weakness, as they much preferred to take revenge on their old enemy than fight for a foreign king who cared little for them.

The tally of Covenanters killed in Montrose's campaign was very bloody, indeed.

Tippermuir	3,000
Aberdeen	800
Fivy	unknown
Inveraray	900
Inverlochy	1,700
Auldearn	2,000
Alford	700
Kilsyth	3,000
Total	12,100 and probably many more.

Archibald Campbell, First Marquis of Argyll

XVI. Archibald Campbell, Eighth Earl, First Marquis of Argyll (1607 - 1661)

Much can be written of the Clan Campbell and its leaders throughout the history of Scotland. Archibald Campbell, Marquis of Argyll, was no different from his ancestors in always seeking to extend his lands and influence. Known as Gillespie Grumach, the Grim, and Glied or squinting Marquis, he held supreme power in Scotland for a time. It was not, therefore, a total surprise that he became a leading Covenanter and also the rival and opponent of the Marquis of Montrose.

In 1633 Argyll handed to King Charles I the Justiciarship of Scotland, which is all except his own lands, and was made Marquis in 1641. Following the National Covenant in 1638, there was a breathing space wherein the King was unable to raise a serious force of arms and he sent the Duke of Hamilton north to parlay. "Flatter them with what hopes you please" were the King's instructions, but "don't call them traitors until the fleet was ready to sail" was the underlying theme. In the event Hamilton had to allow a General Assembly to be called, which he perceived as unrepresentative of the people and called for its dissolution. When he was shouted down, Hamilton walked out followed by all, but one, of the Privy Councilors present - the Earl of Argyll remained and declared, "I take you for members of lawful Assembly." The Assembly, now openly illegal, proceeded to excommunicate the bishops and purged the Kirk of ceremonies, of the Five Articles of Perth, the Canons of 1636 and the Prayer Book of 1637.

With the support of Argyll, the Covenanters had gained a wily politician who was also able to call upon some 5,000 clansmen, if required. Said to have been a man of deep religious conviction and personal power, he was daring in his political decisions. He had much moral courage, but was not a soldier, and this he soon displayed against the brilliant generalship of Montrose. Before then, however, there were the Bishops' Wars in which Argyll worked diligently for the purification of the Kirk - and Clan Campbell aggrandisment. For about six weeks, he engaged in a private war in the Braes of Mar, settled old scores with the Murrays of Atholl; attacked Angus, and Rannoch before he moved on in August to secure Dumbarton Castle against a threat from Ireland.

Inveraray Castle
Ancestral home of the Duke of Argyll, Chief of Clan Campbell

In 1644, when Montrose changed loyalties and joined with Alastair McColl, Argyll was to suffer military defeat and humiliation on three occasions. In his own self-interest, Argyll was vindictive and victorious, attacking the

Ogilvys of Airlie (kinsmen of Montrose) looting and burning their houses at Forther and Airlie. Montrose firstly made a revenge attack on Castle Campbell in the Ochils above Dollar and set it on fire. On 2 Feb 1645 the Campbells were again caught and some 1,500 slaughtered at Inverlochy, and thirdly at Kilsyth on 15 August. After these battles, the military strength of the Campbells would never be the same, but it did not stop Argyll from slaughtering his enemies.

After Montrose's downfall and execution, Argyll sent the armies of the Covenant to deal with old family enemies, the MacDonalds of Kintyre and the MacDougalls of Dunolly. This saw 300 men at the garrison of Dunavertie slaughtered and the burning of the MacDougall strongholds of Dunolly and Gylen. While in Cowal, the lands of the Lamonts were plundered and over 130 of that clan were butchered at Dunoon.

By December 1647 a treaty, known as "The Engagement," was concluded with the moderate wing of the Covenanters, but it was short lived being ended by Cromwell crushing the Engagement's army at Preston on 17 August 1648. This left the radicals to return to power with a vengeance to what they saw as the true revolution. Meanwhile, Argyll was able to sup with Cromwell at Moray House in Canongate, Edinburgh. Six months later his stance changed again, when Charles I was executed, something he and the staunch Covenanters disagreed with as they had always respected the King's person. Within a few days the Scottish parliament proclaimed Charles's son as King, while in England, the monarchy was abolished.

Somewhat unpolitically for him, Argyll used all his cunning and opportunities to ingratiate himself with the new King and established a watchful control over him. There were even proposals that the King should marry the eldest of Argyll's daughters, Lady Anne Campbell. Short of becoming Argyll's son-in-law the King lavished favours on Argyll, including written promises to make him Duke of Argyll and a Knight of the Garter. He was the principal performer at the King's coronation at Scone, placing the crown upon his head on 1 January 1651.

But it was a waiting game as King Charles saw the promised help from Montrose dissolve in defeat at Bonar Bridge (27 April 1650) and Montrose's execution on 21 May 1650. Cromwell's slaughter of Leslie's army at Dunbar on 3 September 1650, where some 4,000 Scots were killed and 10,000 captured, was the turning point for the Covenanters as splits within the Kirk became more bitter and scapegoats were sought for the defeat. The final act of desperation was the ill-fated venture into England which met disaster at Worcester on 3 September 1651. Following this final defeat the King fled "over the water."

The Revolution that had begun in 1637, under the leadership of the nobles, ended with them uncertain of where they stood. The fate of Argyll was fairly typical, he had held the reins of power for twelve years and had placed the crown on Charles II's head at the Parish Kirk of Scone in 1651, but otherwise he feared the threat of Cromwell and invasion of his lands - the very threat that had induced him into politics in 1639. Thus for the next ten years, Argyll wisely kept his head down.

Following the death of Cromwell and the collapse of his son Richard's attempt at government, there followed the Restoration of Charles who was joyfully proclaimed King of all three kingdoms in Edinburgh on 14 May 1660, although he arrived in London on 29 May, his thirtieth birthday. The loyal burghers celebrated at the Mercat Cross in Edinburgh drinking to the king's health and symbolically dashing their glasses to the ground - some three hundred dozen glasses were smashed in this way.

But the King who had sworn to preserve Presbyterianism in Scotland set to work to destroy it. The Covenants were declared illegal, Presbyteries and Sessions were forbidden and, horrors of horrors, bishops were appointed with ministers told that they must accept Episcopacy. There soon followed the search for scapegoats, with Argyll and James Guthrie, the Covenanter minister of

Memorial to the Campbell Martyrs of 1685,
Inveraray

THIS MONUMENT WAS ORIGINALLY
ERECTED IN 1754, IN INVERARAY,
ON A SITE WHICH NOW FORMS PART
OF THE GARDEN BELONGING TO
THE BANK OF SCOTLAND.
THE MONUMENT COMMEMORATES THE
EXECUTION BY THE 1ST MARQUIS OF
ATHOLL, OF SEVENTEEN CAMPBELL
LEADERS IN 1685. IT WAS MOVED TO
ITS PRESENT POSITION IN ORDER
TO MAKE IT MORE ACCESSIBLE TO
THE PUBLIC AND WHERE IT WAS
UNVEILED BY THE 10TH DUKE OF
ATHOLL IN 1985.

Inscription of the Campbell Martyrs Memorial
17 Chiefs executed for rebellion led by the 9th Earl

Greyfriars Kirk, soon to suffer execution. Argyll meanwhile, traveled to London to congratulate the new King despite warnings not to do so and was promptly thrown into the Tower of London. After months of lingering in chains, he was sent back to Scotland in December to stand trial in Edinburgh.

Argyll's fate was seemingly a foregone conclusion, the judges and advocates clearly understanding the King's wishes. Despite all sorts of obstacles put in his way - the leading lawyers of the day were threatened and bullied so none would take up his defence, Argyll acquitted himself well in the months of interrogation ahead. However, in May, the former General Monck, now the Duke of Albemarle, sent old letters to Argyll showing that he had collaborated with Cromwell (to whom he had given his word of honour) and his fate was sealed.

The sentence was soon passed, Argyll having to kneel to hear the ominous words:

Archibald Campbell, Marquis of Argyll, is found guilty of high treason and is adjudged to be execute to the death as a traitor, his head to be severed from his body at the Cross of Edinburgh, upon Monday the twenty seventh instant, and to be affixed in the same place where the Marquis of Montrose's head was formerly.

On the appointed day at 2 pm, the Marquis of Argyll made his goodbye's saying, "I could die like a Roman but I choose rather to die like a Christian." After speaking to James Guthrie, who was to follow him within a week, he went to the Maiden (as the Scottish guillotine was called), made a short speech, saying "I had the honour to set the crown on the King's head, and now he hastens me away to a better crown than his own." He knelt down and gave the signal for the blade to fall. So ended Archibald Campbell, Marquis of Argyll.

Archibald Johnston, Lord Warriston

XVII. Archibald Johnston, Lord Warriston - the Lawyer of the Covenant

Some people seem to be born to follow a particular profession and so it was for Archibald Johnston born to a merchant father, a burgess of Edinburgh, in March 1611. His grandfather Sir Thomas Craig was an advocate of note and the author of a book on Feudal Law. An aunt was the wife of Lord Durie and mother of the second Lord Durie; another uncle by marriage was Sir James Skene, President of the Court of Session. A grandmother, Rachel Arnot, had hidden Robert Bruce the dissident minister of St. Giles and her house was the place of refuge for banished ministers. He was thus aware of both the law and Covenanters from an early age.

He took his degree in Glasgow in 1633 and settled in Edinburgh. He soon married Helen Hay, a judge's daughter, and they had twelve children in their marriage of twenty-seven years. At first his career prospered with a town house in the High Street and a country home at Warriston, seven miles from Edinburgh. By 1638 Johnston had begun to earn a reputation and had already fallen out with Archbishop Laud and King Charles. Thomas Carlyle was to call him a "Canny, lynx - eyed lawyer."

In the protestation and tumult that arose following the introduction of the Service Book on 23 July 1637 very many representatives from all over the Lowlands of Scotland gathered in Edinburgh to petition the Privy

Council. Johnston was responsible for coordinating this opposition and the creation of four permanent committees called "The Tables" made up of the best and ablest representatives from each of four categories. The first Table was composed of the nobility, the second of representatives from the shires, the third of members of the Presbyteries and the fourth of the burghers and townsmen. At the heart coordinating things was the "Central Table" which sat constantly in Edinburgh and negotiated directly with the Privy Council. Archibald Johnston was the Clerk and Secretary of the Central Table with a finger on all the pulses. Early on he was literally to deliver great work to the Assembly when he found the missing Kirk records from 1590. There had been great fears that these historic records had fallen into the hands of the bishops and may have been mutilated or destroyed. The restoration of these records was itself a minor miracle.

With Alexander Henderson, the foremost and most statesmanlike of the Presbyterian ministers of his day, they framed the National Covenant. Henderson had came to notice when he defended himself before the Privy Council for failing to obtain and use the New Liturgy when ordered to do so by the Archbishop of St. Andrews. He did so well that the concerns were reported to London. This skill and tact was the reason for his joining with Johnston in the drafting of the National Covenant.

The Covenant was in three parts, the first reproduced the Old Covenant of 1581 sometimes called the Kings Confession; the second scheduled the enactments against Popery and confirmed the privileges of the Reformed Church; the third was an emphatic protest against the changes in the manner of worship, which had brought about the then current troubles. With the benefit of hindsight and countless examinations by scholars it might be said that the Covenant was a very clever document. It was both long and turgid and to the layman probably unintelligible, with over four thousand words and full of involved legal clauses. But the final part (see Appendix 5) concerning resistance to innovation and support for Law and Order was a trumpet call that could be recognised and subscribed to by all. So it was on 28 February 1638 that Archibald Johnston held up the Covenant in Greyfriars Kirk and read its contents in a clear and distinct voice so that all present might hear.

The Glasgow Assembly of November and December 1638 brought him to the fore when they voted him, almost unanimously, to be the Clerk and he duly took the minutes of that momentous meeting. Despite the order from the Kings representative, the Duke of Hamilton, to disperse, the Assembly continued to work on. The previous Acts ratifying Episcopacy were annulled. The Service Book and the Canons, the Court of High Commission, and the Articles of Perth were swept away. Eight bishops were excommunicated, six more deposed or suspended and the National Covenant was confirmed. All this was overseen by Archibald Johnston.

Soon he was discussing ways and means of supporting the Covenanter Army at Berwick and subsequently was much involved in the negotiations that brought to an end to the First Bishop's War 18 June 1639. He and Henderson were again involved in the Treaty of Ripon, 26 October 1640 that ended the Second Bishop's War. Charles seemed to have a grudging respect for Johnston remarking that "the devil himself could not make a more uncharitable construction or give a more bitter expression" and on leaving the Royal presence Johnston was bid "walk more circumspectly in time coming." Despite these warnings Johnstone prospered and in 1641 was knighted and became a Lord of Session. Later he was one of the eight Scottish Commissioners that went to the Westminster Assembly.

Under Cromwell he very reluctantly accepted office and was one of the Judges appointed to superintend the administration of the law in Scotland. This was well received by the populace because the Judges, four of the seven being English, had no truck for the corruption they found and which was rapidly cleansed. In 1657 he was restored to the dignity of Lord Clerk Register of Scotland, which, among other things, provided him with useful income needed to support a large family. He later joined the English Council of State. However, there was a coming storm as Charles II came to power intent on settling old scores for troublemakers such as Argyll and Warriston who were condemned for cooperating with Cromwell. On 14 July 1660 a warrant for Sir Archibald's arrest was issued.

It seems Sir Archibald had wind of what was coming and had escaped to the Continent. On failing to appear at the summons he was formally summoned by trumpet to surrender himself and a reward of one hundred pounds Scots to any one who might detain him. In an unusual step it was also declared to be treason for anyone to harbour or assist Warriston. On 10 October he was declared a fugitive. In his absence and driven by spite, his offices were declared vacant and estates were forfeit. In February 1661 at the Mercat Cross in Edinburgh the Lyon King of Arms declared him a traitor and tore up his Coat of Arms. Warriston was forced to flee abroad.

In Hamburg he became ill and was severely, some say badly, bled by a Dr. Bates, a physician to King Charles. Howie in *The Scots Worthies* relates that Dr. Bates prescribed poison instead of physic

> *and then caused draw from him sixty ounces of blood ... he was brought near the gates of death, and so far lost his memory, that he could not remember what he had said or done a quarter of an hour before.*

After two years he went to Rouen, France to meet his wife but in January 1663 was seized by one Andrew Murray and taken to imprisonment in the Tower of London, before removal to the Edinburgh Tolbooth in June. On 8 July he was arraigned before the Parliament at which the hearing and sentencing were almost perfunctionary. Warriston's nephew, the historian Bishop Burnet, wrote that he was so disordered both in body and mind that it was a reproach to any government to proceed against him.

Warriston clearly was in desperately poor health and unable to defend himself and a vote was put to defer any sentence but John Maitland, Duke of Lauderdale, aided by Archbishop Sharp and the prelates, finally got his way with his demand for immediate execution. Although allowed a fortnights grace in which to prepare himself, Archibald Johnston was led to the gallows on 22 July 1663. In a final twist the gallows were erected opposite his own house where, with arms uplifted to the sky, he stepped forward to receive the martyr's diadem. His head was cut off and displayed at the Netherbow Gate alongside his friend the Rev. James Guthrie.

The head was later removed following the intercession of Lieutenant General Drummond who had married one of Johnston's daughters, and was buried with the rest of the body in Greyfriars Kirk yard. Another daughter of Warriston was Lady Graden who in turn was sister-in-law of Robert Baillie of Jerviswood. She accompanied Baillie when he was executed, hung drawn and quartered, on 23 December 1684 and witnessed the sorry affair with great fortitude.

James Sharp, Archbishop of St. Andrews

XVIII. Rev. James Sharp, Minister of Crail, Archbishop of St. Andrews - the Turncoat

In Covenanting history, James Sharp was possibly the most reviled of all both for being a turncoat and for his self-interest and greed when accepting the elevation from minister at Crail in Fife, to Archbishop of St. Andrews. He was an ardent pursuer of the Covenanters after his appointment, and his murder on Magus Moor in 1679 was greeted with joy by many extremists. Others saw that there would be a bloody price to pay.

James Sharp was born in 1613 in Banffshire, son of the Sheriff-clerk and factor to the Earl of Findlater, his mother being from the Leslie family. Not especially bright, although possessed of native cunning, he managed to get to university and graduate before spending some time in England at Oxford and London. He became minister in the village of Crail in Fife where he was noticed perhaps more by his absence than his ministry as he spent considerable time in London where he hovered on the fringe of the Court. More interested, it seems, in the machinery of the church than ministering to his parish, he was a schemer, who during the Restoration of King Charles II in 1660 was at the heart of intrigue. During this period he was giving his colleagues in Scotland glowing reports of the King's willingness to support Presbyterianism while placing himself in positions of influence. This duplicity came to head in 1661 when the Privy Council announced the restoration of the bishops.

The decree at the Mercat Cross in Edinburgh on 6 September restored episcopacy, forbade the meeting of the clerical courts and enjoined that non-conformists should be committed to prison. In the following December the Rev. James Sharp, minister of Crail became Archbishop of St. Andrews and wholly subservient to the Crown. There had already been signs of unease from the likes of the Rev. Robert Blair, that James Sharp was becoming a sycophant of the Court, and his elevation confirmed those fears. There were too, tales of satanic intervention even that Sharp received such a visitor late at night. Whatever the truth of such stories, the reality was that he was not trusted and was widely despised.

Among Sharp's early involvements was his revenge on the Rev. James Guthrie whom he called "hare brained" and was executed on 1 June 1661. Conjoined with Sharp was another former Presbyterian supporter - John, Earl of Maitland, the King's Commissioner in Scotland (1667-1680). Maitland was above all else a soldier who had worked his way up from the ranks. He was a zealous Covenanter in 1644 and 1645 then became a confidant of King Charles whom he served valiantly. But he was also a violent and arbitrary man who was a heavy drinker. Earlier, with the aid of his cronies and the Parliament packed with the king's men, the Earl of Middleton began to demolish the Kirk by passing numerous laws - nearly four hundred in the first six months of the Parliament of 1661. Among these was an Act of 11 June 1662, to become known as Middleton's Act, which required ministers who had been ordained after 1649 to be presented by the patron and the appointment to be sanctioned by a bishop.

It may have been the intention only to weed out the die hard Covenanters from their kirks as there was astonishment, and anger from Sharp, when between three and four hundred ministers were "outed." Sharp complained bitterly at the precipitate action and lack of finesse, even though it accomplished one of his objectives. A consequence was the appointment of curates to fill the vacated posts, many of who had little learning or were callow youths. There followed another Act referred to as "The Bishops Drag Net," which imposed heavy fines on those who did not attend the Church. In the same year, 1663, the "Scots Mile Act" was introduced which forbade the outed ministers from living within twenty miles of their former Kirk and within six miles of a city. The latter part of this law is thought to have been added by Sharp in order to force Robert Blair from the vicinity of St. Andrews, such was his spite and fear of the man. The pettiness of the legislation had one great effect - it marked the beginning of the field meetings or "conventicle" and a firming of the Presbyterian resistance especially in the south west of Scotland.

When the Parliament broke up in the autumn of 1663 there was an understanding that they would not be recalled, thereby leaving the government of Scotland to the Privy Council. Sharp immediately sought the King's ear and persuaded him to bring back the obsolete Court of High Commission to deal with the Covenanters by summary law. Sharp was the Court's President and other members included nine prelates and thirty-five laymen. With almost limitless power, the Court could summon virtually anyone before it on vague pretexts; it imposed huge fines, banished and imprisoned outed ministers. Its more ghoulish acts included the whipping of women through the streets, branding on the face with a hot iron and ordering prisoners to be sold as slaves in the Colonies. Even giving a slice of bread to a hunted minister was classed as sedition. This then was the powder keg that would be ignited in 1679 by zealous troopers ill treating an old man who had not paid his fine for non-attendance at Church.

The Battle at Rullion Green in November 1666 gave Sharp the opportunity to show his true colours when, as President of the Court, he addressed eleven prisoners who had surrendered on promise of mercy. To these he said, "You were pardoned as soldiers, but you are not acquitted as subjects." The eleven were peremptorily sentenced to death and ordered that their heads and right arms were to be struck off; the heads to be affixed above the city gates and their arms to be fixed to the prison doors at Lanark. Sharp again showed his spiteful nature when a young minister, Hugh McKail, was tortured with the boot, this was a singularly evil device that was strapped round a limb into which metal wedges were then driven thus gradually crushing the limb. His reason for not intervening when petitioned was that in a sermon at St. Giles, Edinburgh in September 1662, he had been referred to as a Judas. So on 22 December 1666 another martyr gained his diadem while Sharp stood by.

Following the ill fated rising, Sharp and his cohorts increased their rule of violence by doubling and trebling fines; by hunting down the rebels; and by dispensing summary justice at the end of a troopers rifle on their own doorsteps. It was at this time that the Earl of Lauderdale, the King's Secretary, saw that things were getting out of hand and that the severe policies must be restrained. To this end Sharp was brought to a frightened submission and the Earl of Rothes, the King's Commissioner in Scotland, moved to the post of Lord Chancellor. Lauderdale, himself another former supporter of Presbyterianism, then took charge in Scotland. It is not without significance that during his tenure between 1667 and 1678 the executions of Covenanters ceased. But Sharp also continued his attack on Presbyterianism by helping Lauderdale to pass the Act of Supremacy which gave the King absolute control over ecclesiastical matters.

An early attempt on the life of Sharp took place on 11 July 1668 when James Mitchell, a Covenanter who had not laid down his arms and thought by many to be of unsound mind, sought to purge the nation of his presence. He saw Sharp as the person most responsible for the misfortunes of his colleagues and decided that assassination was the solution. To this end he armed himself with a pistol, loaded with three balls, and waited for Sharp's coach to pass by at Blackfriar's Wynd in Edinburgh. Come the moment for action Mitchell fired at the door of the coach but only succeeded in shooting the Archbishop's traveling companion, Honeyman the Bishop of Orkney, who later died. Mitchell escaped and the Privy Council offered a reward of 5,000 merks for information and pardon for any accessories to the crime - there were no takers. There was tragic ending for Mitchell, however, as in 1674 he was found and seized by Sir William Sharp, the Archbishop's brother. There followed a long series of appearances in Court and interviews all aimed at getting a confession since there was no hard evidence from other sources, which was sufficient to convict. He was threatened and ultimately tortured using "the Boot." Sent back to the Tolbooth, he was then sent for a while to the Bass Rock. Suffice to say that through a combination of treachery, lies and perjury and the desire of Sharp for vengeance, Mitchell was convicted and executed in Edinburgh on 18 January 1678.

Magus Muir

Early in 1679, Sharp introduced possibly his most heinous piece of legislation against the Covenanters. This permitted the killing of any person who was armed either going to, at, or coming from a field meeting or conventicle. No trial was required, and persons could be shot on the spot. This was the legislation that heralded the "Killing Time." But Sharp would not live to see the consequences of his vindictiveness as his own demise was soon upon him. He was in Edinburgh and about to set off for London to obtain the King's signature to his latest law but decided that he would first go to St. Andrews. He set out on Friday 2 May 1679 with his eldest daughter and a handful of servants. They stopped the night at Kennoway, about twenty miles from his destination at the home of a Captain

Seatoun. In the morning, the party continued to the Manse at Ceres before moving on again to destiny and death.

Not far away, a group of Covenanters had met to way lay a magistrate by the name of William Carmichael who had been particularly obnoxious in his dealings with the Covenanters. However, their plans came to naught, as the magistrate did not appear. About midday on Saturday 3 May 1679 the party was at Ceres saying their goodbyes prior to dispersing when a farm boy came running to them with the news that the Archbishop Sharp himself would be passing in a few minutes. After brief discussion, David Hackston was elected leader for the new challenge, but he declined on the grounds that he had a known private grievance with Archbishop Sharp to whom he owed money and it would detract from the testimony of the action taken by the Covenanters. John Balfour of Kinloch, nicknamed Burley, who was David Hackston's brother-in-law, took the lead and rode to intercept the coach closely followed by James Russell of Kettle, George Fleming and George Balfour; David Hackston, Andrew and Alexander Henderson, William Daniel and Andrew Gillan. They knew that the Archbishop's daughter, Isabel, was in the coach and were anxious to avoid harm coming to her and demanded that Sharp come out of the coach. But he refused to do so, and in anger Fleming and George Balfour shot at him seated within, while others thrust at him with their swords. Seemingly, despite this onslaught, Sharp was not injured and was given away by his daughter sobbing, "there's life yet."

Balfour told Sharp that they were not slaying him from personal malice but for causing the death of Covenanters. They shot at him again in the coach and one stabbed him. Finally Sharp emerged and crawled to the mounted figure of Hackston to ask for protection. Hackston said that he would not lay a hand upon him and the others with swords drawn turned to complete their deed. Too late, Hackston tried to intercede but the murder on Magus Moor had taken place and there would soon be a terrible vengeance exacted for it. Vengeance soon fell on David Hackston but also on five prisoners taken at Bothwell Brig who had nothing whatsoever to do with the assassination. They were arbitrarily tried, convicted and executed in retribution at Magus Moor on 25 November 1681. The five were Thomas Brown, James Wood, Andrew Sword, John Waddel and John Clyd. A sixth man, David Hardie, was acquitted of a capital charge and not hung alongside his unfortunate colleagues. W M Bryce in his *Flodden Wall* (1910) cites the Records of Justiciary and the declarations or 'confessions' the men made which were used as the only evidence and proof at their trial by the Lord Advocate.

Thomas Brown in Edinburgh, confesses he wer taken prisoner at Bothwelbridge with these were defate then and caryed a sword and declared he hes not freedome to give bond never to ryse in armes against the King and his authoritie. He declares the above wrytten confession to be true, but obstinatlie refuses to subseryve the same tho he cane wreitt.

John Weddall, prisoner, confesses he wes taken prisoner with these were defate at Bothwellbridge. He will not call them rebens, nor will he give bond never to ryse in armes against the King or his authoritic. He confesses he caryd a small sword & declares he cannot wreitt.

David Hardie confesses he wes taken prisoner at the muir beyond Culrosse by the Clerk of Dumblane, & that he hade no armes. He refuses to give bond, &c.

Andrew Sword confesses he wes taken prisoner at Hamilton with those wer defate ther. Declares he caryed a sword, but will not call it a Rebellion he wes in, nor will he give bond never to ryse in armes against the King. Confesses that this is truth, but refuses to subseryve it, tho he cane wreitt.

James Wood in Aird confesses he wes taken prisoner at Bothwelmuir with those wer defate ther; he will not call them rebells, nor will he give bond never to ryse in armes against the King. DeclairefA he cannot wreitt.

John Clyd confesses he wes taken prisoner with the rest that wer defate at Bothwelbridge. He caryed ane sword, and refuses to inact himself never to ryse in armes against the King. Declares he cannot wreitt.

The five unfortunate fellow-prisoners were sentenced

to be caryed to the muir of Magus within the Sherriffdome of Fyff, and that place thereof wher his Grace the late Archbishop of St. Andrews wer murdered, upon Tuesday the eighteint day of November instant betwixt two and four o'clock in the afternoon, and ther to be hanged on ane gibbet till they be dead, and ther bodies to be hung up on chaines in the said Place till they rott, and all ther lands, heretages, goods, and gear to be forfault & escheat to our soveraigne Lords use for the treasonable crymes above specified; which wer pronounced for doom.

It is difficult to gauge if Archbishop Sharp was as bad as he has been painted. At the time, and without benefit of hindsight, he was undoubtedly a morally weak man who would go with the stronger side rather than hold unto death to any great principle. He must have been reasonably clever to represent the Scottish Presbyterians on a number of occasions in London. He was for about ten years a leading member of the moderate 'Resolutioners.' Cromwell called him "Sharp of that Ilk" and recognised his "supple intelligence," That he was duplicitous is borne out by events. Did he deserve to be murdered? We cannot apply our twenty-first century standards to events over three hundred years ago. Reality then was that no other form of justice was available to the wronged who were themselves being murdered with Sharp's connivance. There was neither independent judiciary nor process that could be used, while the Head of State was a King who himself was prejudiced against the Presbyterians. An "eye for an eye" approach seemed apposite in the circumstances.

Alexander Henderson
From the Fordal Portrait

XIX. Rev. Alexander Henderson - Statesman and Scribe

Along with his friend, a brilliant young advocate named Archibald Johnston of Warriston (later Lord Warriston), Alexander Henderson was responsible for the drafting of both the National Covenant in 1638 and the Solemn League and Covenant in 1643. For these acts alone he deserves a niche in Covenanting history. But it fell to Henderson, as Moderator of the General Assembly that met in November 1638 in St. Mungo's Cathedral in Glasgow, to tell the King's representative, the Duke of Hamilton, "Sir, if you must leave, we must remain until our duty is done." Thus began the civil disobedience of the Presbyterians against a meddlesome king.

In his early years, Henderson had studied and then taught philosophy at St. Andrews and had been forced on the unwilling parish of Leuchars in 1612 when almost thirty years of age. At that time he was prelatic and on his ordination found that the door of the church had been nailed closed against him, and was forced to break in through a window. However, he happened upon the Rev. Robert Bruce and was taken with his preaching and the Presbyterian way. Henderson continued for some time in his quiet bookish life and grew in character along with his Presbyterian beliefs, developing not only as a theologian of considerable merit, but a powerful and weighty manner of speaking that simply made people listen to him.

Some have said that he grew in holiness, but it was a small man with great character and presence that was a solitary voice at the Perth Assembly in 1618 when the obnoxious Articles of Perth were enacted. He became a counsellor to the Tables (the ruling body) in Edinburgh and would later be co-author of the Covenants, three times Moderator of the General Assembly and a commissioner to the Divines who drew up the Westminster Confession of Faith. This he was to cram into a span of only nine years.

Henderson was compromised into coming into the open about his support for the Presbyterian way in 1637 when the Archbishop of St. Andrews instructed him to purchase two copies of the New Liturgy for the use of his parish. Henderson went to Edinburgh and stated his objections to the Privy Council and asked that the Archbishop's instruction be cancelled. The Privy Council, swayed by his arguments and that of others, sent reports of the general opposition to the Liturgy to London. Henderson's skill and tact in dealing with the matter did not go unnoticed by his peers as well as his adversaries when events turned to the Covenant.

The National Covenant is in three parts; the first reciting the older Covenant, sometimes called the King Confession, of 1581; the second part listed the various Acts of Parliament which condemned Popery and confirmed the privileges of the Reformed church; and the third part was an emphatic protest against the alien methods of worship which had provoked the troubles of 1638. Archibald Johnston, Lord Warriston authored the second part and Alexander Henderson the third part (Appendix 5).

Henderson was held in the highest regard by his peers, including Rev. Samuel Rutherford and Rev. Dickson who regarded him as the foremost and most statesman like of the Presbyterian clergy of the day. So it was that he was dragged to centre stage and fame by his election as the Moderator of the General Assembly that met in Glasgow from 21 November to 20 December 1638. Henderson's moment came when on 28 November the King's representative, the Duke of Hamilton, protested at the presence of the lay elders (including some of the most powerful noblemen such as Rothes, Lothian, Cassilis, Eglintoun, Montrose, Wemyss and Home). Hamilton also protested at the sentence on the bishops and denied the Assembly had authority to act in Episcopalian matters. If they persisted, he said, he must pronounce the Assembly dissolved and its enactments invalid. It fell to Henderson to calmly reply, "Yes" and said the Assembly had no choice but to remain until their duty was done. The Duke departed and next day issued a proclamation ordering all who were not normally resident in Glasgow to leave the city within twenty-four hours.

It was in Glasgow, at this time, that Henderson spent time in prayer with the Marquis of Argyll and to whom credit is given for conversion of the most powerful man in Scotland. It was Argyll, alone, of the nobles present (he was there as a member of the Privy Council) who made his support clear for the General Assembly and advised them to continue as if nothing had happened. Henderson warmly welcomed the support of the Marquis and the General Assembly proceeded to deal severely with the Acts of previous Assemblies that had ratified Episcopacy; the Service Book, the Canons, the Court of High Commission and the Articles of Perth, were all annulled. Eight bishops were excommunicated and six more deposed or suspended; and, finally, the National Covenant that Henderson had helped to write, was confirmed.

It was not without a hint of irony that in 1641, while in Edinburgh, King Charles went to hear Henderson preach and acknowledged the man's dignity and honesty by making him a royal chaplain. Thus Henderson spent some time both holding services for the King and the royal family in Holywood Palace and also discussed church matters with the King.

Henderson comes to the fore again five years later when the Solemn League and Covenant was sworn in, in 1643. In England the Parliamentary armies were suffering a string of defeats and desperately needed allies and troops. It was with this military help in mind that a deputation went to see The Convention of Estates (the ruling body) in Edinburgh and the General Assembly in St. Andrews. The English deputation was successful and needed some form of written agreement or treaty between them. They were in favour of a political and civil agreement, but the Scots, with an interest in saving souls and a higher objective of religious conformity in the three kingdoms, wanted a religious covenant. So it was that Alexander Henderson drew up the bond between the two countries - the Solemn League and Covenant of 1643 (Appendix 6)

In the summer of 1646, when in the sanctuary of the Scottish camp at Newcastle, King Charles requested that Henderson should come and discuss with him the question of Church government. This Henderson did, although not a well man, he travelled from London to attend on the King. It was in mid July that Henderson decided to leave his lodgings in Newcastle and to make for Leith by ship, wishing to go to his homeland before it was too late. He arrived in Edinburgh a man worn out by nine years of almost unceasing pressure and dedication to the Presbyterian cause, and exhausted in body. He died on 16 August 1646 in his sixty-third year saying, "Never school boy more longed for the breaking up than I do to have leave of this world."

He is buried in Greyfriars Kirk yard beneath a monument inscribed:

Reader bedew thine eyes
Not for the dust here lyes -
It quicken shall again,
And aye in joy remain
But for thyself, the Church and States
Whose woes this dust prognosticates.

Henderson's monument bears the marks of later troubles when, shortly after the Restoration, the inscription was defaced on the order of the Earl of Middleton and traces of bullet marks can be seen from shots fired by the soldiers sent to deface the monument. After the Revolution, the inscription was restored.

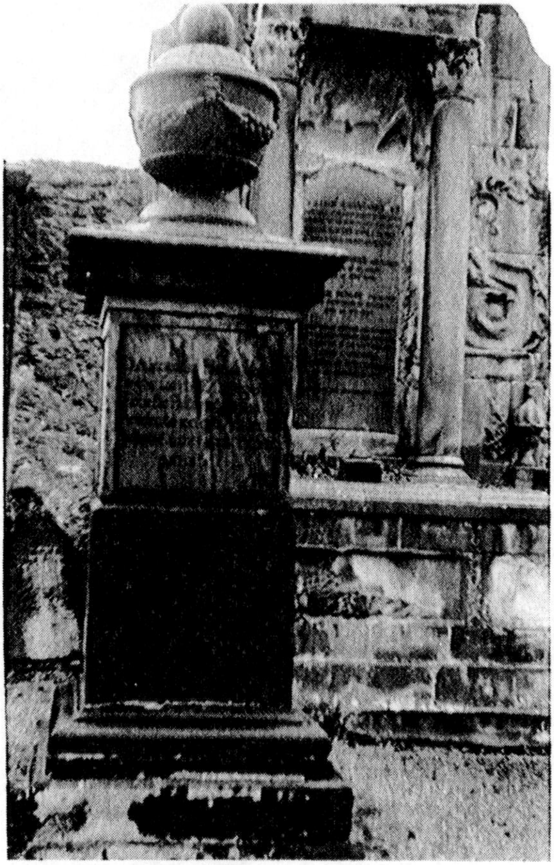

Alexander Henderson monument
Greyfriars Kirk

XX. Rev. Robert Blair - A Godly Man

The Rev. Robert Blair is remembered for his work, and persecution, in both Ulster and Scotland, being one of the first Scottish ministers to cross to Ulster in the time of the Plantation.

The son of John Blair and Beatrix Muir, of Windyedge, he was born in 1593, the youngest child of six. His father, a man devoted to prayer, died when he was about five years old from tuberculosis, a disease that is thought to have contributed to bouts of ill health and ultimately to Robert's death. His mother was of sturdy stuff living as a widow for fifty years and was over one hundred when she died. Robert Blair was able to go to Glasgow University in 1608 where he met his life long friend David Dickson, and continued his education with his brother William Blair, later minister at Dumbarton. He then became a schoolteacher in Glasgow having some 150 pupils allotted to his care. It was in this period that he became acquainted with Dr. Boyd of Trochrig, Principal of Glasgow College, who opened his eyes to the ministry. Blair was subsequently admitted as Regent or Professor of Philosophy and Greek in 1616. Here he was encouraged by colleagues to read the classical authors and the scriptures which opened his mind to the church. He sought to become a minister and began the trials for that role by preaching in the College Kirk where his sermons were well received.

A cloud descended, however, when Dr. Boyd retired and Dr. John Cameron was brought from France as his replacement. Dr. Cameron was of the Episcopalian belief and sought to make Robert Blair conform to the Articles of Perth (which reintroduced ceremony and the rule of the bishops). Blair refused and following some antagonism and pressure from the Archbishop of Glasgow he decided to leave the College in 1623. He was offered several appointments in Glasgow and even in France but very shortly afterwards he received the invitation from Viscount Claneboye to go to Bangor in County Down.

His arrival in Bangor began with the news that the Dean, Rev. John Gibson, was a sick man. Gibson had first gone to Bangor in 1622 and had been appointed Dean of Down by the King. He surprised Blair with the vehemence of his opposition to episcopacy. With the Dean in his sick bed Blair preached at Bangor for three Sabbaths to the satisfaction of the congregation. The Dean soon died and the Rev. Robert Blair had his first hurdle to overcome - that of ordination. The official church was the Church of Ireland and was Episcopalian in practice, thus Blair could not be true to his beliefs and accept ordination by a bishop. However, the early years of the Plantation of Ulster were blessed by an enlightened view, encouraged by Archbishop Ussher, and a way round the quibbles was found. Bishop Knox knew of the reservations that Blair had and proposed that the ordination would be by the laying on of hands by the Rev. Cunningham and other Presbyterian ministers. The Bishop then suggested that he would attend solely as a Presbyter, which Blair was unable to refuse. Thus some simple machinations made it possible for his ordination, which took place on 10 July 1623.

Blair found that his new ministry was both large - over 1,200 persons, and educationally backward. He set to work with great determination and preached four times a week, interspersing this with visiting people in their homes and helping them to read the scriptures and understand them. He also was active in stirring up others to like endeavours and worked most happily with the Rev. Cunningham in nearby Holywood. They preached for one another and celebrated the Communion four times a year in each of their congregations annually.

His ministry in Bangor was not without incident, as John Howie in *Scots Worthies* relates two tales about the Rev. Blair. The first concerned a horse dealer who had sold his horses in Scotland and accepted a bond in payment, which would be redeemed at Martinmas. Come the time the buyer, or as the dealer believed, the Devil, demanded his surrender saying that he had sold himself, not his horses. The Devil demanded that the dealer kill someone and ordered him to kill the Rev. Blair. The dealer called on the minister armed with a dagger but was unable to draw it out and fell trembling to the floor. On learning of the reason for the dealer's visit Blair exhorted him to seek refuge in the Lord. Two weeks later the dealer called for Rev. Blair to attend him in his sick bed and said that the Devil had again appeared to him and was to return to take him body and soul. Blair attended at the time and prayed all night with the man in defiance of the Devil such that the dealer was greatly comforted and passed away peacefully and penitent.

The second tale was of Blair's deliverance from a fire which could have killed him and possibly done severe damage to the house in which he was staying. This came about when his candle burnt out while he was late at his studies and he called for another. When it was brought by the landlady, she saw that a joist of his bed was on fire - had he retired as usual and not been studying he may well have died. The timeous alarm enabled the fire to be put out and all was saved.

But in the autumn of 1631, the bishops shattered the peace by seeking to regain control and to enforce episcopacy. Robert Blair and John Livingston were suspended by the Bishop of Down and Connor, Echlin. However, an appeal to Archbishop Ussher saw their re-instatement much to the displeasure of the Bishop who appealed to Archbishop Laud in London. Laud had authority over all things ecclesiastical and also the ear of the King. Instructions were issued via the Irish government that the four leading Presbyterian ministers - Rev.s Blair, Livingston, Welsh and Dunbar should be re-tried. This time Archbishop Ussher could not intervene as the King had endorsed the order. In May 1632, all four were required to conform to episcopacy and on refusing were deposed from the ministry.

On this occasion Blair took himself to London to seek the intervention of King Charles I. After some delay the King saw Blair and his petition for reinstatement, which he signed and indorsed, "Indulge these men, for they are Scotsmen." It was while in England that Blair had a strange revelation about the impending death of his wife who had been in good health when he left Ireland. The revelation was from Ezekiel 24 v 16 "Son of man, behold, I am about to take the delight of your eyes away from you at a stroke..." Blair's burdens were, however, increased with the appointment of William Wentworth, later Earl of Strafford, as the new Lord Deputy of Ireland Blair soon found that that Wentworth had his own agenda for the Presbyterians and the outlook became black indeed. It was at this time that thoughts turned to the possibility of migrating to the American colonies.

Fate then played a cruel trick on the ministers when in May 1634 Wentworth allowed their reinstatement for six months. This was done at the behest of Lord Castlestuart, a Presbyterian nobleman, to which Wentworth yielded for political advantage. The reinstatement was, however, short lived as Bramhall, Bishop of Derry took great exception and remonstrated with Wentworth. So it was that in the November of 1634 Blair and his colleagues were summoned before Bishop Echlin and the sentence of excommunication passed on them. Blair responded by demanding the Bishop should appear before the Tribunal of Jesus Christ to answer for his deed. A few months later Echlin fell sick and on his deathbed admitted to his physician of the cause, "It is my conscience, man." Echlin died in 1635 and was replaced by Henry Leslie, an equally obstreperous individual, who on 11 August passed sentence of "perpetual silence within this diocese" on five ministers - the Rev.'s Brice, Ridge, Cunningham, Calvert and Hamilton.

Blair had lost his first wife Beatrix, the daughter of Robert Hamilton, a merchant in Edinburgh in 1627 and had been left with the care of three young children. Early in 1635, he sought to marry Catherine Montgomery, daughter of Hugh, Viscount Montgomery of the Ards. Following a visit to Scotland the couple were married in May 1636. After his excommunication Blair had continued to preach in his own house or that of others, but with the ongoing persecution by the bishops he joined with John Livingston and others to go to the New World on board the *Eaglewing*. The little ship of only 150 tons set sail on 9 September 1636, but it was not meant to be as battered by heavy seas, she returned to Ireland on 3 November.

The failed attempt at emigration was a watershed for the Rev. Blair. Soon after the return his son William died and to add to his burden it was learnt that he and John Livingston were to be arrested. Thus they hastily retreated to Irvine where fresh tribulations awaited as he was forbidden to preach. Once again he sought to leave the country and to join a regiment stationed in France, but was frustrated in this. Eventually his first wife's sister, Barbara Hamilton, petitioned the Privy Council and he was allowed to preach once more.

In 1638 Blair was assistant for a while to the Rev. McAnnan in Ayr where he was favourably received, so much so that he disobeyed an order of the General Assembly in 1638 to remove to St. Andrews. In 1639 the Assembly, annoyed at the delay, peremptorily ordered him to go to St. Andrews where he was to minister for some twenty three years. But there was good in the transfer, for at the same time the Rev. Samuel Rutherford of Anwoth, was transferred to become Professor of Divinity at St.

Mary's College in St Andrews. So began some twenty years of companionship and working together.

These were turbulent times and Robert Blair was on a number of occasions called to assist the Church and the Army. In the Bishops' Wars, Blair was with Lord Boyd's force that formed part of Leslie's army at Duns Law. After the victory at Newburn in the Second Bishop's War, he was sent by the Committee of Estates to be wise counsel to the Commissioners at the Treaty of Ripon in October 1641. The negotiations were then transferred to London where he attended with Robert Baillie and George Gillespie.

In 1641 the rebellion in Ireland had driven many ministers from the land and the General Assembly of 1642 received a number of requests for help. Inevitably Robert Blair was one of the ministers who went back to Ireland to preach, sometimes twice a day on the Sabbath and also at field meetings to large gatherings. On returning from Ireland, Blair was appointed to the Committee of the General Assembly and in the autumn of 1643 was instrumental in the drafting of the Solemn League and Covenant.

Blair still had service to give the army when in 1643 he was appointed minister with the Earl of Crawford's regiment and was at many of the engagements in which this regiment took part including Marston Moor in July 1644. After the regiment was withdrawn and sent to deal with the incursions by the Marquis of Montrose, he returned to St. Andrews. In July 1645 he was at the Parliament and Commission of the Kirk sitting in Perth and took the opportunity to preach to the soldiers of the Fife and Midlothian Foot (at Forgandenny on 27 July 1645) when he prophesied that they would be punished for their sins and dissolute ways unless they repented. The soldiers seem not to have done so as on 15 August 1645 the regiment was destroyed by Montrose's forces at Kilsyth. After this defeat, there were moves by some Covenanters to negotiate with Montrose, but Blair strongly opposed this until General David Leslie was able to return from

England and finally defeat Montrose at Philiphaugh on 13 September.

In 1646 Blair was Moderator of the General Assembly and was dispatched with Andrew Cant and Robert Douglas to see King Charles I at Newcastle where Alexander Henderson was already engaged in trying to bring the King to accept Presbytery and the Covenants. Despite great endeavour, the King obstinately refused to accept their agreements and Blair returned to St. Andrews. In August 1646, Alexander Henderson died and the King appointed Blair to replace him as the King's Chaplain in Scotland. With some trepidation, Blair took up the task, and with his usual diligence, prayed twice daily before dinner and supper. He also preached weekdays in the church and took the opportunity to discuss prelacy, liturgies and ceremonials with the King. Both then and later - when again dispatched by the General Assembly to talk to the King, he met obstinacy and refusal.

Although he must have known of the issues, it does not seem that Blair was in the front line in the debate about "the Engagement," a treaty by some Scottish Royalists to support King Charles in the Civil War in England. This treaty came to naught when Oliver Cromwell dealt out a thorough defeat to the Royalist forces at Preston in August 1648. But it was Blair, the Rev. David Dickson and Rev. James Guthrie who were sent to speak with Oliver Cromwell and elicit his views on rule by a monarchy, religious toleration and whether the church should be Episcopal, Independent or Presbyterian. Cromwell declined to answer the last question, which prompted Blair to comment subsequently that Cromwell was "A dissembler and great liar."

The end of King Charles I came in 1649 beneath the headsman's axe and led to a new furore among the Presbyterians who did not support the execution of a Scottish King by the English. The alliance with the English Parliamentarians quickly folded, and was accelerated by the Scots declaration accepting the Crown Prince as King

Charles II of England, Scotland and Ireland. Charles II accepted the terms offered by Scotland, which included swearing the Covenants and extension of Presbyterianism to England and Ireland. He signed the agreement at Breda in Holland, on 1 May 1650 and arrived in Scotland on 23 June. The duplicity of King Charles II was soon dealt with by Cromwell at the battle of Dunbar 3 September 1650; by occupation of Edinburgh 24 December 1650, and routing the royalist forces at Worcester on 3 September 1651. Charles fled to France while the Presbyterians spent the next ten years in bitter argument and counter accusation until the Restoration of Charles II in 1660.

Robert Blair foresaw the dark days ahead when the Rev. James Sharp of Crail, took the bribe of elevation to Archbishop of St. Andrews. Blair was scathing in his criticism of Sharp, despising him for the arch turncoat he was. In 1662 Blair and hundreds of other Presbyterian ministers were "outed" from their ministries and he was confined to his quarters in Edinburgh, then allowed to retire to Inveresk. After a while he was allowed to move around, except to St. Andrews, and went to Kirkcaldy where he continued to preach at private meetings and taught his younger son the Greek language and logic. Here again the pernicious blight and spite of Archbishop Sharp followed him when an act was introduced prohibiting an outed minister residing within twenty miles of a city and thus the archbishop's see. In February 1666 Blair moved to Meikle Couston in the Parish of Aberdour where, surrounded by many friends, he passed away on 27 July. He lies buried in Aberdour Kirk yard.

Perhaps his epitaph is well described by an English merchant, who visited St. Andrews and heard Blair preach, who said,

I heard a sweet majestic man and he showed me the majesty of God.

John Livingston

XXI. Rev. John Livingston of Ancrum and the "Eaglewing"

The stories of the Covenanters and the bloody Killing Time understandably focus on the western shires of Scotland, but it must be remembered that there were Covenanters in other less glamorous parts. Such was John Livingston of Ancrum in the Border country with England. Here, too, the persecutors caused the removal of a gentle man from his ministry in October 1662.

John Livingston was born in Kilsyth in 1603, the son of William and Agnes Livingston, minister at Kilsyth and later in Lanark. One of seven children, the young John was raised in an environment of piety and meekness on his mother's side and his father a zealous worker for the Reformation. As a schoolboy in Sterling he was a member of the church, although his early inclination was to be a doctor. His parents were kind and generous and enjoyed giving hospitality to Christians visiting the area, so he was able to meet many notable men and women of the time. His mother, however, died when he was fourteen, when she was only thirty-two. He continued his education at Glasgow College (as the University was called) graduating in 1621 and in 1625 turned to the ministry - where he soon encountered persecution. For a while he stayed with his father and made visits to preach when he was asked. In April 1626 Lord Kenmuir in Galloway sought him to take the parish of Anwoth, but he did not do so nor was he successful in a call to Torpichen the following year. He then accepted invitations to preach in Lanark, Irvine, and Newmilns

A year of change began in June 1630 which saw John Livingston asked to step in at short notice for a preacher at Kirk O'Shotts, which he reluctantly did. On 30 June the virtually unknown young man stood on a gravestone and began his preaching. As he approached its end, the Heavens opened and there was a downpour that threatened to break up the meeting. But such was Livingston's powerful presence that the assembled crowd stood a further hour as he used the conditions to demonstrate the despair and horror of fire and brimstone in God's judgment upon them. It is said that over 500 people felt a change in their attitudes and became believers as a result of the Kirk O'Shotts revival.

A youthful and able speaker, although diffident about his abilities, he was sought by several congregations to be their minister, but in the five years to 1630, he found none, as on each occasion his way was blocked by the bishops. His first parish was an Irish one, at Killinchy, County Down. This came about through a meeting in Irvine, Ayrshire with the Rev. Robert Cunningham of Holywood, near Belfast and earlier with the Rev. George Dunbar of Larne (formerly of Ayr and a prisoner at Blackness for a while). Both had enquired if he would be interested in going to Ireland and he had indicated on both occasions he would go if he received a clear call and free entry.

About August 1630, he received an invitation from Viscount Claneboye to go to Killinchy. Here he was well received by the congregation and had to be ordained. To achieve this, he went with letters to the Rev. Andrew Knox, Bishop of Raphoe, who well knew what was required and after discussion gave Livingston a book of ordination with instruction to mark that to which he objected. The price sought for ordination was that he should preach at Ramallen where they got but few sermons. He found that the book had already been marked and did not have to do it himself, thus with his conscience clear, he submitted to the Rev. Robert Cunningham and some other ministers to "imposition of the hands" and ordination for the ministry at Killinchy.

Persecution, however, soon came upon him through the vindictiveness of the Irish bishops. The Bishop of Down suspended Robert Blair and Livingston for nonconformity. They were eventually allowed to return to their ministry in 1632 following intervention with the King by Lord Castlestuart. In November 1635, he again fell foul of the bishops and was again suspended, then excommunicated.

With this ongoing persecution of the Presbyterians and no early solution in sight, John Livingston was instrumental in negotiations with landowners - the Clotworthy family especially, and John Winthrop, son of the Governor of Massachusetts concerning a plan to emigrate. From the plan came the building of the ship the "Eaglewing," and the attempt by some 140 brave souls to seek their promised land in 1636. Unfortunately for them, they were forced to return by bad weather and John Livingston was returned to the Covenanting fold, but not before baptising a child born on the return trip to Michael Coltheard and his wife, naming him Seaborn - reminiscent of the child Oceanus Hopkins born on board the Mayflower in that epic voyage in 1620.

For some time, Livingston continued to discharge his duties privately, residing at the home of his mother-in-law, Mrs. Stevenson who owned the iron furnace at Malone, twelve miles from Killinchy where he continued to preach almost every Sabbath. However, a warrant was issued for his arrest and he first retired to Irvine on the Ayrshire coast, and then he went to Edinburgh. In March 1638 he went to London, but the King had apparently heard he was there, and he again had to retreat and return to Scotland by a circuitous route to avoid any pursuers. On 5 July 1638 he was admitted as the minister at Stranraer. While here its is recorded, that large numbers of people came from

Ireland to take Communion from him, on one occasion there was present in excess of 500 people from Co. Down.

He had his home at Stranraer for ten years before he was sent, at the order of the General Assembly, to spend fourteen years at Ancrum in Teviotdale. He found the work at Ancrum hard going, having to contend with an ignorant and loose living peoples and it was some time before there were sufficient people to take Communion. During this time Livingston became a regular representative of the Church and was among those sent to negotiate with King Charles II at Breda in Holland. It was not a task he enjoyed as his preference was for "moderation and sweet reasonableness." He considered that his colleagues sometimes meddled too much in government, or held too many meetings that exposed the Church's divisions. Livingston, who distrusted the King anyway, had his fears confirmed when he observed the King still using the Service Book and leading a dissolute life.

Somewhat diffident of his own abilities, Livingston was nevertheless a very able scholar with a passion for books. He knew Hebrew and Chaldee with some Syrian; he was familiar with French, Italian and Dutch and read the Bible in Spanish and German, although he was forestalled for a while in his desire to learn Arabic by its sheer complexity. What such a linguist might be able to charge for his services in the modern world, one can only guess. Livingston had other hidden talents. As a young man he had a melodious voice and enjoyed singing and was often summoned by the Principal John Boyd, when a student at Glasgow, to sing "setts of musick." In later years he did not sing much, neither did he partake often of another pleasure - that of hunting.

Although appointed to attend on Cromwell in London during 1654, and latterly on the army, he did so reluctantly and was glad to return to Ancrum and his parishioners. When King Charles II was restored to the throne in 1660, he foresaw that trouble lay ahead and in 1662 it duly happened. A proclamation was issued ordering all ministers from 1649 who had not celebrated the holiday of 29 May (to celebrate the King's birthday and Restoration) to acknowledge the prelates or be removed from their posts. He left Ancrum and lingered for a while in Edinburgh where he learnt that a summons to appear before the Council would probably result in banishment (rather than execution) and he appeared before them on 1 December 1662. He declined to take oaths and was sentenced to remove immediately to the north side of the Tay and to leave the Kingdom entirely within two months. On 9 April 1663 he set sail for Rotterdam.

In the years of his banishment, he remained very active, and on many occasions preached to the Scottish congregation in Rotterdam. In December, his wife and two children joined him the other five children were left behind. He was asked three times by the General Assembly to write the history of the Church of Scotland since the Reformation of 1638, but declined to do so. Instead he set himself the task of revising the Latin version of the Old Testament, comparing it throughout with the Hebrew version. He intended to publish it with parallel columns in the two texts, but circumstances prevented it, although as a scholar he had much pleasure in the task.

He was probably seen at his best in two places; firstly in Killinchy where incredibly his stipend was a mere £4 a year, yet there was always a happy welcome for all. He had married in 1635 Janet the eldest daughter of Bartholomew Fleming, an Edinburgh merchant. She was a great support to him through the lean years and the later troubles. Indeed, after he was gone, she was the leader of a group of women, who in 1674, made representations to the Earl of Rothes for fair treatment of ministers, which resulted in her banishment from Edinburgh for a while.

The other place where Livingston was at his best was in the pulpit. Diffident as ever about his abilities, his practice was to make short notes beforehand and to enlarge upon them when the time came. He sought balance in his sermons and at times indulged in a “childish rudimentary”, as he described it, aware not to be too clever nor to omit the telling, saying or word picture that summed up his point. Throughout his sermons he was said to have “the eloquence of the spirit and a throbbing affection for the Heavenly Lord and the souls of men.”

From about 1664 he suffered continuously with a bladder problem, he could not walk far and had shaking hands that made writing difficult. It was perhaps a blessed release when and on 9 August 1672 he died in exile leaving us his solemn declaration,

I die in the Faith that the truths of God, which he hath helped the Church of Scotland to own, shall be owned by him as truths, so long as the sun and moon endure.

William Guthrie, of Fenwick
A Portrait prefixed to some Editions of "The Christian's Great Interest."

XXII. Rev. William Guthrie of Fenwick - Risk Taker and Fisher of Men

Fenwick is a small village to the north of Kilmarnock in Ayrshire, but it sits large in the annals of the Covenanters. A centre for resistance despite the close proximity of military garrisons at Kilmarnock and Newmilns, it was an area subject to repeated raids by the dragoons given testimony by there being more Covenanter gravestones here than any other locality in Scotland, with seven victims of the Killing Times. Also, Captain John Paton, executed in Edinburgh and buried in Greyfriars in May 1684 was from Meadowhead within the parish. A later son of Fenwick was John Howie of Lochgoin, a historian and writer about the Covenanters and author of *Scots Worthies.* To this village, as its first Minister, came the Rev. William Guthrie, a cousin of James Guthrie of Stirling.

William Guthrie was born in 1620 in Pitforthy, near Brechin, Forfarshire. He was the eldest of five boys, no fewer than four of whom became Covenanting ministers - Robert, Alexander and John, as well as William. At St. Andrews he was given a classical and philosophical education aided by his cousin James and the recently appointed Samuel Rutherford. Prepared for the ministry under their guidance, he also took the step of foregoing his inheritance as the eldest son, giving the rights to the brother who did not take up the calling to the kirk.

He was for a while tutor to Lord Mauchline, son of the Earl of Loudon, and while there preached in the town of Galston where some Covenanters from Fenwick heard him. Lord Boyd, a Royalist, who disapproved of anyone recommended by the Earl of Loudon stalled the request for Guthrie to come to Fenwick. The objections were overcome eventually and in November 1644 William Guthrie was ordained minister of Fenwick where he was to faithfully serve for twenty years until the bishops and dragoons forced him out.

He married a distant relative of the Earl of Loudon, Agnes Campbell, daughter of David Campbell of Sheldon in Ayrshire, in August 1645 and settled down to a life of devotion and caring to his parish. By Agnes, William Guthrie had six children, of which two daughters outlived him. One married Miller of Glenlee and the other in 1681 to Peter Warner of Irvine. Peter Warner had two children, William and Margaret. The latter married the Rev. Robert Wodrow, minister at Eastwood and author of *The History of the Sufferings of the Church of Scotland.*

Guthrie was also a risk taker in the course of his beliefs being present with six other ministers at a skirmish on Mauchline Moor in 1648 when some 2,000 armed people at a massed communion were broken up by troopers under Sir James Turner (later to be seized during the Pentland Rising). In 1650 Guthrie was with the army that was routed at Dunbar by Cromwell's forces. He was not a healthy man and this at times gave him a "melancholic" attitude which was reflected in sermons that were grave and sad. He was also a man of mirth and humour who delighted in being friendly, and enjoyed good company.

He had a surprising reputation as a good angler, which was one of his main relaxations, but inevitably it was his calling to be "a fisher of men" within the Parish of Fenwick. The parish was widespread with some people living six miles away in a countryside with few roads and much moorland and morasses. It wasn't easy to get to church, that is for sure, and so much easier to use the

Sabbath as a day of relaxation. To this Guthrie responded with several stratagems, including disguising himself and seeking a night's lodging in a cottage and then spends the evening in discourse with the household. He is said to have offered a well-known poacher half a crown to attend church, which was accepted. But in later weeks the poacher attended without a bribe having learnt that there was greater value to have than a pocketful of coins. On another occasion, he was a guest overnight in a house that did not follow the practice of bringing out "the Books" for evening prayer. He inquired if he might join them in their devotions, but the householder said that he had no gift for prayer, however, before long he was on his knees with his family aided in their prayers by a solicitous Guthrie.

Guthrie was widely travelled in his ministry throughout the western shires as evidenced by the tale of a merchant of Glasgow who was returning from Ireland and found himself stranded on the isle of Arran for the Sabbath. Here he was decidedly unhappy that he would only be able to hear a sermon in Gaelic, but on arriving at church, found the inestimable William Guthrie as the visiting preacher. On another occasion when in Angus to the north, Guthrie sought overnight shelter in the home of a known opponent of the Covenanters and eventually confessed he was a minister and sought permission to pray. Reluctantly allowing it under ancient rules of courtesy, the three daughters of the house joined Guthrie in prayer and were converted such that the next day the local curate was made to stand aside so that Guthrie might preach in his stead.

The consequence of his ministrations was that Fenwick gained a reputation as the place to be, with people moving into the parish and travelling from Glasgow, Paisley, Hamilton and Lanark to hear him preach. It seems that Guthrie's especial gift was to be able to speak to the people in their own dialect. He also had clarity of thought that enabled him to reduce complex arguments to simple prose, which he displayed in a small book, "The Christians Great Interest" that he published in 1659.

Guthrie had never really had much faith in King Charles and foresaw the coming bloodshed, but he was for a while under the protection of friends at Court - the Earl of Eglinton and the Earl of Glencairn. Thus, for four years he continued his ministry with ever growing congregations. He was active too, in the meetings of the Glasgow Synod and favoured a straight spoken address to "the Godless Parliament in Edinburgh."

In July 1664, the blow finally came, when the curate of Calder, accompanied by twelve troopers, arrived to suspend William Guthrie from office and declare his church vacant. At their parting Guthrie warned the curate that he would suffer the Lord's displeasure and to prepare for some stroke coming to him. The curate died a few days later in great torment "of an iliac passion " and his wife and children also died within the year. The five pounds he had been paid to perform the odious task was judged to be blood money and had cost him everything.

Guthrie remained in Fenwick for a few months longer before ill health and the death of the brother to whom he had foregone his inheritance took him back to Pitforthy. He was staying at the house of his brother in law, Lewis Skinner, in Brechin when the end came. There on 10 October 1665, aged only forty-five years, he was released from a troublesome world.

XXIII. Alexander Peden - the Prophet

Alexander Peden was born about 1626 in the house of Auchincloich in the northern part of the Parish of Sorn, Ayrshire. He was the eldest son and heir to his father, a small proprietor of land, who by the standards of the day was quite well off. Thus the young Alexander received a good education - a scholar of the University of Glasgow, - and mixed freely among the gentlemen of the county, which included the Boswell family of Auchinleck. But despite these advantages, he chose a lifetime of loneliness and poverty.

For a while Peden was a teacher in Tarbolton during which time he was falsely accused of wronging a woman. He was at risk of being excommunicated when evidence was produced of his innocence, but the experience left a scar and may well be the reason why he never married. Peden's next step was, in 1659, to seek ordination into the church and no less than five times appeared before the Presbytery of Lanark and Biggar before his licence was granted. He was ordained and appointed to the parish of New Luce in Galloway but his stay was brief as in 1662, along with so many other ministers, he was compelled to leave the church. Thus began twenty-three years of wandering the hills and moors of South West Scotland from the Clyde, through Renfrewshire, his homeland of Ayrshire into the depths of Dumfries and Galloway, and across the Irish Sea in Ulster where he preached at Kells and Glenwherry, Co. Antrim between 1679 and 1681 and made later visits in 1682 and 1684.

He was undoubtedly a gifted preacher and would present it in homely ways that the populace could understand. His manner of delivering a sermon with the occasional halt and aside discussion with an unseen third party, or an apparent conversation aside with God, added to his reputation. A vivid speaker he was credited with almost supernatural powers because he almost routinely escaped the soldiers seeking him out. Not only did he escape pursuers many times, but also it was on occasion because of swirling mists and sudden severe weather cloaking him from the dragoons, thus adding to his mystique. A shrewd assessor of his fellow man and the issues that beset the Covenanters gave meaning to his reputation as a prophet although his forecasts were probably the result of keen observation and wisdom. Among his prophesies were that at Rullion Green and Bothwell Brig "the saints will be broken, killed, taken and fled."

A well-known prophecy of Peden's concerned John Brown, known as "The Christian Carrier," who on 1 May 1685 refused to take the Abjuration Oath and a search of his home revealed treasonable papers and weapons. He was condemned on the spot by Claverhouse. He was shot in front of his wife and children, fulfilling a prophecy that Peden had made in 1682, when he had married them. At that time Peden had said,

You have a good man to be your husband, but you will not enjoy him long; prize his company, and keep linen by you to be his winding sheet, for you will need it when ye are not looking for it, and it will be a bloody one.

The tale is told of a trip to Ulster and County Antrim in 1682 where he took work, threshing corn for local farmer William Stiel at Glenwherry, thereby gaining a modest wage, but also time to think and pray and a bed in the

Mist at Dalveen Pass
Courtesy of A. Pittendreigh

barn. However, a servant told of his praying and he was obliged to reveal his identity only to be received into the house as an honoured guest by the farmer and his family. On another occasion he displayed a brave recklessness by escaping from pursuing dragoons by plunging into an icy river in spate, leaving the pursuers on the far shore afraid to take the plunge. In yet another incident dragoons chased Peden and his party into the hills when he prayed for help with the words, "cast the lap of thy cloak over auld Sandy" a thick mist descended and they escaped under its cover.

Whether Divine Providence or not, tales such as these soon became lore and gained for Peden a reputation which of itself concerned the authorities who feared the power and influence he exercised. This was enhanced by the fact that Peden often used a curious mask to disguise himself in his travels during The Killing Time. Very crude by today's standards, the mask is made of leather, with real teeth fixed in the mouth and human hair attached to the forehead but in the days of flickering oil lamps and candles it must have served its purpose. The mask is today in the National Museum of Scotland in Edinburgh as is Peden's well thumbed Bible.

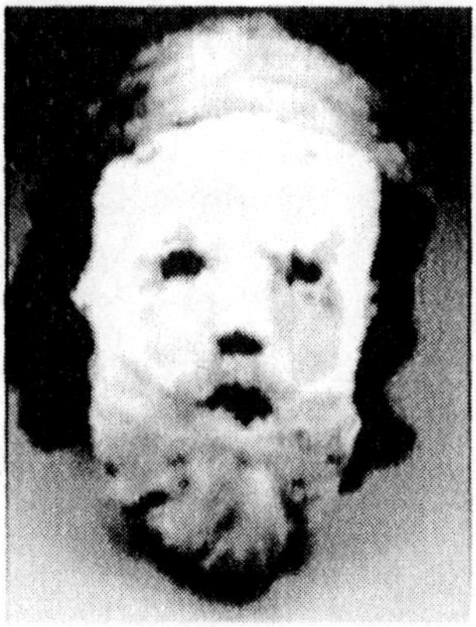

He was not directly involved in the Pentland Rising in 1666, but good fortune ran out in June 1673 when he was captured while holding a conventicle at Knockdow, near Ballantrae in South Ayrshire. He was brought before the Privy Council and sentenced to imprisonment on the Bass Rock where he was held for four years and three months - until October 1677.

From the Bass Rock he was moved to the Tolbooth in Edinburgh where he spent another eighteen months. In

December 1678 he, with sixty-seven others, was sentenced to banishment and put on board the *St. Michael* to be taken to Virginia. This scene was another glimpse into the future, when Peden prayed on behalf of a fellow deportee James Law Lord, "let not James Law's wife miss her husband, until thou return him to her in peace and safety, which we are sure will be sooner than either he or she is looking for." On board ship Peden also reassured his fellows that, "If we were once in London we will all be set at liberty."

However, the ship was delayed five days and when put into London there was nobody to receive them at first. Then the captain of the ship for Virginia refused to take them on board when he found out that they were good Christians and not the thieves and vagabonds he had believed were to be transported. At this the captain of the *St. Michael* declined to provision sixty prisoners and put them ashore. Thus freed, the prisoners were treated well by the people of Gravesend and most of them made their way back to Scotland; fulfilling yet another Peden prophesy.

Peden returned to Scotland where for the next seven years he divided his time between Scotland and Ulster going as he called it "from one bloody land to the other bloody land." He returned for the last time in February 1685. Peden was not in fact a Cameronian, although he was as severe a critic as any of the government and prelacy, and supported the Earl of Argyll's rebellion to remove a Popish king from the throne. For many years he and James Renwick, another Covenanter preacher, held each other in respect even though of differing opinions on some matters, and were reconciled as Peden lay upon his death bed.

The end came for Peden on 26 January 1686 after he had returned to his brother's home at Ten Shilling Side, Auchinleck. There was a concealed cave nearby to which Peden would retire at night. Two days before he died he left the cave and went to his brother's house where his sister-in-law remonstrated with him insisting that he return to the safety of the cave. Peden refused saying, "I have done with that for it is discovered. But there is no matter, for within forty eight hours I will be beyond the reach of all the devil's temptations and his instruments in hell and on earth, and they shall trouble me no more."

Within three hours the troopers came and found the cave, but not Peden who hid in a pile of straw. After the soldiers had gone away Peden told his friends to bury him where they would, he would be lifted again, and in a few hours he died. As he had foretold, there was no peace for him in death as the government continued to hound him. The Boswell family was so concerned for his body that they had it re-interred secretly in their family vault. But some forty days after he had died, and despite protests of the Boswell family and the Countess of Dumfries, soldiers took the body to the place of execution, a hill above Cumnock, and hung it on the gibbet. When it was eventually cut down, the body was buried again, this time at the foot of the gibbet as if a common criminal. Time has been a great healer for little by little the local people buried their loved ones alongside Alexander Peden, thus creating a new and hallowed graveyard.

In 1891 a monument, paid for by public subscription, was erected with the following inscription:

In Memory
of
ALEXANDER PEDEN
[A native of Sorn]

THAT FAITHFUL MINISTER OF CHRIST, WHO FOR HIS UNFLINCHING ADHERENCE TO THE COVENANTED REFORMATION IN SCOTLAND, WAS EXPELLED BY TYRANT RULERS FROM HIS PARISH OF NEW LUCE, IMPRISONED FOR YEARS ON THE BASS ROCK BY HIS PERSECUTORS, AND HUNTED FOR HIS LIFE ON THE SURROUNDING

MOUNTAINS AND MOORS, TILL HIS DEATH ON 26TH JANUARY 1686 IN THE 60TH YEAR OF HIS AGE, AND HERE AT LAST, HIS DUST REPOSES IN PEACE, AWAITING THE RESURRECTION OF THE JUST SUCH WERE THE MEN THESE HILLS WHO TRODE STRONG IN THE LOVE AND FEAR OF GOD DEFYING THROUGH THE LONG DARK HOUR, ALIKE THE CRAFT AND RAGE OF POWER.

ERECTED
IN
1891.

Samuel Rutherfurd
From a Portrait probably by Robert Walker

XXIV. Rev. Samuel Rutherford - The Intellectual Gladiator and Saint

Born in 1600 in the Border village of Nisbet, Samuel Rutherford's father was a fairly prosperous farmer who was able to give his three sons, Samuel, George and James, good educations. Samuel Rutherford was one of the great thinkers of the Reformation and the Covenanting movement. He was also a gifted orator and preacher as well as a prolific writer with some sixteen books published, twelve in London. He left to posterity many examples of his sermons, which had been assiduously copied over the years. The most famous of his works is probably "Lex Rex - the Law and the Prince: A Disputation for the Just Prerogative of King and People," which got him into serious trouble. He was also a great letter writer and has left a rich heritage from his days in exile in Aberdeen. Faith Cook, in her book, *Samuel Rutherford and His Friends,* so aptly describes that he was

> *a faithful counsellor and masterly physician of the soul.*

Rutherford very nearly did not make adulthood, as one day, playing with other children he fell down a well; when his parents arrived they found him wet and cold but alive, sat on a hillock He explained, "A bonnie white Man drew me forth and set me down." He did not enter the Church until he was a grown man having first been to Edinburgh

University in 1617 and graduating with a Master of Arts degree in 1621, then staying as Professor of Latin. He married young but his two children died in infancy and his wife, Eupham, also died about 1631 after a long illness.

He became minister of Anwoth in Galloway in 1627 at the invitation of Sir John Gordon of Lochinvar, later to become Lord Kilmure. Anwoth is a pretty village slightly off today's beaten track but clearly a place of some importance in the past with a church (now a ruin) that goes back to the fourteenth century. Within the churchyard lies the grave of John Bell of Whyteside, a local laird, who was involved in the assassination of Archbishop James Sharp on Magus Muir in 1679 from which time he had been a fugitive. He was one of five men shot out of hand by Sir Robert Grierson of Lag in February 1685 on Kirkconnel Moor. Samuel Rutherford was minister at Anwoth until 1636 when he was exiled to Aberdeen, but in only nine years he garnered a reputation for his caring approach and God fearing sermons. A contemporary, the Rev. James Urquhart of Kinloss is quoted as saying, "Many times I thought he would have flown out of the pulpit when he came to speak of Jesus Christ." The historian, the Rev. Robert Wodrow in his book *The History of the Sufferings of the Church of Scotland* describes Rutherford as, "one of the most moving and affectionate preachers in his time or perhaps in any age of the Church."

In his manse, the *Bush o Bield*, Rutherford rose at three am each morning to pray and study. Perpetually busy, he was always committed to some deed or duty, praying, visiting the sick, teaching in school, writing treatises, reading and studying. He was said to have a

Table Tomb
Of
Covenanter
John Bell
Of
Whyteside
Anwoth Church

John Bell of Whyteside

Around the edge

HERE LYES JOHN BELL
OF WHITESYDE WHO WAS BARBAROUSLY SHOT
TO DEATH IN THE PAROCH
OF TONGLAND AT THE COMMAND OF LAG 1685

Inscription
Of the
Memorial
To
John Bell

The main inscription

THIS MONUMENT SHALL TELL POSTERITY
THAT BLESSED BELL OF WHITESYDE HERE DOTH LY
WHO AT COMMAND OF BLOODY LAG WAS SHOT
A MURDER STRANGE WHICH SHOULD NOT BE FORGOT
DOUGLAS OF MORTON DID HIM QUARTERS GIVE
YET CRUEL LAG WOULD NOT LET HIM SURVIVE
THIS MARTYR SOUGHT SOME TIME TO RECOMMEND
HIS SOUL TO GOD BEFORE HIS DAYS DID END
THE TYRRANT SAID, WHAT, DEVIL! YE'VE PRAY'D ENOUGH
THIS LONG SEVEN YEAR ON MOUNTAIN AND IN CLEUCH
SO INSTANTLY CAUS'D HIM WITH OTHER FOUR
BE SHOT TO DEATH UPON KIRKCONNEL MOOR
SO THUS DID END THE LIVES OF THESE DEARE SANTS
FOR THERE ADHERENCE TO THE COVENANTS.

"strange utterance" a shrill voice, but nevertheless a compelling delivery that made his audience listen. In Anwoth the sermons he gave were published under the titles "The Trial and Triumph of Faith, and Christ Dying and Drawing Sinners to Himself."

Several versions of a tale are told how the Archbishop Ussher, Primate of Ireland, resolved to go to England by way of Scotland so that he might listen to Rutherford preach. Arriving in Anwoth there was no place to stay and he sought shelter at Rutherford's house where he was taken in. Neither Rutherford nor his wife recognised their visitor nor assumed anything from his name. In the evening Mrs. Rutherford was catechising the children and Ussher joined in. He was asked how many Commandments there were and replied eleven, much to his hosts surprise. The following day, the Sabbath, the Archbishop rose early and walked in the fields nearby and came to a place which Rutherford himself used as a place of quiet and contemplation. It was here that Rutherford came upon the Primate at prayer and then realised who he was. Confirming the identity, the pair then agreed to listen to each other preach that day - Rutherford in the morning and the Primate in the afternoon. The Archbishop gave as his sermon "A new Commandment I give unto you, that ye love one another" answering the question that Mrs. Rutherford had earlier posed.

Trouble on the horizon came in the shape of Thomas Sydserff, Bishop of Galloway, who came from the northern diocese of Brechin. Sydserff disliked Rutherford and took exception to a book he had published that had been highly critical of Archbishop Laud, King Charles I's right hand man. Rutherford was first summoned before an ecclesiastical court in Wigtown then tried in Edinburgh. The sycophantic Bishop managed to have him deposed on 27 August 1636, forbidden to preach, and exiled to Aberdeen. Although far from his ministry and friends, he nevertheless kept himself busy writing letters and sent some 220 in the twenty-two months he was in exile.

Memorial plate for Samuel Rutherford
Anwoth Church
Courtesy of A. Pittenreigh

In 1639 his connection with Anwoth was finally broken when the General Assembly expressed their wish that he should take the post of Professor of Divinity at St. Mary's College at St Andrews. Much against his wishes, he went to St. Andrews on condition that he could share the preaching with Rev. Robert Blair. He was later made Principal of the New College and Rector of the University where he became the doyen of Scottish thinkers and teachers. Twice Edinburgh tried to entice him to their university and also twice the city of Utrecht asked him to take their chair of theology. Rutherford's response was typical of the man, "I had rather be in Scotland with an angry Jesus Christ than in any Eden or garden in the earth." In 1640, some five months after taking up his post, Rutherford married Jean McMath.

Between 1643 and 1647 Rutherford was mainly in London working in the Jerusalem Chamber of Westminster, as one of the Scottish Commissioners to the Assembly of Divines. Here he argued the case for church freedom, having an input to the emerging Westminster Confession of Faith, the Directory and Catechisms, and producing more treatises. Typical of the man was his zeal and drive being one of the most active of the 151 members and one of the final committee of four appointed to complete the Shorter Catechism in October 1647. It was while he was in London that his two children died.

"Lex Rex", published in 1644, aimed to show that constitutional government, in which the rights of the people and their rulers are both observed, is the best for all parties. Today we take this as self evident, a truism. But in the seventeenth century, the power and influence of the book is seen in the effect it produced on the enemies of civil and religious liberty. The forty-four chapters or questions asked by Rutherford about the relationship of the Kirk and the Crown, such as that limitless sovereignty was the right of God alone. The book itself, it has been said, is the constitutional inheritance of all countries in modern times. The thrust of what Rutherford wrote can be recognised as appearing again and again in the declarations by Presbyterians in the emerging democracies such as *The Hanover Resolves* in Pennsylvania (4 June 1774), *The Mecklenburg Declaration* in North Carolina (31 May 1775) and in *The Declaration of Independence* (1776) itself.

The Restoration of King Charles II in 1660 saw more oppression as he took his revenge on Scotland and its Church. In September 1660 the Committee of Estates (the ruling body in Scotland) issued a proclamation declaring "Lex Rex" to be full of "seditious and treasonable matter" and ordered that all copies of the book, which could be found, were to be burned at the Mercat Cross in Edinburgh and at the gates of New College in St. Andrews. The public hangman in Edinburgh did this on 16 October 1660. The Drunken Parliament, as it was called, led by the Earl of Middleton, was determined to have the leaders of the Covenanting movement condemned to death - the main targets being the Marquis of Argyll, Rev. James Guthrie of Stirling, Archibald Johnston, Lord Warriston, and Samuel Rutherford.

For Rutherford the spite and revenge of government began by depriving him of his University post as Principal and his stipend was confiscated. He was also confined to his house and ordered to appear before the next parliament to answer a charge of treason. However, he was not to answer the charge, as his long time illness had caught up with him. On receiving the summons Rutherford said

Tell them I have got a summons already before a superior Judge and judicatory, and I behove to answer my first summons, and ere your day come I will be where few kings and great folks come.

Samuel Rutherford died on 29 March 1661, surrounded by his closest friends and at his bedside his eleven-year-old daughter, Agnes, the sole surviving child of the seven born to his second marriage. Had he not died then it is certain that he would have shortly followed the Marquis of Argyll and the Rev. James Guthrie to the scaffold.

He is buried in St. Andrews where his tombstone reads:

M
S R
Here lyes the Rev. Mr. Samuell
Rutherfoord Professor of Divinity in
the University of St. Andreus who died
March the 20 1661.
What tongu what Pen or Skill of Men
Can Famous Rutherfoord Commend
His Learning justly raised his Fame
True GODliness Adorn'd His Name
He did converse with things Above
Acquainted with Emmanuel's Love
Most orthodox He was And sound
And Many Errors did confound
For Zions King and Zions cause
And Scotlands covenanted LAWS
Most constantly he did contend
Until His Time was At An End
Than he wan to the Full Fruition
Of That which He Had seen in vision.

James Guthrie

XXV. Rev. James Guthrie of Stirling - the Scapegoat

It seems so easy to dismiss a person's life and efforts, for whatever cause, in the hindsight of history. The return of King Charles II to the throne in 1660 resulted in the restoration of the King to his throne, his privy council, the Scottish parliament and judiciary and the return of the bishops to the church. In the aftermath of the Restoration there came a growing royalist reaction that sought out scapegoats for the Covenanting past, which led inexorably to the execution of the Marquis of Argyll on 27 May 1661 and the Rev. James Guthrie on 1 June 1661.

Born to the Laird of Guthrie in Forfarshire, the young James was brought up in an Episcopal faith and schooled at Brechin Grammar School where he excelled in classics. From there he went to St. Andrews to study philosophy and had thoughts of entering the church. His scholarship was rewarded, however, with appointment as professor of philosophy and with it the friendship and influence of Samuel Rutherford. Until then he was fond of the ceremonies and procedures of the Episcopal church, but when he left university it was to take up the ministry in a humble Presbyterian church.

He had joined the throng at Greyfriars to sign the National Covenant and took the step that was to see him the victim of a vengeful government twenty-three years later. Of those interim years he spent twenty-two as a minister in charge of two churches at Lauder and Stirling where he moved his home to in 1650. In these years James Guthrie became much involved in the workings of the Presbyterian Church and became a leader in the Synod and the Assembly much respected for his clarity of thought, perception and patience. Among his works was a treatise on Elders and Deacons and a pamphlet called "The Causes of the Lord's Wrath against Scotland" which would be used as evidence against him at a later date.

He was the servant and messenger of the Assembly on many auspicious occasions such as when sent to see the Marquis of Montrose on 20 May 1650, the day before his execution. Forthright in his comments he told Montrose that he was wrong for enlisting Irish help in his campaigns, and wrong to have forsaken the Covenant; to which Montrose expressed regret that any actions of his had been offensive to the Church of Scotland.

On another occasion he was the servant of the Commission of Assembly given the task of excommunicating the Earl of Middleton, the King's Commissioner in Scotland, who had been found out trying to get King Charles to forsake the ruling Presbyterian Committee of Estates. On the Sabbath while on the way to church, Guthrie was met by a messenger with a request from the King, the Committee of Estates and the Commission seeking to delay excommunication. Howie in *Scots Worthies* says a letter handed to him as he entered the pulpit which he did not open until after the service. After wrestling with his conscience and concluding that he must follow the Assembly's verdict (even though some now sought to stop him) he proclaimed John Middleton excommunicated and gained for himself a powerful and unforgiving enemy.

Summoned by the King to Perth, where he was holding Court, Guthrie also crossed swords with him. Following the delivery of a critical sermon, Charles clearly sought to over awe the humble minister, but he was soon put in his place by Guthrie who told him that he recognised the King's authority in civil matters but that he must not meddle with matters of religion. Firmly put in his place, the King responded by making Guthrie remain in Perth for a while, a virtual prisoner.

James Guthrie was again prominent in two encounters with Oliver Cromwell. The first was in 1648 when Cromwell was lodging in the Earl of Moray's house in the Cannongate, Edinburgh. Along with Rev. Robert Blair and Rev. David Dickson they sought Ironsides' views of the role of the monarchy, religious tolerance, and whether the church should be Episcopal, Independent or Presbyterian. Three tough questions with far reaching consequences that Cromwell replied, "Yes", "No", and "give me time to think." The fervent Robert Blair saw the request for time "dissembling" - avoiding the issue. But Guthrie's calm and patience won the day realising that there was nothing whatsoever to be achieved by rant and prejudice against the absolute military ruler.

The second interview with Cromwell was in April 1651 in Glasgow, when he invited representatives of the Church to a conference. The purpose was to respond to sermons and lectures delivered the day before, the Sabbath, which were critical of the Cromwellian approach to religion. Neither side won their debate it appears, but from it arose the label of grudging respect that Cromwell gave James Guthrie - "The short man who could not bow" - meaning that Guthrie would not give in or concede his argument. A mighty testimonial by a mighty man.

The death of Cromwell and the short-lived rule of his son Richard were followed by Restoration of King Charles in 1660. On his restoration, Charles took a very firm line indeed towards the Scots, rejecting his former allegiance to the Presbyterians and packing the Scottish Parliament with his own supporters. An act was passed almost immediately recognising the King's authority in both civil and church matters and restoring prelacy, the rule of the bishops. So began twenty-eight years of torment and persecution of the Presbyterians in Scotland.

For James Guthrie, the Restoration gave him one final task on behalf of the Assembly, which was an address to the King. With the assistance of others, Guthrie drafted "The Paper of 23 August" that prayed for the safety of his Majesty and sought him to conserve the Reformed religion of Scotland. They also reminded him that he had sworn to uphold the Covenant in former times. The King's response was prompt, and almost within hours the ten preachers and one of the two laymen who had drafted the address were imprisoned in Edinburgh Castle. James Guthrie was soon transferred first to Stirling, then to Dundee and then back to Edinburgh pursued by the vindictive Archbishop Sharp, who regarded him as "a harebrain rebel" and the grudge bearing Earl of Middleton.

In February and April of 1661 Guthrie made appearances before the Scottish Parliament and responded to the charges against him, but the conclusion was foregone. In an almost empty House, perhaps ashamed at what was being done, he was sentenced to be hanged at the Mercat Cross on Saturday 1 June, his head to be fixed on the Netherbow gate and his estate confiscated. So it was with hands bound behind him like a common thief, he went to the gallows where he made a short speech and lastly cried, "The Covenants, the Covenants shall yet be Scotland's reviving" as he stepped into eternity.

A poignant ending lays with the tale of William, the four-year-old son of James Guthrie, who would run out from his home nearby the Netherbow Gate to look upon his father's head, suspended above. He would then run home and tell his mother where he had been before locking himself in his room for many long hours. It is said that the boy, although distressed by the sight and memory of his father's death, considered the head that soldiers had fastened up the most beautiful head in the world. The head would remain above the gateway for twenty-seven years as a constant reminder to all of the sheer wickedness of the government and the Godliness of the Rev. James Guthrie. It is not without some irony that the head was taken down and buried by the Rev. Alexander Hamilton, then a student at St. Andrews, who was Guthrie's successor as minister at Stirling.

The last Testimony of James Guthrie is listed as an Appendix in "The Wrestlings of the Church of Scotland for the Kingdom of Christ" which was proclaimed and ordered to be burnt in December 1667. Many copies survived however, and his Testimony is reproduced in "*The Martyr Graves of Scotland*" by the Rev. J. H. Thomson. The final few lines sum up clearly what all the Martyrs of the Covenant died for:

The matters for which I am condemned are matters belonging to my calling and function as a minister of the Gospel - such as the discovery of sin and reproving of sin, the pressing and the holding fast of the oath of God in the Covenant, and preserving and carrying on the work of religion and reformation according thereto, and denying to acknowledge the civil magistrate as the proper competent judge in causes ecclesiastical - that in all these things, which - God so ordering by His gracious providence - are the grounds of my indictment and death, I have a good conscience, as having walked therin accordingly to the light and rule of God's Word, and as did become a minister of the Gospel.

XXVI. Rev. John Blackader - Field Preacher and Prisoner on the Bass Rock

John Blackader was one of the most zealous and popular of the Covenanter's field preachers and he was often in the company of John Welch of Irongray, the great grandson of John Knox.

Like so many of the Covenanter ministers, Blackader came from a reasonably well off family, the Blackaders of Tulliallan, Perthshire, and of a distinguished line of fighters. The original home was in Berwickshire where, in the fifteenth century, his forebear was Cuthbert Blackader who, with his seven sons, was called "The Black Band of the Blackaders" and fought valiantly for the Lancastrians (Red Rose) against the Yorkists (White Rose). Three of the sons and Cuthbert died at the battle of Bosworth on 22 August 1485 but, because of their bravery, King James of Scotland granted their heirs the unique privilege of carrying on their shields the two roses. The Berwickshire branch lost its dominating position and younger sons acquired by marriage the estates of Tulliallan in Perthshire. John Blackader was, in later life, entitled to the title of a baronetcy and the carriage of the badge of honour awarded the family, but he chose not to do so.

John Blackader was born in December 1615 and educated at Glasgow University where his uncle, the Rev. Dr. Strang, was the Principal. He spent many years travelling the country preaching and was thirty-seven years old when he was ordained minister of the parish of Troqueer in the Stewartry of Kirkcudbrightshire in 1652. He had seven children of whom two suffered imprisonment. A younger son was a brave and daring soldier who had joined the Cameronian regiment as a cadet in 1689 and served with the colours under John, Duke of Marlborough, in Flanders and Germany. He retired from the army as Lieutenant Colonel of the 26th or Cameronian Regiment, was Deputy Governor of Stirling Castle in 1711, and died aged sixty-five in 1729.

Troqueer Church Bell Tower
Dumfries

Blackader worked hard for the common people of his parish who were backward and ignorant and some practised "popery." However, by patient application, home visiting, encouraging education and reading the Bible and preaching twice on the Sabbath, he gradually brought his congregation together. But, along with other ministers, he was ejected from his living in 1662 - His family was physically ejected from the family home in his absence by no less a person than Sir James Turner, later to be captured by the Pentland rebels.

Blackader had heard that he was to be arrested and had gone to nearby Dumfries when soldiers arrived at his home and forced his wife and children to leave the house and seek cover in the Parish of Glencairn. In 1665 another attempt to seize him failed because he and his wife were safe in Edinburgh but, again in his absence, the children were turned out of their beds and his house ransacked, the brave troopers even stabbing at the beds with their swords while uttering threats to roast the children on the fire. In the confusion a ten-year-old son escaped and ran in his nightshirt to the Bridgend of Mennihyvie (Moniave) where he was found asleep at the village cross the following morning.

Blackader belonged to a more moderate section of the Presbyterians; disapproving of the Indulgence which aimed to lure ministers back to a modified form of service. But he was unhappy at the use of force and as a result he was not at any of the encounters with the royalist soldiers. Perhaps importantly, he did not accept the die hard position adopted by Richard Cameron in the Sanquhar Declaration. Almost contradictory is that he was among the ministers who encouraged the hard core of prisoners held in the Greyfriars Prison not to sign bonds for good behaviour. The leader of the prisoners, a Robert Garnock, a blacksmith from Stirling, was influenced by a letter from Blackader but was hanged for his resistance.

He did not, at first, commence field preaching and kept a low profile, but the barbarous behaviour of the troopers seemed to convince Blackader that an offensive was needed. He soon became prominent amongst the field preachers and helped organise conventicles. Under his influence, there emerged an underground church with regular committee meetings and even its own church court.

From the government view point, he was becoming a dangerous nuisance since he also preached in private houses, which were more difficult to detect and meant that persons of influence were being drawn to congregations.

He preached for some twenty years wherever and whenever opportunity afforded itself, whether in houses, barns or fields. He ranged far afield preaching in Fifeshire, the Lothians, Lanarkshire, in Carrick and Cunningham in Ayrshire and among the hills of Galloway. During this time he preached at Fenwick in January 1669 where there had been no Presbyterian teaching since the Pentland Rising three years before. He established a new congregation at Bo'ness and had a crowd of 1,200 hanging on his every word at Paisley. At Dunscore in the midst of deep snow it is said that he sat on a chair in the open and preached to the populace who pulled up lumps of heather on which to sit and listen.

At the Hill of Beath near Dunfermline in the summer of 1670, he and John Dickson preached to a large crowd during which a lieutenant in the militia road up dismounted and listened to the sermon, which then happened to be about brotherly love and was not treasonable. Being satisfied, the lieutenant went to remount and was surrounded by belligerent members of the congregation. Blackader stopped his sermon and intervened, allowing the soldier to be on his way. This conventicle is also remembered as one of the first at which people carried pistols and swords for defence, so it was a lucky lieutenant who rode away unscathed. It says something of the demand on the physical man that Blackader took over seven hours to ride home from this conventicle, having to go the long way round via Stirling, as there was no boatman to take him across the estuary from Dunfermline to Edinburgh.

Blackader preached with the outed John Welch of Irongray on several occasions, notably so in 1678 at what have been called the Communion Stones at Skeoch Hill near Irongray. Here rows of stones in an amphitheatre in the hills are a natural setting, surrounded by high hills from which lookouts could keep watch for the troopers. At Skeoch some 14,000 people attended over a period of three days and 3,000 took Communion. Another remembered Communion was that at East Nisbet in the Borders conducted in idyllic surroundings, in a field next a stream where sixteen tables were set up, each seating one hundred communicants, so that about 3,200 took communion that day.

He spent some time in Holland in 1680 and was eventually arrested at his home in Edinburgh on 6 April 1681. He was arraigned before General Dalziel and then before a Committee of the Privy Council who ordered his immediate incarceration. Blackader was sentenced to imprisonment on the Bass Rock where he was duly committed the next day there was such haste to be rid of him. With his health failing, a bid was made to get him released but he died there in December 1685 before this could be done. He is buried in North Berwick Churchyard where his gravestone inscription begins:

Here lies the body of
Mr. John Blackader, minister of the
Gospel at Troqueer, in Galloway, who
died on the Bass after five years impri-
sonment, Anno Dom 1685, and of his age
sixty three years.

A memorial plague in Troqueer parish church bears the following inscription:

To the Glory of God in memory of
The Rev. John Blackader
Born 1615
Ordained minister of the Parish of Troqueer 1653
Extruded 1662. Outlawed for preaching in the fields 1674
Imprisoned on the Bass Rock 1681
Died after a cruel confinement 1685
"Faithful unto death"
Erected AD 1902.

XXVII. Rev. Donald Cargill - the Administrator

In every group or society there is always someone that all turn to for advice or guidance on a topic and so it was with the Rev. Donald Cargill. By nature said to be timid and shrinking from confrontation yet this belies the steel in his backbone that enabled him to be a constant source of guidance, direction and authorship of Declarations by the strong principled Cameronians.

The son of Laurence Cargill, a notary and gentleman of Rattray in Perthshire, he was born about 1619. His father had some difficulty in getting the young Donald to study divinity but perseverance finally resulted in graduation. It was not until 1655 that he was ordained for the ministry of the Barony Church in Glasgow and even then he was reluctant to take up the position. On a preliminary visit to the church he had made up his mind to leave Glasgow fearing that he was not up to the task. It is said that he was in the act of mounting his horse when a local woman berated him for leaving, because he had

appointed a meal for poor hungry people, and will ye go away and not give it?

He stayed on in Glasgow but was among the 300 ministers who were ejected from their churches by the Earl of Middleton's Act of Presentation and Collation in 1662.

He and his family were ordered not to live anywhere on the south side of the River Tay and to take what belonged to him out of Glasgow by the first of November 1662, else he would be liable to imprisoned as "a seditious person."

It seems that any early timidity and concern of being a minister had left him by the time he was outed but was compounded by the sad loss of his wife, Margaret Brown, after only one year of marriage. Left with no real family ties, he became very active in field preaching and private prayer meetings interspersed with only a short break in Holland. In this time the field preaching or "conventicles" became more and more frequent and of concern to the government such that by 1670 they were being declared illegal. In 1678 an Act was passed to enable military forces to be raised for the suppression of conventicles. With this came a hated tax, called the cess, to pay for the maintenance of the troops. But undaunted, the conventicles continued - in one area of Lanark in February to April 1679 twenty consecutive Sabbath meetings were without disruption.

A feature of conventicles in the 1670s was the increasing number of armed members of the congregation, and perhaps not surprisingly, the soldiers tended to leave very large meetings alone. This however, also gave rise to problems of conscience and some ministers felt that there needed to be an explanation and justification for this action. So it was, following a conventicle at Avondale, 25 May 1679, that the leaders - Robert Hamilton, David Hackston, John Balfour of Kinloch, consulted with Donald Cargill. The result was the issue of another Declaration on Thursday 29 May, a day set aside for the celebration of King Charles' birthday and restoration to the throne.

On this occasion Robert Hamilton and some eighty horsemen set off to issue the Declaration in Glasgow, but found the way too strongly guarded. They ended up at the market cross in the royal burgh of Rutherglen where the document was read. The party then cast into the celebratory bonfires copies of the Act Recissory (that had annulled all the acts of Parliament from 1640 to the Reformation in 1660); the Act of Supremacy which asserted the king was superior in all things; the Declaration which condemned the Covenants; the Act rejecting the Presbyterian Church and establishing prelacy and the Act of Presentation and Collation. When this was done a copy of the Declaration was hung on the market cross, a prayer said and the party returned to Avondale.

Although in relatively mild language, the Declaration at Rutherglen alarmed the government and two days later John Graham of Claverhouse was given full powers to look for its authors. Thus it was that he arrived in Hamilton on the evening of Saturday 31 May and unleashed his soldiers on the town. They found the Rev. John King in bed and he and other people were seized. From this action it seems that Claverhouse learned of the conventicle at Drumclog where the Covenanters put him to flight the next day.

Donald Cargill was again involved with trying to sort out policy as the Covenanters argued and fell out with one another in the period before the defeat at Bothwell Brig. Again the Covenanters favoured a Declaration, but this time they were debating whether to adopt the softer line of the Indulged (those ministers who accepted a compromise of some forms of prelacy and "owned" the King). Cargill was representative of the majority who rejected the softer line of John Welch. However, despite having been out voted, Welch had his version of the Declaration published at Hamilton, Glasgow, Lanark, Ayr and Irvine and became known as the "Hamilton Declaration." The result was yet another drafting task for Donald Cargill to reject the Hamilton Declaration.

Between 19 and 21 June there was constant coming and going between the two parties with Donald Cargill chief among the negotiators. There then followed a peculiar turn of events when Welch and his group prepared a Supplication to present to the Duke of Monmouth who had meanwhile arrived with 15,000 royalist troops. In this the Rev. John Blackader was sent to Sir Robert Hamilton to get his signature on the document and to say that Donald Cargill begged him to subscribe to it. Hamilton signed believing that Cargill had genuinely asked and was therefore duped by Welch. However, the Supplication came to nothing with Hamilton rejecting the terms of surrender sent by the Duke of Monmouth and the Covenanters fell into defeat.

Another phase began for Donald Cargill after the disaster of Bothwell Brig with his short relationship with the fearless Richard Cameron, who had returned from Holland in the spring of 1679. In the heated persecution after Bothwell, Cargill and Thomas Douglas were two of the few who were brave enough to join Cameron, and the three united in services at Darmead in Cambusnethan and at Auchengilloch a secluded glen south of Strathhaven. It was at these meetings that discussion took place about a statement to the world renouncing allegiance and disowning Charles II as a tyrant and usurper.

The Declaration of Sanquhar on 22 June 1680 is a major declaration of faith, and a declaration of war. It is often ascribed to Richard Cameron, but it is very likely that Donald Cargill was responsible for its actual writing. But before this there was another document of great moment that was not in fact published by the Covenanters. This was "The Queensferry Papers."

On 3 June 1680 Donald Cargill was in Queensferry along with Henry Hall, of Haughhead, a long time companion. Hall was a gentleman of some property and lived in the parish of Eckford about six miles south of Kelso, and was related to the Earl of Roxburgh. Not far from their lodgings in Queensferry resided Middleton, the Governor of the nearby Blackness Castle which was used as a prison for Covenanters. Middleton was informed by the curates of Borrowstounnes and Carriden of the presence of Cargill and Hall and he immediately sought them out.

By cunning and subterfuge, Middleton ingratiated himself with them and bought wine. After taking a drink,

Middleton demanded that they regard themselves as his prisoners. Henry Hall restrained Middleton while Cargill escaped. In the struggle, Thomas George, an excise man, wounded Hall by striking him on the head with a carbine. Some women took him to a country house and doctors were brought, but Dalziel of the Binns, of Rullion Green fame, who also lived nearby, came with guards and seized him. Although it was plain to see that Hall was dying, Dalziel took him away to Edinburgh, but his prisoner died on the way. It was in the search of his clothing that the highly incriminating papers were found. Thus its existence came to public notice from the government and was not published by the Covenanters.

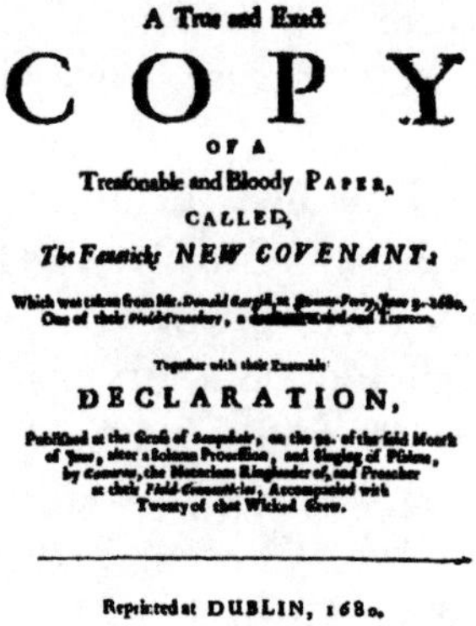

A True and Exact

COPY

OF A

Tresonable and Bloody PAPER,

CALLED,

The Fanaticks NEW COVENANT:

[illegible]

[illegible]

DECLARATION,

[illegible]

Reprinted at DUBLIN, 1680.

Frontispiece of the Queensferry Papers

The Queensferry Papers was a strongly worded and skilfully written policy document or manifesto, which attained its title from the place in which it was discovered. It was a confession of faith and also a rejection of sinful and wicked rulers and the tyranny that came from government by a single person, i.e., the King. As such it was a bold and dangerous document, which meant certain death for the authors.

The Sabbath after the Ayrsmoss battle of 22 July 1680 at which Richard Cameron and his brother Michael had fallen, Donald Cargill preached the sermon choosing as his text, "Know ye not that there is a prince and a great man fallen this day in Israel." But there was soon to follow a momentous meeting at Torwood, between Larbert and Stirling, in October 1680. Here he preached a sermon based on "Thus saith the Lord God, Remove the diadem and take off the Crown." When he had done preaching Cargill solemnly continued to excommunicate Charles Stuart, King of England; James, Duke of York; James, Duke of Monmouth; John, Duke of Lauderdale; John, Duke of Rothes; Sir George MacKenzie (the King's Advocate also known as Bluidy MacKenzie); and Thomas Dalziel of the Binns.

Cargill preached his last sermon at Dunsyre, and it was the following morning, 12 July 1681 at Covington Mill, where he had been resting, that James Irvine of Bonshaw captured him and his companions, Walter Smith and James Boig. They were taken first to Glasgow then to Edinburgh with their captor no doubt anxious to collect the 5,000 merks reward for Cargill. They were soon sentenced to be executed and on 27 July 1681 Donald Cargill climbed the ladder saying, "I go up this ladder with less fear, confusion, or perturbation of mind, than ever I entered a pulpit to preach."

After the execution, as was the custom for traitors, his head was hacked off and suspended above the Netherbow Gate alongside that of his great friend Richard Cameron.

XXVIII. David Hackston - the Soldier

Although a lesser light among the Covenanters in terms of preaching, David Hackston of Rathillet, stands tall among the soldiers of the Covenant as the leader of "The Cameronians," as his armed supporters became known. Hackston came from an old Scottish and reasonably well off family in the Parish of Kilmany, Fife whose ancestry goes back to Sir John de Haukerston who swore fealty to King Edward I in 1296. The area is also known as Halkertoun and the family name was often given as Halkerston. David Hackston, or Halkerston, became laird when his father James died on 3 March 1670. On his own death in 1680, the estates passed to his nephew Robert Halkerston. David Hackston was present at two Declarations - the Sanquhar Declaration and the Rutherglen Declaration, and was likely to have been at many other important events doing his duty as the able lieutenant and bodyguard. As a soldier of the Covenant he was present at the Magus Moor assassination of Archbishop Sharp; he fought valiantly at Drumclog; Bothwell Brig and Ayrsmoss. But he rests in memory as having suffered a dreadful death for doing his duty.

Magus Moor Saturday 3 May 1679

We first come across David Hackston the soldier in 1679 when he was a member of a group of Covenanters who had determined to chastise William Carmichael, a drunken and dissolute magistrate that Archbishop Sharp had appointed to be Sheriff depute of Fife and who had been particularly energetic pursuing Covenanters. It is not clear whether they intended to kill the Sheriff or merely frighten him off, but on the day, Saturday 3 May 1679, fortune seemed to conspire against them and their quarry eluded them.

The group was breaking up to go their various ways when information was received that Archbishop Sharp himself would be passing shortly. The group decided to attack the Archbishop, David Hackston was elected leader but declined the leadership as he owed Sharp money and it would appear that the attack was motivated by that rather than as the vengeance of the Covenanters. John Balfour of Kinloch, David Hackston's brother-in-law, led the attack.

During the attack Sharp asked Hackston for protection to which he replied that he would not lay a hand upon him. The others finished the deed with their swords and generated a shock wave that reverberated through the Church of Scotland, the majority of the Presbyterian ministers, and the government. By 1679 many of the outed ministers, were beginning to come to terms with episcopacy and saw the murder as unnecessary For the government the murder was reason enough to give up any policy that sought reconciliation, and to intensify military action against the Covenanters. For Hackston it meant that he would suffer a grisly execution even though he had not actively participated in the murder.

Drumclog Sunday 1 June 1679

On 29 May 1679 at about seven o'clock in the evening some seventy or eighty armed men appeared in the streets of Rutherglen led by Robert Hamilton, in whose company rode David Hackston, John Balfour and James Russell. It was a day of celebration for the King's Restoration and a bonfire was blazing in the street, which the men doused.

They went to the Town Cross and there read a declaration condemning the government for its actions since 1660 and then, lighting their own fire, burnt the Acts of Parliament and of the Privy Council which had been against the Covenanters.

John Claverhouse and his troops were at Falkirk and, hearing of the demonstration, immediately set out to arrest the perpetrators. On the way he seized a Presbyterian chaplain and some fourteen other people who were tied together in pairs and driven along in front of the horsemen. They had stopped for the night at Strathaven when Claverhouse learnt of a proposed conventicle nearby at Loudon Hill, where Thomas Douglas was due to preach and he decided to attack it the following morning, Sunday 1 June.

However, Claverhouse was surprised to find that there was an armed look out who gave warning to the assembled throng, and that there were others present with arms. These included Robert Hamilton with his Rutherglen bodyguard, Henry Hall of Haughead, William Cleland of Douglas, John Balfour, James Russell and David Hackston. In all there were some forty horsemen, fifty footmen carrying guns and about 150 with ancient halberds and farm pitchforks who had girded their loins to do battle with roughly the same number of troops.

The Covenanters had chosen their ground well and the bog that lay between them and Claverhouse came quickly to their assistance. Claverhouse's troopers were unable to find a way through and struggled in the morass while the Covenanters, knowing their way through the bog charged upon them furiously. In no time at all the troopers were overcome and they turned and fled with Claverhouse among them, not stopping until they had reached Glasgow and the protection of Lord Ross's regiment. Thus ended the Covenanter victory at Drumclog.

Bothwell Brig Sunday 22 June 1679

Now filled with the taste of victory, the numbers of the Covenanting army grew rapidly to about 6,000. With hindsight, one wonders if the gallant band had pursued Claverhouse into Glasgow, where the Covenanters had supporters, they might have forced him to flee to Edinburgh. But they did not and before the Covenanters returned to Glasgow, Lord Ross had time to barricade the main streets and placed musketeers at vantage points. On Monday morning the Covenanters appeared and split into two parties, but their assault was futile and was repulsed.

There followed a lull in activity until the morning of Friday 6 June when the strengthened Covenanter forces drew up outside Glasgow and awaited the orders of their leader, Robert Hamilton. What followed, however, was great dissension among the people brought about by Hamilton's stubborn insistence that he would not accept in the army those who had accepted the Indulgences (concessions by the Crown that allowed Presbyterian ministers to return to their churches and preach under certain severe conditions.) While the arguments and dissension went on, the Royalist numbers increased to about 15,000 as support arrived from London led by King Charles's son, the Duke of Monmouth.

Despite last minute entreaties, Hamilton finally gave battle even though his force had shrunk by several thousands because of his stubborn refusal of help from other more moderate Presbyterians. The Covenanters did their best, but poorly led and unsupported in the field it was left to the likes of David Hackston to hold the Bothwell Brig for many hours. With but 300 men of Galloway, they fought most valiantly to hold their ground; they begged for reinforcements, but none came; they pleaded for more ammunition but none came. Hamilton finally gave the order to fall back and Hackston and his warriors did so followed, much to Hackston's discontent, by the Royalist artillery that they had fought so hard to contain and which would soon cut the Covenanters to pieces.

It has to be said that Bothwell Brig was lost through bad management, stubborn pride, divisiveness and self-interest. Over 400 Covenanters died, and about 1,100 were taken prisoner. Two ministers were executed at the Mercat Cross. There followed the ordeal of imprisonment in the Greyfriars Kirk Yard from which some escaped, and several hundred were released on their pledge of good behaviour. Two hundred and fifty seven prisoners were condemned to slavery in the American colonies and sent aboard the ill-fated *Crown* that foundered off of Orkney and 211 prisoners were drowned.

Ayrsmoss

So we come to the last battle of David Hackston, who was in the bodyguard totalling about sixty that travelled with Richard Cameron. They had stayed the night at the farmhouse of William Mitchel in Meadowhead at the Water of Ayr, but an informer disclosed their location. On Thursday 22 July 1680 at about four o'clock in the afternoon they were surprised at the eastern end of Ayrsmoss by about 120 troops under Bruce of Earlshall. In the moments before the battle Cameron led a short prayer in which he repeated several times "Lord, spare the green, and take the ripe." Seeking the best ground the Covenanters drew up with eight horsemen led by Cameron to the right and fifteen horsemen led by Hackston to the left. Those on foot formed up in the centre. In the ensuing fight the troopers advanced and opened fire wounding several, and in the hand-to-hand fighting Richard Cameron and his brother Michael were killed along with seven others. Five Covenanters were captured of whom two died of their wounds.

Those killed at Ayrsmoss were:

Rev. Richard Cameron
Michael Cameron
John Gemmel
John Hamilton
James Gray
Robert Dick
Capt. John Fowler
Thomas Watson
Robert Paterson

Among the prisoners was David Hackston who, in the fight, had wounded many and was finally taken by three dragoons who attacked from behind while he fought another with sword in hand. In no time the prisoners were taken to Edinburgh in a caravan of soldiers rejoicing in their victory and displaying the hacked off head of Richard Cameron to the people. Another head, said to be that of Michael Cameron was displayed although it was actually the head of John Fowler. Two prisoners died on the way leaving Archibald Alison of Evandale and John Malcolm of St. Johns Dalry who were executed on 13 August 1680. An especially grisly execution was ordered for their leader David Hackston.

A warrior's death

The Rev. J. H. Thomson in *The Martyr Graves of Scotland* quotes the Court's judgment. David Hackston was sentenced to a barbarous and revengeful death:

to be drawn backwards on a hurdle to the Mercat Cross and there at the cross of Edinburgh, and there upon a high scaffold erected a little above the cross have his right hand struck off and after some time to have his left hand struck off, and then to be hanged up and cut down alive, and the bowels taken out, and his heart to be shown to the people by the hand of the hangman, and his heart and bowels to be burnt in the presence of the people, in a fire prepared for that purpose upon the scaffold, and afterwards to have his head cut off, and his body divided into four quarters, and his head to be affixed on the Netherbow, and one of his quarters with both of his hands to be affixed at St. Andrews, another quarter at Glasgow, the third at Leith, the fourth at Burntisland, and that none presume to be in mourning for him, nor he to have a coffin, and that none be on the scaffold with him but two baillies, four officers, the executioner and his servants, and this sentence to be put in execution against him this thirtieth day of July instant, betwixt three and five o'clock in the afternoon. And ordained his name, fame, memory; and honours to be extinct, and his arms to be riven and delete furth of the books of arms, so that his posterity may never be able to bruick [hold] or joyse [enjoy] any lands, heritage, titles of dignities within this realm in time comming.

Hackston's head was fixed alongside Richard Cameron's at the Netherbow Gate and both were lifted higher than other martyred souls displayed there. How perverse it is that this vile manner of execution by hanging, drawing and quartering, seems to be reserved for the bravest of the brave like David Hackston who had this death in common with another Scottish warrior, the great Sir William Wallace.

XXIX. Rev. James Hamilton - an Ulster Covenanter

The Ulster Plantation and the earlier settlements in Co. Down and Co. Antrim by Sir Hugh Montgomery (later Viscount Montgomery of the Ards) and Sir James Hamilton (later Lord Claneboye) had established a strong Scottish presence and with it the desire for Presbyterian ministers. This was slowly satisfied in the years to 1630 as more ministers, trained in Scotland, became available. An undoubted help was a peaceful coexistence and compromise with the Bishops of the established church and the tolerance of Archbishop Ussher. The atmosphere changed dramatically in 1633, however, with the appointments of Archbishop Laud in England and Thomas Wentworth, later the Earl of Strafford, as Lord Deputy in Ireland, the shadow of persecution fell once more on Ireland.

The momentum of reform in Scotland was equally felt in Ireland with several of the early ministers still seeking return to a stricter Presbyterian way. Among these was Robert Blair, who was invited to Ireland by Lord Claneboy and ordained on 10 July 1623. Blair succeeded to Dean Gibson at Bangor where he had among his congregation a young James Hamilton, nephew of Sir James. The young James had been tutored in Scotland under the care of his uncle Archibald Hamilton of Halcraig, Lanarkshire, and on return to Ireland had begun working for Lord Claneboye as his chamberlain. He was competent in his tasks and highly regarded by Lord Claneboye. Meanwhile it was with circumspection that Rev. Blair and Rev. Robert Cunningham of Holywood encouraged the young James in his religious studies and to engage in preaching.

The private papers of the family, assembled as the Hamilton Manuscripts, tell us that James'

> *... disposition and private diligences moved towards the Ministry, which he so carefully concealed, and prudently, that my Lord and his good Lady were never 'ware of it till they saw and heard him preach in the pulpit at Bangor. My Lady was pleased to compliment him thus: 'James, I think your gown and pulpit become you very well; I will bestow the gown, and my Lord (if he will be advised by me) shall bestow the pulpit.'*

So it was in 1625 that the Rev. James Hamilton was ordained to the ministry at Ballywalter and entered into the annals of the Covenanters.

James married Elizabeth Watson, daughter of Rev. David Watson of Killeavy near Newry who bore him fifteen children although only a few reached maturity. A son, Archibald, was prominent in the Presbyterian Church in Ireland becoming minister at Benburb in 1668. At Ballywalter the Rev. James enjoyed ten years of peaceful ministry until he was caught up in the machinations of Thomas Wentworth, Lord Deputy, and the Bishop of Derry (Dr. Bramhall). In July 1636 he and Rev. Brice of Broadisland; Rev. Ridge of Antrim; Rev. Cunningham of Holywood; and Rev. Colvert of Oldstone declined to accept the new canons when asked by the new Bishop of Down and Connor, Henry Leslie. Subsequently in a public debate with Leslie Bishop Bramhall intervened and James Hamilton was deposed from Ballywalter on 12 August 1636. James Hamilton, along with Livingstone, Blair and McClelland were among the group who set sail on the Eaglewing on 3 September 1636 hoping to reach the

American colonies. Forced back by bad weather he and his family then fled to Scotland where he settled in the ministry at Dumfries, in what was to become the heartland of the hard line Covenanters. He remained there for another ten years.

Following the momentous events at Greyfriars Kirk of 28 February 1638, the National Covenant was widely broadcast and subscribed to in Ireland. But it was with the Solemn League and Covenant of 25 September 1643 that the Rev. James Hamilton made his return having been chosen by the Committee of Estates in Edinburgh to undertake the task of supervising the administration of the Covenant in Ulster. Appointed with him were the Rev. Hugh Henderson of Dalry in Ayrshire, Rev. William Adair of Ayr and the Rev. John Weir of Dalserf in Lanarkshire.

The purpose of the visit was to have all persons over eighteen years old to subscribe to the Covenant. Within the Scottish regiments the task was undertaken by their own chaplains. It was significant that among the few who declined to sign was a certain Major Dalziel, later to be an arch persecutor of the Covenanters in Scotland. Among the people, those who had taken the Black Oath were compelled to renounce it publicly before being admitted to the Covenant. Troopers frequently accompanied the ministers since there was still trouble with the native Irish rebels but they covered an enormous amount of ground in the three months given to them. They held meetings at Belfast, Comber, Newtownards, and Bangor in Co. Down; Broadisland, Island Magee and other places in Co. Antrim; Derry; Raphoe, Ramelton and Enniskillen in the North. On returning to Belfast they then administered Communion to congregations at Newtownards, Hollywood and Ballywalter. In all, about 16,000 people subscribed to the Solemn League and Covenant in Ireland.

It was no surprise therefore that the punishing schedule, and travel over poor to non-existent roads in all weathers began to have a toll on the ministers. The Rev. Adair developed a fever that laid him low, suffering relapses at Newtownards and Stranraer as he made his way home. But Rev. James Hamilton, Rev. Weir and Rev. Watson (father-in-law of Rev. Hamilton) were subject of a cruel fate. The Irish leader Alastair McColl, on board the Wexford frigate the *Harp,* seized their ship on 3 July 1644. McColl was on his way with 2,000 seasoned troops to attack the Argyll lands at Ardnamurchan in support of the Marquis of Montrose against the Covenanters. Landing in Argyll on 8 July the Irish quickly plundered the area and moved on with their prisoners to the castle at Mingarrie.

The three ministers were among the prisoners taken by McColl for possible exchange for his father and two brothers held by the Marquis of Argyll. Also taken were Thomas Jordan, a preacher; the Rev. Weir's pregnant wife; William Hamilton of Glasgow; William Irving of Dumfries; and Archibald Bruce. The prisoners were held aboard the frigate until 15 July before being cast into a single dungeon where they remained together until 23 September. During that time the Marquis of Argyll tried to liberate them by force, but after seven weeks and no success he abandoned them to their fate. The prisoners suffered much deprivation having only rainwater to drink and coarse rye grains to eat, which they had to grind between two slates.

McColl realised he could not afford so many captives and on 3 September he released Mrs. Weir, now close to having her child. The three merchants, Hamilton, Irving and Bruce were released on 23 September on giving their bond to pay a ransom. Thomas Jordan was released as he had not been a minister in Scotland, having only preached in Ireland. But McColl ordered that the three remaining ministers were to be "kept close" and were not to be released. In such circumstances, there was little prospect of relief for the prisoners and both their spirits and their health sank. The Rev. Weir first complained of illness on 2 October and died on the 16th, aged thirty-four years, leaving Rev. Hamilton and his father-in-law to suffer the cold of winter. In March of 1645, the Rev. Watson also died. In May of 1645, after an imprisonment of ten months, the Rev. James Hamilton was released in an exchange of prisoners.

On his release, and perhaps by way of compensation for his great efforts in Ireland and suffering in prison, the General Assembly transferred James Hamilton from Dumfries to Edinburgh, where he served for fifteen years. During this time he was appointed by the General Assembly to be a chaplain to the King. It was the cause for yet another imprisonment when he was taken prisoner at Eliot in Angus, by troopers under the command of General Monck - who had just taken Dundee. For two years Hamilton lingered in the Tower of London before he was released with no explanation or apology. As with other ministers, at this time, he withdrew from the ministry in Edinburgh and retired to the quiet of the countryside. He died in Edinburgh on 10 March 1666.

The pedigree of the Rev. James Hamilton shows that he is descended from the Duke of Hamilton's family through his great grandfather Archibald Hamilton of Raplock, Lanarkshire; grandfather Rev. Hans Hamilton, Vicar of Dunlop (eldest son of Archibald Hamilton) and father Gawin Hamilton, of Ballygawly, third son of Hans, a merchant in Coleraine who drowned in an accident before his thirtieth birthday. The Rev. James Hamilton came from a family that gave at least thirteen members of the dynasty to the Church while many more served King and Country in high office as members of the Privy Council; Members of Parliament, and gallant soldiers and sailors in the far lands of the British Empire.

Statue of James Renwick
Courtesy of A. Pittendreigh

XXX. James Renwick - the Preacher

Another stalwart of the Covenanters was James Renwick who was born on 15 February 1662 in the village of Moniave, in Nithsdale. His father, Andrew, was a weaver by trade, and his mother Elizabeth Corsan had several children who died young. He was brought up in a Christian family with his mother wholely convinced that he would go into the ministry Perhaps precocious the young James had learned to read the Bible by the time he was six years old and was content to read his book in preference to any other activity. Later he was encouraged to mix with gentlemen's sons and to learn about the world before going to university. His father died 1 February 1679 yet despite this loss at an important time in his young life, he managed to graduate from the University of Edinburgh. A sign of things to come perhaps, but Renwick declined to take the oath of allegiance as part of the graduation ceremony because he was so afraid of offending God and was later graduated privately in Edinburgh

After leaving university he continued his biblical studies and attended both private prayer meetings and conventicles. It was then that he determined for himself the iniquities and defections of some of the ministers of the church. With a new found zeal he decided to be a witness for the Covenant, the turning point coming on 27 July 1681 when he was at the Mercat Cross and watched the execution of Donald Cargill. Here he saw and heard a brave man declare his faith before he was executed, and whose head and hands were hacked off and positioned on the Netherbow Gate alongside Richard Cameron.

Renwick resolved that he would take up the ways of Cargill and Cameron and was soon in contact with the Societies, an eager advocate to do battle against tyranny. In October 1681 he attended a meeting of the Societies and expressed his concern that none were giving formal testimony against hearing the curates, cess paying and owning the king as supreme head of the church. His offer to assist was eagerly accepted and he was soon involved in the working of the Societies and in the publication of "The Act and Apolgetic Declaration of the true Presbyterians of the Church of Scotland" at Lanark on 12 January 1682.

He was sent to Holland, - to Rotterdam, Groenigen and Leeuwarden, to complete his studies as a preacher. Aged twenty-one he was ordained but only after he had convinced the Dutch ministers that he could not accept their Catechism because had sworn a covenant that subscribed to the Confession and Catechism of the Church of Scotland. His was the first ordination in this manner and was an important precedent for the future supply of ministers. Returning to Scotland in 1683 he was very much the patriot burning with fervour ready to adopt the mantel of Richard Cameron and anxious to pursue his ministry. He was soon to be recognised not only as a fervent believer but a fluent and gracious preacher well able to get his point across to the crowds who came to listen to him.

His first conventicle was at Darmead, in the parish of Cambusnethan, Lanarkshire in November 1683 where he preached from the text of the Book of Isaiah that Donald Cargill had used at his last gathering. People came from up to sixteen miles to hear him and began for Renwick four years of ministry before he too was cut down by his persecutors. Into that short life he crammed awe-inspiring deeds. Constantly preaching, he baptised some 600 children in his first year and roamed far and wide to preach at conventicles.

The government saw that the Covenanters had a new leader and began another cycle of repression and persecution of notable figures including Sir Hew Campbell of Cessnock, who was sent to the Bass Rock prison. Captain John Paton of Fenwick was taken and hung in Edinburgh on 9 May 1684 despite the intervention of General Tam Dalziel. Generally there was an increase in demands to take Oaths of loyalty which were enforced by the presence of troops, and liability to heavy fines.

A more invidious weapon of government was to spread lies and slanders about Renwick in which they were aided by the 'Indulged' ministers. He was variously accused of excommunicating all the ministers in Scotland, even some who were dead. He was also accused of promoting schism, of being Sectarian, Independent, an Anabaptist, a blasphemer and a supporter of the Gibbites - a small sect given to strange practices. The general outcry was that he had no mission at all It was against this background that James Renwick issued his "Apologetical Declaration and Admonitory Vindication against Intelligencers and Informers" on 28 October 1684 defending his creed and supporters against many slanders that had been made, and threatening death to spies and collaborators. The declaration was posted by fixing on church doors.

The response from the government was a particularly odious Abjuration Oath, which was cleverly drawn up as a "catch all" measure. The oath enabled any person refusing "on demand" to swear it, to be put to death on the spot in the presence of two witnesses. The application of the new law was at first directed at Covenanters, but within a short time it began to be applied to all Presbyterians in sometimes dubious conditions - such as the use of it to convict and execute the two Margarets (MacLachlan and Wilson) at Wigtown. So began "The Killing Time."

Renwick was not a sturdy man by any means being rather delicate and fragile. Thus the excessive travel, night wanderings, broken sleep and irregular diet were soon to catch up with him and show itself in consumption. Despite poor health, he persevered in preaching at conventicles and had his share of escapes from capture. One such occasion was in July 1684 near Dungavel when he and three companions were surprised by about twenty troopers. His companions were captured but Renwick drove his horse pell-mell towards the crown of a hill where, just before the crest, he threw himself into a hollow in the heather. He fully expected his pursuers to find him but there he lay until sunset when he was able to make his way to a friendly farm about four miles away.

A traditional tale of Renwick is that of travelling to a conventicle in Galloway and putting up the night before at an inn at Newton Stewart. The authorities knew of the imminent gathering and a troop of dragoons had been dispatched to search it out. The commanding officer of the troop, who some say was lost, arrived at the inn and sought shelter for the night but, it being early evening, he then asked if there was company to be had for conversation to pass the time away. Surprisingly, Renwick joined the officer and they passed the evening enjoyably talking of many things. The following morning the officer inquired after his companion of the previous evening and was told that he had left earlier to seek a "hiding place," whereupon it was disclosed that it had been his quarry James Renwick. It is said that the officer was so surprised to learn that Renwick was a harmless and discreet person that he resolved not to pursue him further and returned to his barracks.

On another occasion, Renwick travelled to the village of Balmaclellan in Galloway where he was to preach at a conventicle in a secret place. On the morning the day was clouded and heavy showers were falling in the hills swelling the hill streams and the rivers into which they flowed. Even so the people gathered for the conventicle only to be found by troopers as they began to pray. Renwick and two companions, John McMillan and David Ferguson, fled towards the river Ken intending to cross and go to friends in the Parish of Penninghame. On reaching the river they found it flooded and decided to stop and pray, which they did in the shelter of some bushes. On rising from their knees and about to enter the surging river they were astonished to see pursuing troopers landing on the other side of the river. It seems that the troopers had ridden past the men in the gloom and hurried across the river before it became impassable; whereas if the three had not stopped for prayer they might well have been caught in midstream. Providential intervention, it may well have been, but a second intervention was to follow.

McMillan and Ferguson left Renwick at the river and returned whence they came. Renwick made his way downstream and sought cover for the night, eventually settling on the rock to sleep. He was, however, wakened by the sound of singing and traced it to a shepherd's cottage further down the valley. The owner of the cottage was a James McCulloch, who was not a friend of the Covenanters, but imbued with drink he welcomed Renwick into the home. McCulloch was suspicious, but his wife, a God fearing woman, drew Renwick to one side and made him comfortable in an adjoining bedroom.

Awakening early, he searched for his clothes without success. Mrs. McCulloch had taken them to dry them out and gave him some of her husband's old clothing in the meantime - which was to save his life. Mr. McCulloch had departed the cottage early to take sheep to safer pastures following the night's downpour. Renwick took the opportunity to walk outside and enjoy the air. In passing out of the cottage, he threw across his shoulder an old plaid and was joined by one of the dogs. Thus attired and relaxed enjoying the morning air, he suddenly found himself surrounded by troopers who asked if he was the master of the cottage. Truthfully Renwick said he was not and told them where he might be found. After some conversation about rebels and fugitives the troopers concluded that the river in full flood would have prevented fugitives getting across and they departed leaving a thankful Renwick delivered to safety twice in twenty-four hours.

On 4 September 1684 the Privy Council issued letters of intercommuning against Renwick which required all persons to aid in his arrest, and none were to offer him help or victuals or have "any intelligence with him by word, writ or message ... under pain of being esteemed art and part with him in the crimes aforesaid." It is a measure of the respect that the populace had for him that he eluded capture for over three years after the proclamation.

It was on 28 May 1685 that Renwick with an entourage of some 200 men rode into Sanquhar, as did his predecessor Richard Cameron five years before, to issue a "Protestation and Apologetical Admonitory Declaration" that was similar in content but was particularly to witness against the accession to the throne by James II, a devout Catholic. Renwick then spent some time in the north of England preaching wherever opportunity afforded itself before returning to Scotland in December 1686 to take part in the General Meeting of the United Societies.

Meanwhile the slanders and false accusations continued and had even reached Renwick's supporters in Holland where the Dutch Divine Koelman was turned against him. Elsewhere there was a cool relationship with Alexander Peden, who was also misled by the propaganda. This relationship was, however, mended in a famous reconciliation on Peden's deathbed, and his admission that he was a faithful servant of the Lord.

But there was yet more trouble for Renwick following the proclamations in 1687 tolerating Presbyterians to meet in private houses (12 February). Further proclamations on 28 June and 5 October extended the tolerance to preaching in any house and finally declaring all preachers and hearers in the open fields should be prosecuted with the utmost severity. Renwick now found that he had to bear witness against the granters of the toleration and also the accepters. This led to a veritable storm of invective and

Inscription
on
James Renwick Memorial
Moniaive
Courtesy of A. Pittendreigh

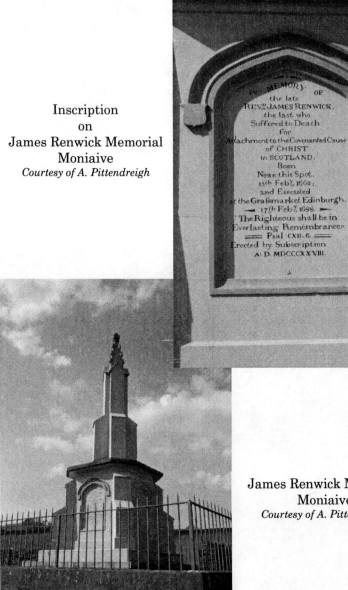

IN MEMORY OF
the late
REVD. JAMES RENWICK,
the last who
Suffered to Death
For
Attachment to the Covenanted Cause
of CHRIST
in SCOTLAND:
Born
Near this Spot,
15th Feby. 1662;
and Executed
at the Grassmarket Edinburgh.
17th Feby. 1688.
"The Righteous shall be in
Everlasting Remembrance"
Psal. CXII. 6.
Erected by Subscription
A: D. MDCCCXXVIII.

James Renwick Memorial
Moniaive
Courtesy of A. Pittendreigh

accusations that he had done more to hurt the Church of Scotland than its enemies had in the past twenty years.

The time finally came when in December 1687 he was overheard in an Edinburgh house and recognised. This came about because he had lodged with a friend in Castle Hill who was a smuggler and was under observation by Customs officers. A John Justice, officer, heard the family at prayer and recognised their visitor. The next day access was made to the house on the pretence of searching for uncustomed goods. Renwick fled from the house but was seized and handed over to the City Guard who dispatched him to prison.

Renwick was highly-strung and fearful of torture, unsure that he could sustain the pain but his accusers, the Privy Council, were mindful of his martyrdom and effect on the people. He was condemned on three charges - refusal to accept the King's authority; refusal to pay the cess (tax) to his Majesty; and, counselling his followers to come to meetings armed. Renwick pleaded guilty and declined offers of pardon and release right to the end. Curiously he was allowed to say whatever he wished in his appearances before the Privy Council and the justiciary. In prison itself he was visited by very many people including the Lord Advocate, various Indulged ministers, friars and bishops. Given this exceptional treatment and the history of duplicity by the government it is suspected that there was an ulterior motive possibly to turn Renwick and get him to recant. He was even requested by the chief jailor not to make a speech at his execution and offered him his life if he would sign a petition. Renwick replied that he had never read in the Scriptures "that martyrs petitioned for their lives, when called to suffer for truth."

Several times attempts were made to interrupt his last words but he persevered in explaining why he was to die for his faith, his objections to the usurper, James II, the paying of a tax that was collected specifically to fund religious oppression, and for teaching that it was lawful for people to carry arms in order to defend themselves. Thus on 17 February 1688, just three days after his twenty-sixth birthday, he was executed in the Grassmarket, Edinburgh. His head and hands were affixed above the Netherbow Gate alongside other Martyrs of the Covenant.

Before the year was out, the Stuarts were in exile and persecution had ended. Although Renwick was the last of the preachers to die for their faith, the very last Covenanter to be martyred was a sixteen-year-old youth, George Boyd, shot down by a trooper in an Ayrshire field in the summer of 1688.

A final word on Renwick comes from Viscount Tarbet, one of his prosecutors, who said

> *He was one of the stiffest maintainers of his principles that ever came before us ... we could never make him yield or vary in the least ... if he had lived in Knox's day (he) would not have died by any laws then in being.*

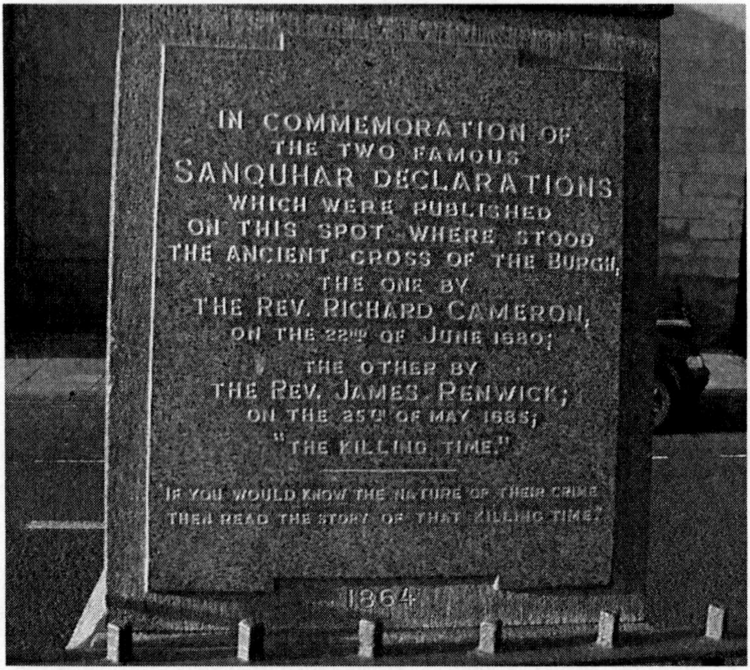

Inscription of the
Cameron and Renwick Memorial
Sanquhar
Courtesy of A. Pittendreigh

XXXI. Richard Cameron - The Lion of the Covenant

The Battle of Bothwell Brig on 22 June 1679 had a great effect upon the Covenanters in general and a silence seemed to come down on their protestations with the government. To many it resolved into bickering between themselves and temporarily few voices were raised in support of the ideals of the Covenant. Richard Cameron, later to be called "The Lion of the Covenant," was one voice that rose loud and clear.

Richard Cameron was born circa 1648 in the ancient town of Falkland in Fifeshire where his father, Allan Cameron, was a merchant. His mother was Margaret Paterson. He had two younger brothers, Michael and Alexander, and a sister Marion. After graduating from university in 1665 he was a schoolmaster in Falkland where he became interested in the field preachers. In particular he attended a number of conventicles at which John Welsh of Irongray, preached which resulted in his conversion to the Covenanter beliefs. Cameron was convinced that it was a sin to accept the Indulgences (concessions given by the King) and became a vociferous "root and branch" believer and amongst the most inflexible members of the movement.

For a while he continued as tutor to the family of Sir William Scot of Harden in Roxburghshire, but he left to join with John Welsh who urged him to become a licensed preacher. This was done at the home of Henry Hall of Haughhead and he was sent to begin his preaching in Annandale. Cameron gained a reputation for being outspoken and this sometimes created concern among colleagues who reproved him and urged that he preach on the evangelical themes to which they all agreed. It appears that Cameron was keen to be ordained and knew that it would be easier to do this abroad, thus in May 1679 (before Drumclog and Bothwell Brig), he went to Holland and joined with the exiled ministers John Brown of Wamphray and Robert MacWard.

Despite his reputation for attacking the Indulgence, Cameron preached well and was ordained in Rotterdam by the Dutch divine, Pastor James Koelman, Brown and MacWard. Here, again, was a prophetic statement made when at the laying on of hands during ordination, MacWard was the last to remove his hands and before doing so said,

> *Behold, all ye beholders, here is the head of a faithful minister and servant of Jesus Christ who shall lose the same for his Master's interest, and shall be set up before sun and moon in the public view of the world.*

In October 1679 Cameron returned to Scotland and began his ministry in Clydesdale and Ayrshire. He had occasional help from other ministers but, following the battle at Bothwell Brig, there was very great pressure on ministers and none would publicly preach. Cameron, therefore, became a mainly solitary figure preaching at conventicles throughout the south west of Scotland. His principal colleagues in these difficult times were Donald Cargill and Thomas Douglas. Many of his conventicles took place on Darmead Linn, a hill to the south of Shotts, near the village of Forth. It was here that he drafted the Sanquhar Declaration, which he and his brother Michael posted in the town on 22 June 1680. A bold and uncompromising document, its closing words make clear that war had been declared:

As also we, under the banner of our Lord Jesus Christ, the Captain of Salvation, do declare a war with such a tyrant and usurper, and all the men of these practices, as enemies to our Lord Jesus Christ and His cause and covenant.

There was also a maturity about his ministry as he became the man who denounced the despotism of the Royal house, directing his wrath against the worst offenders in the land. It also meant that there was a reward for him dead or alive.

Richard Cameron preached his last sermon on 18 July at Kype Water about seven miles south of Strathaven where his sermon was "Be still, and know that I am God." On 21 July 1680, Cameron spent the night at the farm of William Mitchell of Meadowhead, Water of Ayr. With him were his bodyguard of about forty persons on foot and twenty-three horsemen who rested on the moor nearby. The tale is told that rising in the morning Cameron washed his face and hands in the trough outside and remarked prophetically that, "This is their last washing. I have need to make them clean, for there are many to see them."

Cameron knew that there was a party looking for him and meanwhile, Sir John Cochrane of Ochiltree informed Bruce of Earlshall, a Fife property owner, where they might be found. At about four o'clock on the afternoon of Thursday 22 July some 120 troops under the command of Bruce came upon Cameron and his group at Ayrsmoss, a bleak stretch of open moorland being over 650 feet in altitude at one end and rising to nearly 730 feet at the other. There was no escaping and the band gathered round Richard Cameron to pray, ending in the three times repeated cry, "Lord, spare the green and take the ripe."

Turning to his brother, Michael, he remarked, "... this is the day we will get the Crown."

With only twenty-three horsemen in Cameron's small force, eight were posted to the right under Robert Dick and fifteen under the command of the redoubtable David Hackston of Rathillet to the left. As the troopers neared, some twenty were seen to dismount and started to encircle to attack from the rear. A party on foot was sent to intercept while the main group advanced with Hackston leading the fight. Despite a valiant stand the Covenanters were outnumbered and nine horsemen lay dead, including Richard Cameron aged barely thirty-two, and his brother Michael.

Five prisoners were taken - Manual of Shotts who died of his wounds at the Tolbooth in Edinburgh, John Vallance who died the next day; Archibald Alison and John Malcolm who were executed at the Grassmarket, Edinburgh on 13 August; and David Hackston who was to suffer the most brutal of executions. But chief amongst the battle's trophies were the head and hands of Richard Cameron, which were delivered in triumph to the Privy Council in Edinburgh. Old Allan Cameron, the father, was then a prisoner in the Tolbooth. He had been locked up for assisting conventicles to be held near his home in Falkland. He was shown the head and hands and was left weeping for his son as they took the trophies to be fixed above the Netherbow Gate with the hands in prayer beneath the severed head - a gruesome warning for all Covenanters.

Others who died at Ayrsmoss were John Gemmel; John Hamilton; James Gray, eldest son of Gray of Chryston; Robert Dick; Captain John Fowler; whose head was taken to Edinburgh having been mistaken for Michael Cameron; Thomas Watson and Robert Paterson of Kirkhill in the parish of Cambusnethan - a pious and zealous youth.

Little is known of the other brother Alexander, save that he became a Covenanting minister studying theology in Holland, where he remained until 1688 when he was in

Utrecht. The sister Marion and two companions were brutally murdered by Claverhouse's troopers who had caught them as they fled across the moors towards Daljig, a farm near New Cumnock. It is said that the troopers callously offered to let the girls go if they burned their Bibles, knowing full well that they would not do so. Inevitably the dragoons then charged their rifles and shot them down on the spot.

With the wonderful sense of hindsight, we might question why Richard Cameron pursued such a violent campaign and the need for his death. There is no doubt that the King really had broken pledges and promises and given every reason for the people to renounce allegiance. A less direct confrontation with the government might have given time for the people to rally to the cause and saved Richard Cameron from an early death. Be that as it may, his death at Ayrsmoss helped the more cautious to focus on the need for reform and sent signals of a revolution that was to occur in 1689.

XXXII. John MacMillan of Balmaghie - First Minister of the Reformed Presbyterian Church

Although the "Killing Times" had passed and Presbyterianism in Scotland was firmly established with the succession of William and Mary to the throne, there were still rumblings in the Church. There was the wish, by some to maintain a strict form of worship and management as propounded by Richard Cameron and James Renwick, and their successors, the Societies. In time, a new leader was to emerge in the form of the Rev. John MacMillan.

John MacMillan was born at Barncauchlaw, Minnigaff in 1669 and graduated from Edinburgh University in June 1697. He was ordained on 18 September 1701 and was in fact the second of that name to be a minister in the parish of Balmaghie, in Galloway. His predecessor was not related and seems to have been a sickly man who died 26 July 1700 aged only thirty-seven years. But John MacMillan, often referred to as "alter" (meaning second), was industrious with a high regard for doing his duty. An early task, for example, was to review the arrangement and duties of the elders; determine what property there was belonging to the church and the arrangements for collecting and handling charitable donations and welfare of the poor. Today we might compare this to a new tenant checking the inventory for all the property for which he was responsible.

In 1702 the Synod of Galloway requested ministers to explain the National Covenant of 1638 to their congregations, which John MacMillan did, but he also explained to them the nature and objectives of the Solemn League and Covenant of 1643. The distinction he made was that the National Covenant was intended to counter Popery while the Solemn League and Covenant was of wider scope being for religion, King and the "peace and safety" of the three kingdoms. He was opposed in principle to the "Revolution Settlement" of 1690 because and in spite of Presbyterianism being the religion of Scotland, there was still prelacy in England and Ireland, and Catholicism was granted considerable toleration. In Scotland, the General Assembly could not meet without royal approval. This situation was not what the hardened Covenanters thought was right and was the reason for MacMillan's stand. In July 1703, he petitioned the Presbytery to assert the Divine Right of Presbyterian Church Government - the right of the Church courts to manage their own affairs and the Headship of Christ over the Church.

The fall out from Revolution had hardly settled before King William III died on 8 March 1702. This left Queen Anne on the throne and raised the hopes of the Jacobites and ushered in yet another round of civil interference in the Presbyterian Church. This began with a letter to the General Assembly from the Queen in 1703, which seemed to deny that the scriptures underpinned Presbyterianism and the way it was organised in church courts. The Assembly replied that Presbyterianism was agreeable to the Word of God and most conducive to the advancement of true religion and godliness. Later, while in session reviewing the actions of the Synods and about to approve them, the Queen's Commissioner, Lord Seaforth abruptly dissolved the Assembly. As one would expect, this attempt to control the proceedings of the courts of the Church caused alarm among the earnest evangelical ministers such as John MacMillan.

The Presbytery was not of such stern stuff and sought to get John MacMillan to withdraw his petition, and when he would not, they appointed a visitation of his congregation to take place on 30 December 1703. The purpose of this visit was not visitation, but to charge him with libel and following divisive policies. MacMillan did not know of the action, but when the charge was passed to the Presbytery officer to be read out, he got hold of it, read it to his audience and demanded that they produce evidence if they had any. None was forthcoming and the meeting eventually broke up with MacMillan continuing to defy the visitation members.

There then followed a disgraceful act, where some members went to the neighbouring Crossmichael church, reconvened the meeting of the Presbytery and deposed MacMillan from his ministry. That they did this without summoning him before the meeting was completely illegal and served to show the Jacobite sympathies and the malleability of the new Moderatism that was creeping into the Church. MacMillan responded to the Presbytery with apologies and remained silent for about a year but, despairing of getting any redress, stood up after the sermon one Sabbath and declared that he would preach the following week.

From then on, for some twenty-six years, he ministered within the parish, simply ignoring the committee and its ruling, and continuing to preach and live in the manse. Notably, the congregation stayed with him and when a new minister was sought to replace MacMillan in 1710 only nine parishioners signed his call - some eighty-seven heads of households and young men protested against the appointment. During this time he also married Mary Gordon, daughter of Sir Alexander Gordon of Earlstoun and widow of Edward Goldie of Craigmuie, an event that would not have been possible if the charges made against him had any substance.

Shortly after his deposition, the General Meeting of the Societies invited him to a meeting, which he attended.

Several more meetings took place and on 10 October 1706 he received a call to be their minister. MacMillan saw where his duty lay and on 2 December 1706 he began by preaching at Crawfordjohn. Although the members of the Society were widely scattered, MacMillan visited them regularly, but it was the widespread nature of his new parish that stretched from Galloway to Fife that eventually caused him to leave Balmaghie in 1729 and reside in Dalry.

The break from the Established Church can be dated from when he and John McNeil published, on 29 September 1708, a "Protestation Declinature and Appeal" which was sent to Edinburgh setting out in strong terms the evils of the Church and the State. MacMillan continued preaching, assisted by John McNeil until he died in 1722 having been a licentiate, i.e., not ordained a minister for sixty-three years. MacMillan continued alone for the next twenty-one years until he was joined in the ministry by the Rev. Thomas Nairn. Expelled from the Associate Presbytery for holding similar views to MacMillan, Nairn's coming allowed for the formation of the Reformed Presbytery on 1 August 1743 at Braehead.

An important event for both the Societies in Scotland and their brethren in Ulster was the decision to renew the National Covenant and the Solemn League and Covenant in 1712. This took place at Auchensaugh and was because they objected to the Union between Scotland and England (1707) and the Act of Toleration (1712) which gave legal protection to Episcopalian worship in Scotland. This took several days to effect as each member swore with uplifted hands to each and every article of the two Covenants. These Covenants were renewed again in 1745.

MacMillan's ministry was of an old style and characterised by his incessant visiting of his parishioners, not for social chitchat but for prayer and catechising. This he did both in Balmaghie and in his greater parish of the Society. He also, for a time, preached in the fields, houses and barns and was much sought after to lay hands on babies, even though some might then be baptised by a regular minister. The physical drain on MacMillan, who was on his own from 1722, was enormous. Although viciously attacked in assorted pamphlets over the years, MacMillan seems to have bitten his tongue, or turned the other cheek perhaps. One can only guess that these vitriolic criticisms, even libelous statements, received the contempt they deserved.

MacMillan died at his brother's house at Broomhill, Bothwell on 1 December 1753 in his eighty-fourth year, and was buried in Dalserf where he had resided since moving from Clydesdale in August 1727. John MacMillan had no children from his first marriage to Jean Gemble, who died in 1711, aged thirty-eight years. The passing of his second wife on 5 May 1723, aged forty-three years, left MacMillan on his own once more. He then married circa 1725 to Grace Russell by whom he had five children.

Josias, born 1726, died 7 February 1740, aged thirteen years

Kathren, born 1727, died 17 February 1736, aged eight years.

John, born 1729

Grizel, born 1731, died 1767.

Alexander Jonita (Janet), born 1734 and died aged six months.

Josias, Kathren and Janet are buried in Dalserf churchyard.

Grizel MacMillan married John Galloway of Sandyhills, near Glasgow and had two sons and a daughter, Elizabeth, who married John Grieve, a surgeon in Inverkeithing. When John Galloway died in 1764, Grizel married the Rev. John Thorburn, minister at the Reformed Presbyterian Church in Pentland. Grizel died in 1767 leaving an infant daughter.

John MacMillan II, born in 1729, married twice, having six children by his first marriage and twelve by the second.

A daughter married the Rev. Thomas Rowatt, minister at Scaurbridge Cameronian Church in Penpont. His ministry is memoralized in Shettleston churchyard where a monument records that he died 11 February 1808 aged seventy-nine years, and in the fifty-eighth year of his ministry.

John MacMillan III, son of John MacMillan, of Sandhills was born in 1750 and became minister at Sterling. He died 20 October 1818. Like his father and grandfather before him, he preached the firm line of the Covenant.

It is not often that a man can leave a living monument, but in John MacMillan's case, his son the Rev. John MacMillan of Sandhills, and his grandson, the Rev. John MacMillan of Stirling, followed him as ministers, between them giving over 100 years of continuous preaching of the Covenanted gospel.

Campbelltown Harbour
from which many migrants sailed the twenty-one miles to Ulster

Part III
The Ulster Scots and Presbyterianism

XXXIII. The Ulster Scots - a Historical Snapshot

It's a tangled web the Ulster Scots weave. To understand their widespread migration it is necessary to be aware of the changes that were taking place in England, Scotland and Ireland in the sixteenth, seventeenth and eighteenth centuries. Not only was there religious discrimination depending on whether the King or Queen was Catholic or Protestant but Ireland had become part of the English lands under Henry VII. This meant that until 1707 Scotland was a foreign country. Thus England was concerned with its safety along its borders with Scotland and Ireland whilst there was the ever-present threat of war with France, Holland and Spain. In some ways the English Parliament tended to regard Ireland as a sideshow and this contributed to the problems.

There had been a long tradition of the "galloglass" or mercenary Scots soldiers employed in Ireland since the thirteenth century; and, there was a regular flow of people across the twenty-one miles of sea between Scotland and Ireland. It was not therefore, too surprising that when King James VI of Scotland became King James I of England in 1603, there was a major change of direction in Ireland. He saw that by placing loyal Scottish Protestants into Ireland, he could also remove a lot of his problems on the Scottish - English border where the "Border Reivers", (reiver means thief) had run riot for generations. Also called "the riding clans" there were a number of families involved, including Armstrong, Elliott, Irvine, Graham, Nixon, and Johnson, who lived by pillaging the populace on both sides of the Border. James dealt with the Reivers very harshly, transporting some to Connacht in the west of Ireland, and hanging others. He also saw the opportunity to encourage the Presbyterian "Dissenters" in Scotland to move across the Irish Sea. When the Irish Earls fled from Ireland in 1607, their lands were seized and redistributed to people that would be loyal to the throne. This became the Plantation of Ulster.

The Montgomery and Hamilton settlement of Co. Antrim and Co. Down

The Scottish migration to Ireland was initiated by the granting of land to two Scottish families - Hugh Montgomery, Sixth Laird of Braidstone, Ayrshire, and Sir James Hamilton from Ayr. They were courtiers who used their position close to the King to privately acquire land in Counties Down and Antrim before the formal Plantation scheme commenced in 1610. There was much wheeling and dealing after the first allotments were made in 1603, but, by 1606 the situation was resolved and settlement began in earnest with both taking Scottish settlers with them to their new estates. Their efforts were rewarded by the exclusion of these two counties from the later Plantation scheme, because they had already accomplished the substantial Scottish - Protestant settlement that James I of England (VI of Scotland) desired.

Sir James Hamilton, later Viscount Clandeboye, came from the Dunlop area of Ayrshire, where his father was the Rev. Hans Hamilton. The family had owned lands in Raploch, Lanarksshire for some 400 years, which they seemed to have lost at some stage hence James's enthusiasm for taking up as much he could in Antrim and Down. He was the eldest of six sons James, Archibald,

Gawin, John, William and Patrick. He was largely tutored by James Ussher, later the Bishop of Meath and Archbishop of Armagh.

Hugh Montgomery was the eldest son of Adam, fifth Earl of Braidstane born ca. 1560 and made Viscount Montgomery of the Great Ards in 1622. The Montgomery lands and the lordship of Braidstane were in the bailliary of Kyle, in Ayrshire. Until the middle of the seventeenth century, the lands were within the Parish of Beith, consisting of two divisions - Braidstane and Giffen. There were changes to boundaries after 1649.

The Montgomery Manuscripts, written as memoirs by William Montgomery, son of Hugh, quotes some details of tenants. He says that, "No lists of original settlers can be found." Among them were several named Orr, who originally settled in the town lands of Ballyblack and Ballykeel, and were the progenitors of a very numerous connexion of this surname throughout the Ards. This is borne out by the genealogy of James Orr and Janet McClement by Gawin Orr ca. 1828 now in the Linen Hall, Belfast. A later work by Ray A Jones (1977), entitled *Ulster Pedigrees, Descendants, in Many Lines, of James Orr and Janet McClement, Who emigrated from Scotland to Northern Ireland ca. 1607* builds on Gawin Orr's earlier work and is a valuable reference for the Orrs. The families related to the Orrs by marriage are listed at Appendix 9.

The Montgomery Manuscripts go on to record that in June 1606, settlers began to arrive, including the brothers of Sir James Hamilton - Gawin and John. Other families included Maxwell, Rose, Barclay, More and Baylie. On the Montgomery lands, settlers included John (or James) Shaw of Greenock, brother of Sir Hugh's wife Elizabeth Shaw; Patrick Montgomery of Black House or Craigbowie (husband of Christian Shaw, sister of Elizabeth, and thus Hugh Montgomery's brother-in-law) and Cunningham of Glengarnock - related to the Shaws. George Montgomery, brother of Hugh, was appointed to bishoprics of Derry, Raphoe and Clogher in 1605. Significantly (for the

Montgomery's) in 1607, tenants began to arrive to settle church lands. Proclamations in Glasgow, Ayr, Irvine, Greenock and other southwestern parts of Scotland, especially around Braidstone, declared leased land on easy terms. This drew numbers of Scots to Donegal and Londonderry

The main destination for the Scottish settlers during the seventeenth century was the former MacDonnell lands in Antrim and the Baronies of Dunluce and Glenarm. In Co. Down, the Hamilton and Montgomery estates were the main Scottish locations up to about 1614. Hamilton recruited tenants for his Cavan estates from Clandeboye, while some lands passed to tenants, who themselves recruited Scots. Thereafter, further land disputes probably adversely influenced further growth. This period also saw the Incorporation of Bangor, Newtown and Killyleagh to ensure there was a protestant majority.

Most of the burgesses came from the Scottish Lowlands with about 200 - 300 males in Co. Down by 1614. In all it is estimated that some 10,000 Scotsmen were brought to Ireland by the Montgomery and Hamilton plantations. Under the patronage of George Montgomery, more influence in the Church was exercised by the appointment of Scottish Bishops - Andrew Knox became Bishop of Raphoe, in 1610. There were seven ministers from Scotland in 1612 and fifteen ministers, of which twelve were from Scotland, in 1622.

An important side issue was the denizations granted to Scots. Denization was a patent from the King giving the rights and privileges of an Englishman and therefore making the person eligible to have title to land. Thus there were some 300 denizations approved and 300 Scots families planted in 1619. The Montgomery Manuscripts lists many 'substantial persons' who were granted denization in 1617 and settled on Sir Hugh Montgomery's estate ten years earlier (Appendix 8).

Scottish land allocations 1610

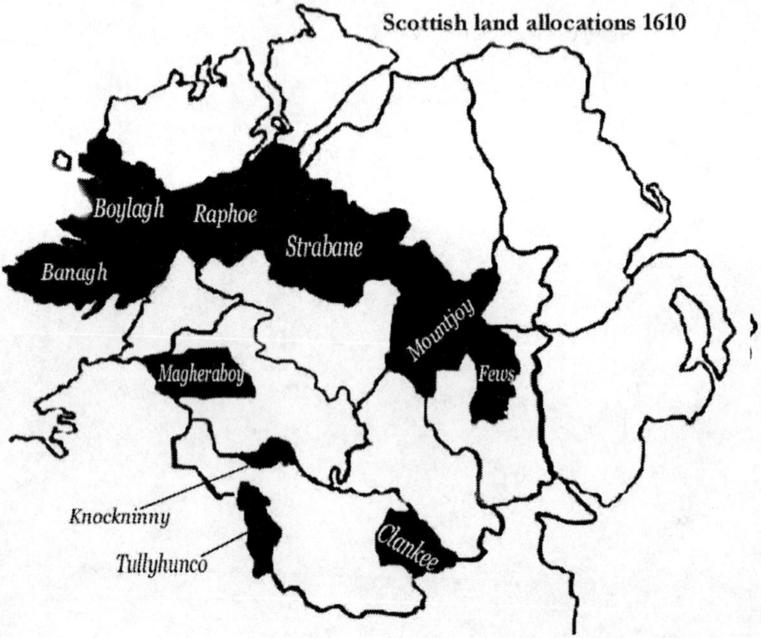

The Plantation Scheme 1610 - 1630

The principle of "Planting" peoples on sequestered land evolved from Henry VIII's accession to the throne of Ireland in 1541 and it was under his policy of "Surrender and Regrant" of lands that the Irish princes received English titles - O'Neill became Earl of Tyrone; O'Brien Earl of Thomond; and Macwilliam Burke of Galway, Earl of Clanrickard. Under Edward VI, a more aggressive policy led to seizure of lands in reprisal for insurrection and in 1556, under Queen Mary, a plantation scheme for most of Leix and Offaly was declared with the counties being renamed Queens County and Kings County. The policy of seizure and grant to English landlords continued under Elizabeth I.

On 4 September 1607 the Earls of Tyrone and Tyrconnel, with thirty relatives and sixty friends and followers, fled into exile. These included Maquire, owner of half Fermanagh, It was decided that all the lands of Shane O'Neill were forfeit and as a result, large portions of Tyrone Donegal, Coleraine, Armagh, Cavan and Fermanagh became available for plantation. On 29 September 1607 the Privy Council approved the Plantation scheme.

A rebellion, of sorts, by Sir Cahir O'Dogherty on 19 April 1608 led to the sacking of Londonderry and the use of Scottish levies from Ayr to take Carrickfergus - the first use of Scottish troops by the English for conquest abroad. The troops remained and became a further source of tenants. When Derry was granted to the City of London in 1610, among the southwestern Scots who were compensated were Boyd, Patterson and Wray. In January 1609 proposals were made for the plantation of Tyrone, which evolved and became the plan for the division of all the escheated lands in the six Counties. This led to the 1610 Scheme.

A Proclamation of the Plantation in Ulster was made by the Scottish Council on 8 March 1609. The applicants tended to come from within twenty-five miles of Edinburgh; and were generally persons of substance. They were also seen to be by way of family ventures with mutual action taken as cautioners or guarantors for one another. It was the urban middle class and petty gentry who were most enthusiastic. In all, the Scottish undertakers received some 81,000 acres. The nine baronies set aside for the Scots were mainly around the periphery of the seized lands. They were Boylagh, Banagh and Portlough in Donegal; Strabane and Mountjoy in Tyrone; Knockninny, Magheraboy in Fermanagh; Clankee and Tullyhunco in Cavan; and, the northern half of The Fews in Armagh.

The Plantation "Undertakers," were so called because they had to undertake to build fortified barns and houses and populate the land with English and Scottish Protestants. These same settlers, of course, formed a loyal armed force - yeoman soldiers, in times of disturbance. This was a device to keep the indigenous people and the Catholics under control. Thousands of Scots went to Ulster with the Plantation. At much the same time in Scotland, there was religious discrimination against Presbyterians in particular who dissented from the official faith and rule by the bishops. There was also a deliberate and ongoing policy of repressing the Gaelic traditions and language while also "clearing" the Highlands with many small crofters forced off their land. In 1650 there was another major redistribution of lands in Ireland, when Cromwell offered land in lieu of wages to his soldiery - many took the offer and sold the lands on without themselves even visiting their allotment. In later years, many of these Ulster Scots, subsequently migrated to the English Colonies in America.

The Scottish origin of the undertakers influenced migration, and to a large degree, the family location of many Scots. In the early days these were:

Donegal	-	Cunningham, Campbell
Fermanagh		Home, Johnston, Armstrong, Elliot, Little Irving, Beaty - all Border

	names.
Tyrone	Stewart, Hamilton, Elliott, Armstrong, Johnson, Graham, Scot, Irving.
Antrim	Stewart, Boyd, Hamilton
Down	In the 1630 muster: 53 Montgomerys, 44 Hamiltons, then Campbells (Ayrshire - Hamilton estates) Johnston, Kennedy, Scot, Bell, Maxwell, Gibson, Dixon, McKee - mainly from the vicinity of Ayr, Renfrew, Wigtown and Lanark.

The Muster Rolls of 1630 provide a basis for analysing the extent of Scottish migration. The extant Rolls show a total of 13,147 adult males, which suggests a total population in excess of 30,000 of which about sixty per cent were Scottish.

The early settlers were by no means going to a land of milk and honey. While it is true there was fertile land that would yield good crops they first had to construct a home and learn to handle the attacks and stealing by the native Irish 'wood kerne'. The *Montgomery Manuscripts* tells that Sir Hugh "brought with him divers artificers, as smiths, masons, carpenters etc. They soon made cottages and booths for themselves, because sods and saplins of ashes, alders and birch trees (above 30 years old) with rushes for thatch, and bushes for wattles, were at hand." In the north of County Down, in the area of Newtownards, the Montgomery settlers were fortunate to have available building stone from quarries at Scrabo and slate quarries were opened at Greyabbey, Bangor, Ballywalter and Ballydunlady in Castlereagh. The result was that the town of Newtownards was exceptional for its day with neat houses and paved streets. Elsewhere the houses were often built of 'cage work' with large trees used to make the frames and the smaller branches for wattles to fill the spaces in between, then sods of earth would be overlaid.

This method was learnt from the native Irish who adopted this sort of dwelling so that they could easily follow the herds of cattle.

The 'wood kerne' were Irish who had over generations been driven off the land as far back as the Anglo Norman times, and forced to live in the woods. From their refuge they made sorties on farms stealing cattle and anything else that took their fancy. They were not averse to murder, often as revenge on the new occupants of 'their' land. At the time of the Plantation there were also soldiers who had served under Hugh O'Neill hiding in the woods which exacerbated the problem. The existence of the 'wood kerne' was the reason for building strong farm buildings and the high walled yards, called bawns, to hold the cattle safely overnight.

XXXIV. Presbyterians in Ireland - So many Oaths to take

Presbyterianism was not new to Ireland as there had been members of the faith in prominent posts since the time of Queen Elizabeth I. It began as an organised faith with ministers brought to Ulster by the Montgomery and Hamilton families to County Antrim and County Down Although the Presbyterian Covenanters were essentially Scottish and were bloodily persecuted in the later years of the seventeenth century, their Presbyterian brethren who migrated to Ireland were also subjected to persecution by those in authority and suffered their own "Killing Time" in 1641. With hindsight, it is quite remarkable just how many times successive governments cynically sought to use an Oath as a device for coercing the Presbyterians, surely knowing that it would be rejected and thereby give them the option to resort to force.

The *Montgomery Manuscripts* mention that Sir Hugh Montgomery brought with him from Scotland two or three chaplains. These were probably David McGill and James Montgomery. The third was probably David Maxill of Gray Abbey who is mentioned in a grant of 1629.

Yet among all this care and indefatigable industry for their families, a place of God's honour to dwell in was not forgotten or neglected, for indeed our forefathers were more pious than ourselves, and so soon as said stump of the old castle was so repaired (as it was in spring time, i6o6), as might be shelter for that year's summer and harvest, for Sir Hugh and for his servants that winter, his piety made some good store of provisions in those fair seasons, towards roofing and fitting the chancel of that church, for the worship of God; and therein he needed not withdraw his own planters from working for themselves, because there were Irish Gibeonets and Garrons [ponies] enough in his woods to hewand draw timber for the sanctuary ; and the general free contribution of the planters, some with money, others with handicraft and many with labouring, was so great and willingly given, that the next year after this, viz. in 1607, before winter it was made decently serviceable, and Sir Hugh had brought over at first two or three chaplains with him for these parishes. In summer, 1608, some of the priory walls were roofed and fitted for his Lady and children and servants (which were many) to live in.

The settlers were mainly from Ayrshire and would have sought a pastor of their choosing at an early date. The *Hamilton Manuscripts* record that Sir James Hamilton, later the Viscount Claneboye, settled ministers in all six parishes within his estates. The first full time minister was Edward Brice, who came to Broadisland in 1613, having been forced to flee persecution in Scotland because of his vehement objections to episcopacy and an alleged charge of adultery.

Bearing in mind that one of the main objections of the Presbyterians was the rule of the bishops; their early years in Ulster enjoyed the benign influence of Archbishop James Ussher. As Professor of Divinity at Trinity College in Dublin, he had drawn up a Confession of Faith in 1615, which was adopted by convocation of the clergy. This Confession was Calvinistic in many ways admitting the validity of ordination by presbyters and made no demand for superiority of episcopacy. The Irish Church, therefore, presented itself as Presbyterian in theory and Episcopalian in form with bishops willing to act as presbyters for the ordination of ministers. Indeed ministers from Scotland were accepted without the need for preordination such as William Dyall who went to the Parish of Donoghenry (Stewartstown) in 1615.

First Presbyterian Congregation of Larne,

NOW KNOWN AS THE

Old Presbyterian Congregation of Larne and Kilwaughter.

The Old Meeting House, Larne Congregation founded ca 1625

This set of compromises allowed the Presbyterians to conduct their worship, receive the church tithes and to coexist with the established church. Soon Edward Brice was joined by Robert Cunningham at Holywood and Craigavad (1615); John Ridge at Antrim (1619); Josias Welsh, the grandson of John Knox, first at Oldstone then at Templepatrick (1626); the Rev. John Hubbard from Southwark, London, who brought his congregation with him to Carrickfergus (1621); James Glendinning who replaced Hubbard at Carrickfergus (1623); Robert Blair at Bangor (1623): George Dunbar at Larne (1625); James Hamilton at Ballywalter (1625); Andrew Stewart at Donegore (1627); Henry Colwort (or Calvert) at Oldcastle (1630) and John Livingston at Killinchy (1630). There were also Irish born ministers who were Presbyterians, such as

Jeremiah O'Quinn and Owen O'Conolly, who in 1641 saved Dublin Castle from falling into the hands of the rebels. Some of these ministers accepted Church of Ireland livings, although Blair, Welsh and Livingston ministered for many years in the Presbyterian form and without an organised Presbytery.

The peaceful coexistence of the Presbyterian ministers with the Church of Ireland was shattered by the resurgence of the bishops seeking control. At the centre of the drama were Robert Blair and John Livingston who were suspended by Bishop Echlin in 1632. Things came to a head in August 1636 when five of the ministers - Brice, Ridge, Cunningham, Calvert and Hamilton were summoned before the Bishop of Down and required to explain their refusal to accept episcopacy. They were unable, in all conscience, to accept the bishop's rule and were sentenced to "perpetual silence within this diocese." Against this background, Livingston, Blair, McClelland and Cunningham had meanwhile been exploring the possibilities with other Presbyterians and the Massachusetts colony of migration and had organised the building of the ship, the "*Eaglewing.*" But even here they were thwarted in 1636 by bad weather and the migrants had to return to Ireland and a growing persecution.

The Black Oath

The arrival of Thomas Wentworth, later Earl of Strafford, as Lord Lieutenant of Ireland in 1633 saw the onset of his agenda to drive Presbyterians out of Ulster. People began to be persecuted for simply being Presbyterian - a Mrs. Pont, a minister's wife, was sent to prison for three years. Lady Clotworthy was summoned before a court to explain herself; Sir Robert Adair was indicted for treason, lost all his property and had to flee to Scotland; Henry Stewart, a wealthy landowner, was fined a total of £16,000 - a huge amount of money at that time (over one million pounds sterling or one and a half million US dollars at today's values).

The Presbyterians were then subjected to the "Black Oath" which required an open-ended declaration of loyalty to the King to follow any of his commands, and denouncing all covenants including the National Covenant. The oath originated from King Charles I who saw it as a further means to secure his cause in Ulster. It was suggested to Wentworth in January 1639 who then agreed with the king that failure to swear to the oath should result in the seizure of their lands. In a proclamation on 26 May 1639 it was ordered that all Scottish residents in Ulster over the age of sixteen was required to take the oath and was imposed equally on men and women. The only exception was those Scots who professed to be Roman Catholics.

This was followed up by Episcopalian ministers and churchwardens having to produce a return of all Scots who lived in their vicinity and whether they had taken the Oath. Those who had not sworn or who declined especially the latter part of the oath regarding 'any commands' were reported to the authorities. There followed many imprisonments and people began seeking refuge in the forests and caves. Thousands fled to Scotland leaving their houses and properties to ruin and the harvest not taken in.

The wording of the Black Oath given in *The Hamilton Manuscripts* is:

I --- do faithfully swear, profess and promise, that I will honour and obey my sovereign lord King Charles and will bear faith and true allegiance unto him, and defend and maintain his Royal power and authority, and that I will not bear arms, or do any rebellious or hostile act against him, or protest against any of his Royal commands, but submit myself in all due obedience thereunto: and that I will not enter into any covenant, oath or bond of mutual defence and assistance against any persons whatsoever, by force, without his Majesty's sovereign and regal authority.

And I do renounce and abjure all covenants, oaths and bands whatsoever, contrary to what I have herein sworn, professed, and promised. So help me God, in Christ Jesus.

By 1630 the Plantation programme was faltering badly not least because of money problems in the City of London. In Ulster, undertakers had not done enough to set up fortifications and bawns (fortified yards to keep cattle safe from four legged wolves and two legged rustlers), nor had quotas of British settlers been met, rents were high; customs duties at the main ports were high and trade was declining. A cause celebre at this time was the trial of the City of London and the associated Irish Society for mismanagement and neglect of the Londonderry Plantation. The trial occurred between 28 January and 28 February 1635 before the infamous 'Star Chamber' court. The City of London was fined £70,000 and lost their patents for the lands in and around Londonderry. It took a complaint to the English Parliament on 30 November 1640 before the lands were restored on making a loan of £40,000 to fund the war against the Scots. The King still meddled in the affair, however, and it was not until Cromwell's intervention that the lands were in fact restored.

The failure of the Plantation generally and the tribulations of Londonderry in particular are important because they led to the impeachment and execution of Strafford on 12 May 1641. He was accused of being a warmonger and a meddler in the affairs of others, and of misusing his closeness to the king to advance dangerous policies. The allegations against him by the Puritan John Pym were rebutted but the charge was changed and an Act of Attainder proposed. This was a simple decree of treason based on a general presumption of guilt. The decision to execute Strafford came as a severe blow to King Charles I who was assuring his minion that all would be well. But a sacrifice was necessary to appease the public and the Parliament and the courtiers for once agreed. Faced with the weight of opinion Charles gave in and hurriedly signed the Act of Attainder. Straffords' comment was "Put not your trust in princes nor in the sons of men, for in them there is no salvation."

The failure of the Plantation also encouraged the aspirations of the native Irish to rebel on 22 October 1641, with the objective of recovering of the seized lands. It also alienated the City of London financiers from the King and put them behind the Parliamentarians in the English Civil War that broke out in August 1642.

XXXV. The Irish "Killing Time"

The persecution of the Presbyterians, and the widespread problems of the Plantation, had sown the seeds for rebellion by the native Irish under Sir Phelim O'Neill who sought to rid themselves of British rule and recover forfeited lands. Theirs was a festering resentment as the native Irish had only received a small share of the seized lands and that was the poor uplands. The Old English were concerned about the policy of Wentworth, Earl of Strafford, who sought to recover any lands where the title was in doubt. Their holdings were dependent on ancient law and they foresaw trouble, hence their association with the Irish. The pertinent point is that the 1641 Rebellion was more than just Catholic versus Protestant, there was a complex web of other issues involving the position of the Church of Ireland which was alien to the Catholics yet held considerable areas of land, and Civil War in England and Scotland as well as fears of war with France. If that was not enough, there were bad harvests in 1640 and 1641, in part due to lack of labour because so many Scots had fled back to Scotland to avoid the persecution emanating from the Dublin government. Profit, politics and prejudice certainly coloured the reports of the rebellion.

The initial outbreak on 23 October 1641 was to seize Dublin Castle but this failed. A secondary objective was to take Charlemont Castle, commanded by Sir Toby Caulfield. Such was the element of surprise that he thought that O'Neill was actually calling by to have dinner with him. Elsewhere the general populace were also surprised probably having been lured into a sense of false security after many years of reasonable and peaceful coexistence. However, the insurgents ransacked towns and massacred their inhabitants, with Protestants, of any faith, a primary target. This then was the "Killing Time" in Ireland which lasted until the autumn of 1642 when Owen Roe O'Neill, a distinguished soldier on the continent, took command of the Irish Confederate army and directed that the war should be conducted according to civilized rules of war. Thereafter the discontent rumbled on as part of the Eleven Years War which did not end until Cromwell's forces took Limerick in October 1651 and Galway in April 1652.

Some of the major towns, such as Enniskillen, Londonderry, Coleraine, Carrickfergus, Lisburn and Belfast, received timely warning and were able to prepare for and repulse attack. But, other small towns and the countryside in general were ravaged. Plundering and pillaging of Protestant homes and farms, and livestock was common. The excesses occurred with churches and ministers' houses which were torched and the occupants stripped naked and left cowering in the hedgerows in what was one of the severest winters in memory. It was said that the river Blackwater in Co. Tyrone turned red with the blood of the murdered populace.

There is much debate that the 1641 Rebellion was not as bad as some might paint it. However, there are thirty-two volumes of sworn depositions in the library of Trinity College, Dublin that give a horrific description of events. These tell of children having their brains dashed out against a brick wall, or being thrown into pots of boiling water, of people having their eyes gouged out, hands and ears cut off; of being buried alive; of women stripped naked and cut up with knives; and even strips of flesh cut from a victims who were roasted alive. Whatever the actual numbers of people who were brutalised, the fact that *any* of the inhumane actions took place at all is simply horrific. Where the truth lies is difficult, if not impossible, to quantify, but 4-6,000 killed is probably nearer the truth than the 154,000 that has been claimed by the Irish justices. Research by Hilary Simms (*Ulster 1641* Ed B Mac Cuarta.) into the killings in Co Armagh, the worst hit of all the nine counties then in Ulster, makes the telling point that if the worst case numbers in Armagh (1259) are multiplied up by nine the total for the whole of Ulster comes to less than 12,000.

At Loughgall, some 300 men, women and children were allegedly stripped of their clothing and locked in the church. They were then selectively assaulted and brutalised, raped, butchered, broiled over hot gridirons and hung drawn and quartered. At Portadown, it was reported that 196 persons were hurled into the river and drowned in one day; and that about 1,000 in all suffered in this way.

Ministers of the church were particularly dealt with extreme cruelty, hung, dismembered, and one, Thomas Murray of Killyleagh, was actually crucified, with the bodies of two English gentlemen suspended either side of him in mockery of the Crucifixion. The *Hamilton Manuscripts* quotes from the records of the General Assembly of the Church of Scotland that his widow presented a petition at St Andrews in 1642 testifying

> *that he was actually crucified on a tree; her two sons killed, and cut to pieces before her eyes; her own body frightfully cut, and maimed in sundry parts; her tongue half cut out; and that she was kept in prison and inhumanly used by the rebels;*

In the fields and hedgerows multitudes suffered privation, cold and disease. Bodies lay where they were and the smell of death pervaded everything. A plague broke out and it is said that 6,000 died in Coleraine, while Belfast, Carrickfergus and Lisburn also suffered badly.

Into the fray then came Major General Munro and 10,000 Scottish troops, who arrived in Carrickfergus in February 1642. Importantly the soldiers were accompanied by their own chaplains who were to play a prominent part in the Presbyterian re birth in Ireland. These chaplains organised a Session in each regiment, and when there were four they created the first regular Presbytery on 10 June 1642. The ministers were Hugh Cunningham, who settled at Ray, Co. Donegal; Thomas Peebles at Dundonald and Holywood; John Baird at Dervock; John Aird and John Scott who later returned to Scotland. Support from Scotland soon helped the reestablishment of Presbyterian congregations, but more tribulations were to follow.

An interesting event, involving the Covenanters, occurred in May 1644. The English Parliament appointed General Munro commander in chief of all the English and Scottish forces in Ireland on 27 April 1644. Sir James Montgomery, knowing of this, called his officers together on 12 May with a view to arranging the hand over of command to Munro who was, at the time, in Carrickfergus. Scouts, sent out, were captured and, under orders from Munro, deliberately misreported no sign of movement towards Belfast and the guard was relaxed. But, Munro had speedily marched through the night and caught Belfast by surprise, much to the amazement of the English Colonels. Munro's excuse was that he did not feel safe in the town without his own troops, and besides, there those, meaning Colonel Chichester and his regiment, who had declined to accept the Solemn League and Covenant.

In the course of this seizure of Belfast, a troop of soldiers of Col. Arthur Chichester's regiment had been stood down at Stranmillis, on the outskirts of Belfast. Munro had ordered that they march with drums beating and colours flying to the Market Place and there they were required to ceremonially shred their colours as an indication of obedience to the Scottish army and the Covenant. The duplicity seems to have been unnecessary as the English Colonels placed themselves under his command forthwith, but the incident is indicative of the mistrust that existed between the so-called allies.

The Representation

The Solemn League and Covenant of 1643 was the agreement between the Scottish Presbyterians and the English Parliamentarians for extension of the Presbyterian faith into England, Ireland and Wales. It was taken to Ireland by the Rev. James Hamilton in 1644, widely disseminated and sworn to with enthusiasm. As a by-product of the swearing of the Covenant there was a growth to over thirty congregations with ministers by 1647.

Yet again, the Presbyterian conscience was troubled both by the way a majority in the English Parliament was achieved (by locking up dissenting Members so they could not vote) and by the decision to execute King Charles in January 1649. On 15 February the Presbytery met in Belfast and drew up a "Representation," objecting to the King's death, which was ordered to be read from every pulpit. This change of allegiance understandably soured relationships with the English Parliamentarians. Meanwhile in Ireland there were five factions, each with an army, who were scrambling for alliances and prolonging the war. Into the arena came Oliver Cromwell as Lord Lieutenant of Ireland, landing at Dublin on 15 August 1649 from where he launched his swift and sometimes bloody campaign to subdue Ireland.

XXXVI. Cromwell and the Restoration in Ireland

There were two agreements entitled "The Engagement," the first being in 1647 between Charles I and Scottish nobles in which the King agreed to the Solemn League and Covenant and adoption of the Presbyterianism faith. The Church of Scotland never approved the agreement and after the defeat at Preston by Cromwell, power returned to the hard line Covenanters. The second engagement was with Cromwell in Ireland.

Cromwell's campaign in Ireland was relatively brief and bloody and probably reflected his impatience with the long drawn out conflict and a determination to punish the rebels. The rebellion had been dragging on in various ways since 1641 with several changes in the composition of the alliances. The Irish Confederacy was divided in both their objectives and military strategy and their leaders were jealous of one another. The Papal Nuncio, Rinuccini interfered in alliances on orders from Rome where the Pope was warily watching the ambitious manoeuvrings of Louis XIV of France. Perhaps most significant was that the rebels has overestimated the resources available to them As to Cromwell's tactics, the time was ripe for a swift and decisive campaign against a disorganised enemy and he grasped the opportunity offered him.

Historians reviled Cromwell for his bloody deeds but it is important to understand that the seventeenth century military ethos was to deal harshly with belligerent defenders who did not accept an offer to surrender. Defenders had but one chance and little quarter was expected or given in much the same way as Montrose had dealt with the Covenanter armies in 1644-5. Prisoners were a burden, they took up scarce resources and tied up soldiers for guard duty who would otherwise be fighting. Moreover, a dead enemy did not come back to fight another day.

The battle at Drogheda went on for about twelve days in and around the town and the end result was carnage with some 3,000 soldiers from the garrison slaughtered. Among the dead were the clergy although there is debate if many civilians were in fact massacred. The delay at Drogheda was mainly due to the time it took for the artillery train to arrive which has been sent by ship. The absence of heavy guns in the initial assaults may have misled the defenders, but such is the fortune of war. The garrisons at Trim and Dundalk saw what treatment they too might receive and they fled, offering no resistance. Next in line was Wexford where an abrupt surrender of the fort guarding the river entrance led to panic by the defenders and another slaughter by Cromwell's troops. The no nonsense approach effectively broke the back of the rebellion. By the end of 1649 the towns of New Ross, Youghal, Cork, Kinsale and Bandon had been taken. Cromwell's force was resisted at Waterford, but in the spring of 1650 he took Kilkenny and Clonmel. In May Cromwell handed over the war to his lieutenants Broghill in Munster, Coote in Ulster and Henry Ireton with the main army. By May 1652, and the taking of Galway, the rebellion was over and the country subdued.

Another oath arose from Cromwell's subjugation also called "The Engagement," This renounced the claim of Charles Stuart, the heredity claims of King Charles's line, and bound signatories to be true and faithful to the Commonwealth, as Cromwell's government was known. The Irish Presbyterians refused to take the oath and were subject of more severe punishments with very many fleeing to Scotland. Only a handful of ministers remained in Ireland, ministering to their flocks through the "conventicle" - the clandestine open air meeting. The vacant ministries were filled with other non-conformist ministers, Baptist and Independents, from England.

The Dublin Parliament proposed to banish the leading Presbyterians from counties Antrim and Down and to remove some 260 of them to the Province of Munster. The replanting was accompanied by the promise of cheap land and "freedom of conscience." There were two categories - those who went voluntarily under negotiated terms and were assisted i.e. allotted land; and others who did not have agreements with the government and negotiated their own land purchases. Those with agreements 'on account with the Commonwealth' would go to Kilkenny and Tipperary; those who were 'not provided for by the Commonwealth' would go to Leinster. Waterford was removed from the list of destinations because the Presbyterians claimed it was too remote, but merchants who wished to could remove to Cork.

The moves were not wholely arbitrary in the sense that virtually all the Presbyterian's requirements were agreed. They were, for example, allowed to receive the profits from their existing lands and harvests; to live rent-free for two years on the new property; they were allowed to keep weapons and allowed to follow their religion. A list of Presbyterians required to move to Kilkenny, Tipperary was produced on 23 May 1653 at Carrickfergus. (Appendix 10)

Before lasting damage could be done to the Ulster Presbyterians and their ownership of land, Cromwell realised that they were essentially law abiding and would not otherwise give him much trouble, so persecution ceased. The *Hamilton Manuscripts* records that Cromwell was coming under pressure from the army who were

wholly against the government being settled on any single person this motion of the Governors here in Ireland had no bottom to rest upon and, therefore, their project of transplanting the Scotch to Tipperary, did evanish within a little time; and the ministers and people in this country began to have a quiet calm for all the former storms which they had endured.

Cromwell had seen the opportunity to plant a Protestant population in the Provinces of Munster and Leinster by banishing priests and forcing Catholic landowners to move to Connaught and Clare. The forfeited land was then used to pay the one thousand or so adventurers who had financed the war and his thirty five thousand soldiers. The land was identified in an extensive 'Civil Survey' which began in 1654 which, with two other earlier surveys, covered thirty two counties of Ireland. In Leinster some eleven million acres of land was confiscated of which about eight million acres was deemed to be profitable. Later, more land in Mayo and Sligo was confiscated. Much of the land given to the soldiers was quickly sold on to whomsoever wanted it. About a quarter of the soldiers actually took up residence and many intermarried with the local Irish.

Land confiscations 1653-1665

Extracted from *An Atlas of Irish History* by R E Edwards

Assigned to	County	Percent of County
Adventurers &	Antrim	41
Soldiers	Down	26
	Armagh	34
	Meath	76
	West Meath	75
	Kings Co.	46
	Queens	43
	Tipperaray	77
	Limerick	57
	Waterford	52

Additional for	Londonderry	14
adventurers &	Tyrone	4
soldiers	Fermanagh	15
	Monaghan	38
	Cavan	43
	Louth	65
	Kilkenny	58
	Wexford	60
	Kerry	59
Arrears from	Donegal	11
1649	Leitrim	39
	Longford	61
	Wicklow	35
Reserved for	Dublin	46
Government use	Kildare	49
	Carlow	72
	Cork	65
For the Irish	Sligo	58
excluding coast	Mayo	80
and river strips	Roscommon	68
	Galway	91
	Clare	80

An important consequence was that land ownership in Ireland changed significantly placing it in Protestant hands. The land held by Catholics in Ireland fell from about 90 percent in 1603 to fourteen percent after the Treaty of Limerick in 1691. The Penal Laws in the 1700s further reduced the Catholic land holding to about five percent. Over the years there was a gradual decrease in Protestant owners, many of them absentees, but an increase in Catholic tenants. In the towns and cities their government became a Protestant monopoly. Combined, these two factors stored up resentment and problems for the future.

By the end of 1653, there was a gradual increase in Presbyterian ministers, rising from about twenty-four to seventy. All ministers who applied received an endowment of around £100 and there were soon five Presbyteries with some eighty congregations under seventy ministers ruled by a General Synod, which met four times a year. Appendix 11 gives the details of ministers who received salaries and or tithes between 1655 and 1661. Cromwell died in September 1658 and after a short attempt at government by his son Richard Cromwell, the door was reopened to another time of repression. This was the Restoration of King Charles II to the throne and his duplicity when he reneged on his earlier oath and acceptance of Presbyterianism and the Covenants.

Restoration of Charles II. Another phase of persecution

Charles II was declared King in Dublin on 14 May 1660. One of his first acts was to settle the many land disputes and by declaration confirmed the allocations made to Cromwell's soldiers and the 'Adventurers' (settlers). But as fickle as ever, Charles then brought out the Act of Explanation which restored a third of the lands to the native Irish. This indecision was a major destabilising factor for everyone in Ireland whether Presbyterians, Cromwellians, Old English, New English or colonists from Europe.

The enforcement of prelacy in 1661 was ahead of similar action which would take place the following year in England and Scotland. The action caused some sixty-four Presbyterian ministers to refuse acceptance of the bishops and were ejected from their ministry (see Appendix 13). It is of note that the women of Comber in County Down were enraged by the ejection of their minister and the appointment of an Episcopalian in his stead. They took a leaf out of Janet Geddes book, pulled him from the pulpit and tore his surplice to ribbons. One of the women was later prosecuted at Downpatrick Assizes where she freely admitted "These are the hands that pu'd the white sark over his heid."

Seven ministers were seized and imprisoned in Carlingford Castle and expelled to Scotland; ministers were excommunicated and Bishop Robert Leslie of Raphoe caused four ministers to be incarcerated for six years simply because they were Presbyterians. The four were John Hart of Taughboyne; Thomas Drummond of Ramelton; William Semple of Letterkenney; and Adam White of Fannet. They were eventually released on a petition being made to the king in October 1670.

The cause of Presbyterians was not helped by an attempt at rebellion in 1663 led by a Captain Blood, the brother-in-law of William Lecky, a Presbyterian minister. The plot was betrayed and Blood escaped while two other alleged conspirators. Mr. John Crookshanks and Mr. Andrew McCormack fled to Scotland only to be killed at the battle of Rullion Green in 1666. William Lecky was tried and executed, but there remained the suspicion that other ministers had been involved and ten ministers were imprisoned in Carrickfergus and seven in Carlingford Castle. There followed another period where the Bishops pursued the Presbyterians for non compliance. In 1665 the Irish Parliament directed the adoption of the English Liturgy and any minister must be ordained according to the Episcopalian rite by 29 September 1667 or be disqualified from having an ecclesiastical benefice. Non-conformist ministers were liable to a fine of one hundred pounds if they celebrated the Communion. Despite these privations, there was still the common man who assisted in making barns available for services or provided shelter and sustenance to the surviving ministers. Fortunately, the truth of the Blood rebellion was revealed and by 1668 the government was tolerant of small, albeit crude, meeting houses that were being constructed. It seems it had dawned on the government that the Presbyterians were not the problem that the prelates vociferously claimed. The Bishop of Down, for example, summoned twelve ministers with the intention of excommunicating them but Sir Arthur Forbes intervened for them and the persecution fell through.

A curious anomaly was the granting, by King Charles II, in 1672, of the "Regium Donum" (the King's Gift) of £1,200, which was later reduced to £600, as that was all which was available. This was the work of Sir Arthur Forbes who sowed the seed with the king in 1672 and was an open recognition of the Church and its work. Yet at the same time the Bishops continued to make life as difficult as they could by fining the populace for non attendance at an Episcopalian church and for not using the approved Prayer Book. This endowment was enjoyed by the Irish Presbyterian Church, with some breaks, until 1869. A list of ministers who shared the "Regium Bonum" for the Christmas Quarter in 1712 during Queen Anne's reign is in Appendix 11, where some 113 ministers shared the net sum available of £286, each therefore receiving about £2.10s.4d. (Equivalent today to about £225 sterling or about $320 US. Dollars).

XXXVII. James II - the Siege of Londonderry and the Boyne

Persecution returned in strength after Charles died in February 1685, and his brother, the Catholic, James II, came to the throne and with it wholesale changes in government and all positions of power both in England and Ireland. The Catholics of Ireland had great expectations of James II and were soon receiving benefit of appointments to official posts, including the army in England. This alarmed many and was exacerbated by his Declaration of Indulgence, which gave religious freedom for all, including the Catholics, and his direction that the Indulgence should be read in the churches. Many resented this and seven English bishops who objected were sent to the Tower, but later acquitted.

James had been tolerated largely because he was an old man and the assumption was that his daughter Mary, a Protestant, would succeed him. But the King surprised all by having a son who it was thought would be brought up a Catholic. This led to the political parties in Parliament uniting and sending an invitation to William, Prince of Orange and his wife Mary, to accept the throne. William of Orange was the son of the eldest daughter of Charles I and William II of the Netherlands and therefore nephew and son in law of James II. King William landed at Torbay in the south of England on 5 November 1688. Meanwhile the Catholic supporters of James were arguing among themselves during which John Churchill, the future Duke of Marlborough deserted with his troops. There followed some futile negotiations with James who left London on 18 December 1688.

James escaped by rowing boat down the river Thames during which he threw away the Great Seal which was used to indicate the King's assent to important documents. He proceeded to Sheerness, a naval dockyard at the mouth of the river Thames and the river Medway but the ship he transferred to was unable to sail because of stormy weather. There followed a bizarre attack on the ship by some sailors who robbed Charles and the other passengers and took him to an inn at Rochester where he was recognised and returned to London. Surprisingly he was welcomed back by the people. William ordered that Charles should be returned to Rochester where, it appears, he was allowed to escape a second time. This is likely as William realised that no good purpose was served by Charles' presence in the country; if he stayed the revolution would probably end in bloodshed.

William III and Mary II, took the throne jointly with William having the executive power. Their accession marks the end of the Stuart Catholic sympathies and the struggle for absolute monarchy. Since then no King or Queen of England has been Catholic or been able to rule without the consent of Parliament. In 1689 a Bill of Rights enacted these conditions which were read out at William and Mary's coronation.

The Siege of Londonderry

In Ireland the Catholics under the patronage of the Catholic Lord Deputy, Richard Talbot, Earl of Tyrconnel, (nicknamed 'Lying Dick') saw them appointed to all positions of power. Protestants were dismissed from the army and the Catholic replacements given their arms. The judges were said to distinguished more for their "brogue and their blunders." Virtually all Catholics now carried swords and displaced Protestants from jobs wherever they could. The armed peasantry committed outrages on their neighbours, homes of the aristocracy were ransacked and about a million cattle were taken from the Protestant farmers. It is estimated that the damage to property in this period was in the order of five million pounds (about one half billion pounds or two billion dollars at today's values). There were, of course, great fears of a repeat of the 1641 massacres and it came to a head in December 1688.

On 3 December 1688 a letter addressed to the Earl of Mount Alexander was found in the street of Comber, County Down. This spoke of a plan to massacre all the Protestants on the 9th of the month. There was no truth in the matter, which Tyrconnel himself declared to the Protestant representatives, but it was believed by the populace at large. The result was that the Ulster Presbyterians declared for King William.

The main Protestant strongholds at the time were Londonderry and Enniskillen to which the frightened colonists fled for safety. Londonderry was a town of about two thousand population, while Enniskillen was a village of about eighty houses on an island in Lough Erne. The presence of an Irish contingent in the vicinity of Enniskillen caused the Rev. Robert Kelso, the minister, to advocate resistance. The eighty or so men, augmented by refugees from the south west of Ireland, came upon the Irish officers dining with Captain Corry, a local landlord and magistrate who was trying to negotiate terms. With no officers to command them the Irish insurgents broke up and fled. The Enniskillen contingent elected Gustavus Hamilton to be their Governor and continued to carry on a highly successful campaign against the Irish Catholic forces until the war was over.

Londonderry was built on a slope and the summit of a hill about one hundred and twenty feet above the river level. It had a fifteen-foot wall round it and was defended with a number of cannons which had been donated by the London Guilds. On 7 December a copy of the Mount

Alexander letter was received by Alderman Tomkins, the Mayor's deputy, in Londonderry and at the same time a letter was received from Limavady saying that a regiment of Catholics had been raised by Lord Antrim and was on the way to the city. The alarm was raised and with it cries of defeatism by Dr Ezekiel Hopkins, the Episcopalian Bishop of Derry, who decried resistance against James, the lawful and 'anointed' king. But nine out of ten Presbyterians were in favour of resistance which was supported by the Rev. James Gordon, minister of Glendermot, whose advice was simple and precise "Shut the gates and keep them out." As the forces of Lord Antrim approached the gates (they were about sixty yards away) thirteen young men, the apprentices of Derry, ran forward and slammed the gates shut. The thirteen were:

Henry Campsie	William Crookshanks
Robert Sherrard	Daniel Sherrard
Alexander Irwin	James Steward
Robert Morrison	Alexander Cunningham
Samuel Hunt	James Spike
John Cunningham	William Cairns
Samuel Harvey	

Much of Ulster was already in Catholic hands and the capture of Londonderry was a prime objective. In the city some Protestant forces under a Colonel Lundy were admitted but the Presbyterians still mustered their own troops. Lundy was the official governor and an Episcopalian turncoat who had professed support for William but favoured the Catholic cause. He was responsible for gathering all the Protestant forces from outlying districts, including the garrison from Coleraine, into Derry where he alleged there was adequate stores. Once assembled, he then said there were insufficient stores and sought to surrender the city. He also caused two ships with English troops on board, which had been sent to help the Protestants, to be sent back to England.

James II had landed at Kinsale on 12 March 1689 and was in Dublin on the 24th March He arrived at the city gates of Londonderry on 17 April and demanded its surrender. The pleas and demands of Governor Lundy, and the Bishop were rejected with the cry that has echoed down the years 'No Surrender.'

Outside the walls Providence in the shape of Captain Adam Murray, arrived from Culmore with a party of cavalry. A Presbyterian elder whose family came from Philiphaugh, Scotland, he learned that Lundy was trying to surrender and he hurried to the city gates. Entrance was at first refused but the gates were opened by a Captain Morrison. Murray stormed into the council demanding to know what was going on and accused Lundy of treachery, then he left the room to go and marshal the city's defence. Lundy sought to get some Presbyterian ministers to advise Murray to surrender but they declined to do so. Meanwhile a Major Henry Baker was selected to be the new Governor. His authority now overthrown Lundy slipped out of the city under cover of night disguised as a private soldier carrying firewood.

Much credit is given to Captain, later Colonel Adam Murray for subsequent organisation of the city, its defences and essential support services. He declined the offer of the Governor's job and valiantly led sorties against the Catholic forces including one in which he killed the French commanding general Maumont. At one point the Catholic forces seized Murray's eighty-year-old father and threatened to hang him. But the old man advised his son to hold out, which Murray did, and the old man was allowed to return home unharmed. A Rev. George Walker, rector of Donoughmore and Lissan, was put in charge of the stores and subsequently claimed to have been the Governor and saviour of Londonderry. When Murray had first arrived at the city walls he had offered to hoist him over the walls by rope but was not disposed to admit the cavalry. This was in character for a man who was something of a charlatan and liar who had no involvement whatsoever in the fighting and was not the Governor. He was later dismissed from King William's service.

The people of the city suffered greatly during the siege from bombardment and shortage of rations. Soon they were starving and had to resort to cats, dogs, rats and even tallow for food. Coupled with this was a growing shortage of ammunition but the citizens held out, even when Protestant hostages were herded under the outer wall and threatened with death by General Rosen. The response to this threat was to raise a large gallows on the ramparts in full view of the attackers and ready twenty prisoners for execution. Five of the prisoners wrote to Rosen and begged him not to have them executed as common criminals. A stalemate was achieved, with nobody executed, and the siege went on for several more weeks. Rosen was soon replaced as commander on the order of King James who was annoyed at his behaviour and treatment of prisoners.

Meanwhile a frigate, the *Dartmouth*, and three ships containing desperately needed supplies were anchored in Lough Foyle, prevented from approaching the city by a massive chain and log boom across the river. The commander of the relief squadron was a Major General Kirke who was exceedingly reluctant to bring his ships under fire but the Rev. James Gordon somehow got out from the city and made strong representations to shame him into action. Great bravery and seamanship, especially by Captain Leake of the *Dartmouth*, and the small longboat from the *Swallow* which cut the boom, enabled the *Mountjoy* and *Phoenix* to break through and make it to the city quayside. The third supply ship, the *Jerusalem* was ordered to stay where it was pending the attempt. The crew of the *Swallow*'s longboat were subsequently rewarded with £10 per man for their gallantry - the crew was Robert Kells, Jeremy Vincent, James Jamison, John Young, Alexander Hunter, Henry Breman, William Welcome, John Field and Miles Tonge.

With the lifting of the siege King James II and his army took stock of their position and on 1 August were in full retreat. The siege of Londonderry and its 30,000 inhabitants had lasted one hundred and five days. The garrison had lost about 2,800 men mostly from sickness, and only about 80 killed in action. Of the non-combatants about 7,000 died. The Irish army lost about 9,000 with a large proportion in the field. When the siege was lifted they had about 6,000 men left in arms.

The tragedy of the siege was that the Presbyterians were cruelly treated by Major General Kirke who assumed the role of Governor. He refused assistance to people attacked by marauders, stopped assistance being sent to Limavady which was burnt the week after Londonderry was delivered; seized the cattle of Protestant farmers and even seized Murray's horse and saddle. He generally treated the defenders of Londonderry as if they had been enemies. The treatment by the government was as bad. A committee appointed by the English Parliament accepted that £195,091 sterling was due in pay to the Londonderry and Enniskillen regiments but only £9806 was ever paid. A further £138,349 was owed to officers of those regiments for the provision of food, horses and equipment which was taken from them by a less than grateful government. Besides this, the landlords continued to demand their rents and the rectors their tithes from the Presbyterian farmers. To rub salt in the wound, Kirke sent the charlatan Walker with a loyal address to King William. Walker was feted and given the Freedom of Glasgow and Edinburgh; an award of £5,000 from Parliament and the offer of a bishopric. It was said that the only blood he shed throughout the siege was "the blood of the grape."

The Boyne

King James summoned a Parliament to meet in May 1689 which was attended almost entirely by Catholic supporters, the Protestants being afraid to appear. The Parliament proceeded to repeal the Act of Settlement of 1662 which had confirmed estates to Protestants, and forfeited them to Catholics. The Penal Laws were repealed and most of the land was returned to Catholics. Technically the land was restored to those who possessed it before 23 October 1641, and another clause forfeited estates if the owner had held correspondence with anyone in arms against the King. It was a blow that hit just about every Protestant landowner in Ireland - if the estate had come to the family before 1641 it was forfeit by one provision, and if after 1641 it was confiscated by another provision.

An Act of Attainder named persons accused of treason unless they surrendered for trial before a specified day, but the Act was kept secret until after that day. The result was that 2461 persons were declared traitors. The tithes payable by Catholics were transferred to their own clergy and James issued debased coinage made from brass utensils and old cannon which was not accepted abroad. Fortunately James rejected the French ambassador's suggestion of slaughtering all Protestants, as he realised he would stand no hope of regaining the crown of England if he pursued such a policy.

On 13 August 1689 General Schomberg and 10,000 soldiers landed at Groomsport and marched to take Carrickfergus. He moved south as quickly as he could through Belfast and then on to Dundalk where he waited the arrival of his cannons and supplies. This took some time during which his army was beset with illness. Having lost about a third of his troops he moved headquarters to Lisburn. Schomberg's presence in the North of Ireland brought reassurance to the Presbyterians who returned to their farms and began rebuilding homes. Elsewhere a reinforced Catholic army was engaged in Sligo and Dungannon and was itself divided by quarrels between the French and Irish officers. In the event no serious fighting took place through the winter of 1689. In February 1690 Wolseley, who was at Belturbet, surprised the Irish at Cavan, captured the town and destroyed a vast amount of supplies before he retreated and took Killeshandra Castle on his return journey. In May Schomberg took possession of Charlemont Fort, a stronghold that was considered to be one of the most important in Ulster.

King William meanwhile found that the English were impatient with the war and he took personal charge, landing at Carrickfergus on 14 June. He was greeted with joyous crowds when he arrived in Belfast, most of whom were Presbyterians and received a deputation of Presbyterian ministers - Rev. Patrick Adair of Belfast; Rev Archibald Hamilton of Armagh; and Rev. William Adair of Ballyeaston. As he passed along the country William was favourably impressed with the appearance of the country, which he declared was a land worth fighting for. At Loughbrickland he reviewed the army of some 36,000 men - English, Irish, Scots, Dutch, Danish and French Huguenots. On the 25th June he reached Newry and by the 30th was close to the Irish army of some 35,000 at Drogheda on the bank of the Boyne.

William rode round his positions despite some musket fire and was lucky not to be killed. He was struck by a musket ball which tore his jacket and nicked the flesh, but he rode off to get treatment remarking there was "no great need for the bullet coming any nearer." The next day, split into three divisions, William's army forced their way with great difficulty across the river Boyne. The first division crossed at Slane and put the Irish cavalry to flight, killing Sir Neal O'Neill their commander. When reinforcements arrived the infantry was then put to flight. The Dutch supported by the Enniskillen men, the men of Derry, the Danes and the French Huguenots crossed at the centre but on arriving at the other side Schomberg was surrounded and killed. William led the third division across at Drogheda where they faced a storm of bullets, and took command of the centre which had become disorganised with Schomberg's death.

A minor disaster almost happened when William led the Enniskillen men forward and at the last moment turned aside to avoid hand to hand fighting. His turning misled the following troops who soon realised their mistake and charged forward. William then went forward with a Dutch regiment which captured Richard Hamilton, the Irish commander, and son of Sir George Hamilton of Strabane. The battle was now won but the Irish retreated in good order and James, watching from Dunore Hill soon departed with cavalry escort to Dublin where he arrived in the evening. A defeated James II took ship at Kinsale the following day and fled to France.

In the Battle of the Boyne the Irish Catholics lost about one thousand five hundred men, and the Protestants about five hundred. William was welcomed in Dublin by Protestants assembled on College Green and the news of victory was received with delight in England, Holland and Austria. Surprisingly the news was also received with a modicum of pleasure in Rome as the Pope was strongly opposed to the ambitions of King Louis of France, and favoured Austria in the ongoing European war. The Austrians were allies of the English. Among the dead was Rev. George Walker, recently elevated to Bishop of Derry. When told of his death William remarked "what took him there?" almost to say "serves the fool right."

Ireland was not yet subjugated and Limerick was besieged for a while in August 1690 until William decided to lift the siege, put his army in winter quarters and he returned to England. The Earl of Marlborough meanwhile besieged Cork, which surrendered in September 1690, and he went on to take Kinsale in October. There followed a long drawn out siege of Athlone in June 1691, an attack on Aughrim in July 1691, and a return to Limerick in August 1691 to face a force led by the French General St Ruth. The Treaty of Limerick was signed on 3 October and ended the war.

A consequence of the peace was the departure of about eleven thousand officers and men from the Irish Army to the continent. They were welcomed by Louis XIV of France and formed the Irish Brigade. This brigade and others in Europe were reinforced over the years by thousands of

Irishmen and were known as the 'Wild Geese' About half a million men joined the French Army between 1691 and 1791. The Catholic historian Abbe MacGeoghegan was a chaplain in the Irish Brigade and from the French War Department records he estimated that 450,000 Irishmen died in the service of France between 1691 and 1745.

XXXVIII. The Legacy of a Century of Struggle

It would have been justice if the Presbyterians had prospered following their hardships and efforts on behalf of King William, and they at least expected liberty to exercise their religion according to their conscience. However, it was not to be. The Episcopalian party became the oppressors and another melancholy chapter in Ireland's religious squabbles began.

Within Ireland there would soon be accusations and recriminations over the keeping of the Treaty of Limerick. The first article had promised that the Irish Catholics would be no worse off than they had been under Charles II. The Ninth article agreed that the Catholics should be required to swear an oath of allegiance only and not to matters of religion. The Treaty was ratified by the Lords Justices of Ireland and by William and Mary under the Great Seal of England. Disgracefully there followed the imposition on the Irish Catholics a mass of new and penal legislation in direct contravention of the Treaty. The "Act to prevent the further growth of Popery" in 1703 was the seed corn for generations of oppression and resentment.

The Separation of the Covenanters

There were still ministers who preached the strict adherence to the Covenant, one of whom was Rev. David

Houston, who became a thorn in the side of several Presbyteries. Born in Glasgow in 1633, he came to Ulster in 1660. He was several times admonished for his Covenanting principles and was formally suspended by the Route Presbytery in 1672. However, he continued in his ways, both in Ulster and in Scotland, and he was formally deposed in 1687 by which time he was firmly committed to the Scottish Covenanting Societies. In 1689, Houston was living in Newtownards and latterly at Armoy, Co. Antrim where he died in 1696. His contribution to the Reformed Presbyterianism was significant, and through his work he united the many disparate Societies into a cohesive fellowship.

Apart from Houston, there were others who wished to retain their attachment to the Covenant and they began to hold separate meetings for fellowship - apart from both the established Church of Ireland and the Presbyterian Church. To these separatists there came the likes of Alexander Peden, who preached to them at Kells and Glenwherry in Co. Antrim in 1679 and 1681. These separatists formed themselves into Societies and were known also as "Mountain Men." They corresponded with the Covenanting Societies of Scotland who followed Richard Cameron and James Renwick. By doing so they perpetuated the testimony of the Covenant in Ireland and were the seed from which the Reformed Presbyterian Church in Ireland grew.

A major event was the renewal of the Covenants of 1638 and 1643 by the Rev. John MacMillan at Auchensaugh, in 1712 at which the Irish Societies were represented. Thus the Societies continued to meet for fellowship and worship, and while they had no pastor, in the accepted sense, elders and occasional visitors helped to keep the ministry alive until they could be brought fully into the fold consequent to the First Reformed Presbytery that was set up in Scotland in 1743. From 1744 the Irish Covenanters at last had a link with an organised body of church government to guide them.

The Test Act

The supremacy, of King William following the Battle of the Boyne in 1690, was not as advantageous to the Presbyterians as it might have been because as a constitutional monarch, he could not do all that he wished for them. Thus, until his death in 1702, William was able only to influence existing law while the Irish Bishops, who represented about half of the membership of the Irish House of Lords, continued their vindictive actions against Presbyterians. Despite this, by 1702 there were nine Presbyteries under three sub synods of Belfast, Monaghan and Lagan and an annual Synod that met in June.

Yet, again, there was trouble in store, as in 1704 the Test Act was introduced, not this time an oath, but a requirement for all appointees to public office to take the Communion in an Episcopal church within three months or lose their position. It is possible that the government thought that they could obtain converts to Episcopacy by this act but it was not to be. In Londonderry, ten of the twelve Aldermen were Presbyterians and lost their office, while fourteen of the twenty-four burgesses were expelled. In Belfast, nine of thirteen burgesses lost their seats. Over the country, generally, public office holders such as magistrates, postmasters and town councillors were ejected for their faith. There was too, a positive discrimination with landlords encouraged to charge Presbyterians higher rents; they were banned from being school teachers, the leases for church lands prohibited letting to a Presbyterian tenant or building of a Presbyterian church; and in the towns of Antrim, Downpatrick and Rathfriland the doors of the churches were nailed shut to prevent services being held.

There was also a persecution, called the Non Juring controversy, where a few ministers declined to take the Abjuration Oath, not that they sided with the Jacobites, but because of the phraseology used. Three ministers - Rev.

McBride of Belfast; Rev. McCracken of Lisburn and a Rev. Riddell, had warrants issued against them and had to leave the country. The Rev. McCracken was apprehended in 1713 and placed in Carrickfergus gaol. He was fined £500 and imprisoned for six months and spent two and a half years in prison in total. But generally throughout Ireland there was little support for the Jacobite causes in either 1715 or 1745. Indeed it was so quiet that Scottish troops were recalled to the mainland to help deal with the rebellions.

Moderatism

Meanwhile the Irish Presbyterians began to argue amongst themselves over the moderatism that was creeping in from Scotland and doctrinal issues raised by the Belfast Society founded in 1705. This was a group of younger ministers led by Rev. John Abernethy of Antrim. Other members included Rev. William Taylor of Randalstown, Rev. Alexander Brown of Donegore, Rev. James Kirkpatrick of Templepatrick, Rev. Thomas Orr of Comber, and Rev. Alexander Colville. The Society debated issues that would otherwise be for the presbyteries to decide on eg sincerity of the individual was the proper test for his or her belief. Soon the Society was debating major doctrinal matters such as the subscription to the Westminster Confession. This in turn resulted in the New Light versus Old Light debates, the Seceder issues and Subscribing and Non Subscribing divisions.

The Toleration Act

Persecution by the prelates continued throughout the reign of Queen Anne, who died in 1714. Curiously Queen Anne also paid the "Regium Bonum" (Appendix 12) although the prelates sought to prevent it. Under King George I, things began to improve and a Toleration Act, in

1719, was passed that exempted the ministers from penalties to which they had been liable for celebration of their worship. But the Test Act remained in force until 1780.

The contribution of the Ulster Scots Presbyterians to the community is much easier to state. There is little doubt that they helped turn a backwater of Ireland from bogs and forests into a veritable garden. Their thrift, industry, and organisation saw the creation of an infrastructure of farms and farming communities that helped feed a nation. The development of flax spinning and weaving founded the linen industry for which Ulster is famous. And it was a Presbyterian mill owner from Belfast, Andrew Mulholland, who introduced steam power to these trades and enabled a huge leap in production to meet the demands for linen from abroad.

XXXIX. Migration to the Colonies

There was almost constant turmoil in Ireland through the seventeenth and eighteenth centuries with assorted rebellions in 1641, 1650 (Cromwell), 1690 (Battle of the Boyne), 1798 and 1803 Rebellions. There were also increasing pressures from landlords, many of them absentees from Ireland, who were racking up the rents; bad harvests; plague; and persecution and discrimination on religious grounds. Add to this political mismanagement from London by politicians who did not understand the issues and who delegated government to a biased Dublin Parliament. There was ample cause for the Ulster Scots to seek a new promised land.

A saving grace perhaps was that many of the ministers of the church went with, or followed after, their congregation when the latter migrated. In the American colonies, there was for a long time, resentment against Catholics, but the Presbyterians and other non-conformists enjoyed freedom of religion and thrived there. Ireland was also a destination for many other dissenters, such as the Huguenots, who were integrated into the population or joined the exodus to the New World.

It should be remembered that until the Declaration of Independence in 1776 America (both the United States to be and Canada) was just another state or county of Britain As such the settlers from Ulster were simply moving across the county line. There was no passport requirement or legislation that required the movement of people generally to be reported. Often the only evidence of their going might be family correspondence, a local church record, non renewal of tenancies in landlord's estate records, local newspapers at place of embarkation and arrival, records of ship and migration agents or the ships manifest. There was considerable migration with sailings from all round Ireland and from English ports. The younger people sometimes went via England where they worked to get their passage money before migrating. Another point to bear in mind is that prior to the Famine in 1845-50 the majority of migrants were Ulster Protestants. In the fifty years pre Famine there were about one million Irish migrants of which about half were Catholic. From the Famine to the current times there have been about six million Irish emigrants from the other three provinces of Connacht, Leinster, Munster, who were mostly Catholic

There were regular movements from Ireland to England through the ports of Londonderry, Portrush, Larne, Belfast, Portpatrick, Warrenpoint, Dundalk, and Drogheda to Glasgow, Liverpool, Fleetwood, Ardrossan, Greenock and London. From Dublin, Cork, Wexford and Waterford, the main English destinations were Bristol, Liverpool, Glasgow and Plymouth. The vessels to America were cargo carrying sailing ships - passenger ships came along in the nineteenth century, and pre the American Revolution were engaged in trade as their priority. They had little provision for passenger comforts and passengers often suffered at the expense of the cargo sleeping on open decks. There was also the probability that a ship might end up at a different port than originally intended as they were at the mercy of the wind and Atlantic storms.

Migration from Ulster to America was very heavy early in the eighteenth century as a result of the Penal Laws against Catholics which created great resentment towards all Protestants. This harsh climate among neighbours was exacerbated by harvest failures in 1726, deprivation of franchise for Catholics and an increased tax of four shillings in the pound on absentee landlords (who then raised rents) in 1728. There was a large wave of migrants to the colonies in 1729 as the problems increased. In 1744 the potato and oats crops failed in Ulster driving more small farmers from the land. Surprisingly the Jacobite rebellions of 1715 and 1745 in Scotland did not spill over into Ulster primarily because the Irish Catholics had learnt their lesson from the unfulfilled promises of the Stuart kings. Migration came to a halt in the summer of 1775 with the firing of Lexington and Concord and was virtually at a standstill for the next eight years, restarting in August 1783.

The prime driver for emigration to the new democracy of the United States was commerce, which was aided by a series of enactments in the US after 1783, when Ulster enjoyed a virtual free trade status. Another significant change was in the type of person emigrating. Broadly, before 1770 many migrants were or became indentured servants and were employed as labourers to do the hard and dangerous jobs in the new frontiers. The indenture was usually for a period of 4 - 7 years and for some it became a form of slavery. The lucky ones might be rewarded on completion of their service with a sum of money and a few acres of land. There was also a period when transportation was used to punish wrong doers. After 1783, the emigrants became more fare paying and whole families travelled together. Importantly they were often skilled tradesmen with money in their pockets who were not only populating the new lands, but going to carry on a trade and therefore invest in their new homeland.

It was in the eighteenth century that there were positive moves to encourage settlement in lands as far apart as South Carolina, where land was given to immigrants, and efforts were made to recruit settlers for Prince Edward Island in Canada. Even as late as 1888, there were Emigration agents in most towns in Ireland. However, the letter home was as an effective recruiting medium as any.

Tracing ancestors in the United States and Canada is sometimes complicated because many immigrants stayed for a while in the vicinity of their place of arrival, such as New York and Philadelphia. From there they sometimes took another ship to Canada or South Carolina because they had heard of the free land that was available; or they went up the Ohio Valley and migrated west. Some migrants went to Canada after the Revolutionary War because they were "Royalists" and later returned to the United States. Others found life so hard and bleak in places such as Prince Edward Island and Nova Scotia that they moved on to places new.

Perhaps the thing to remember is that these immigrants had known the most difficult times and had nothing to lose, but their lives. They were prepared to go anywhere that offered even half a chance of a living and prosperity. It is not surprising to find them in the Gold Rushes to Alaska or Ballarat in Australia, or in the mines digging lead and coal, or excavating the subways of New York. Many, perhaps most, came from farming and home weaving backgrounds and would have followed that tradition., But they were adaptable and turned a hand to anything that needed doing.

The Presbyterians generally had an advantage from a good education at an early age and could turn to record keeping as clerks, or land surveyors, post office and store proprietors, and other positions of modest authority in the new communities. Many became law officers, lawyers, judges, and in later years entered into local and national politics. Many Scots were involved in the tobacco, rum and sugar trades in the West Indies and could well have followed this trade with migration to Virginia, Georgia and other southern states.

Early settlers in America

The main Scots and Ulster Scots migration to the American colonies began around 1714 with the earliest known migration in 1652. Many went to the western counties of Pennsylvania, between the Susquehanna River and the Allegheny Mountains. A large group went down the Shenandoah Valley in 1732 and spread into the southeast United States. Others went down the Cumberland, Ohio and Tennessee River valleys. It is fair to say that the Ulster Scots were the major group of early arrivals in North America prior to 1800.

State	Settlement years	No. of settlements
Delaware	1692-1750	14
Georgia	1732-1798	20
Kentucky	1775-1793	42
Maine	1736-1785	13
Maryland	1649-1715	8
	1720-1788	20
Massachusetts	1652	1
	1718-1783	18
New Hampshire	1719-1776	16
New Jersey	1700-1775	60
New York	1640-1768	70
	1741-1796	9
North Carolina	1683	5
	1719-1800	67
Pennsylvania	1698-1800	150
South Carolina	1684-1799	76
Vermont	1763-1778	13
Virginia	1603-1798	80
West Virginia	1737-1798	19

Note: Information extracted from *A Genealogical and Historical Atlas of the United States of America* by E. Kay Kirkham, 1976

XL. America and the Declaration of Independence

It was 1752 before the supply of a permanent preacher for the Ulster dissenters would be met; meanwhile the Rev. John Cuthbertson who had been licensed and ordained by the Reformed Presbytery to preach in America, was diverted from his appointment to help out in Ireland. Cuthbertson soon went to America landing in Pennsylvania in August 1751 where he spent the next twenty-two years visiting the Societies and preaching to the Presbyterians in Pennsylvania and New York. In 1774 he was a member of the first American Reformed Presbytery which united with the American Associate Presbytery in 1782 and formed the Associate Reformed Church. In 1858 there was union with the Associate Synod of North America to become the United Presbyterian Church of North America.

There had been earlier ministers of the Kirk who had migrated to the American Colonies. Prominent among them was the Rev. Francis Makemie, a licentiate from the Presbytery of Lagan, who set out for Barbados in 1683 from where he went to Maryland and settled in East Virginia. He built up several congregations and was responsible for the foundation of the Presbyterian Church amongst the English speaking peoples of America. He was responsible for the creation of the first Presbytery in 1706 which had seven ministers, three of whom came from

Ireland. He was also at the centre of persecution when in January 1707; he was refused permission to preach in New York, But having then held a prayer meeting in a private house, he was pursued by Governor Cornbury on the grounds that he had preached without his permission. Rev. Makemie was found not guilty and acquitted under the Toleration Act of 1688, but, he was hit financially by having to pay costs of £83-7s-6d - a year's salary in those days. However, his stand for the right to preach unmolested was an important precedent in the new lands.

The Rev. Makemie was shortly joined by the Rev. William Trail of Ballindrait and the Rev. William Tennent, founder of the "log college," which was instrumental in supplying educated ministers to the burgeoning American church. Rev. Tennent was married to a daughter of the Rev. Gilbert Kennedy of Dundonald and had previously been an Episcopal minister in Ireland. Others with Ulster connections were the Rev. John Hampton from Burt who was the first Moderator of the first Synod; the family of Rev. John Rodgers, first Moderator of the General Assembly, came from Derry City; the second Moderator, the Rev. Robert Smith, was born in Derry. The dedicated work of these ministers must not be under-estimated as by 1760, there were some 300 Presbyterian congregations.

It would not be amiss to mention the down to earth approach to their work by the early preachers. Having memories of the open-air conventicles of the Covenanters stood them in good stead as they road their "circuit" on the frontier. These preachers would hold services wherever there was need, in barns or clearings in the woods, often riding hard to avoid Indians, armed only with their Bible and an indomitable faith. A later Ulsterman was the Rev. John Elder, who was minister at Derry in Pennsylvania from 1736 - 1771, who carried his rifle with him to church.

It is noteworthy that as early as 1743 the Presbyterian Covenanters in America had denounced King George II and renewed the Covenants of 1638 and 1643. A new link was forged that would see the Ulster Scot Presbyterians making their contribution to Declarations of Independence such as *The Hanover Resolves* in Lancaster Co., Pennsylvania on 4 June 1774, which includes the stirring words:

That it is the bounden duty of the people to oppose every measure which tends to deprive them of their just prerogatives. That in the event of Great Britain attempting to force unjust laws upon us by the strength of arms, our cause we leave to heaven and our rifles.

The later *Mecklenburg Declaration of Independence*, at Charlotte Town, North Carolina, on 20 and 31 May 1775 pursues further the theme of independence.

That we, the citizens of Mecklenburg county, do hereby disolve the political bonds which have connected us with the mother country, and absolve ourselves from all allegiance to the British crown, abjuring all political connection with a nation that has wantonly trampled on our rights and liberties and inhumanly shed the innocent blood of Americans at Lexington. That we do hereby declare ourselves a free and independent people, that we are and of right to be, a sovereign and self-governing people under the power of God and the general Congress; to the maintenance of which independence we solemnly pledge to each other our mutual cooperation, our lives, our fortunes, and our most sacred honour.

If we look into the shade of times past we may see the influence of the Scottish tradition of people banding themselves together by solemn oaths for mutual protection and to pursue and promote their objectives. There was the early cry for democracy in the Band of 1557 seeking that the election of ministers "should be made by the people" which was subscribed to by the feudal "Lords of the Congregation." The National Covenant of 1581 extended to defending the King and "...liberties of our country, ministration of justice and punishment of iniquity...."

Archibald Johnston, the advocate, and Alexander Henderson, the theologian, carefully set out the law and the rights of the people for a free religion in the National Covenant of 1638. The Solemn League and Covenant of 1643 continued the theme while in 1644 Samuel Rutherford published his *Lex Rex* with its axioms of democracy

The law is not the king's own but is given to him in trust. Power is a birthright of the people borrowed from them; they may let it out for their good, and resume it when a man is drunk with it; A limited and mixed monarchy hath glory, order, unity from a monarch; from the government of the most and wisest hath safety of counsel, stability, strength; from the influence of the Commons it hath liberty, privileges, promptitude of obedience.

There was the use of Committees of Correspondence to keep one another informed thus banding together for united action. And the final step by desperate and determined men like Richard Cameron and Donald Cargill declaring their right of armed resistance in the Declaration of Sanquhar in 1680.

It sounds familiar and there can be no doubt that the martyrs of the Presbyterian Kirk would have joyfully subscribed to another "National Covenant," for that is what the *Declaration of Independence* of 4 July 1776 is, and the famous tenets there declared:

When in the Course of human Events it becomes necessary for one People to dissolve the Political Bands which have connected them with another, and to assume among the Powers of the Earth the separate & equal Station to which the Laws of Nature and of Nature's God entitle them, a decent Respect to the Opinions of mankind requires that they should declare the causes which impel them to the Separation.

We hold these truths to be self evident, that all men are created equal, that they are endowed by their Creator with certain umalienable rights, that among these are Life, Liberty, and the pursuit of happiness.

In the War of Independence the Presbyterians were strongly anti British. A particular thorn in the British side was William Martin of Rocky Creek whose church was burned down by troops and he was arrested for preaching sedition. He was brought before the Governor, Lord Cornwallis, who charged him with preaching rebellion against King George III. Martin was sentenced to death but was at the last moment pardoned through the intervention of a Colonel Philips whom he had known in Ireland. Martin's reply to the charges laid against him sums up the Presbyterian contribution -

The Declaration of Independence is but a reiteration of what our Covenanting forefathers have always maintained. I am thankful you have given me liberty to speak and I will abide by your pleasure whatever it be.

Statue of Margaret Wilson
Knox College Canada
Courtesy of Bill Blain

Part IV
Epilogue

XLI. The Solway Martyrs - Controversy Returns

Over three hundred years later, in 1992, Margaret Wilson was again at the centre of a dispute. This time over a statue of her tied to a stake that was donated to the Presbyterian Knox College in Toronto, Canada in 1938. On this occasion, the blight and prejudice of political correctness deemed the beautiful marble statue to promote bondage and violence against women. In a knee jerk reaction, the statue was removed from the public rotunda of the college to a private boardroom.

A prolonged battle by the Kirk Session at Knox, Waterdown, through the formal channels of the Presbyterian Church to the ultimate authority of the General Assembly finally achieved an order to return the statue to the public area. Even then, dissenters sought to appeal to the following annual General Assembly and a Special Commission was appointed to investigate the matter. After a battle of some four years, the statue was returned to the public space and an explanation of the statue provided that informs the ignorant of the reason for it being there.

It is rather sad that the commemoration of a historical event of great moment, that displayed the highest dedication to faith, should be considered unfit for the common person to see. The removal of the statue in such circumstances seems to confirm an absence of knowledge and understanding of the facts and the whole affair was fueled by the blight of the twentieth century, political correctness.

Yes, Margaret Wilson was dishevelled after living rough on the moors, then incarcerated for some eight weeks in a seventeenth century prison, with all help and succour banned by law.

Yes, she was bound to a post - for execution by drowning by order of the court and the earlier direction of the highest court of Appeal in the land, the Privy Council.

Yes, she was a victim of cruel and brutal men, who were responsible for carrying out the court's judgment.

Yes, Margaret Wilson gained her diadem through a steadfastness and dedication to her faith that is an example to behold.

Yes, she was so nearly lost for a second time upon the altar of prejudice.

It is to be hoped that both Margarets and all others who suffered for their belief; rest peacefully assured that their strength and spirit lies in the safe keeping of the common people of the Kirk who understand and revere their sacrifice.

The statue

The story behind the Margaret Wilson statue at Knox College, Toronto is also of interest. The statue was a gift to the College by Senator A. C. Hardy of Brockville in 1938 and for sixty-two years the College has considered it to be a "copy by a now unknown artist." Research in Canada by my good friend Bill Blain turned up several interesting pieces of information.

A search in the Archives of the Presbyterian Church uncovered Hardy's 1938 letter offering the statue to the College and in it he states that he acquired the statue from the estate of John Morgan Richards (1841 - 1918). Richards was an American businessman who resided at Steep Hill Castle, Ventnor, Isle of Wight and in London, England from 1867 until his death and who took considerable interest in the arts. His daughter, Pearl Mary Craigie, who wrote under the name John Oliver Hobbes, was an author and dramatist.

Inquiries, circulated to many organizations from Chicago to Edinburgh, about the "unknown artist" brought a response from the National Gallery of Canada that Charles Bell Birch, A. R. A. (1832 - 1893) was the likely sculptor having displayed a virtually identical study at the Royal Academy Exhibition in London, England in 1889. This was confirmed by the Royal Academy who supplied a picture of the statue from the 1889 Exhibition Catalogue. It was also discovered that Birch displayed a bust of Mrs. J. M. Richards at the Royal Academy the following year. Birch was born in Brixton, London, England. He studied at the Somerset House School of Design, the Berlin Royal Academy and was made an Associate of the Royal Academy, London where from 1852 on he exhibited many works. The works of Birch may be found in several cities in the UK, in Perth, Australia and his George Brown Memorial, dedicated in 1884, in Queen's Park, Toronto is located only about three blocks from his statue of Margaret Wilson at Knox College.

Is the statue a "copy?" The National Gallery explained that the nineteenth century technique for sculpture was to first produce a plaster model. Doubtless this was what was displayed at the Royal Academy Exhibition in 1889. If a commission resulted, as came in this case from Richards, the sculptor would then reproduce the plaster model in a more durable material, in this case, marble. Often assistants were employed by the sculptor to help with the carving and this sometimes resulted in slight differences in detail. It can fairly be concluded that the statue at Knox College is a copy only in the sense that it follows the original plaster model and that, in reality, it is an original Victorian statue from the early 1890's by C. B. Birch, a respected sculptor of the period.

One mystery remains - in his 1938 letter Hardy indicated the statue had been displayed at the World's Fair in Chicago. There have been two World's Fairs in Chicago: 1933-4 and 1893 and neither the Art Catalogues from them nor a search of internet information about the two art displays has turned up any mention of this statue. Possibly Hardy was misinformed.

The Painting

It is strange that the story of Margaret Wilson should again come to the fore with an article in the Liverpool Daily Post (England) of 24 February 2000, reporting on a painting of her by Sir John Everett Millais, called the "Martyr of the Solway." On this occasion it was to tell that an X - ray examination of the painting revealed that originally it was of a partly nude Margaret. It seems that the person commissioning the painting about 1871, George Holt, a Liverpool shipping magnate, was a staunch churchman who may have objected to the half clad painting, and a pink blouse was added. Given the morals of the 1870s, it is understandable that an addition was made to the painting, moreover, if that was what the client wanted then who was to argue.

I live only twenty miles from the Walker Art Gallery, Liverpool, where the painting is currently on display, and I can say that it is a beautiful painting of a beautiful young woman. At the end of the day I do not think it matters one jot whether or not Margaret went to her death clothed or unclothed, the fact to be remembered is that she died for her faith - as did a part clothed Jesus Christ.

Appendix 1

Time Line: The Scottish Church 1528 - 1690

Kings & Queens of Scotland and England from 1603 through to 1820.

	Ascended	Died
James V	1513	1542
Mary	1542	1587
James VI	1567	1625
(James I)	1603	1625
Charles I	1625	1649

Commonwealth Declared 19 May 1649

Oliver Cromwell	1653	1658
Richard Cromwell	1658	1659

Stuart Restoration

Charles II	1660	1685
James II (VII)	1685	1688

Interegnum 11 Dec 1688 - 13 Feb 1689

William III &	1689	1702
Mary II	1689	1694
Anne	1702	1714

House of Hanover

George I	1714	1727
George II	1727	1760
George III	1760	1820

1528 Patrick Hamilton, the first martyr, burnt at the stake. Scotland almost totally Catholic, except for followers of John Wycliffe (the Lollards) in the southwest of Scotland.

1542 James V dies. The baby, Mary Stuart, became Queen of Scots, aged one week. The Reformation takes shape with preaching by George Wishart (martyred in 1546).

1547 John Knox captured by the French and made a galley slave, freed ca. 1549, preaches in England for seven years.

1554 The Earl of Arran, (who supported the Reformation), Regent for the child Mary, hands over to the Catholic French Queen Mother, Mary of Guise. Mary Tudor Queen of England, a strenuous Catholic, Protestant ministers flee to Scotland.

1555 - 56 John Knox visits Scotland but returns to Geneva (comes back in 1559).

1556 Band by the "Gentlemen of Mearns" led by John Knox.

1557 Protestant nobility draw up The First Religious Covenant (a Band to renounce Popery and defence of the Gospel) and become known as the Lords of the Congregation. Alliance with the Protestant English government of Queen Elizabeth I in 1560. French military in Scotland expelled.

1559 Knox returns 2 May, preaches at Dundee and Perth. The Second Covenant or "Band for Mutual Defence" signed at Perth 31 May 1559. Third Covenant at Stirling on 1 August. Queen Regent dies.

1560 Knox urges Scottish Parliament to declare the Reformed Faith (Presbyterianism) the national religion. Popery is condemned and the first General Assembly meets 20 December 1560. Fourth Covenant or "Band for expelling the French" signed in Edinburgh 27 April 1560.

1561 The young Queen Mary Stuart arrives from France in August and tries to revert to Catholicism.

1562 Fifth Covenant by the Barons and Gentlemen of Kyle, Carrick and Cunningham.

1567 Queen Mary forced to abdicate in favour of her infant son James VI. Government by Regents until 1578. Attempts made to introduce Bishops to the church.

1572 Sixth Covenant by the citizens of Edinburgh.

1572 - 74 Knox dies. Mantle of leadership falls on Andrew Melville on his return from the Continent (1574).

1578 James VI, aged twelve, is led by courtiers to resist Presbyterianism. He wishes to be head of an Episcopal church with Bishops controlling it and the General Assemblies.

1580 Protestant leaders promise support for the Reformed faith and discipline in a National Covenant written by Rev. John Craig of Edinburgh at the request of King James VI and signed by him in 1580 - known as "The King's Confession"

1584 Royalist supporters in Parliament enact that no assemblies can take place without the King's consent, and all ministers must accept Bishops as their superiors. Called the Black Acts and repealed in 1592.

1596 The National Covenant of 1581 is renewed 30 March and a General Assembly held at Edinburgh (the last till 1638).

1603 - 18 James VI of Scotland becomes King James I of England and comes under the influence of English courtiers. He reintroduces Bishops and exiles leading Presbyterians.

1610 - 30 The Plantation of Ulster, with thousands of Presbyterian Scots migrating to the Province of Ulster, followed by a gradual build up of ministers from Scotland.

1618 The Articles of Perth try to make Scottish worship the same as in England.

1625 - 30 Revivals gather strength in Ireland and Scotland led by the preaching of Robert Blair in Ireland, and John Livingston and David Dickson in Scotland. Kirk o Shotts meeting by Livingston has 500 converts. Charles I succeeds to throne in 1625 and continues anti Presbyterian policies with the assistance of Archbishop Laud.

1632 Bishops and Thomas Wentworth, later Earl of Strafford, persecute Presbyterians in Ireland.

1636 The "*Eaglewing*" sets sail for Massachusetts 9 September, but is forced back by extreme weather conditions and lands the would be migrants 3 November.

1637 New form of service prepared by Laud is rejected. Janet Geddes said to have thrown a stool at the Dean in St. Giles Church, Edinburgh 23 July.

1638 The National Covenant renewed 28 February at Greyfriars Kirk. King Charles forced to allow a General Assembly, which removes the Bishops and re-asserts an independent Presbyterianism.

1639 - 40 King Charles tries to seize control by force but is defeated in both the First Bishops' War (Treaty of Berwick 18 June 1639) and the Second Bishops' Wars (Treaty of Ripon 26 October 1640)

1641 Rebellion in Ireland by the native Irish, the Irish Killing Time. Thousands murdered; very many Protestants flee to Scotland. General Munro returns with 10,000 Scottish troops in 1642. Skirmishes rumble on till 1647. Cromwell finally silences opposition at Limerick 1651 and Galway 1652

1642 - 43 Civil War in England. English Parliamentarians and Scottish Presbyterians form an alliance and sign the Solemn League and Covenant in 1643.

1644 Irish land in Argyll 8 July. Montrose's golden year of triumphs for the King - Tippermuir 1 September, Aberdeen 13 September, Fivy 28 October, Inveraray December.

1645 Montrose continues winning - Inveraray; Inverlochy 2 Feb, Auldearn 9 May, Alford 2 July, Kilsyth 15 August and meets disaster at Philiphaugh 13 Sep. Charles defeated at Naseby 14 June by Cromwell. Disagreement about the treatment of the King breaks the alliance (the Scots had no objection to the King as Head of State provided he did not meddle in the church and its affairs).

1649 Second Civil War in which the Scots fight for the King. They resent his execution 30 Jan 1649 and declare his son, Charles II, the lawful heir to the throne.

1650 Cromwell defeats Scots at Dunbar 3 Sep. Edinburgh surrenders 24 December

1651 Charles II crowned at Scone 1 January. Cromwell again victor at Worcester 3 Sep and becomes overlord of the three kingdoms. Charles II flees. Presbyterians enjoy reasonable tolerance, as do other non-conformist faiths.

1658 Cromwell dies. His son Richard takes over but is not successful.

1660 Restoration of Charles II rejects the former allegiance to the Presbyterians and the Covenant. He assumes the role of head of the church and reintroduces the Bishops.

1661 Over 60 Presbyterian ministers ejected from their churches in Ireland

1662 - 65 Over 300 ministers thrown out of their churches and begin preaching in the open field called "conventicles." Replaced by government appointed curates; attendance at church enforced with fines and military force.

1666 The Pentland Rising - by Presbyterians in the southwest who march on Edinburgh and are routed at Rullion Green 28 November. First show or organised militancy by the Covenanters. Excuse for greater persecution.

1669 An Act of Indulgence offers some relief but splits the Presbyterians into the "indulged" and the "not indulged."

1670 Conventicles banned and deemed treasonable, death penalty for ministers preaching at them. Conventicles start to be armed.

1678 Declaration at Rutherglen 29 May. Celebratory bonfires for the King doused. Acts of Parliament against Covenanted Reformation burnt.

1679 Archbishop Sharp murdered at Magus Moor 3 May. Another rising in Galloway results in a minor battle at Drumclog on 1 June and victory for the Covenanters. But they fail to take advantage of the moment and do not seize Glasgow. Bickering and stubbornness splits the forces who lose the help of the "indulged" and are beaten at Bothwell Brig on 22 June. Over 1,000 prisoners locked in Greyfriars Kirk Yard.

1680 The extremists begin to hold that by breaking his oaths made at Scone in 1651, the King had forfeited all rights to civil obedience. Led by Richard Cameron and Donald Cargill, armed resistance becomes a tactic. Declaration of Sanquhar by Cameron 22 June - a declaration of war.

1684 - 85 The Killing Time. Suspects executed on the spot without a trial. Some thirty-one executions in Edinburgh and 113 known executions in the countryside. 211 prisoners were drowned while being transported to the Colonies in the wreck of the Crown, off of Orkney. King Charles II dies February 1685 and is succeeded by his Catholic brother, James II.

1685 - 88 James Renwick continues holding conventicles, but captured and executed in Edinburgh 17 Feb 1688. George Wood, a sixteen-year-old lad from Sorn, the last Covenanter to be executed - shot in June 1688 by trooper John Reid. Glorious Revolution in England leads to James II fleeing and Protestant William of Orange and Mary II succeeding to the throne. Presbyterianism and the Church of Scotland have their liberty and freedom restored but not to the satisfaction of the Societies or Cameronians who remained outside the Revolutionary Church.

Appendix 2

The Five Articles of Perth

A General Assembly met in Perth on 25 August 1618, at which the Archbishop of St. Andrews, Spottiswoode, took the Moderator's chair on the grounds that as the Assembly was meeting in his diocese, he had the right to preside. The meeting had been appointed on the order of the King and was packed out with subservient Bishops, nobility and gentry, with the Presbyterian ministers forced to stand at the back of the hall.

When the Articles were to be voted on, Spottiswoode sought to brow beat the ministers by saying that the vote would be recorded and the name of those voting against adoption would be notified to the King. In the event some forty-five ministers voted against although there was a substantial majority for adoption of the Articles. They were:

1 The Holy Communion to be received in a kneeling position.

2. Private Communion could be given to the sick.

3. Private Baptisms could be given as necessary.

4. Young children should be catechised, and subsequently blessed by a Bishop.

5. Holidays must be observed at Christmas, Good Friday, Easter, Ascension and Pentecost. These were ruled as holy days of the whole Kirk of the World and not merely Roman Catholic practices.

Appendix 3

The Westminster Confession of Faith

THE CONFESSION OF FAITH, *Agreed upon by the Assembly of Divines at Westminster: Examined and approved, Anno 1647, by the General Assembly of the Church of Scotland; and ratified by Acts of Parliament 1649 and 1690.*

CHAP I. - *Of the Holy Scripture.*

I. Although the light of nature, and the works of creation and providence, do so far manifest the goodness, wisdom, and power of God, as to leave men inexcusable; yet they are not sufficient to give that knowledge of God, and of his will, which is necessary unto salvation. Therefore it pleased the Lord, at sundry times, and in divers manners, to reveal himself, and to declare that his will unto his church; and afterwards, for the better preserving and propagating of the truth, and for the more sure establishment and comfort of the church against the corruption of the flesh, and the malice of Satan and of the world, to commit the same wholly unto writing: which maketh the holy Scripture to be most necessary; those former ways of God's revealing his will unto his people being now ceased.

II. Under the name of Holy Scripture, or the Word of God written, are now contained all the books of the Old and New Testaments, which are these:

Old Testament
Genesis Exodus Leviticus Numbers Deuteronomy Joshua

Judges Ruth 1 Samuel 2 Samuel 1 Kings 2 Kings 1 Chronicles 2 Chronicles Ezra Nehemiah Esther Job Psalms Proverbs Ecclesiastes Song of Songs Isaiah Jeremiah Lamentations Ezekiel Daniel Hosea Joel Amos Obadiah Jonah Micah Nahum Habakkuk Zephaniah Haggai Zechariah Malachi

New Testament

Matthew Mark Luke John Acts Romans 1 Corinthians 2 Corinthians Galatians Ephesians Philippians Colossians 1 Thessalonians 2 Thessalonians 1 Timothy 2 Timothy Titus Philemon Hebrews James 1 Peter 2 Peter 1 John 2 John 3 John Jude Revelation

All which are given by inspiration of God to be the rule of faith and life.

III. The books commonly called Apocrypha, not being of divine inspiration, are no part of the canon of the Scripture, and therefore are of no authority in the church of God, nor to be any otherwise approved, or made use of, than other human writings.

IV. The authority of the holy Scripture, for which it ought to be believed, and obeyed, dependeth not upon the testimony of any man, or church; but wholly upon God (who is truth itself) the author thereof: and therefore it is to be received, because it is the Word of God.

V. We may be moved and induced by the testimony of the church to a high and reverent esteem of the Holy Scripture. And the heavenliness of the matter, the efficacy of the doctrine, the majesty of the style, the consent of all the parts, the scope of the whole (which is, to give all glory to God), the full discovery it makes of the only way of man's salvation, the many other incomparable excellencies, and the entire perfection thereof, are arguments whereby it doth abundantly evidence itself to be the Word of God: yet notwithstanding, our full persuasion and assurance of the infallible truth and divine authority thereof, is from the inward work of the Holy Spirit bearing witness by and with the Word in our hearts.

VI. The whole counsel of God concerning all things necessary for his own glory, man's salvation, faith and life, is either expressly set down in Scripture, or by good and necessary consequence may be deduced from Scripture: unto which nothing at any time is to be added, whether by new revelations of the Spirit, or traditions of men. Nevertheless, we acknowledge the inward illumination of the Spirit of God to be necessary for the saving understanding of such things as are revealed in the Word: and that there are some circumstances concerning the worship of God, and government of the church, common to human actions and societies, which are to be ordered by the light of nature, and Christian prudence, according to the general rules of the Word, which are always to be observed.

VII. All things in Scripture are not alike plain in themselves, nor alike clear unto all: yet those things which are necessary to be known, believed, and observed for salvation, are so clearly propounded, and opened in some place of Scripture or other, that not only the learned, but the unlearned, in a due use of the ordinary means, may attain unto a sufficient understanding of them.

VIII. The Old Testament in Hebrew (which was the native language of the people of God of old), and the New Testament in Greek (which, at the time of the writing of it, was most generally known to the nations), being immediately inspired by God, and, by his singular care and providence, kept pure in all ages, are therefore authentical; so as, in all controversies of religion, the church is finally to appeal unto them. But, because these original tongues are not known to all the people of God, who have right unto, and interest in the Scriptures, and are commanded, in the fear of God, to read and search them, therefore they are to be translated into the vulgar language of every nation unto which they come, that, the Word of God dwelling plentifully in all, they may worship him in an acceptable manner; and, through patience and comfort of the Scriptures, may have hope.

IX. The infallible rule of interpretation of Scripture is the Scripture itself: and therefore, when there is a question about the true and full sense of any Scripture (which is not manifold, but one), it must be searched and known by other places that speak more clearly.

X. The supreme judge by which all controversies of religion are to be determined, and all decrees of councils, opinions of ancient writers, doctrines of men, and private spirits, are to be examined, and in whose sentence we are to rest, can be no other but the Holy Spirit speaking in the Scripture.

CHAP II. - *Of God, and the Holy Trinity.*

I. There is but one only, living, and true God, who is infinite in being and perfection, a most pure spirit, invisible, without body, parts, or passions; immutable, immense, eternal, incomprehensible, almighty, most wise, most holy, most free, most absolute; working all things according to the counsel of his own immutable and most righteous will, for his own glory; most loving, gracious, merciful, long-suffering, abundant in goodness and truth, forgiving iniquity, transgression, and sin; the rewarder of them that diligently seek him; and withal, most just, and terrible in his judgments, hating all sin, and who will by no means clear the guilty.

II. God hath all life, glory, goodness, blessedness, in and of himself; and is alone in and unto himself all-sufficient, not standing in need of any creatures which he hath made, nor deriving any glory from them, but only manifesting his own glory in, by, unto, and upon them. He is the alone fountain of all being, of whom, through whom, and to whom are all things; and hath most sovereign dominion over them, to do by them, for them, or upon them whatsoever himself pleaseth. In his sight all things are open and manifest, his knowledge is infinite, infallible, and independent upon the creature, so as nothing is to him contingent, or uncertain. He is most holy in all his counsels, in all his works, and in all his commands. To him is due from angels and men, and every other creature, whatsoever worship, service, or obedience he is pleased to require of them.

III. In the unity of the Godhead there be three persons, of one substance, power, and eternity: God the Father, God the Son, and God the Holy Ghost: the Father is of none, neither begotten, nor proceeding; the Son is eternally begotten of the Father; the Holy Ghost eternally proceeding from the Father and the Son.

CHAP III. - *Of God's Eternal Decree.*

I. God, from all eternity, did, by the most wise and holy counsel of His own will, freely, and unchangeably ordain whatsoever comes to pass: yet so, as thereby neither is God the author of sin, nor is violence offered to the will of the creatures; nor is the liberty or contingency of second causes taken away, but rather established.

II. Although God knows whatsoever may or can come to pass upon all supposed conditions, yet hath he not decreed anything because he foresaw it as future, or as that which would come to pass upon such conditions.

III. By the decree of God, for the manifestation of His glory, some men and angels are predestinated unto everlasting life; and others foreordained to everlasting death.

IV. These angels and men, thus predestinated, and foreordained, are particularly and unchangeably designed, and their number so certain and definite, that it cannot be either increased or diminished.

V. Those of mankind that are predestinated unto life, God, before the foundation of the world was laid, according to his eternal and immutable purpose, and the secret counsel and good pleasure of his will, hath chosen, in Christ, unto everlasting glory, out of his mere free grace and love, without any foresight of faith, or good works, or perseverance in either of them, or any other thing in the creature, as conditions, or causes moving him thereunto; and all to the praise of his glorious grace.

VI. As God hath appointed the elect unto glory, so hath he, by the eternal and most free purpose of his will, foreordained all the means thereunto. Wherefore, they who are elected, being fallen in Adam, are redeemed by Christ, are effectually called unto faith in Christ by his Spirit working in due season, are justified, adopted, sanctified, and kept by his power, through faith, unto salvation. Neither is any other redeemed by Christ, effectually called, justified, adopted, sanctified, and saved, but the elect only.

VII. The rest of mankind God was pleased, according to the unsearchable counsel of his own will, whereby he extendeth or withholdeth mercy, as he pleaseth, for the glory of his sovereign power over his creatures, to pass by; and to ordain them to dishonor and wrath for their sin, to the praise of his glorious justice.

VIII. The doctrine of this high mystery of predestination is to be handled with special prudence and care, that men, attending the will of God revealed in his Word, and yielding obedience thereunto, may, from the certainty of their effectual vocation, be assured of their eternal election. So shall this doctrine afford matter of praise, reverence, and admiration of God; and of humility, diligence, and abundant consolation to all that sincerely obey the gospel.

CHAP IV. - *Of Creation.*

I. It pleased God the Father, Son, and Holy Ghost, for the manifestation of the glory of his eternal power, wisdom, and goodness, in the beginning, to create, or make of nothing, the world, and all things therein whether visible or invisible, in the space of six days; and all very good.

II. After God had made all other creatures, he created man, male and female, with reasonable and immortal souls, endued with knowledge, righteousness, and true holiness, after his own image; having the law of God written in their hearts, and power to fulfill it: and yet under a possibility of transgressing, being left to the liberty of their own will, which was subject unto change. Beside this law written in their hearts, they received a command, not to eat of the tree of the knowledge of good and evil; which while they kept, they were happy in their communion with God, and had dominion over the creatures.

CHAP V. - *Of Providence.*

I. God the great Creator of all things doth uphold, direct, dispose, and govern all creatures, actions, and things, from the greatest even to the least, by his most wise and holy providence, according to his infallible foreknowledge, and the free and immutable counsel of his own will, to the praise of the glory of his wisdom, power, justice, goodness, and mercy.

II. Although, in relation to the foreknowledge and decree of God, the first Cause, all things come to pass immutably, and infallibly; yet, by the same providence, he ordereth them to fall out, according to the nature of second causes, either necessarily, freely, or contingently.

III. God, in his ordinary providence, maketh use of means, yet is free to work without, above, and against them, at his pleasure.

IV. The almighty power, unsearchable wisdom, and infinite goodness of God so far manifest themselves in his providence, that it extendeth itself even to the first fall, and all other sins of angels and men; and that not by a bare permission, but such as hath joined with it a most wise and powerful bounding, and otherwise ordering, and governing of them, in a manifold dispensation, to his own holy ends; yet so, as the sinfulness thereof proceedeth only from the creature, and not from God, who, being most holy and righteous, neither is nor can be the author or approver of sin.

V. The most wise, righteous, and gracious God doth oftentimes leave, for a season, his own children to manifold temptations, and the corruption of their own hearts, to chastise them for their former sins, or to discover unto them the hidden strength of corruption and deceitfulness of their hearts, that they may be humbled; and, to raise them to a more close and constant dependence for their support upon himself, and to make them more watchful against all future occasions of sin, and for sundry other just and holy ends.

VI. As for those wicked and ungodly men whom God, as a righteous Judge, for former sins, doth blind and harden, from them he not only withholdeth his grace whereby they might have been enlightened in their understandings, and wrought upon in their hearts; but sometimes also withdraweth the gifts which they had, and exposeth them to such objects as their corruption makes occasions of sin; and, withal, gives them over to their own lusts, the temptations of the world, and the power of Satan, whereby it comes to pass that they harden themselves, even under those means which God useth for the softening of others.

VII. As the providence of God doth, in general, reach to all creatures; so, after a most special manner, it taketh care of his church, and disposeth all things to the good thereof.

CHAP VI. - *Of the Fall of Man, of Sin, and of the Punishment thereof.*

I. Our first parents, being seduced by the subtlety and temptation of Satan, sinned, in eating the forbidden fruit. This their sin, God was pleased, according to his wise and holy counsel, to permit, having purposed to order it to his own glory.

II. By this sin they fell from their original righteousness and communion with God, and so became dead in sin, and wholly defiled in all the parts and faculties of soul and body.

III. They being the root of all mankind, the guilt of this sin was imputed; and the same death in sin, and corrupted nature, conveyed to all their posterity descending from them by ordinary generation.

IV. From this original corruption, whereby we are utterly indisposed, disabled, and made opposite to all good, and wholly inclined to all evil, do proceed all actual transgressions.

V. This corruption of nature, during this life, doth remain in those that are regenerated; and although it be, through Christ, pardoned, and mortified; yet both itself, and all the motions thereof, are truly and properly sin.

VI. Every sin, both original and actual, being a transgression of the righteous law of God, and contrary thereunto, doth, in its own nature, bring guilt upon the sinner, whereby he is bound over to the wrath of God, and curse of the law, and so made subject to death, with all miseries spiritual, temporal, and eternal.

CHAP VII. - *Of God's Covenant with Man*

I. The distance between God and the creature is so great, that although reasonable creatures do owe obedience unto him as their Creator, yet they could never have any fruition of him as their blessedness and reward, but by some voluntary condescension on God's part, which he hath been pleased to express by way of covenant.

II. The first covenant made with man was a covenant of works, wherein life was promised to Adam; and in him to his posterity, upon condition of perfect and personal obedience.

III. Man, by his fall, having made himself incapable of life by that covenant, the Lord was pleased to make a second, commonly called the covenant of grace; wherein he freely offereth unto sinners life and salvation by Jesus Christ; requiring of them faith in him, that they may be saved, and promising to give unto all those that are ordained unto eternal life his Holy Spirit, to make them willing, and able to believe.

IV. This covenant of grace is frequently set forth in Scripture by the name of a testament, in reference to the death of Jesus Christ the Testator, and to the everlasting inheritance, with all things belonging to it, therein bequeathed.

V. This covenant was differently administered in the time of the law, and in the time of the gospel: under the law, it was administered by promises, prophecies, sacrifices, circumcision, the paschal lamb, and other types and ordinances delivered to the people of the Jews, all fore signifying Christ to come; which were, for that time, sufficient and efficacious, through the operation of the Spirit, to instruct and build up the elect in faith in the promised Messiah, by whom they had full remission of sins, and eternal salvation; and is called the Old Testament.

VI. Under the gospel, when Christ, the substance, was exhibited, the ordinances in which this covenant is dispensed are the preaching of the Word, and the administration of the sacraments of Baptism and the Lord's Supper: which, though fewer in number, and administered with more simplicity, and less outward glory, yet, in them, it is held forth in more fullness, evidence and spiritual efficacy, to all nations, both Jews and Gentiles; and is called the New Testament. There are not therefore two covenants of grace, differing in substance, but one and the same, under various dispensations.

CHAP VIII. - *Of Christ the Mediator.*

I. It pleased God, in his eternal purpose, to choose and ordain the Lord Jesus, his only begotten Son, to be the Mediator between God and man, the Prophet, Priest, and King, the Head and Savior of his church, the Heir of all things, and Judge of the world: unto whom he did from all eternity give a people, to be his seed, and to be by him in time redeemed, called, justified, sanctified, and glorified.

II. The Son of God, the second person in the Trinity, being very and eternal God, of one substance and equal with the Father, did, when the fullness of time was come, take upon him man's nature, with all the essential properties, and common infirmities thereof, yet without sin; being conceived by the power of the Holy Ghost, in the womb of the virgin Mary, of her substance. So that two whole, perfect, and distinct natures, the Godhead and the manhood, were inseparably joined together in one person, without conversion, composition, or confusion. Which person is very God, and very man, yet one Christ, the only Mediator between God and man.

III. The Lord Jesus, in his human nature thus united to the divine, was sanctified, and anointed with the Holy Spirit, above measure, having in him all the treasures of wisdom and knowledge; in whom it pleased the Father that all fullness should dwell; to the end that, being holy, harmless, undefiled, and full of grace and truth, he might be thoroughly furnished to execute the office of a mediator, and surety. Which office he took not unto himself, but was thereunto called by his Father, who put all power and judgment into his hand, and gave him commandment to execute the same.

IV. This office the Lord Jesus did most willingly undertake; which that he might discharge, he was made under the law, and did perfectly fulfill it; endured most grievous torments immediately in his soul, and most painful sufferings in his body; was crucified, and died, was buried, and remained under the power of death, yet saw no corruption. On the third day he arose from the dead, with the same body in which he suffered, with which also he ascended into heaven, and there sitteth at the right hand of his Father, making intercession, and shall return, to judge men and angels, at the end of the world.

V. The Lord Jesus, by his perfect obedience, and sacrifice of himself, which he, through the eternal Spirit, once offered up unto God, hath fully satisfied the justice of his Father; and purchased, not only reconciliation, but an everlasting inheritance in the kingdom of heaven, for all those whom the Father hath given unto him.

VI. Although the work of redemption was not actually wrought by Christ till after his incarnation, yet the virtue, efficacy, and benefits thereof were communicated unto the elect, in all ages successively from the beginning of the world, in and by those promises, types, and sacrifices, wherein he was revealed, and signified to be the seed of the woman which should bruise the serpent's head; and the Lamb slain from the beginning of the world; being yesterday and today the same, and forever.

VII. Christ, in the work of mediation, acts according to both natures, by each nature doing that, which is proper to itself; yet, by reason of the unity of the person, that which is proper to one nature is sometimes in Scripture attributed to the person denominated by the other nature.

VIII. To all those for whom Christ hath purchased redemption, he doth certainly and effectually apply and communicate the same; making intercession for them, and revealing unto them, in and by the Word, the mysteries of salvation; effectually persuading them by his Spirit to believe and obey, and governing their hearts by his Word and Spirit; overcoming all their enemies by his almighty power and wisdom, in such manner, and ways, as are most consonant to his wonderful and unsearchable dispensation.

CHAP IX. - *Of Free Will.*

I. God hath endued the will of man with that natural liberty, that it is neither forced, nor, by any absolute necessity of nature, determined to good, or evil.

II. Man, in his state of innocence, had freedom, and power to will and to do that which was good and well pleasing to God; but yet, mutably, so that he might fall from it.

III. Man, by his fall into a state of sin, hath wholly lost all ability of will to any spiritual good accompanying salvation: so as, a natural man, being altogether averse from that good, and dead in sin, is not able, by his own strength, to convert himself, or to prepare himself thereunto.

IV. When God converts a sinner, and translates him into the state of grace, he freeth him from his natural bondage under sin; and, by his grace alone, enables him freely to will and to do that which is spiritually good; yet so, as that by reason of his remaining corruption, he doth not perfectly, nor only, will that which is good, but doth also will that which is evil.

V. The will of man is made perfectly and immutably free to good alone, in the state of glory only.

CHAP X. - *Of Effectual Calling.*

I. All those whom God hath predestinated unto life, and those only, he is pleased, in his appointed and accepted time, effectually to call, by his Word and Spirit, out of that state of sin and death, in which they are by nature, to grace and salvation, by Jesus Christ; enlightening their minds spiritually and savingly to understand the things of God, taking away their heart of stone, and giving unto them a heart of flesh; renewing their wills, and, by his almighty power, determining them to that which is good, and effectually drawing them to Jesus Christ: yet so, as they come most freely, being made willing by his grace.

II. This effectual call is of God's free and special grace alone, not from anything at all foreseen in man, who is altogether passive therein, until, being quickened and renewed by the Holy Spirit, he is thereby enabled to answer this call, and to embrace the grace offered and conveyed in it.

III. Elect infants, dying in infancy, are regenerated, and saved by Christ, through the Spirit, who worketh when, and where, and how he pleaseth: so also are all other elect persons who are incapable of being outwardly called by the ministry of the Word.

IV. Others, not elected, although they may be called by the ministry of the Word, and may have some common operations of the Spirit, yet they never truly come unto Christ, and therefore cannot be saved: much less can men, not professing the Christian religion, be saved in any other way whatsoever, be they never so diligent to frame their lives according to the light of nature, and the laws of that religion they do profess. And, to assert and maintain that they may, is very pernicious, and to be detested.

CHAP XI. - *Of Justification.*

I. Those whom God effectually calleth, he also freely justifieth: not by infusing righteousness into them, but by pardoning their sins, and by accounting and accepting their persons as righteous; not for anything wrought in them, or done by them, but for Christ's sake alone; nor by imputing faith itself, the act of believing, or any other evangelical obedience to them, as their righteousness; but by imputing the obedience and satisfaction of Christ unto them, they receiving and resting on him and his righteousness, by faith; which faith they have not of themselves, it is the gift of God.

II. Faith, thus receiving and resting on Christ and his righteousness, is the alone instrument of justification: yet is it not alone in the person justified, but is ever accompanied with all other saving graces, and is no dead faith, but worketh by love.

III. Christ, by his obedience and death, did fully discharge the debt of all those that are thus justified, and did make a proper, real, and full satisfaction to his Father's justice in their behalf. Yet, inasmuch as he was given by the Father for them; and his obedience and satisfaction accepted in their stead; and both, freely, not for anything in them; their justification is only of free grace; that both the exact justice and rich grace of God might be glorified in the justification of sinners.

IV. God did, from all eternity, decree to justify all the elect, and Christ did, in the fullness of time, die for their sins, and rise again for their justification: nevertheless, they are not justified, until the Holy Spirit doth, in due time, actually apply Christ unto them.

V. God doth continue to forgive the sins of those that are justified; and, although they can never fall from the state of justification, yet they may, by their sins, fall under God's fatherly displeasure, and not have the light of his countenance restored unto them, until they humble themselves, confess their sins, beg pardon, and renew their faith and repentance.

VI. The justification of believers under the Old Testament was, in all these respects, one and the same with the justification of believers under the New Testament.

CHAP XII. - *Of Adoption.*

I. All those that are justified, God vouchsafeth, in and for his only Son Jesus Christ, to make partakers of the grace of adoption, by which they are taken into the number, and enjoy the liberties and privileges of the children of God, have his name put upon them, receive the spirit of adoption, have access to the throne of grace with boldness, are enabled to cry, Abba, Father, are pitied, protected, provided for, and chastened by him, as by a Father: yet never cast off, but sealed to the day of redemption; and inherit the promises, as heirs of everlasting salvation.

CHAP XIII. - *Of Sanctification.*

I. They, who are once effectually called, and regenerated, having a new heart, and a new spirit created in them, are further sanctified, really and personally, through the virtue of Christ's death and resurrection, by his Word and Spirit dwelling in them: the dominion of the whole body of sin is destroyed, and the several lusts thereof are more and more weakened and mortified; and they more and more quickened and strengthened in all saving graces, to the practice of true holiness, without which no man shall see the Lord.

II. This sanctification is throughout, in the whole man; yet imperfect in this life, there abiding still some remnants of corruption in every part; whence a riseth a continual and irreconcilable war, the flesh lusting against the Spirit, and the Spirit against the flesh.

III. In which war, although the remaining corruption, for a time, may much prevail; yet, through the continual supply of strength from the sanctifying Spirit of Christ, the regenerate part doth overcome; and so, the saints grow in grace, perfecting holiness in the fear of God.

CHAP XIV. - *Of Saving Faith.*

I. The grace of faith, whereby the elect are enabled to believe to the saving of their souls, is the work of the Spirit of Christ in their hearts, and is ordinarily wrought by the ministry of the Word, by which also, and by the administration of the sacraments, and prayer, it is increased and strengthened.

II. By this faith, a Christian believeth to be true whatsoever is revealed in the Word, for the authority of God himself speaking therein; and acteth differently upon that which each particular passage thereof containeth; yielding obedience to the commands, trembling at the threatenings, and embracing the promises of God for this life, and that which is to come. But the principal acts of saving faith are accepting, receiving, and resting upon Christ alone for justification, sanctification, and eternal life, by virtue of the covenant of grace.

III. This faith is different in degrees, weak or strong; may be often and many ways assailed, and weakened, but gets the victory: growing up in many to the attainment of a full assurance, through Christ, who is both the author and finisher of our faith.

CHAP XV. - *Of Repentance unto Life.*

I. Repentance unto life is an evangelical grace, the doctrine whereof is to be preached by every minister of the gospel, as well as that of faith in Christ.

II. By it, a sinner, out of the sight and sense not only of the danger, but also of the filthiness and odiousness of his sins, as contrary to the holy nature, and righteous law of God; and upon the apprehension of his mercy in Christ to such as are penitent, so grieves for, and hates his sins, as to turn from them all unto God, purposing and endeavoring to walk with him in all the ways of his commandments.

III. Although repentance be not to be rested in, as any satisfaction for sin, or any cause of the pardon thereof, which is the act of God's free grace in Christ; yet it is of such necessity to all sinners, that none may expect pardon without it.

IV. As there is no sin so small, but it deserves damnation; so there is no sin so great, that it can bring damnation upon those who truly repent.

V. Men ought not to content themselves with a general repentance, but it is every man's duty to endeavor to repent of his particular sins, particularly.

VI. As every man is bound to make private confession of his sins to God, praying for the pardon thereof; upon which, and the forsaking of them, he shall find mercy; so, he that scandalizeth his brother, or the church of Christ, ought to be willing, by a private or public confession, and sorrow for his sin, to declare his repentance to those that are offended, who are thereupon to be reconciled to him, and in love to receive him.

CHAP XVI. - *Of Good Works.*

I. Good works are only such as God hath commanded in his holy Word, and not such as, without the warrant thereof, are devised by men, out of blind zeal, or upon any pretense of good intention.

II. These good works, done in obedience to God's commandments, are the fruits and evidences of a true and lively faith: and by them believers manifest their thankfulness, strengthen their assurance, edify their brethren, adorn the profession of the gospel, stop the mouths of the adversaries, and glorify God, whose workmanship they are, created in Christ Jesus thereunto, that, having their fruit unto holiness, they may have the end, eternal life.

III. Their ability to do good works is not at all of themselves, but wholly from the Spirit of Christ. And that they may be enabled thereunto, beside the graces they have already received, there is required an actual influence of the same Holy Spirit, to work in them to will, and to do, of his good pleasure: yet are they not hereupon to grow negligent, as if they were not bound to perform any duty unless upon a special motion of the Spirit; but they ought to be diligent in stirring up the grace of God that is in them.

IV. They who, in their obedience, attain to the greatest height which is possible in this life, are so far from being able to supererogate, and to do more than God requires, as that they fall short of much which in duty they are bound to do.

V. We cannot by our best works merit pardon of sin, or eternal life at the hand of God, by reason of the great disproportion that is between them and the glory to come; and the infinite distance that is between us and God, whom, by them, we can neither profit, nor satisfy for the debt of our former sins, but when we have done all we can, we have done but our duty, and are unprofitable servants: and because, as they are good, they proceed from his Spirit; and as they are wrought by us, they are defiled, and mixed with so much weakness and imperfection, that they cannot endure the severity of God's judgment.

VI. Notwithstanding, the persons of believers being accepted through Christ, their good works also are accepted in him; not as though they were in this life wholly unblamable and unreprovable in God's sight; but that he, looking upon them in his Son, is pleased to accept and reward that which is sincere, although accompanied with many weaknesses and imperfections.

VII. Works done by unregenerate men, although for the matter of them they may be things which God commands; and of good use both to themselves and others: yet, because they proceed not from an heart purified by faith; nor are done in a right manner, according to the Word; nor to aright end, the glory of God, they are therefore sinful, and cannot please God, or make a man meet to receive grace from God: and yet, their neglect of them is more sinful, and displeasing unto God.

CHAP XVII. - *Of the Perseverance of the Saints.*

I. They, whom God hath accepted in his Beloved, effectually called, and sanctified by his Spirit, can neither totally nor finally fall away from the state of grace, but shall certainly persevere therein to the end, and be eternally saved.

II. This perseverance of the saints depends not upon their own free will, but upon the immutability of the decree of election, flowing from the free and unchangeable love of God the Father; upon the efficacy of the merit and intercession of Jesus Christ, the abiding of the Spirit, and of the seed of God within them, and the nature of the covenant of grace: from all which ariseth also the certainty and infallibility thereof.

III. Nevertheless, they may, through the temptations of Satan and of the world, the prevalency of corruption remaining in them, and the neglect of the means of their preservation, fall into grievous sins; and, for a time, continue therein: whereby they incur God's displeasure, and grieve his Holy Spirit, come to be deprived of some measure of their graces and comforts, have their hearts hardened, and their consciences wounded; hurt and scandalize others, and bring temporal judgments upon themselves.

CHAP XVIII. - *Of Assurance of Grace and Salvation.*

I. Although hypocrites and other unregenerate men may vainly deceive themselves with false hopes and carnal presumptions of being in the favor of God, and estate of salvation (which hope of theirs shall perish): yet such as truly believe in the Lord Jesus, and love him in sincerity, endeavoring to walk in all good conscience before him, may, in this life, be certainly assured that they are in the state of grace, and may rejoice in the hope of the glory of God, which hope shall never make them ashamed.

II. This certainty is not a bare conjectural and probable persuasion grounded upon a fallible hope; but an infallible assurance of faith founded upon the divine truth of the promises of salvation, the inward evidence of those graces unto which these promises are made, the testimony of the Spirit of adoption witnessing with our spirits that we are the children of God, which Spirit is the earnest of our inheritance, whereby we are sealed to the day of redemption.

III. This infallible assurance doth not so belong to the essence of faith, but that a true believer may wait long, and conflict with many difficulties before he be partaker of it: yet, being enabled by the Spirit to know the things which are freely given him of God, he may, without extraordinary revelation, in the right use of ordinary means, attain thereunto. And therefore it is the duty of everyone to give all diligence to make his calling and election sure, that thereby his heart may be enlarged in peace and joy in the Holy Ghost, in love and thankfulness to God, and in strength and cheerfulness in the duties of obedience, the proper fruits of this assurance; so far is it from inclining men to looseness.

IV. True believers may have the assurance of their salvation divers ways shaken, diminished, and intermitted; as, by negligence in preserving of it, by falling into some special sin which woundeth the conscience, and grieveth the Spirit; by some sudden or vehement temptation, by God's withdrawing the light of his countenance, and suffering even such as fear him to walk in darkness, and to have no light: yet are they never utterly destitute of that seed of God, and life of faith, that love of Christ and the brethren, that sincerity of heart, and conscience of duty, out of which, by the operation of the Spirit, this assurance may, in due time, be revived; and by the which, in the meantime, they are supported from utter despair.

CHAP XIX. - *Of the Law of God.*

I. God gave to Adam a law, as a covenant of works, by which he bound him and all his posterity to personal, entire, exact, and perpetual obedience, promised life upon the fulfilling, and threatened death upon the breach of it, and endued him with power and ability to keep it.

II. This law, after his fall, continued to be a perfect rule of righteousness; and, as such, was delivered by God upon Mount Sinai, in ten commandments, and written in two tables: the four first commandments containing our duty towards God; and the other six, our duty to man.

III. Beside this law, commonly called moral, God was pleased to give to the people of Israel, as a church under age, ceremonial laws, containing several typical ordinances, partly of worship, prefiguring Christ, his graces, actions, sufferings, and benefits; and partly, holding forth divers instructions of moral duties. All which ceremonial laws are now abrogated, under the New Testament.

IV. To them also, as a body politic, he gave sundry judicial laws, which expired together with the state of that people; not obliging any other now, further than the general equity thereof may require.

V. The moral law doth forever bind all, as well justified persons as others, to the obedience thereof; and that, not only in regard of the matter contained in it, but also in respect of the authority of God the Creator, who gave it. Neither doth Christ, in the gospel, any way dissolve, but much strengthen this obligation.

VI. Although true believers be not under the law, as a covenant of works, to be thereby justified, or condemned; yet is it of great use to them, as well as to others; in that, as a rule of life informing them of the will of God, and their duty, it directs and binds them to walk accordingly; discovering also the sinful pollutions of their nature, hearts, and lives; so as, examining themselves thereby, they may come to further conviction of, humiliation for, and hatred against sin, together with a clearer sight of the need they have of Christ, and the perfection of his obedience. It is likewise of use to the regenerate, to restrain their corruptions, in that it forbids sin: and the threatenings of it serve to show what even their sins deserve; and what afflictions, in this life, they may expect for them, although freed from the curse thereof threatened in the law. The promises of it, in like manner, show them God's approbation of obedience, and what blessings they may expect upon the performance thereof: although not as due to them by the law as a covenant of works. So as, a man's doing good, and refraining from evil, because the law encourageth to the one, and deterreth from the other, is no evidence of his being under the law; and, not under grace.

VII. Neither are the aforementioned uses of the law contrary to the grace of the gospel, but do sweetly comply with it; the Spirit of Christ subduing and enabling the will of man to do that freely, and cheerfully, which the will of God, revealed in the law, requireth to be done.

CHAP XX. - *Of Christian Liberty, and Liberty of Conscience.*

I. The liberty which Christ hath purchased for believers under the gospel consists in their freedom from the guilt of sin, the condemning wrath of God, the curse of the moral law; and, in their being delivered from this present evil world, bondage to Satan, and dominion of sin; from the evil of afflictions, the sting of death, the victory of the grave, and everlasting damnation; as also, in their free access to God, and their yielding obedience unto him, not out of slavish fear, but a childlike love and willing mind. All which were common also to believers under the law. But, under the New Testament, the liberty of Christians is further enlarged, in their freedom from the yoke of the ceremonial law, to which the Jewish church was subjected; and in greater boldness of access to the throne of grace, and in fuller communications of the free Spirit of God, than believers under the law did ordinarily partake of.

II. God alone is Lord of the conscience, and hath left it free from the doctrines and commandments of men, which are, in anything, contrary to his Word; or beside it, if matters of faith, or worship. So that, to believe such doctrines, or to obey such commands, out of conscience, is to betray true liberty of conscience: and the requiring of an implicit faith, and an absolute and blind obedience, is to destroy liberty of conscience, and reason also.

III. They who, upon pretense of Christian liberty, do practice any sin, or cherish any lust, do thereby destroy the end of Christian liberty, which is, that being delivered out of the hands of our enemies, we might serve the Lord without fear, in holiness and righteousness before him, all the days of our life.

IV. And because the powers which God hath ordained, and the liberty which Christ hath purchased, are not intended by God to destroy, but mutually to uphold and preserve one another; they who, upon pretense of Christian liberty, shall oppose any lawful power, or the lawful exercise of it, whether it be civil or ecclesiastical, resist the ordinance of God. And, for their publishing of such opinions, or maintaining of such practices, as are contrary to the light of nature, or to the known principles of Christianity (whether concerning faith, worship, or conversation), or to the power of godliness; or, such erroneous opinions or practices, as either in their own nature, or in the manner of publishing or maintaining them, are destructive to he external peace and order which Christ hath established in the church, they may lawfully be called to account, and proceeded against, by the censures of the church, and by the power of the civil magistrate.

CHAP XXI. - *Of Religious Worship, and the Sabbath-day.*

I. The light of nature shows that there is a God, who has lordship and sovereignty over all, is good, and does good unto all, and is therefore to be feared, loved, praised, called upon, trusted in, and served, with all the heart, and with all the soul, and with all the might. (Rom. 1:20, Acts 17:24, Psalm 69:68, Jer. 10:7, Psalm 31:23, Psalm 18:3, Rom. 10:12, Psalm 62:8, Josh. 24:14, Mark 12:33) But the acceptable way of worshiping the true God is instituted by himself, and so limited by his own revealed will, that he may not be worshiped according to the imaginations and devices of men, or the suggestions of Satan, under any visible representation, or any other way not prescribed in the Holy Scripture. (Deut. 12:32, Matt. 15:9, Act 17:25, Matt. 4:9-10, Deut. 15:1-20, Exod. 20:4-6, Col. 2:23)

II. Religious worship is to be given to God, the Father, Son, and Holy Ghost; and to him alone; (Matt. 4:10, John 5:23, 2 Cor. 13:14) not to angels, saints, or any other creature: (Col. 2:18, Rev. 19:10, Rom. 1:25) and, since the fall, not without a Mediator; nor in the mediation of any other but of Christ alone. (John 14:6, 1 Tim. 2:5, Col.3:17)

III. Prayer, with thanksgiving, being one special part of religious worship, (Phil. 4:6) is by God required of all men: (Psalm 65:2) and, that it may be accepted, it is to be made in the name of the Son, (John 14:13-14, 1 Pet. 2:5) by the help of his Spirit, (Rom. 8:26) according to his will, (1 John 5:14) with understanding, reverence, humility, fervency, faith, love, and perseverance; (Psalm 47:7, Eccl. 5:1-2, Heb. 12:28, Gen. 18:27, James 5:16, James 1:6-7, Mark 11:24, Matt. 6:12-15, Col. 4:2, Eph 6:18) and, if vocal, in a known tongue. (1 Cor. 14:14)

IV. Prayer is to be made for things lawful; (1John 5:14) and for all sorts of men living, or that shall live hereafter: (1Tim. 2:1-2, John 17:20, 2 Sam. 7:29, Ruth 4:12) but not for the dead, (2 Sam. 12:21-23, Luke 16:25-26, Rev. 14:13) nor for those of whom it may be known that they have sinned the sin unto death. (1 John 5:16)

V. The reading of the Scriptures with godly fear, the sound preaching and conscionable hearing of the Word, in obedience unto God, with understanding, faith, and reverence, singing of psalms with grace in the heart; as also, the due administration and worthy receiving of the sacraments instituted by Christ, are all parts of the ordinary religious worship of God: beside religious oaths, vows, solemn fastings, and thanksgivings upon special occasions, which are, in their several times and seasons, to be used in an holy and religious manner.

VI. Neither prayer, nor any other part of religious worship, is now, under the gospel, either tied unto, or made more acceptable by any place in which it is performed, or towards which it is directed: but God is to be worshiped everywhere, in spirit and truth; as, in private families daily, and in secret, each one by himself; so, more solemnly in the public assemblies, which are not carelessly or willfully to be neglected, or forsaken, when God, by his Word or providence, calleth thereunto.

VII. As it is the law of nature, that, in general, a due proportion of time be set apart for the worship of God; so, in his Word, by a positive, moral, and perpetual commandment binding all men in all ages, he hath particularly appointed one day in seven, for a Sabbath, to be kept holy unto him: which, from the beginning of the world to the resurrection of Christ, was the last day of the week; and, from the resurrection of Christ, was changed into the first day of the week, which, in Scripture, is called the Lord's day, and is to be continued to the end of the world, as the Christian Sabbath.

VIII. This Sabbath is then kept holy unto the Lord, when men, after a due preparing of their hearts, and ordering of their common affairs beforehand, do not only observe an holy rest, all the day, from their own works, words, and thoughts about their worldly employments and recreations, but also are taken up, the whole time, in the public and private exercises of his worship, and in the duties of necessity and mercy.

CHAP XXII. - *Of lawful Oaths and Vows.*

I. A lawful oath is a part of religious worship, wherein, upon just occasion, the person swearing solemnly calleth God to witness what he asserteth, or promiseth, and to judge him according to the truth or falsehood of what he sweareth.

II. The name of God only is that by which men ought to swear, and therein it is to be used with all holy fear and reverence. Therefore, to swear vainly, or rashly, by that glorious and dreadful Name; or, to swear at all by any other thing, is sinful, and to be abhorred. Yet, as in matters of weight and moment, an oath is warranted by the Word of God, under the New Testament as well as under the Old; so a lawful oath, being imposed by lawful authority, in such matters, ought to be taken.

III. Whosoever taketh an oath ought duly to consider the weightiness of so solemn an act, and therein to avouch nothing but what he is fully persuaded is the truth: neither may any man bind himself by oath to anything but what is good and just, and what he believeth so to be, and what he is able and resolved to perform.

IV. An oath is to be taken in the plain and common sense of the words, without equivocation, or mental reservation. It cannot oblige to sin; but in anything not sinful, being taken, it binds to performance, although to a man's own hurt. Nor is it to be violated, although made to heretics, or infidels.

V. A vow is of the like nature with a promissory oath, and ought to be made with the like religious care, and to be performed with the like faithfulness.

VI. It is not to be made to any creature, but to God alone: and, that it may be accepted, it is to be made voluntarily, out of faith, and conscience of duty, in way of thankfulness for mercy received, or for the obtaining of what we want, whereby we more strictly bind ourselves to necessary duties; or, to other things, so far and so long as they may fitly conduce thereunto.

VII. No man may vow to do anything forbidden in the Word of God, or what would hinder any duty therein commanded, or which is not in his own power, and for the performance whereof he hath no promise of ability from God. In which respects, popish monastical vows of perpetual single life, professed poverty, and regular obedience, are so far from being degrees of higher perfection, that they are superstitious and sinful snares, in which no Christian may entangle himself.

CHAP XXIII. - *Of the Civil Magistrate.*

I. God, the supreme Lord and King of all the world, hath ordained civil magistrates, to be, under him, over the people, for his own glory, and the public good: and, to this end, hath armed them with the power of the sword, for the defense and encouragement of them that are good, and for the punishment of evil doers.

II. It is lawful for Christians to accept and execute the office of a magistrate, when called thereunto: in the managing whereof, as they ought especially to maintain piety, justice, and peace, according to the wholesome laws of each commonwealth; so, for that end, they may lawfully, now under the New Testament, wage war, upon just and necessary occasion.

III. The civil magistrate may not assume to himself the

administration of the word and sacraments, or the power of the keys of the kingdom of heaven; yet he hath authority, and it is his duty, to take order, that unity and peace be preserved in the church, that the truth of God be kept pure and entire, that all blasphemies and heresies be suppressed, all corruptions and abuses in worship and discipline prevented or reformed, and all the ordinances of God duly settled, administered and observed. For the better effecting whereof, he hath power to call synods, to be present at them, and to provide that whatsoever is transacted in them be according to the mind of God.

IV. It is the duty of people to pray for magistrates, to honor their persons, to pay them tribute or other dues, to obey their lawful commands, and to be subject to their authority, for conscience' sake. Infidelity, or difference in religion, doth not make void the magistrates' just and legal authority, nor free the people from their due obedience to them: from which ecclesiastical persons are not exempted, much less hath the pope any power and jurisdiction over them in their dominions, or over any of their people; and, least of all, to deprive them of their dominions, or lives, if he shall judge them to be heretics, or upon any other pretense whatsoever.

CHAP XXIV. - *Of Marriage and Divorce.*

I. Marriage is to be between one man and one woman: neither is it lawful for any man to have more than one wife, nor for any woman to have more than one husband, at the same time.

II. Marriage was ordained for the mutual help of husband and wife, for the increase of mankind with legitimate issue, and of the church with an holy seed; and for preventing of uncleanness.

III. It is lawful for all sorts of people to marry, who are able with judgment to give their consent. Yet it is the duty of Christians to marry only in the Lord. And therefore such as profess the true reformed religion should not marry with infidels, Papists, or other idolaters: neither should such as are godly be unequally yoked, by marrying with such as are notoriously wicked in their life, or maintain damnable heresies.

IV. Marriage ought not to be within the degrees of consanguinity or affinity forbidden by the Word. Nor can such incestuous marriages ever be made lawful by any law of man or consent of parties, so as those persons may live together as man and wife. The man may not marry any of his wife's kindred nearer in blood than he may in his own, nor the woman of her husband's kindred nearer in blood than of her own.

V. Adultery or fornication committed after a contract, being detected before marriage, giveth just occasion to the innocent party to dissolve that contract. In the case of adultery after marriage, it is lawful for the innocent party to sue out a divorce: and, after the divorce, to marry another, as if the offending party were dead.

VI. Although the corruption of man be such as is apt to study arguments unduly to put asunder those whom God hath joined together in marriage: yet, nothing but adultery, or such willful desertion as can no way be remedied by the church, or civil magistrate, is cause sufficient of dissolving the bond of marriage: wherein, a public and orderly course of proceeding is to be observed; and the persons concerned in it not left to their own wills, and discretion, in their own case.

CHAP XXV. - *Of the Church.*

I. The catholic or universal church, which is invisible, consists of the whole number of the elect, that have been, are, or shall be gathered into one, under Christ the head thereof; and is the spouse, the body, and the fullness of him that filleth all in all.

II. The visible church, which is also catholic or universal under the gospel (not confined to one nation, as before under the law), consists of all those throughout the world that profess the true religion; and of their children: and is the kingdom of the Lord Jesus Christ, the house and family of God, out of which there is no ordinary possibility of salvation.

III. Unto this catholic visible church Christ hath given the ministry, oracles, and ordinances of God, for the gathering and perfecting of the saints, in this life, to the end of the world: and doth, by his own presence and Spirit, according to his promise, make them effectual thereunto.

IV. This Catholic Church hath been sometimes more, sometimes less visible. And particular churches, which are members thereof, are more or less pure, according as the doctrine of the gospel is taught and embraced, ordinances administered, and public worship performed more or less purely in them.

V. The purest churches under heaven are subject both to mixture and error; and some have so degenerated, as to become no churches of Christ, but synagogues of Satan. Nevertheless, there shall be always a church on earth, to worship God according to his will.

VI. There is no other head of the church but the Lord Jesus Christ. Nor can the pope of Rome, in any sense, be head thereof; but is that antichrist, that man of sin, and son of perdition, that exalteth himself in the church against Christ, and all that is called God.

CHAP XXVI. - *Of Communion of Saints.*

I. All saints, that are united to Jesus Christ their head, by his Spirit, and by faith, have fellowship with him in his graces, sufferings, death, resurrection, and glory. And being united to one another in love, they have communion in each other's gifts and graces; and are obliged to the performance of such duties, public and private, as do conduce to their mutual good, both in the inward and outward man.

II. Saints by profession are bound to maintain a holy fellowship and communion in the worship of God, and in performing such other spiritual services as tend to their mutual edification; as also in relieving each other in outward things, according to their several abilities and necessities. Which communion, as God offereth opportunity, is to be extended unto all those who in every place call upon the name of the Lord Jesus.

III. This communion which the saints have with Christ, doth not make them in any wise partakers of the substance of his Godhead; or to be equal with Christ in any respect: either of which to affirm is impious and blasphemous. Nor doth their communion one with another, as saints, take away, or infringe the title or propriety which each man hath in his goods and possessions.

CHAP XXVII. - *Of the Sacraments.*

I. Sacraments are holy signs and seals of the covenant of grace, immediately instituted by God, to represent Christ, and his benefits; and to confirm our interest in him; as also, to put a visible difference between those that belong unto the church, and the rest of the world; and solemnly to engage them to the service of God in Christ, according to his Word.

II. There is, in every sacrament, a spiritual relation, or sacramental union, between the sign and the thing signified: whence it comes to pass, that the names and effects of the one are attributed to the other.

III. The grace which is exhibited in or by the sacraments rightly used, is not conferred by any power in them; neither doth the efficacy of a sacrament depend upon the piety or intention of him that doth administer it: but upon the work of the Spirit, and the word of institution, which contains, together with a precept authorizing the use thereof, a promise of benefit to worthy receivers.

IV. There be only two sacraments ordained by Christ our Lord in the gospel; that is to say, Baptism, and the Supper of the Lord: neither of which may be dispensed by any, but by a minister of the Word lawfully ordained.

V. The sacraments of the Old Testament, in regard of the spiritual things thereby signified and exhibited, were, for substance, the same with those of the New.

CHAP XXVIII. - *Of Baptism.*

I. Baptism is a sacrament of the New Testament, ordained by Jesus Christ, (Matt. 28:19) not only for the solemn admission of the party baptized into the visible church; (1 Cor. 12:13) but also, to be unto him a sign and seal of the covenant of grace, (Rom. 4:11, Col. 2:11,12) of his ingrafting into Christ, (Gal. 3:27, Rom. 6:5) of regeneration, (Tit. 3:5) of remission of sins, (Mark 1:4) and of his giving up unto God, through Jesus Christ, to walk in newness of life: (Rom. 6:3,4) which sacrament is, by Christ's own appointment, to be continued in his church until the end of the world. (Matt. 28:19,20)

II. The outward element to be used in this sacrament is

water, wherewith the party is to be baptized, in the name of the Father, and of the Son, and of the Holy Ghost, by a minister of the gospel, lawfully called thereunto. (Matt. 3:11, John 1:33, Matt. 28:19,20)

III. Dipping of the person into the water is not necessary; but Baptism is rightly administered by pouring, or sprinkling water upon the person. (Heb. 9:10,19,20,21,22, Acts 16:33, Mark 7:4)

IV. Not only those that do actually profess faith in and obedience unto Christ, (Mark 26:15,16, Acts 8:37,38) but also the infants of one, or both, believing parents, are to be baptized. (Gen 17:7,9, Gal. 3:9,14, Col. 2:11,12, Acts 2:38,39, Rom. 4:11,12, 1 Cor. 7:14, Matt. 28:19, Mark 10:13,14,15,16, Luke 18:15)

V. Although it be a great sin to contemn or neglect this ordinance, (Luke 7:30, Exod. 4:24,25,26) yet grace and salvation are not so inseparably annexed unto it, as that no person can be regenerated, or saved, without it; (Rom. 4:11, Acts 10:2,4,22,31,45,47) or, that all that are baptized are undoubtedly regenerated (Acts 7:13,23)

VI. The efficacy of Baptism is not tied to that moment of time wherein it is administered; (John 3:5,8) yet, notwithstanding, by the right use of this ordinance, the grace promised is not only offered, but really exhibited, and conferred, by the Holy Ghost, to such (whether of age or infants) as that grace belongeth unto, according to the counsel of God's own will, in his appointed time. (Gal. 3:27, Tit. 3:5, Eph. 5:26, Acts 2:38,41)

VII. The sacrament of Baptism is but once to be administered unto any person (Tit. 3:5)

CHAP XXIX. - *Of the Lord's Supper.*

I. Our Lord Jesus, in the night wherein he was betrayed, instituted the sacrament of his body and blood, called the Lord's Supper, to be observed in his church, unto the end of the world, for the perpetual remembrance of the sacrifice of himself in his death; the sealing all benefits thereof unto true believers, their spiritual nourishment and growth in him, their further engagement in and to all duties which they owe unto him; and, to be a bond and pledge of their communion with him, and with each other, as members of his mystical body.

II. In this sacrament, Christ is not offered up to his Father; nor any real sacrifice made at all, for remission of sins of the quick or dead; but only a commemoration of that one offering up of himself, by himself, upon the cross, once for all: and a spiritual oblation of all possible praise unto God, for the same: so that the popish sacrifice of the mass (as they call it) is most abominably injurious to Christ's one, only sacrifice, the alone propitiation for all the sins of his elect.

III. The Lord Jesus hath, in this ordinance, appointed his ministers to declare his word of institution to the people; to pray, and bless the elements of bread and wine, and thereby to set them apart from a common to an holy use; and to take and break the bread, to take the cup, and (they communicating also themselves) to give both to the communicants; but to none who are not then present in the congregation.

IV. Private masses, or receiving this sacrament by a priest, or any other, alone; as likewise, the denial of the cup to the people, worshiping the elements, the lifting them up, or carrying them about, for adoration, and the reserving them for any pretended religious use; are all contrary to the nature of this sacrament, and to the institution of Christ.

V. The outward elements in this sacrament, duly set apart to the uses ordained by Christ, have such relation to him crucified, as that, truly, yet sacramentally only, they are sometimes called by the name of the things they represent, to wit, the body and blood of Christ; albeit, in substance and nature, they still remain truly and only bread and wine, as they were before.

VI. That doctrine which maintains a change of the substance of bread and wine, into the substance of Christ's body and blood (commonly called transubstantiation) by consecration of a priest, or by any other way, is repugnant, not to Scripture alone, but even to common sense, and reason; overthroweth the nature of the sacrament, and hath been, and is, the cause of manifold superstitions; yea, of gross idolatries.

VII. Worthy receivers, outwardly partaking of the visible elements, in this sacrament, do then also, inwardly by faith, really and indeed, yet not carnally and corporally but spiritually, receive, and feed upon, Christ crucified, and all benefits of his death: the body and blood of Christ being then, not corporally or carnally, in, with, or under the bread and wine; yet, as really, but spiritually, present to the faith of believers in that ordinance, as the elements themselves are to their outward senses.

VIII. Although ignorant and wicked men receive the outward

elements in this sacrament; yet, they receive not the thing signified thereby; but, by their unworthy coming thereunto, are guilty of the body and blood of the Lord, to their own damnation. Wherefore, all ignorant and ungodly persons, as they are unfit to enjoy communion with him, so are they unworthy of the Lord's table; and cannot, without great sin against Christ, while they remain such, partake of these holy mysteries, or be admitted thereunto.

CHAP XXX. - *Of Church Censures.*

I. The Lord Jesus, as king and head of his church, hath therein appointed a government, in the hand of church officers, distinct from the civil magistrate.

II. To these officers the keys of the kingdom of heaven are committed; by virtue whereof, they have power, respectively, to retain, and remit sins; to shut that kingdom against the impenitent, both by the Word, and censures; and to open it unto penitent sinners, by the ministry of the gospel; and by absolution from censures, as occasion shall require.

III. Church censures are necessary, for the reclaiming and gaining of offending brethren, for deterring of others from the like offenses, for purging out of that leaven which might infect the whole lump, for vindicating the honor of Christ, and the holy profession of the gospel, and for preventing the wrath of God, which might justly fall upon the church, if they should suffer his covenant, and the seals thereof, to be profaned by notorious and obstinate offenders.

IV. For the better attaining of these ends, the officers of the church are to proceed by admonition; suspension from the sacrament of the Lord's Supper for a season; and by excommunication from the church; according to the nature of the crime, and demerit of the person.

CHAP XXXI. - *Of Synods and Councils.*

I. For the better government, and further edification of the church, there ought to be such assemblies as are commonly called synods or councils:

II. As magistrates may lawfully call a synod of ministers, and other fit persons, to consult and advise with about matters of religion; so if Magistrates were open enemies to the church, the ministers of Christ, of themselves, by virtue of their office, or they, with other fit persons upon delegation from their churches, may meet together in such assemblies.

III. It belongeth to synods and councils, ministerially to determine controversies of faith, and cases of conscience; to set down rules and directions for the better ordering of the public worship of God, and government of his church; to receive complaints in cases of maladministration, and authoritatively to determine the same: which decrees and determinations, if consonant to the Word of God, are to be received with reverence and submission; not only for their agreement with the Word, but also for the power whereby they are made, as being an ordinance of God appointed thereunto in his Word.

IV. All synods or councils, since the apostles' times, whether general or particular, may err; and many have erred. Therefore they are not to be made the rule of faith, or practice; but to be used as a help in both.

V. Synods and councils are to handle, or conclude nothing, but that which is ecclesiastical: and are not to intermeddle with civil affairs which concern the commonwealth, unless by way of humble petition in cases extraordinary; or, by way of advice, for satisfaction of conscience, if they be thereunto required by the civil magistrate.

CHAP XXXII. - *Of the State of Men after Death, an of the Resurrection of the Dead.*

I. The bodies of men, after death, return to dust, and see corruption: but their souls, which neither die nor sleep, having an immortal subsistence, immediately return to God who gave them: the souls of the righteous, being then made perfect in holiness, are received into the highest heavens, where they behold the face of God, in light and glory, waiting for the full redemption of their bodies. And the souls of the wicked are cast into hell, where they remain in torments and utter darkness, reserved to the judgment of the great day. Beside these two places, for souls separated from their bodies, the Scripture acknowledgeth none.

II. At the last day, such as are found alive shall not die, but be changed: and all the dead shall be raised up, with the selfsame bodies, and none other although with different qualities, which shall be united again to their souls forever.

III. The bodies of the unjust shall, by the power of Christ, be raised to dishonor: the bodies of the just, by his Spirit, unto honor; and be made conformable to his own glorious body.

CHAP XXXIII. - *Of the Last Judgment.*

I. God hath appointed a day, wherein he will judge the world, in righteousness, by Jesus Christ, to whom all power and judgment is given of the Father. In which day, not only the apostate angels shall be judged, but likewise all persons that have lived upon earth shall appear before the tribunal of Christ, to give an account of their thoughts, words, and deeds; and to receive according to what they have done in the body, whether good or evil.

II. The end of God's appointing this day is for the manifestation of the glory of his mercy, in the eternal salvation of the elect; and of his justice, in the damnation of the reprobate, who are wicked and disobedient. For then shall the righteous go into everlasting life, and receive that fullness of joy and refreshing, which shall come from the presence of the Lord; but the wicked who know not God, and obey not the gospel of Jesus Christ, shall be cast into eternal torments, and be punished with everlasting destruction from the presence of the Lord, and from the glory of his power.

III. As Christ would have us to be certainly persuaded that there shall be a day of judgment, both to deter all men from sin; and for the greater consolation of the godly in their adversity: so will he have that day unknown to men, that they may shake off all carnal security, and be always watchful, because they know not at what hour the Lord will come; and may be ever prepared to say, Come Lord Jesus, come quickly, *Amen.*

Appendix 4

The Covenant of 1581 'The Kings Confession'

We all and everie one of us underwritten protest, that after long and dew examination of our owne consciences in matteris of true and false religioun, are now throughly resolved in the trueth by the worde and spirit of God, and therefore we beleve with our heartis, confesse with our mouthes, subscryve with our handis, and constantly affirme before God and the whole world, that this onely is the true Christiane fayth and religion pleasing God and bringing salvation to man, quhilk is now by the mercy of God reveled to the World by the preaching of the blessed evangell, and is receaved, beleved and defended by manie and sindrie notable kyrkis and realmes, but chiefly by the kyrk of Scotlarnd, the kingis majestie, and three estatis of this realme, as Godis eteternall trueth and onely ground of our salvation, as more perticulerly is expressed in the confession of our fayth stablished and publictly confirmed by sindrie actis of perlamentis, arid now of a long tymie had bene openly professed by the kingis Majestie and whole body of this realime both in brught and land: To the quhilk confession and formie of religion we willingly aggree in our conscience in all poyntis as unto Godis undoubted trueth and veritie grounded onely upon his written worde. Arid therefore we abhorre and detest all coritrarie religion and doctrine, but chiefly all kynd of papistrie in generall arid pertictiler headis even as they are now damned and confuted by the worde of God and kyrk of Scotland; but in speciale we detest and refuse the usurped authoritie of that Roman Antichrist upon the scriptures of God, upon the kyrk, the civille magistrate and conscience of men: All his tyrannous laes made upon indifferent thingis, agaynst our. cliristiane libertie; his erroneous doctrine agaynst the sufficiencie. of the written worde, the perfection of the lawe, the office of Christ, and his blessed evangell; his corrupted doctrine coricernyng origirnall synne, ou naturall inabilitie and rebellion to God's Law, our justification by fayth onely, oiir imperfect sanctification, and obedience to the lawe; the nature, number, and use of the holie sacramentis; his fyve bastard sacramentis, with all his ritis, ceremoneis, and false doctrine added to the ministration of the true sacramentis without the worde of God; his cruell judgement agaynst infantis deperting without the sacrament, his absolute necessitie of baptisme, his bIasphemous opinion of transubstantiation. or reall presence of Cliristis body in the elementis, and receaving of the same by the wicked. or bodeis of men, his dispensationeis with solemnit othes, perjuries, and degrees of mariage forbidden in the worde, his crueltie agaynst the innocent devorced; his divilish mes, his blasphemous priesthead, his prophane sacrifice for the synnes of the dead and quyck, his canonization of men, calling upon angellis, or sainctis deperted, worshipping of imagrie, relics and croces, dedicating of kyrkis, altaris, dayis, vowes to creatures, his purgatorie, prayeris for the dead, praying or speaking in a strange language, with his processioneis and blasphemous letanie, and multitude of advocattis or mediatoreis; his manyfold ordoures, auricular confession, his despered and uncertayne repentance, his generall and doubtsome fayth, the satisfactioneis of men for their synnes; his justification by workis, his opus operatum, workes of supererogation, meritis,perdones, peregrinationes, and stationeis; his holy water, baptisyng of bellis, cungering of spirits, crocing, saning, anoynting, conjuring, hallowing of Godis good creatures with the superstitious opinion joyned therewith; his worldly monarchy and wicked hierarchie, his three solemnit vowes with all his shavelings of syridrie sortes; his erroneous and bloodie decretes made at Trent, with all the subscyveris and approveris of that cruell and bloodie band conjured agaynst the kyrk of God; and fynally we detetst all his vane allegories, ritis, signes and traditioneis broght in the kyrk without or agaynst the worde of God and doctrine of this true reformed kyrk, to the quhilk we join ourselves willingly in doctrine, faytlh religion, discipline, and use of the holie sacramentis, as lyvely memberis of the same in Christ our head, promising and swearing by the great name of the Lord our God that we shall continue in the obedience of the doctrine and discipline of this kyrk and shal defend the dame according to our vocation 'and power all the dayes of our lyves, under the panes conteyned in the law, and danger both of body and saule in the day of God's fearfull jusgement. Arid seing that manie are styrred tip by Satan and that Roman Antichrist to promise, swear, subscryve and for a tyme use the holie scaramentis in the kyrk deceatfully agaynst there owne conscience, mynding thereby fyrst, under the externall clok of the religion to corrupt and subvert secretly God is true religion within the kyrk, and afterward, when tyme may serve, to become open ennemeis and persecutorsis of the same, under vane hope of the papis dispensation, divised agaynst the worde of God to his greater confusion and theyr dowble condemnation in the day of the Lord Jesus, we therefore, willing to tak away all suspition of hypocrisie and of syk dowble dealing with and his kyrk, protest and call the searcher of all heartis for witnes, that ourmyndis and heartis do fullely aggree with this our confession, promise, othe, and subscription; so that we are not moved for any worldly respect, but are persuaded onely in our conscience through the knowledge and love of God is true religion prented in heartis by the holie spirit, as we shall answer to himin the day when the secretis of all heartis shal be disclosed. And because we perceave that the quitness and stabilitie of our religion and kyrk doth depend upon the savetie and good behaviour of the kynges majestie as upon ane confortable instrument of Godis mercy graunted to this contrey for the maintaining of this kyrk and ministration of justice amongis us, we protest and promis solemnetly with our heartis under the same othe, hand writ, and panes, that we shall defend his persone and authoritie with our goodis, bodyes, and lyves in the defence of Christis evangell, libertie of our contrey, ministration of justice, and punishment of iniquitie, agaynst all enemeis within this realme or without, as we desyre our God to be a strong and mercyfull defender to us in the day of our death and coming of Lord Jesus Christ, to whome with the Father and Holie Spirit be all honour and glorie. Amen

Appendix 5

The National Covenant Signed in Greyfriars Kirk, Edinburgh 28 February 1638

The complete document was in three parts:

1. A recital of the Covenant of 1581, sometimes called the Kings Confession. (See Appendix 4)

2. A reprise of the legislation that had been enacted since 1581 that sets out the rights of the Reformed Kirk of Scotland.

3. The 1638 Covenant, which is reproduced below.

The Confession of Faith of the Kirk of Scotland, subscribed at first by the King's Majesty and his household in the year of God 1580; thereafter by persons of all ranks in the year 1581, by ordinance of the lords of tlie. Secret council and acts of the general assembly; subscribed again by all sorts of persons in the year 1590, by a new ordinance of the council, at the desire of the general assembly; with a general band for the maintenance of the true religion and the king's person, and now subscribed in the year 1638 by us noblemen, barons, gentlemen, burgesses, ministers and commons undersubscribirig; together with our resolution and promises for the causes after specified, to maintain the said true religion, and the King's Majesty according to the confession aforesaid and acts of parliament: the tenor whereof here followeth.

In obedience to the Commandment of God, conform to the practice of the godly in former times, and according to the laudable example of our Worthy and Religious Progenitors, & of many yet living amongst us, which was warranted also by act of Council, commanding a general band to be made and subscribed by his Majesty's subjects, of all ranks, for two causes: One was, For defending the true Religion, as it was then reformed, and is expressed in the Confession of Faith above written, and a former large Confession established by sundry acts of lawful general assemblies, & of Parliament, unto which it hath relation, set down in publick Catechismes, and which had been for many years witli a blessing from heaven preached, and professed in this Kirkand Kingdome, as Gods undoubted truth, grounded only upon his written Word. The other cause was, for maintaining the Kings Majesty, his Person, and Estate: the true worship of God and the Kings authority, being so staidly joined, as that they had the same friends, and common enemies, and did stand and fall together. And finally, being convinced in our minds, and confessing with our mouths, that the present and succeeding generations in this land, are bound to keep the foresaid national Oath and Subscription inviolable, Wee Noblemen, Barons, Gentlemen, Burgesses, Ministers & Commons under subscribing, considering divers times before & especially at this time, the danger of the true reformed Religion, of the Kings honour, and of the publick peace of the Kingdome: By the manifold innovation and evils generally contained, and particularly mentioned in our late supplications, complaints, and protestations, Do hereby profess, and before God, his Angels, and the World solemnly declare, That with our whole hearts we agree and resolve, all the days of our life, constantly to adhere unto, and to defend the foresaid true Religion, and (forswearing the practice of all novations, already introduced in the matters of the worship of God, or approbation of the corruptions of the publick Government of the Kirk, or civil places and power of Kirk-Men, till they be tried and allowed in free assemblies, and in Parliaments) to labour by all means lawful to recover the purity and liberty of the Gospel, as it was established and professed before the foresaid Novations: and because, after due examination, we plainly perceive, and undoubtedly believe, that the Innovations and evils contained in our Supplications,

Complaints, and Protestations have no warrant of the Word of God, are contrary to the Articles of the Foresaid Confessions, to the intention and meaning of the blessed reformers of Religion in this Land, to the above written Acts of Parliament, & do sensibly tend to the reestablishing of the Popish Religion and Tyranny, arid to the subversion and ruin of the true Reformed Religion, and of our Liberties, Lawes and Estates, We also declare, that the Foresaid Confessions are to be interpreted, and ought to be understood of the Foresaid novations and evils, no less than if every one of them had been expressed in the Foresaid confessions, and that we are obliged to detest and abhorre them amongst other particular heads of Papistry abjured therein. And therefore from the knowledge and consciences of our duty to God, to our King and Country, without any worldly respect or inducement, so farre as humane infirmity will suffer, wishing a further measure of the grace of God for this effect, we promise, and swear by the Great Name of the Lord our God, to continue in the Profession and Obedience of the Foresaid Religion: That we shall defend the same, and resist all these contrary errours and corruptions, according to our vocation, and to the uttermost of that power that God hatli put in our hands, all the days of our life: and in like manner with the same heart, we declare before God and Men, that we have no intention nor desire to attempt anything that may turn to the dishonour of God, or to the diminution of the Kings greatness and authority: But on the contrary, we promise arid swear, that we shall, to the uttermost of our power, with our means and lives, attend to the defence of our dread Sovereign, the Kings Majesty, his Person, and Authority, in the defence and preservation of the foresaid true Religion, Liberties and Lawes of the Kingdome: As also to the mutual defence and assistance, every one of us of another in the same cause of maintaining the true Religion and his Majesty's Authority, with our best counsel, our bodies, means, and whole power, against all sorts of persons whatsoever. So that whatsoever shall be done to the least of us for that cause, shall be take as done to us all in general, and to every one of us in particular. And that we shall neither directly nor indirectly suffer ourselves to be divided or withdrawn by whatsoever suggestion, allurement, or terrour from this blessed and loyal Conjunction, nor shall cast in any let or impediment, that may stay or hinder any such resolution as by common consent shall be found to conduce for so good ends. But on the contrary, shall by all lawful means labour to further and promote the same, and if any such dangerous & divisive motion be made to us by Word or Writ, We, and every one of us, shall either suppress it, or if need be shall incontinent make the same known, that it may be timeously obviated: neither do we fear the foul aspersions of rebellion, combination, or what else our adversaries from their craft arid malice would put upon us, seeing that what we do is so well warranted, and ariseth from an unfeigned desire to maintains the true worship of God, the Majesty of our King, arid peace of the Kingdome, for the common happiness of our selves, and the posterity. And because we cannot look for a blessing from God upon our proceedings, except with our Profession and Subscription we join such a life and conversation, as beseemeth Christians who have renewed their Covenant witli God; We, therefore, faithfully promise, for ourselves, our followers, and all other under us, both in publick, in our particular families, and personal carriage, to endeavour to keep our selves within the bounds of Christian liberty, and to be good examples to others of all Godliness, Sobernesse, and Righteousness and of every duty we owe to God and Man. And that this our Union and conjunction may be observed without violation we call the living God, the Searcher of our hearts to witness, wlio knoweth this to be our sincere Desire, and unfained Resolution, as we shall answer to Jesus Christ, in the great day, and under the pain of God's everlasting wrath, and of infamy, and loss of all honour and respect in this World, most humbly beseeching the Lord to strengthen us by his holy Spirit for this end, and to bless our desires and proceedings with a happy success, that Religion and Righteousness may flourish in the Land, to the glory of God, the Honour of our King, and peace and comfort of us all. In witness whereof we have, subscribed with our hands all the premises, &c.

Appendix 6

The Solemn League and Covenant 1643

The Solemn League and Covenant for Reformation and Defence of Religion, the Honour and Happiness of the King, and the Peace and Safety of the Three Kingdoms of Scotland, England, and Ireland; Agreed upon by Commissioners from the Parliament and Assembly of Divines in England, with Commissioners of the Convention of Estates, and General Assembly in Scotland; approved by the General Assembly of the Church of Scotland, and by both Houses of Parliament and assembly of Divines in England, and taken and subscribed by them, *Anno* 1643; and thereafter, by the said authority, taken and subscribed by all Ranks in Scotland and England the same year; and ratified by Act of the Parliament of Scotland, *Anno* 1644: And again renewed in Scotland with an Acknowledgement of Sins, and Engagement to Duties, by all Ranks, *Anno* 1648, and by Parliament 1649; and taken and subscribed by *King Charles II, at Spey, June 23, 1650;* and at *Scoon, January 1, 1651.*

We Noblemen, Barrons, Knights, Gentlemen, Citizens, Burgesses, Ministers of the Gospel, and Commons of all sorts, in the Kingdoms of Scotland, England, and Ireland, by the providence of GOD, living under one king, and being one reformed religion, Having before our eyes the glory of GOD, and the advancement of the kingdom of our Lord and Saviour JESUS CHRIST, the honour and Happiness of the King's Majesty and his posterity, and true publick liberty, safety, and peace of the kingdoms, wherein every one's private condition is included: And calling in mind the treacherous and bloody plots, conspiracies, attempts, and practices of the enemies of GOD, against the true religion and professors thereof in all places, especially in these three kingdoms, ever since the reformation of religion; and how much their rage, power, and presumption are of late, and at this time, increased and exercised, whereof the deplorable state of the church and kingdom of Ireland, the distressed estate of the church and kingdom of England, and the dangerous estate of the church and kingdom of Scotland, are present and public testimonies; we have now at last, (after other means of supplication, remonstrance, protestation, and sufferings,) for the preservation of ourselves and our religion from utter ruin and destruction, according to the commendable practice of these kingdoms in former times, and the example of GOD'S people in other nations, after mature deliberation, resolved and determined to enter into a mutual and solemn League and Covenant, wherein we all subscribe, and each one of us for himself, with our hands lifted up to the most High GOD, do swear,

1. That we shall sincerely, really, and constantly, through the grace of GOD, endevour, in our several places and callings, the preservation of reformed religion in the Church of Scotland, in doctrine, worship, discipline, and government, against our common enemies; the reformation of religion in the kingdoms of England and Ireland, in doctrine, worship, discipline, and government, according to the word of GOD, and example of the best reformed Churches; and shall endevour to bring the Churches of God in the three kingdoms to the nearest conjunction and uniformity in religion, confession of faith, form of church-government, directory for worship and catechising: that we and our posterity after us, may, as brethren, live in faith and love, and the Lord may delight to dwell in the midst of us.

2. That we shall in like manner, without respect of persons, endeavour the extirpatation of Popery, Prelacy, (that is, Church-government by Archbishops, Bishops, their Chancellors, and Commissaries, Deans, Deans and Chapters, Archdeacons, and all other ecclesiastical Officers depending on that hierarchy,) superstition, heresy, schism, profaneness, and whatsoever shall be found contrary to sound doctrine and the power of godliness, lest we partake in other men's sins, and thereby be in danger to receive of their plagues; and that the Lord may be one, and his name one, in three kingdoms.

3. We shall, with the same sincerity, reality, and constancy, in our several avocations, endeavour, with our estates and lives, mutually to preserve the rights and privileges of the Parliaments, and the liberties of the kingdoms; and to preserve and defend the King's Majesty's person and authority, in the preservation and defence of the true religion, and liberties of the kingdoms; that the world may bear witness with our consciences of our loyalty, and that we have no thoughts or intentions to diminish hi Majesty's just power and greatness.

4. We shall also, with all faithfulness, endeavour the discovery of all such as have been or shall be incendiaries, malignants, or evil instruments, by hindering the reformation of religion, dividing the king and his people, or one of the kingdoms from another, or making any faction or parties amongst the people, contrary to this League and Covenant; that they may be brought to publick trial, and receive condign punishment, as the degree of their offences shall require or deserve, or the supreme judicatories of both kingdoms respectively, or others having power from them for that effect, shall judge convenient.

5. And whereas the happiness of a blessed peace between these kingdoms, denied in former times to our progenitors, is, by the good providence of GOD, granted unto us, hath been lately concluded and settled by both parliaments; we shall each one of us, according to our place and interest, endevour that they may remain conjoined in a firm peace and union to all posterity; and that justice may be done upon the willful opposers thereof, in manner expressed in the precedent article.

6. We shall also, according to our places and callings, in this common cause of religion, liberty, and peace of the kingdoms, assist and defend all those who enter into this League and Covenant, in the maintaining and pursuing thereof; and shall not suffer ourselves, directly or indirectly, by whatsoever combination, persuasion, or terror, to be divided and withdrawn from this blessed union and conjunction, whether to make defection to the contrary part, or to give ourselves to a detestable indifference or neutrality in this cause which so much concerneth the glory of GOD, the good of the kingdom, and honor of the King; but shall, all the days of our lives, zealously and constantly continue therein against all opposition, and promote the same, according to our power, against all opposition, and promote the same, according to our power, against all lets and impediments

whatsoever; and, what we are not able ourselves to suppress or overcome, we shall reveal and make known, that it may be timely prevented or removed: And all which we shall do in the sight of GOD.

And, because these kingdoms are guilty of many sins and provocations against GOD, and his Son JESUS CHRIST, as is to manifest by our present distresses and dangers, the fruits thereof; we profess and declare, before GOD and the world, our unfeigned desire to be humbled for our own sins, and for the sins of these kingdoms: especially, that we have not as we ought valued the inestimable benefit of the gospel; that we have not labored for the purity and power thereof; and that we have not endeavoured to receive CHRIST in our hearts, nor to walk worthy of him in our lives; which are the causes of other sins and transgressions so much abounding amongst us: and our true and unfeigned purpose, desire, and endeavour for ourselves, and all others under our power and charge, both in publick and in private, in all duties we owe to GOD and man, to amend our lives, and each one to go before another in the example of a real reformation; that the Lord may turn away his wrath and heavy indignation, and establish these churches and kingdoms in truth and peace. And this Covenant we make in the presence of ALMIGHTY GOD, the Searcher of all hearts, with a true intention to perform the same, as we shall answer at that great day, when the secrets of all hearts shall be disclosed; most humbly beseeching the Lord to strengthen us by his HOLY SPIRIT for this end, and to bless our desire and proceedings with such success, as may be deliverance and safety to his people, and encouragement to other Christian churches, groaning under, or in danger of, the yoke of antichristian tyranny, to join in same or like association and covenant, to the glory of GOD, the enlargement of the Kingdom of JESUS CHRIST, and the peace and tranquility of Christian kingdoms and commonwealths.

Appendix 7

Table of Martyrs and Covenanters with date of imprisonment or execution

Note: Names may be repeated but in some cases may be father and son with the same name. Spelling of names and places is per source records.

Name		Prison	Ship	Place died	Cause	Date died	Place Origin
William	ADAM			Wellwood	Shot	Mar 1685	
Robert	ADAM		H&F				
John	ADDIE		Crown	Orkney	Drown	10 Dec 1697	Torpichen
William	AISDALE		H&F	d at sea			
James	AITCHISON		Crown	Orkney	Survived	10 Dec 1697	Nethen
Teviotdale							
James	AITCHISON	DU		Dunnottar	in escape	1685	
John	AITKEN		Crown	Orkney	Drown.	10 Dec 1697	Shotts Lanarks
Andrew	AITON		Crown	Orkney	Drown.	10 Dec 1697	Evandale
James	ALGIE			Paisley	Hung	3 Feb 1685	Kennishead
Robert	ALISON		Crown	Orkney	Drown.	10 Dec 1697	Evandale
William	ALISON		Crown	Orkney	Drown.	10 Dec 1697	Evandale
Isobel	ALISON			Edinburgh	Exec.	26 Jan 1681	Perth
Colin	ALISONE	GT,DU				20 May 1685	
Adam	ALLAN	GF					Aire
John	ALLAN		Crown	Orkney	Drown.	10 Dec 1697	Torpichen

George	ALLAN			Tynron,	Shot	1685	
Archibald	ALLISON			Edinburgh	Exec.	13 Aug 1680	Evandale
Isabel	ALLISON						
William	ANDERSON	GF					Livingstone
Robert	ANDERSON		Crown	Orkney	Drown.	10 Dec 1697	Kilmarnock
James	ANDERSON		Crown	Orkney	Drown.	10 Dec 1697	Kilmarnock
John	ARBUCKLE		H&F				
Thomas	ARCHER			Edinburgh	Exec.	21 Aug 1685	
James	ARCHIESON	CT,DU				20 May 1685	
Archibald Campbell	ARGYLL	Marquise		Edinburgh	Exec.	27 May 1661	Inveraray
Archibald Campbell	ARGYLL	9th Earl		Edinburgh	Exec.	30 Jun 1685	Inveraray
George	ARNOT	GF					Arlarie
Andrew, Capt.	ARNOT			Edinburgh	Exec.	7 Dec 1666	
James	ATCHISON	DU		Dunnottar	in escape	20 May 1685	
Lady	ATHUNIE		H&F	at sea			
Robert or William	AUCHENLECK			Carlingwark		1685	
William	AUCHINLOSE		Crown	Orkney	Drown.	10 Dec 1697	Paisley
Robert	AULD		Crown	Orkney	Drown.	10 Dec 1697	Kilbride
Andrew	AYTOUN			Cupar	Exec.	3 May 1679	Cupar
Robert	BAILLIE			Edinburgh	Exec.	23 Dec 1684	Jerviswood
James	BALFOUR	GF					Gilstoun
Alexander	BALFOUR	GF					Gilstoun
James	BALFOUR	GF					Gilstoun
Alexander	BALFOUR	GF					Gilstoun
John	BALMAMOON	GF					Glasgow
John	BALMANNO	GF					Glasgow

Alexander	BARCLAY	GF					Blair
Robert	BARCLAY	GT, DU				20 May 1685	
John	BARRIE			Strathaven	Shot	Apr 1685	Strathaven
Thomas	BARTON		Crown	Orkney	Drown.	10 Dec 1697	Monkland
James	BEAL		Crown	Orkney	Drown.	10 Dec 1697	Newburn
Samuel	BECK		Crown	Orkney	Drown.	10 Dec 1697	Kirkmabreck
Janett	BELL	DU				20 May 1685	Dumfries
John	BELL		Crown	Orkney	Drown.	10 Dec 1697	Livingstoun
John	BELL			Kirkconnel	Shot	21 Feb 1685	Whiteside
John	BENNETT	GF					Leslie
James	BENNOCH			Ingleston	Shot	28 Apr 1685	Glencairn
Robert	BIRD	GF					Kirkcaldie
Alexander	BISHOP		Crown	Orkney	Drown.	10 Dec 1697	Torpichen
Alexander	BISSETT		Crown	Orkney	Drown.	10 Dec 1697	East Calder
David	BITCHET		Crown	Orkney	Drown.	10 Dec 1697	FenwickAyr
William	BITCHET		Crown	Orkney	Drown.	10 Dec 1697	FenwickAyr
John	BLACK	DU				20 May 1685	Water of Or
Walter	BLACK	DU				20 May 1685	
Thomas	BLACK	GT, DU				20 May 1685	Hawick
John	BLACK		H&F				
John	BLACKADER	Bass		Bass	Illness	1685	Troqueer
James	BLACKWOOD			Irvine	Hung	31 Dec 1666	FenwickAyr
Hugh	BLAIR	GT, DU				20 May 1685	Kilmacolm
Robert	BOG		Crown	Orkney	Drown.	10 Dec 1697	Strathmiglo
Robert	BOGIE	GF					Newbigging
James	BOGLE	GT, DU				20 May 1685	

William	BOICK			Glasgow	Exec.	14 Jun 1683	Auchinreoch
James	BOIG			Edinburgh	Exec.	27 Jul 1681	
Bessie	BORDON		H&F				
Thomas	BORTHWICK		Crown	Orkney	Drown.	10 Dec 1697	Linlithgow
James	BOUSTON		Crown	Orkney	Drown.	10 Dec 1697	Dreghorn
William	BOYD	GT,DU				20 May 1685	
Thomas	BRADIE	GT, DU				20 May 1685	Lochwinnoch
Robert	BRADIE	GT, DU				20 May 1685	Lochwinnoch
Robert	BRADIE	GT, DU				20 May 1685	Lochwinnoch
John	BRADIE	GT, DU				20 May 1685	Lochwinnoch
William	BREADIE	GT, DU		Dunnottar	in escape	20 May 1685	
William	BREAKENRIG		Crown	Orkney	Drown.	10 Dec 1697	Bothwell
Robert	BRICE		Crown	Orkney	Drown.	10 Dec 1697	Borgue
John	BRICE		Crown	Orkney	Drown.	10 Dec 1697	Borgue
John	BRICE		Crown	Orkney	Drown.	10 Dec 1697	Kirkmichael
John	BRICE			Mauchline		5 Jun 1685	
Andrew	BRODIE			Forgandenny	Shot	Oct 1678	Forgandenny
William	BROUN	GT, DU		Dunnottar	in escape	20 May 1685	Crawford Mure
George	BROUN	GT, DU				20 May 1685	
Thomas	BROWN	GF		Magus Moor	Hung	18 Nov 1679	Edinburgh
Thomas	BROWN	GF					Edinburgh
Thomas	BROWN	GF					Edinburgh
William	BROWN	GF					Kilmarnock
John	BROWN	GT, DU				20 May 1685	
Thomas	BROWN			Magus Moor	Hung.	18 Nov 1679	Edinburgh
Thomas	BROWN		Crown	Orkney	Drown.	10 Dec 1697	Gargunnock

William	BROWN		Crown	Orkney	Drown.	10 Dec 1697	Kilmarnock
Robert	BROWN		Crown	Orkney	Drown.	10 Dec 1697	Kirkmabreck
John	BROWN		Crown	Orkney	Drown.	10 Dec 1697	Mid Calder
John	BROWN			Priesthill	Shot	1 May 1685	Priesthill
John	BROWN			Blackwood	Shot	Mar 1685	
George	BROWN		H&F				
William	BROWN			Craignorth	Shot		
John	BROWNING			Mauchline		6 May 1685	
Thomas	BROWNLEE		Crown	Orkney	Drown.	10 Dec 1697	Evandale
Arthur	BRUCE			Edinburgh	Exec.	30 Nov 1683	Dalserf
John	BRUNING			Mauchline	Hung	1685	
John	BRYCE			Mauchline	Hung	6 May 1685	West Calder
William	BUCHAN		Crown	Orkney	Drown.	10 Dec 1697	Paisley
John	BUCHANAN	GT, DU				20 May 1685	Glasgow
James	BUCHANNAN		Crown	Orkney	Drown.	10 Dec 1697	Gargunnock
Andrew	BUCKLE		Crown	Orkney	Drown.	10 Dec 1697	Fenwick
Robert	BUNTINE			Glasgow	Hung	19 Dec 1666	Fenwick
Alexander	BURDEN		Crown	Orkney	Drown.	10 Dec 1697	Barr
John	CAIRNDUFF		Crown	Orkney	Drown.	10 Dec 1697	Evandale
Thomas	CAIRNS		Crown	Orkney	Drown.	10 Dec 1697	Sprouston
Robert	CALDOW		Crown	Orkney	Survived	10 Dec 1697	Balmaghie
William	CALDWEL		Crown	Orkney	Drown.	10 Dec 1697	Girvan
William	CAMERON	GF					Dalmellington
Hugh	CAMERON		Crown	Orkney	Survived	10 Dec 1697	Dalmellington
Michael	CAMERON			Ayrsmoss	Battle	22 Jul 1680	Falkland
Richard	CAMERON			Ayrsmoss	Battle	22 Jul 1680	Falkland

William	CAMPBELL	GT, DU				20 May 1685	Muirkirk
Hew, Sir	CAMPBELL	Bass					Cessnock
John	CAMPBELL	GT, DU				20 May 1685	Muirkirk
John	CAMPBELL					1683	Barr
George	CAMPBELL		Crown	Orkney	Drown.	10 Dec 1697	Galston
John	CAMPBELL		Crown	Orkney	Drown.	10 Dec 1697	Muirkirkr
George	CAMPBELL			Orkney	Drown.	10 Dec 1697	
Robert	CAMPBELL		H&F				
John	CAMPBELL		H&F				
David	CAMPBELL		H&F				
William	CAMPBELL		H&F				
Donald	CARGILL			Edinburgh	Exec.	27 Jul 1681	Perth
John	CARSAN	DU				20 May 1685	Nithsdale
James	CARSAN		Crown	Orkney			Kirkcudbright
James	CARSELL	GF					Malmaghie
Jean	CASSILLS	DU				20 May 1685	
John	CASSON		H&F				
Christian	CAVIE	DU				20 May 1685	
Christian	CAVIE	H&F					
Robert	CHALMERS		Crown	Orkney	Drown.	10 Dec 1697	Shotts
John	CHRIGHTOUN	DU				20 May 1685	Dalry
John	CHRISTISON		Crown	Orkney	Drown.	10 Dec 1697	Kilmadock
James	CLARK		Crown	Orkney	Drown.	10 Dec 1697	Kilbride
John	CLARK		Crown	Orkney	Drown.	10 Dec 1697	Kilbride
Andrew	CLARK			Edinbh	Hung	15 Aug 1684	Leadhills
Andrew	CLARK		Crown	Orkney	Survived	10 Dec 1697	Lochrutan

James	CLEMENT			Kirkconnel	Shot	21 Feb 1685	
Katherin	CLERK		DU			20 May 1685	
John	CLEYD	GF		Magus Moor		18 Nov 1679	Kilbryd
John	CLYD			Magus Moor	Exec.	18 Nov 1679	
Mungo	COCHRAN	DU				20 May 1685	
James	COCHRAN	GT, DU				20 May 1685	
John	COCHRAN		Crown	Orkney	Drown.	10 Dec 1697	Evandale
John	COCHRAN			Edinburgh	Exec.	30 Nov 1683	Lesmahagow
William	COCHRANE			Edinburgh	Hung	15 Dec 1682	Evandale
Humphrey	COLQUHOUN			Edinburgh	Exec.	22 Dec 1666	
James	COLVIL		Crown	Orkney	Drown.	10 Dec 1697	Glencairn
James	COLVIN		Crown	Orkney			Glencairn
Thomas	COOK			Polmadie	Shot	11 May 1685	Cathcart
Andrew	COOK		Crown	Orkney	Drown.	10 Dec 1697	Melross
John	CORBET		H&F	Tinwald	1685		Tynwald
Andrew	CORBET		H&F				
John	CORBETT	CT, DU	H&F			20 May 1685	Tynwald
Andrew	CORBETT	LT, DU				20 May 1685	
Agnes	CORHEAD	DU				19 May 1685	Dumfries
Agnes	CORHEAD		H&F	at sea			
James	CORSAN		Crown	Orkney	Drown.	10 Dec 1697	Kirkcudbright
Elizabeth	CORSE	DU				20 May 1685	
George	CORSON			New Cumnock	Shot	Apr 1685	
James	COUPER		Crown	Orkney	Drown.	10 Dec 1697	Carnwath
Barbara	COWAN	DU				19 May 1685	Dumfries
Marjorie	COWAN	DU				20 May 1685	Dumfries

Barbara	COWAN		H&F				
Marjory	COWAN		H&F				
John	CRAIG		Crown	Orkney	Drown.	10 Dec 1697	Glassford
George	CRAUFORD			Edinburgh	Exec.	14 Dec 1666	
Paul	CRAW or CRAWAR			St Andrews	Burned	1433	Bohemia
John	CREICHTON					19 Jun 1684	Kirkpatrick
Thomas	CRICHTON		Crown	Orkney	Drown.	10 Dec 1697	Carnwath
John	CRICHTON		H&F				
Thomas	CRIGHTOUN	GF					Carnwath
John	CROOKSHANK			Rullion Green	Battle	28 Nov 1666	Ulster
Patrick	CUNINGHAME	DU				20 May 1685	
Daniel	CUNNINGHAM		Crown	Orkney	Drown.	10 Dec 1697	Drummond
James	CUNNINGHAM		Crown	Orkney	Drown.	10 Dec 1697	Eastwood
William	CUNNINGHAM		H&F	at sea			
Patrick	CUNNINGHAM		H&F				
David	CURRIE	GF	Crown	Orkney	Drown.	10 Dec 1697	Fenwick
James	CUSTON		Crown	Orkney	Drown.	10 Dec 1697	Sudon
John	CUTHBERTSON		Crown	Orkney	Drown.	10 Dec 1697	Kilmarnock
John	CUTHBERTSON		Crown	Orkney	Drown.	10 Dec 1697	Kilmarnock
William	CUTHILL			Edinburgh	Exec.	27 Jul 1681	Bo`ness
Alexander	DALGLEISH	GT, DU		Dunnottar	Torture	1685	
Andrew	DANNIELL	GF					Codziam
James	DAVIE			Blackdub	Shot	Apr 1673	Bathgate
Quintan	DICK	ET, DU				20 May 1685	Dalmellington
John or James	DICK			Edinburgh	Exec.	5 Mar 1684	Edinburgh
Robert	DICK			Ayrsmoss	Battle	22 Jul 1680	

William	DINGWALL			Drumclog	Wounds	1 Jun 1679	Strathaven
Thomas	DINWIDDIE						
Alexander	DOGLEISH	DU				20 May 1685	
Andrew	DONALDSON		Crown	Orkney	Drown.	10 Dec 1697	Girthon
James	DONALDSON		Crown	Orkney	Drown.	10 Dec 1697	Kelton
John	DONALDSON		Crown	Orkney	Drown.	10 Dec 1697	Kincardine
Alexander	DONING	CT, DU				20 May 1685	
Charles	DOUGLAS	CT, DU				20 May 1685	
William	DOUGLAS	DU				20 May 1685	Bridge of Ken
Samuel	DOUGLAS		Crown	Orkney	Drown.	10 Dec 1697	Cavers
John	DOUGLAS		Crown	Orkney	Drown.	10 Dec 1697	Kirkmichael
Charles	DOUGLAS		H&F				
William	DOUGLAS		H&F				
George	DRAFIN		Crown	Orkney	Survived	10 Dec 1697	Lesmahagow
George	DRAPHAN	GF					Lesmahago
Peter	DREDEN	CT, DU				20 May 1685	
William	DRIPS		Crown	Orkney	Drown.	10 Dec 1697	Mauchlin
David	DUN			Cumnock	Shot	Apr 1685	Glass
Margaret	DUN			Cumnock	Shot	Apr 1685	Glass
James	DUN			Caldons/Trool	Shot	23 Jan 1685	Minniegaff
Robert	DUN			Caldons/Trool	Shot	23 Jan 1685	Minniegaff
George	DUNBAR		Crown	Orkney	Survived	10 Dec 1697	Craigie
Isabel	DURIE		H&F				
Katherin	DYKES		DU			20 May 1685	Dumfries
James	EASTON		Crown	Orkney	Drown.	10 Dec 1697	Torpichen
John	EASTON		Crown	Orkney	Survived	10 Dec 1697	Torpichen

Andrew	EASTON		Crown	Orkney	Drown.	10 Dec 1697	Torpichen
Mungo	ECCLES		Crown	Orkney	Drown.	10 Dec 1697	Maybole
John	EDGAR		Crown	Orkney	Survived	10 Dec 1697	Balmaclellan
Robert	EDGAR			Ingleston	Shot	28 Apr 1685	Glencairn
Batholomow	EISTOUNE	GF					
John	ELLIOT		Crown	Orkney	Drown.	10 Dec 1697	Sudon
Ebenezer	ERSKINE	Bass					
Robert	EWART	GF					Glasgow
David	FARRIE			Edinburgh	Exec.	10 Dec 1697	
John	FERGUSHILL			Midland	Shot	Nov 1685	Fenwick
Elspith	FERGUSON	DU				20 May 1685	
Janet	FERGUSON	DU				20 May 1685	
John	FERGUSON		Crown	Orkney	Drown.	10 Dec 1697	Glencairn
William	FERGUSON		Crown	Orkney	Survived	10 Dec 1697	Glencairn
Robert	FERGUSON			Auchencloy Hill	Shot	18 Dec 1684	
Janet	FERGUSON		H&F				
Elspeth	FERGUSON		H&F				
Andrew	FERGUSON						
Elizabeth	H.FERGUSON			in transit		1685	
John	FERGUSON		Crown	Orkney			
Robert	FERGUSON or FERGUS			Auchencloy Hill	Sword	18 Dec 1684	
Mary	FERRETT		H&F	at sea			
William	FIDDISON			Mauchline	Hung	6 May 1685	
Christian	FIFFE	DU				20 May 1685	Dumfries
Alexander	FINDLAY	GF					Kilmarnock
David	FINDLAY			Newmilns	Shot	Apr 1685	Newmilns

James	FINDLEY	GF					Cuninhame
Thomas	FINLATER		H&F				
Thomas	FINLAY		Crown	Orkney	Drown.	10 Dec 1697	Kilmarnock
Thomas	FINLAY		Crown	Orkney	Drown.	10 Dec 1697	Kilmarnock
John	FINLAY			Edinburgh	Hung	15 Dec 1682	Kilmarnock
James	FINLAYSON		Crown	Orkney	Drown.	10 Dec 1697	New Kilpatrick
Thomas	FLEMMING			Drumclog	Wounds	1 Jun 1679	Loudon
Thomas	FLEMMING			Drum	Shot	1 Jun 1679	Loudon
John	FOORD	CT, DU				20 May 1685	
John	FORD		H&F				
John	FOREMAN		H&F				
James	FORK		Crown	Orkney	Drown.	10 Dec 1697	Crichtoun
John	FORMAN	DU				20 May 1685	
Patrick	FORMAN			Edinburgh	Exec.	10 Dec 1697	Alloa
Margerat	FORREST	DU				20 May 1685	
Thomas	FORREST			St Andrews	Burned	1538	Dollar
James	FORSYTH	GT, DU		Dunnottar		20 May 1685	Lochmaben
James	FORSYTHE		H&F				
Andrew	FOULIS	GF					Stewartoun
John, Capt.	FOWLER or FULLER			Ayrsmoss	Battle	22 Jul 1680	
William	FRAM		Crown	Orkney	Survived	10 Dec 1697	Calder
James	FRASER	Bass					Brea
John	FRASER	DU				20 May 1685	
John	FRASER	DU					Alness Ross
John	FRAZER		H&F				
Janett	FUMERTOUN	DU				20 May 1685	Dumfries

Mrs	GAIRDNER	DU				20 May 1685	
James	GALBRAITH		Crown	Orkney	Drown.	10 Dec 1697	Kippen
Grisel	GAMBLE		H&F				
John	GARDNER		Crown	Orkney	Survived	10 Dec 1697	Monklands
Robert	GARNOCK			Edinburgh	Exec.	10 Dec 1697	Stirling
James	GAVIN						Douglas
John	GEBBIE			Drumclog	Wounds	1 Jun 1679	Newmilns
William	GED		H&F	at sea			
John	GEDDE	GF					
John	GEMIL		Crown	Orkney	Drown.	10 Dec 1697	Cumnock
Peter	GEMMEL			Midland	Shot	Nov 1685	Fenwick
John	GEMMEL			Ayrsmoss	Battle	22 Jul 1680	
Grissell	GEMRIE	DU				19 May 1685	Dumfries
Thomas	GERMONT		Crown	Orkney	Drown.	10 Dec 1697	Kirkoswald
John	GIB		Crown	Orkney	Drown.	10 Dec 1697	Abercorn
James	GIB		Crown	Orkney	Drown.	10 Dec 1697	Abercorn
John	GIBB	GF					Pittendreich
John	GIBS			Engleston	Shot	28 Apr 1685	Glencairn
Mary	GIBSON	DU		Dunnottar	in escape	20 May 1685	Dumfries
John	GIBSON			Ingleston	Shot	28 Apr 1685	Ingleston
Robert	GILCHRIST	DU				20 May 1685	Dalgarnoch
Cuthbert	GILCHRIST	DU				20 May 1685	Dalgarnochs
Patrick	GILCHRIST	GF					Kippen
Thomas	GILCHRIST		Crown	Orkney	Drown.	10 Dec 1697	Calder
Patrick	GILCHRIST		Crown	Orkney	Drown.	10 Dec 1697	Gargunnock
Robert	GILCHRIST		H&F				

John	GILFILLAN	GT, DU				20 May 1685	
John	GILFILLAN		H&F				
Peter	GILLIES			Mauchline	Hung	6 May 1685	Skirling
William	GILMORE	GT, DU				20 May 1685	
Robert	GILMORE	GT, DU				20 May 1685	
James	GIUTHRIE Rev						
John	GIVAN	GF					Neilstoune
James	GLASGOW		Crown	Orkney	Survived	10 Dec 1697	Cavers
William	GLASGOW		Crown	Orkney	Survived	10 Dec 1697	Cavers
John	GLASS	GF					
James	GLEN	GT, DU				20 May 1685	
Agnes	GLENCORSES	DU				20 May 1685	Dumfries
Janet	GLENDONEING	DU				20 May 1685	Dumfries
James	GLOVER	ET			illness	1685	Tynwald
Robert	GOODVINE	GT, DU				20 May 1685	Glasgow
Annabell	GORDON	DU				20 May 1685	Dumfries
Issobell	GORDON	DU				20 May 1685	Dumfries
Jean	GORDON	DU				20 May 1685	Dumfries
Edward	GORDON			Irongray	Hung	3 Mar 1685	Blacke
William	GORDON						Earlston
William	GORDON			Bothwell	Shot	22 Jun 1679	Earlston
John	GORDON			Lochenkit	Shot	2 Mar 1685	Garryhorn
John	GORDON			Edinburgh	Exec.	7 Dec 1666	Knockbreck
John	GORDON			Rullion Green	Wounds	6 Jan 1685	Largmore
William	GORDON			Rullion Green	Battle	28 Nov 1666	Largmore
Roger	GORDON						Largmore

John	GORDON					Wounds	6 Jan 1685	Largmore
William	GORDON				Rullion Green	Battle	28 Nov 1666	Roberton
John	GORDON				Lochenkit	Shot	2 Mar 1685	
Robert	GORDON				Edinburgh	Exec.	7 Dec 1666	
Edward	GORDON				Irongray	Hung	12 Mar 1685	
Annabel	GORDON			H&F				
Bessie	GORDONE		DU				19 May 1685	Dumfries
William	GOUGAR				Edinburgh	Exec.	11 Mar 1681	Bo'ness
John	GOVAN	GF						Kirklistoun
John	GOVAN			Crown	Orkney	Drown.	10 Dec 1697	Kirklistoun
John	GOVAN			Crown	Orkney	Drown.	10 Dec 1697	Neilston
William, Lt.	GOVAN				Edinburgh	Exec.	1 Jun 1661	
Katharine	GOVAN		H&F					
Margaret	GRACIE				Tynron Allan's Cairn	Shot	1685	
William	GRAHAM				Crossmichael	Shot	15 Mar 1682	Crossmichael
John	GRAHAM				Ayr	Hung	27 Dec 1666	Midtoun
James	GRAHAM				Edinburgh	Exec.	9 Dec 1684	
Thomas	GRAHAM			H&F	at sea			
Robert	GRAHAME		GF					
John	GRAY		DU				20 May 1685	
Charles	GRAY		DU				20 May 1685	
James	GRAY		GF					West Calder
James	GRAY				Ayrsmoss	Battle	22 Jul 1680	Chryston
James	GRAY			Crown	Orkney	Drown.	10 Dec 1697	FenwickAyr
Robert	GRAY				Edinburgh	Exec.	19 May 1682	Nthhmbld

Thomas	GRAY		H&F	at sea			
John	GRAY		H&F				
James	GRAZE		Crown	Orkney	Drown.	10 Dec 1697	Calder
John	GREENSHIELDS		Crown	Orkney	Drown.	10 Dec 1697	Cavers
Fergus	GREIR	DU				20 May 1685	Dalry
James	GREIR	DU				20 May 1685	Dalry
Jean	GRIER	DU				19 May 1685	Dumfries
John	GRIER			Dumfries	Hung	2 Jan 1667	Dumfries
Robert	GRIER					1685	Lochenkit
Fergus	GRIER	H&F					
James	GRIER	H&F					
Robert	GRIERSON			Ingleston	Shot	28 Apr 1685	Balmaclellan
John	GRIERSON			Auchencloy Hill	Shot	18 Dec 1684	Dalry
William	GRIERSON			Dumfries	Hung	2 Jan 1667	Dumfries
James	GRIEVE	GF					Mahill
William	GRINDLAY	GF					Monkland
William	GRINLAW		Crown	Orkney	Drown.	10 Dec 1697	Monklands
Andrew	GUILLINE			Edinburgh	Exec.	13 Jul 1683	Balmerino
James	GUTHRIE			Edinburgh	Exec.	1 Jun 1661	Stirling Stirling
David	HACKSTON			Edinburgh	Exec.	30 Sep 1680	Kilmany
John	HAIR			New Cumnock	Shot	Apr 1685	
Agnes	HAIRSTAIN	DU				20 May 1685	Dumfries
Henry	HALL			Queensferry	Wounds	3 Jun 1680	Eckford Kelso
John	HALLAM			Kirkcudbright	Hung	1685	Tongland
David	HALLIDAY			Twynholm	Shot	11 Jul 1685	Glengap
David	HALLIDAY			Kirkconnel	Shot	21 Feb 1685	Mayfield

Robert	HAMILTON	GF					Ardrie
James	HAMILTON			Edinburgh	Exec.	7 Dec 1666	Kithemoor
Patrick	HAMILTON		Crown	Orkney	Drown.	10 Dec 1697	Livingstoun
Gavin	HAMILTON			Edinburgh	Exec.	7 Dec 1666	Maudslie
John	HAMILTON			Ayrsmoss	Battle	22 Jul 1680	
Patrick	HAMILTON,			St Andrews	Burned	Feb 1528	Ferme
William	HANNA	CT, DU				20 May 1685	Tundergarth
John	HANNA (Y)	DU				20 May 1685	Traquair
Samuel	HANNAY		Crown	Orkney	Drown.	10 Dec 1697	Kirkmabreck
David	HARDIE	GF					Fife
William	HARDIE	GF					Kelso
David	HARDIE	GF					Lesly
William	HARDIE		Crown	Orkney	Drown.	10 Dec 1697	Kelso
Agnes	HARESTANES	DU					
Thomas	`White Hose` HARKNESS			Edinburgh	Hung	15 Aug 1684	Locherben
James	`Long Gun` HARKNESS						Locherben
John	HARPER	LT, DU				20 May 1685	
John	HARRIS		H&F				
John	HART			Glasgow	Hung	19 Dec 1666	Glassford
Marion	HARVEY			Edinburgh	Exec.	26 Jan 1681	Bo'ness
William	HARVEY			Lanark	Exec.	2 Mar 1682	
John	HARVIE		H&F				
John	HARVY	GT, DU				20 May 1685	Dalserf
Franceis	HASTIE	GF					
Laurence	HAY			Edinburgh	Exec.	13 Jul 1683	Cupar
Katherin	HENDERSON	DU				20 May 1685	Dumfries

John	HENDERSON	DU				20 May 1685	
William	HENDERSON		Crown	Orkney	Drown.	10 Dec 1697	Livingstoun
John	HENDERSON		H&F				
Robert	HENDRIE		Crown	Orkney	Drown.	10 Dec 1697	Airth
William	HENRYSON	GF					Linlithgowshire
William	HERD		Crown	Orkney	Drown.	10 Dec 1697	Ashkirk
Alexander	HERIOT	ET, DU				20 May 1685	
William	HERON			Lochenkit	Shot	2 Mar 1685	Glencairn
William	HERVI			Hamilton	Hung	2 Mar 1682	Lanark
Janett	HILL	DU				20 May 1685	Dumfries
Andrew	HISLOP			Craighaugh	Shot	11 May 1685	Windshields
James	HOBKIRK		Crown	Orkney	Drown.	10 Dec 1697	Cavers
John	HODGE	CT, DU				20 May 1685	
John	HODGE		H&F	at sea			
Thomas	HOG	Bass					Kiltearn
Alexander	HOME			Edinburgh	Exec.	21 Dec 1682	Humetoun
Charles	HONYALL		H&F				
Adam	HOOD	DU				20 May 1685	
Adam	HOOD	H&F					
Thomas	HORN		Crown	Orkney	Drown.	10 Dec 1697	MayboleAyr
James	HOUSTON		Crown	Orkney	Drown.	10 Dec 1697	Balmaghie
David	HOUSTON						
Walter	HUMPER		Crown	Orkney	Drown.	10 Dec 1697	Dalmellington
Walter	HUMPER Jr		Crown	Orkney	Survived	10 Dec 1697	Dalmellington
John	HUMPHREY			Corsegellioch Hill	Shot	Apr 1685	
James	HUNTER	DU				20 May 1685	Nithsdale

John	HUNTER	LT, DU				20 May 1685	
Andrew	HUNTER				illness	1685	Dumfries
Elizabeth G	HUNTER			Holland	illness		Dumfries
John	HUNTER			Beef Tub, Moffat	Shot	1685	Tweedsmuir
William	HUNTER			Kirkcudbright	Hung	Dec 1684	
Robert	HUNTER			Kirkcudbright	Hung	1684	
George	HUTCHESON		Crown	Orkney	Drown.	10 Dec 1697	Straiton
John	HUTCHIESON	GT, DU				20 May 1685	Hairlaw
John	HUTCHINSON		H&F	at sea			
Issobell	HWISON	DU				20 May 1685	Dumfries
Thomas	INGLES		Crown	Orkney	Drown.	10 Dec 1697	Livingstoun
William	INGLIS	GF					
Arthur	INGLIS			Stocklton Dyke	Sword	Jul 1679	Netherton
Annabell	JACKSON		DU			20 May 1685	Dumfries
John	JACKSON	GT, DU				20 May 1685	
George	JACKSON			Edinburgh	Exec.	9 Dec 1684	Nether Pollock
Thomas	JACKSON		H&F				
William	JACKSON		H&F				
John	JAMESON			Corsegellioch Hill	Shot	Apr 1685	
James	JOHNSTON			Glasgow	Exec.	19 Mar 1684	Cadder
William	JOHNSTON			Wigtown	Hung	1685	Penninghame
George	JOHNSTON		H&F				
George	JOHNSTONE	GT, DU				20 May 1685	Midlecather
John	JOHNSTONE		H&F				
John	JOHNSTONE						
James	JUNCK	GT, DU				20 May 1685	

James	JUNK		H&F				
Mungo	KAIP			Edinburgh	Exec.	22 Dec 1666	Evandale
Patrick	KEIR	GF					Kincardin
Patrick	KEIR		Crown	Orkney	Drown.	10 Dec 1697	Kincardine
Katherin	KELLIE	DU				20 May 1685	Dumfries
John	KELLIE	ET, DU				20 May 1685	
John	KELLIE		H&F				
Katherine	KELLIE		H&F	at sea			
John	KENNEDY		Crown	Orkney	Drown.	10 Dec 1697	Closeburn
Alexander	KENNEDY					ca 1528-40	Glasgow
John	KENNEDY		Crown	Orkney	Drown.	10 Dec 1697	Nithsdale,
John	KENNIE		H&F				
John	KERR			Edinburgh	Exec.	22 Feb 1684	Hounam
John	KID Rev			Edinburgh	Exec.	14 Aug 1679	
James	KIDD Rev			Edinburgh	Exec.	14 Aug 1679	
John	KILLEN		Crown	Orkney	Drown.	10 Dec 1697	Shotts
John	KINCAID	DU				20 May 1685	
John	KINCAID		H&F				
John	KING		H&F				
John	KING Rev	GT, DU				20 May 1685	
John	KING Rev			Edinburgh	Exec.	14 Aug 1679	
John	KIPPAN		H&F	at sea			
Robert	KIRK	GF					Burghlie
John	KIRK		Crown	Orkney	Drown.	10 Dec 1697	Ceres
James	KIRK		Crown	Orkney	Drown.	10 Dec 1697	Largo
Robert	KIRK		Crown	Orkney	Survived	10 Dec 1697	Orwel

James	KIRK or KIRKO			Dumfries	Shot	13 Mar 1685	Keir
Sara	KIRKLAND	DU				20 May 1685	Dumfries
John	KIRKLAND		H&F	at sea			
James	KIRKWOOD	DU				20 May 1685	
James	KIRKWOOD		H&F				
Margaret	LACHLAN or MacL..			Wigtown	Drown.	11 May 1685	Kirkinner
Alexander	LAMB			Crown Orkney	Drown.	10 Dec 1697	Straiton
Robert	LAMB				Hung	ca 1528-40	
Robert	Mrs LAMB				Drown.	ca 1528-40	
Thomas	LAUCHLAN			Edinburgh	Exec.	16 Aug 1682	
William	LAUTA	GT, DU				20 May 1685	
John	LAW			Newmills	Shot	Apr 1685	Kilmarnock
James	LAWSON			Glasgow	Exec.	24 Oct 1684	
James	LEARMONT			Edinburgh	Exec.	27 Sep 1678	
Joseph, Maj.	LEARMONT	Bass					
James	LEIDON		Crown	Orkney	Survived	10 Dec 1697	Cavers
Robert	LENNOX			Kirkconnel	Shot	21 Feb 1685	Irlandton
Peter	LERMONT		Crown	Orkney	Drown.	10 Dec 1697	Shotts
Margerat	LESLIE	DU				20 May 1685	Dumfries
Margaret	LESLIE		H&F				
James	LILBURN		Crown	Orkney	Drown.	10 Dec 1697	Kinross
James	LILBURNE	GF					Kinrossie
James	LILEBURN	GF					Kinross
Alexander	LIN(N)			Craigmodie	Shot	1685	New Luce
Margerat	LINLITHGOW	DU				20 May 1685	Dumfries
Janet	LINTHRON		H&F				

Janett	LINTOUN	DU				20 May 1685	Dumfries
James	LOCHART	GT, DU				20 May 1685	Lee
Robert	LOCKHART			Eaglesham	Shot	1 May 1685	Eaglesham
Gawen	LOCKHART		H&F				
Robert	LOGAN	GT, DU				20 May 1685	
John	LYNDSAY	GF					Kilbryde
John	LYNDSAY	GF					
William	LYNDSAY	GF					
George	MacCARTNEY			Ayr	Hung	27 Dec 1666	Blairkennie
John	MacCARTNEY		Crown	Orkney	Survived	10 Dec 1697	Kirkcudbright
Alexander	MacCULLOCH			Ayr	Hung	27 Dec 1666	Cairsphairn
John	MacGEAGHAN			Bellopath	Shot	28 Jul 1688	Auchengibbert
John	MacGIE		Crown	Orkney	Survived	10 Dec 1697	Kirkcudbright
Robert	MacGILL		Crown	Orkney	Survived	10 Dec 1697	Gallshiels
Thomas	MacGIRR						
Matthew	MACHAN	GT, DU				20 May 1685	
David	MacKERVALL		Crown	Orkney	Drown.	10 Dec 1697	Glencairn
John	MacLAMROES						
James	MacMILLAN			Ayr	Exec.	27 Dec 1666	Marduchat
David	MacMILLAN			Edinburgh	Exec.	16 May 1683	
Andrew	MacQUHAN		Crown	Orkney	Survived	10 Dec 1697	Kirkcudbright
Adam	MacQUHAN			Kells	Exec.	6 May 1685	
John	MacTAGART		Crown	Orkney	Drown.	10 Dec 1697	Penningham
Adam	MacWHAN			Kells	Shot	11 May 1685	New Galloway
Elpith	MAIDLINE	DU				20 May 1685	
John	MAIN			Glasgow	Exec.	19 Mar 1684	Old Monkland

John	MALCOLM		Crown	Orkney	Survived	10 Dec 1697	Dalry
John	MALCOLM			Edinburgh	Exec.	13 Aug 1680	St Johns, Dalry
	MANUAL			Edinburgh	Wounds	21 Jul 1680	Shotts
Marcus	MARSCHAELL	GT, DU				20 May 1685	
John	MARSCHALL	DU				20 May 1685	
George	MARSHALL	GF					Balwairdmylne
James	MARSHALL	GF					Newforgane
Edward	MARSHALL			Edinburgh	Exec.	4 Dec 1685	Muiravonside
Michael	MARSHALL		H&F				
John	MARSHALL		H&F				
John	MARTIN		Crown	Orkney	Survived	10 Dec 1697	Borgue
George	MARTIN			Edinburgh	Exec.	22 Feb 1684	Old Dailly
John	MARTIN		H&F				
John	MARTINE	DU				20 May 1685	
John	MARTINE	GF					Pittendreich
Agnes	MATHER	DU				20 May 1685	
John	MATHER		Crown	Orkney	Drown.	10 Dec 1697	Jedburgh
Thomas	MATHIE		Crown	Orkney	Drown.	10 Dec 1697	Monklands
John	MATHIESON					19 Jun 1684	Closeburn
Quintin	McADAM		Crown	Orkney	Survived	10 Dec 1697	Dalmellington
Gilbert	McADAM			Kirkmichael	Shot	1685	
William	McALMOND	ET, DU				20 May 1685	
John	McBRAICKNEY	GF					Kirkcudbright
James	McCALL	DU				20 May 1685	Nithsdale
Andrew	McCALL or McAULEY			Caldons/Trool	Shot	23 Jan 1685	Minniegaff
William	McCALMONT		H&F				

John	McCHISHOLM					19 Jun 1684	Spittle
John	McCLELLEN		Crown	Orkney	Drown.	10 Dec 1697	Colmonel
James	McCLIVE or McCLURE			Caldons/Trool	Shot	23 Jan 1685	Minniegaff
Thomas	McCLORGAN			Old Dailly	Shot	Apr 1685	Old Dailly
Thomas	McCLURG		Crown	Orkney	Drown.	10 Dec 1697	Colmonel
Robert	McCOLME	DU				20 May 1685	
James	McCONNELL		Crown	Orkney	Drown.	10 Dec 1697	Kirkmichael
Andrew	McCORMICK Rev			Rullion Green	Battle	28 Nov 1666	Ulster
John	McCORNOCK		Crown	Orkney	Drown.	10 Dec 1697	Colmonel
John	McCOULL			Irvine	Hung	31 Dec 1666	Carsphairn
	McCROY			Carsphairn	Shot	c 1685	Garryhorn
Alexander	McCUBBIN			Irongray	Hung	3 Mar 1685	Glencairn
David	McCUBIN		Crown	Orkney	Drown.	10 Dec 1697	Dalry
Alexander	McCUBIN			Irongray	Hung	19 Feb 1685	Glencairn
William	McCULLOCH	GF					Dalie
William	McCULLOCH		Crown	Orkney	Drown.	10 Dec 1697	Dalry Ayr
John	Major, McCULLOCH			Edinburgh	Exec.	7 Dec 1666	
Samuel	McEWEN			Edinburgh	Hung	15 Aug 1685	Glencairn
John	McEWEN		H&F				
Robert	McEWEN		H&F				
Walter	McEWEN		H&F				
John	McEWIN	CT, DU				20 May 1685	
James	McGACHIN					19 Jun 1684	Dalry
Robert	McGARRON		Crown	Orkney	Drown.	10 Dec 1697	Maybole
John	McGEACHAN			Stonepark	Exec.	20 Jun 1688	
John	McGHIE	DU				20 May 1685	

John	McGHIE		H&F				
Jean	McGIE	GT, DU				20 May 1685	Govan
Robert	McGILL	GF					Gallosheills
Robert	McGILL	GF					Galloshiells
Robert	McGILL	GF					Gallowshiels
Andrew	McGILL			Ayr	Exec.	Nov 1684	Ballantrae
Andrew	McGILL			Ayr		Nov 1684	
John	McGILLIGEN	Bass					Foddert
Thomas	McHAFFIE/McHASSIE			Straiton	Shot	1686	Largs
John	McHARIE		Crown	Orkney	Drown.	10 Dec 1697	Maybole
Matthew	McILWRAITH			Colmonell	Shot	1685	Colmonell
Pat	McJORE	DU				20 May 1685	Dalry
Hugh	McKAIL Rev			Edinburgh	Exec.	22 Dec 1666	
Walter	McKECHNIE		Crown	Orkney	Drown.	10 Dec 1697	Glasgow
Edward	McKEEN			Barr	Shot	28 Feb 1685	
John	McKENNAN		H&F		at sea.		
Thomas	McKENZIE	GT, DU				20 May 1685	Kilpatrick
Thomas	McKENZIE		Crown	Orkney	Survived	10 Dec 1697	Liberton
William	McKERGUE			Blairquhan		1685	
George	McKERTNY			Ayr	Hung	27 Dec 1666	
James	McKIE		Crown	Orkney	Drown.	10 Dec 1697	Denny
William	McKINN	GF					
Margaret	McLELAN	DU				19 May 1685	Dumfries
Andrew	McLELAN	DU		in transit		20 May 1685	
Robert	McLELAN	GT, DU				20 May 1685	Balmagachien
Robert	McLELLAN	LT					Barmagechan

Robert	McLELLAN			H&F	at sea			
Margaret	McLELLAN			H&F	at sea			
Daniel	McMICHAEL				Dalveen	Shot	31 Jan 1685	Blairfoot
James	McMICHAEL				Auchencloy Hill	Sword	18 Dec 1684	
Alexander	McMILLAN				Ayr	Hung	27 Dec 1666	
James	McMILLAN				Ayr	Hung	27 Dec 1666	
William	McMILLAN			H&F	at sea			
William	McMILLEN		CT, DU				20 May 1685	Galloway
Walter	McMIN		DU				20 May 1685	Bitle
James	McMURRIE			Crown	Orkney	Drown.	10 Dec 1697	Straiton
Nicolas	McNEIGHT		DU				19 May 1685	Dumfries
John	McNURE			Crown	Orkney	Drown.	10 Dec 1697	St Ninians
Andrew	McQUEEN		GT, DU				20 May 1685	Drimen
John	McQUEEN			H&F				
Andrew	McROBERT				Kirkconnel	Shot	21 Feb 1685	Twynholm
John	McTIRE			Crown	Orkney	Drown.	10 Dec 1697	Kirkmichael
Donald	McVEY	CT, DU					20 May 1685	
Robert	McWHAE				Kirkandrews	Shot	1685	Borgue
Adam	McWHAN				New Galloway	Shot	11 May 1685	
John	McWHIRTER			Crown	Orkney	Drown.	10 Dec 1697	Maybole
John	MEIKLE		GF					Evandaleboune
Daniel	MEIKLEWRICK				Altercannoch	Shot	1685	Altercannoch
Walter	MILL				St Andrews	Burned	28 Apr 1558	
William	MILLAR		GF					Barony
Robert	MILLAR		GF					Watterfoot
Margaret	MILLER		DU				20 May 1685	Dumfries

Robert	MILLER	GF					Waterford
Robert	MILLER	GF					Watterfoot
Thomas	MILLER		Crown	Orkney	Survived	10 Dec 1697	Ceres
Thomas	MILLER		Crown	Orkney	Drown.	10 Dec 1697	Gargunnock
William	MILLER		Crown	Orkney	Drown.	10 Dec 1697	GlasgowLanarks
John	MILLER		Crown	Orkney	Drown.	10 Dec 1697	Glassford
William	MILLER		Crown	Orkney	Drown.	10 Dec 1697	Monklands
Robert	MILLER			Edinburgh	Exec.	23 Jan 1685	Rutherglen
Christopher	MILLER			Edinburgh	Exec.	11 May 1681	
Thomas	MILLIGAN		Crown	Orkney	Drown.	10 Dec 1697	Closeburn
Robert	MILLIGAN		Crown	Orkney	Drown.	10 Dec 1697	Glencairn
John	MILLIGAN		Crown	Orkney	Survived	10 Dec 1697	Glencairn
William	MILROY						Castle Stewart
John	MILROY			Wigtown	Hung	1685	Penninghame
Gilbert	MILROY					1685	Penninghame
James	MIRRIE		Crown	Orkney	Drown.	10 Dec 1697	Cumnock
Andrew	MITCHELL	GF					
Robert	MITCHELL			Ingleston	Shot	28 Apr 1685	Cumnock
James	MITCHELL			Edinburgh	Exec.	18 Jan 1678	
Jean	MOFFAT		H&F				
Jean	MOFFATT/MUFFET		DU	Dunnottar	in escape	20 May 1685	Dumfries
Gilbert	MONERG		H&F	at sea.			
Hugh	MONTGOMERIE		Crown	Orkney	Survived	10 Dec 1697	Falkirk
	MORE		Crown	Orkney	Survived	10 Dec 1697	Bothwell
John	MORISON		Crown	Orkney	Drown.	10 Dec 1697	Airth
Robert	MORRIS			Craignorth	Shot		

John	MORTON			Drumclog	Battle	1 Jun 1679	Newmilns
	MOWAT			Fleet - Dee		1685	
James	MUIR			Edinburgh	Exec.	22 Feb 1684	Cessford
George	MUIR		H&F				
John	MUIRE		Crown	Orkney	Drown.	10 Dec 1697	Glendovan
Andrew	MUIRE		Crown	Orkney	Drown.	10 Dec 1697	Glendovan
James	MUIRHEAD			Ayr	Hung	27 Dec 1666	Irongray
James	MUIRHEAD		H&F				
John	MUIRHEAD		H&F				
James	MUNCIE	ET		In prison	illness	1685	
John	MUNDELL	ET		In prison	illness	1685	
John	MURCHIE			Altercannoch	Shot	1685	Barrhill
John	MURDOCH		Crown	Orkney	Survived	10 Dec 1697	Glencairn
Andrew	MURDOCH		Crown	Orkney	Drown.	10 Dec 1697	Kinneil
George	MURE	GT, DU				20 May 1685	
James	MUREHEAD	CT, DU				20 May 1685	
George	MUREHEAD	GT, DU				20 May 1685	
Alexander	MURRAY		Crown	Orkney	Drown.	10 Dec 1697	Mid Calder
Alexander	MURRAY		Crown	Orkney	Survived	10 Dec 1697	Penningham
William	NAIRN	GT, DU				20 May 1685	Edinburgh
John	NEILSON			Edinburgh	Exec.	14 Dec 1666	Corsock
John	NEILSON		Crown	Orkney	Drown.	10 Dec 1697	St Ninians
George	NEIVING	GF					Piqwhonartie
William	NEVIN		H&F				
Andrew	NEWBIGGING	GF					Merse
Andrew	NEWBIGGING		Crown	Orkney	Drown.	10 Dec 1697	Bandon

Symon	NICCOLL	GT, DU				20 May 1685	
James	NICOL			Edinburgh	Hung	27 Aug 1684	Peebles
James	NIMMO						
John	NISBET			Kilmarnock	Exec.	14 Apr 1683	Knowe
James	NISBET			Glasgow	Exec.	5 Jun 1684	Highside
John	NISBET			Kilmarnock	Hung	4 Apr 1683	Kilmarnock
John, Capt.	NISBET			Edinburgh	Exec.	4 Dec 1685	Loudon
Samuel	NISBET		Crown	Orkney	Drown.	10 Dec 1697	Nethen
William	NIVING	CT, DU				20 May 1685	
William	OLIPHANT	DU				20 May 1685	
William	OLIPHANT		H&F				
Thomas	OLIVER	GF					Jedburgh Forrest
John	OLIVER		Crown	Orkney	Drown.	10 Dec 1697	Hobkirk
John	OR	CT,DU				20 May 1685	
James	OR	GT, DU				20 May 1685	
John	PARK	GF					Lanaerk
John	PARK			Paisley	Hung	3 Feb 1685	Kennishead
John	PARKER			Edinburgh	Exec.	7 Dec 1666	Kirkbride
James	PATERSON	CT, DU				20 May 1685	
Andrew	PATERSON	GT, DU				20 May 1685	Hamilton
Robert	PATERSON			Ayrsmoss	Battle	22 Jul 1680	Kirkhill
Alexander	PATERSON		Crown	Orkney	Drown.	10 Dec 1697	Muirkirk
William	PATERSON			Strathaven	Shot	Apr 1685	Strathaven
Simon	PATERSON			Cumnock	Shot	Apr 1685	
James	PATON	GF					Inverkeithing
James	PATON			Edinburgh	Exec.	9 May 1864	Fenwick

John, Capt.	PATON			Edinburgh	Exec.	9 May 1684	Fenwick
Matthew	PATON			Glasgow	Hung	19 Dec 1666	Newmiln
William	PATON						
Andrew	PATTERSON		H&F				
James	PATTON	GF					Inverkeithing
Alexander	PEDEN .	Bass			Illness	26 Jan 1686	Sorn
John	PENDER		Crown	Orkney	Survived	10 Dec 1697	Torpichen
James	PENMAN		Crown	Orkney S	Survived	10 Dec 1697	Quathquhan
Thomas	PHALP		Crown	Orkney	Drown.	10 Dec 1697	Morrenside
Adam	PHILIP			Edinburgh	Exec.	13 Jul 1681	Fife
Margerat	PHILP	DU				20 May 1685	
William	PICAT	GF					Glasgow
Alexander	PIRIE		Crown	Orkney	Drown.	10 Dec 1697	Glasgow
Andrew	PIRIE ?		Crown	Orkney	Drown.	10 Dec 1697	Largo
Andrew	PITULLOCH			Edinburgh	Exec.	13 Jul 1681	Largo
John	POLLOCK	GT, DU				20 May 1685	
Robert	POLLOCK			Edinburgh	Exec.	23 Jan 1685	East Kilbride
John	POLLOCK		H&F				
John	POTTER			Edinburgh	Exec.	1 Dec 1680	Uphall
Thomas	PRINGLE	GF					Stow
John	PRINGLE		Crown	Orkney	Drown.	10 Dec 1697	Castletoun
Thomas	PRINGLE		Crown	Orkney	Drown.	10 Dec 1697	Stow
John	RAINY	DU				20 May 1685	
David	RALSTON		Crown	Orkney	Drown.	10 Dec 1697	Bathgate
Robert	RAMSAY		Crown	Orkney	Drown.	10 Dec 1697	Kirkmichael
John	RANKIN		Crown	Orkney	Drown.	10 Dec 1697	Biggar

John	RANN	H&F		at sea			
William	REID		Crown	Orkney	Drown.	10 Dec 1697	Mauchlin
William	REID		Crown	Orkney	Drown.	10 Dec 1697	Musselburgh
Marian	RENNIE		H&F	at sea			
John	RENWICK		H&F	at sea			
James	RENWICK Rev			Edinburgh	Hung	17 Feb 1688	Moniave
James	RESBY Priest				Burned	1407	England
James	RESTING	GT, DU				20 May 1685	
James	RESTON		H&F				
William	RETCHARDSON		GF				Stenhouse
Thomas	RICHARD			Cumnock	Shot	4 Apr 1685	Greenock
John	RICHARDSON	GF					Stenhouse
John	RICHARDSON		Crown	Orkney	Survived	10 Dec 1697	Borgue
Andrew	RICHMOND		Crown	Orkney	Drown.	10 Dec 1697	Auchinleck
Andrew	RICHMOND			Galston	Shot	Jun 1679	Galston
John	RICHMOND			Glasgow Cross	Exec.	19 Mar 1684	Knowe
Archibald	RIDDELL Mrs		H&F	at sea			
Archibald	RIDDELL Rev	LT					
Archibald	RIDDELL Rev		H&F	at sea.			
William	RIGG	H&F		at sea			
William	RITCHARDSON	GF					Stenhouse
James	RITCHIE	GT, DU				20 May 1685	
James	ROBERTSON			Edinburgh	Hung	15 Dec 1682	Stonehouse
Thomas	ROBERTSON			Edinburgh	Exec.	9 Dec 1684	
Alexander	ROBERTSON			Edinburgh	Exec.	14 Dec 1666	
John	ROBIESON	GT, DU				20 May 1685	

James	ROBSON						
William	RODGER		Crown	Orkney	Drown.	10 Dec 1697	Kilbride
William	RODGER		Crown	Orkney	Drown.	10 Dec 1697	Maybole
Thomas	ROSPER		Crown	Orkney	Drown.	10 Dec 1697	Glencairn
John	ROSS			Edinburgh	Hung	7 Dec 1666	Mauchline
Thomas	ROSS	Bass					Morayshire
Margaret	ROWAN	DU				20 May 1685	
Gilbert	RULE	Bass					
Richard	Col. RUMBOLD			Edinburgh	Exec.	26 Jun 1685	
Alexander	RUSSEL		Crown	Orkney	Drown.	10 Dec 1697	Calder
Peter	RUSSELL	DU				20 May 1685	
James	RUSSELL	DU				20 May 1685	
Robert	RUSSELL	GF					Shotts
James	RUSSELL	GT, DU		Dunnottar	in escape	20 May 1685	
Thomas	RUSSELL	GT, DU				20 May 1685	
Alexander	RUSSELL			Edinburgh	Exec.	10 Dec 1697	
Gavin	RUSSELL			Edinburgh	Exec.	12 Aug 1685	
Peter	RUSSELL		H&F				
Thomas	RUSSELL		H&F	at sea			
Jerome	RUSSELL					ca 1528-40	Glasgow
George	RUTHERFOORD	GF					Ancrum
David	SAMUEL		Crown	Orkney	Survived	10 Dec 1697	East Calder
James	SANDS		Crown	Orkney	Survived	10 Dec 1697	Gargunnock
Robert	SANDS		Crown	Orkney	Survived	10 Dec 1697	Orwel
Robert	SANGSTER			Edinburgh	Exec.	11 May 1681	Stirlingshire
Christane	SCOT	DU				20 May 1685	Dumfries

John	SCOT	DU				20 May 1685	Dumfries
John	SCOT	GF					Etterick Fores
Andrew	SCOT	GT, DU				20 May 1685	
William	SCOT		Crown	Orkney	Drown.	10 Dec 1697	Castletoun
John	SCOT		Crown	Orkney	Drown.	10 Dec 1697	Etrick/Forrest
David	SCOTT	DU				20 May 1685	
Robert	SCOTT			Glasgow	Hung	19 Dec 1666	Dalserf
Margaret	SCOTT			H&F at sea			
George	SCOTT		H&F	at sea			
Eupham	SCOTT		H&F	at sea.			
William	SCULAR		Crown	Orkney	Survived	10 Dec 1697	Cambusnethan
Jane	SEMPLE	DU				20 May 1685	Dumfries
John	SEMPLE			Edinburgh	Exec.	24 Nov 1684	Glassford
John	SEMPLE			Old Dailly	Shot	1685	Old Dailly
John	SETON		H&F				
Thomas	SHELSTON		H&F				
Alexander	SHIELDS	Bass					
John	SHIELDS or SHEILLS			Edinburgh	Hung	7 Dec 1666	Titwood
Ralph	SHIELLS			Edinburgh	Exec.	22 Dec 1666	Ayr
William	SHILLILAU			Woodhead	Shot	Jul 1685	Tarbolton
George	SHORT			Tongueland	Shot	11 Jul 1685	Balmaghie
John	SHORT			Ayr	Hung	27 Dec 1666	Dalry
Hugh	SIMPSON		Crown	Orkney	Drown.	10 Dec 1697	Dalmellington
John	SINTON	CT, DU				20 May 1685	
Robert	SITLINGTON			in transit		illness	
	Dunscore						

Thomas	SITLINGTON						
James	SITTINGTOWN		H&F				
James	SKENE			Edinburgh	Exec.	1 Dec 1680	
Robert	SLOSS	ET, DU				20 May 1685	
Thomas	SMALL			Ecclesmagirdle		1 Sep 1645	Ecclesmagirdle
John	SMITH	DU				20 May 1685	Water of Or
Elizabeth	SMITH		DU			20 May 1685	Dumfries
Alexander	SMITH	GT, DU				20 May 1685	
John	SMITH	GT, DU				20 May 1685	
John	SMITH		Crown	Orkney	Survived	10 Dec 1697	Dalry
James	SMITH			Bank of Burn Ann	Shot	Apr 1685	East Threepwood
John	SMITH		Crown	Orkney	Survived	10 Dec 1697	Glencairn
William	SMITH			Miniave Moss	Shot	29 Mar 1685	Moniave
James	SMITH			Lesmahagow	Hung	14 Jun 1683	Inchbelly
James	SMITH			Glasgow	Exec.	14 Jun 1683	Lesmahagow
William	SMITH			Muirmallen	Murdered	1666	Moremellen
John	SMITH			Lesmahagow	Shot	Feb 1685	Muirkirk
James	SMITH			Ayr	Hung	27 Dec 1666	Old Crachan
Walter	SMITH			Edinburgh	Exec.	27 Jul 1681	
John	SMITH		H&F	at sea			
Robert	SMITH.			Kirkcudbright	Hung	Dec 1684	Kirkcudbright
William	SMYTH	GF					Glasgow
James	SMYTH	GF					
Andrew	SNODGRASS		Crown	Orkney	Drown.	10 Dec 1697	Govan
Andrew	SNODGRASSE	GF					Glasgow

David	SOMERWEL	GF				East Calder	Midlothian
William	SPRAT		H&F				
Andrew	SPROT		Crown	Orkney	Drown.	10 Dec 1697	Borgue
William	SPROULL		H&F				
William	SPROUT	ET, DU				20 May 1685	
James	STEEL		Crown	Orkney	Drown.	10 Dec 1697	Calder
David	STEEL			Skellyhill	Shot	20 Dec 1686	Lesmahagow
Alexander	STEVEN	GF					Bothwel
John	STEVEN		Crown	Orkney	Drown.	10 Dec 1697	Livingstoun
Agnes	STEVENS		H&F				
Robert	STEVENSON			Caldons/Trool	Shot	23 Jan 1685	Straiton
Thomas	STEVENSONS			Caldons/Trool	Shot	23 Jan 1685	Minniegaff
John	STEVENSONS			Caldons/Trool	Shot	23 Jan 1685	Minniegaff
Robert	STEWART			Auchencloy Hill	Shot	18 Dec 1684	Dalry
Archibald	STEWART			Auchencloy Hill	Shot	18 Dec 1684	Auchencloy
William	STEWART			Lochenkit	Shot	2 Mar 1685	Crofts
Archibald	STEWART			Glasgow	Exec.	19 Mar 1684	Lesmahagow
Archibald	STEWART			Edinburgh	Exec.	1 Dec 1680	Lesmahagow
James	STEWART			Edinburgh	Exec.	10 Dec 1697	
George	STOBBIE	GF					Meiklecairnie
Thomas	STODHART			Edinburgh	Hung	12 Aug 1685	
John	STOT	LT, DU		Dunnottar	in escape	20 May 1685	Dumfries
Cristall or Christopher	STRANG	DU				20 May 1685	
Cristall	STRANG			Edinburgh	Exec.	7 Dec 1666	Kilbride
Christian	STRANG			H&F			
David	STRATTON			Edbgh	Burned	ca 1528-40	Angus

John	STRUTHERS		Crown	Orkney	Drown.	10 Dec 1697	Kilbride
Thomas	SWAN		Crown	Orkney	Survived	10 Dec 1697	Carstairs
William	SWANSTON		Crown	Orkney	Survived	10 Dec 1697	Sudon
John	SWINTON		H&F	at sea			
Andrew	SWORD	GF					Borg
Andrew	SWORD	GF		Magus Moor		18 Nov 1679	
Andrew	SWORD			Magus Moor	Exec.	18 Nov 1679	Borgue
William	SYME	GF					Leny
Janet	SYMINGTON		H&F				
Arthur	TACKET or TAIKET			Edinburgh	Hung	30 Jul 1684	Hamilton
John	TARGAT		H&F				
James	TENNENT	CT, DU				20 May 1685	
Robert	THOM			Polmadie	Shot	11 May 1685	Cathcart
John	THOMSON	GF					Bothwelmuir
John	THOMSON	GF					Shots
Andrew	THOMSON	GF					Sauchie
Andrew	THOMSON	GF					Sauchie
Retchard	THOMSON	GF					Shotts
Joseph	THOMSON	GF					
Joseph	THOMSON	GT, DU				20 May 1685	
William	THOMSON		Crown	Orkney	Drown.	10 Dec 1697	Borgue
John	THOMSON		Crown	Orkney	Drown.	10 Dec 1697	Dalmannie
Andrew	THOMSON		Crown	Orkney	Survived	10 Dec 1697	Dundonald
Gabriel	THOMSON			Eaglesham	Shot	1 May 1685	Eaglesham
James	THOMSON		Crown	Orkney	Drown.	10 Dec 1697	Quathquhan
John	THOMSON		Crown	Orkney	Survived	10 Dec 1697	Shotts

Thomas	THOMSON		Crown	Orkney	Survived	10 Dec 1697	St Ninians
Andrew	THOMSON		Crown	Orkney	Survived	10 Dec 1697	St Ninians
James	THOMSON			Drumclog	Wounds	1 Jun 1679	Stonehouse
John	THOMSON		Crown	Orkney	Drown.	10 Dec 1697	Torpichen
William	THOMSON			Edinburgh	Exec.	27 Jul 1681	Fife
Gabriel	THOMSON			Edinburgh	Exec.	24 Nov 1684	
Eupha	THREPLAND	DU					
James	TINTO		Crown	Orkney	Drown.	10 Dec 1697	Temple
James	TOD		Crown	Orkney	Drown.	10 Dec 1697	Dunbar
Robert	TOD		Crown	Orkney	Drown.	10 Dec 1697	Fenwick
Andrew	TORRENCE		Crown	Orkney	Drown.	10 Dec 1697	Evandale
Robert	TRAIL Snr	ET					Edinburgh
Robert	TRAIL Jr	Bass					Edinburgh
John	TRIPNAY	GT, DU				20 May 1685	Glasgow
William	TRUMBLE	CT, DU				20 May 1685	
William	TURNBULL		H&F				
John	TURPINE		H&F				
	Unknown			Rullion Green	Wounds	29 Nov 1666	Black Law
	Unknown			Old Dailly	Shot	1685	Black Clauchrie
	Unknown			Old Dailly	Shot	1685	Killoup
	Unknown			Windshields		1685	
John	UNNES		Crown	Orkney	Drown.	10 Dec 1697	Castletoun
John	URIE			Polmadie	Shot	11 May 1685	Cathcart
Patrick	URIE		H&F				
John	VALLANCE			Edinburgh	Wounds	22 Jul 1680	
John	VERNOR		H&F				

Mrs	VERNOR		H&F				
Margaret	VRIE	DU				20 May 1685	
Patrick	VRIE	GT, DU				20 May 1685	
John	VRIE	GT, DU				20 May 1685	
James	VRIE	GT, DU				20 May 1685	
Alexander	WADDEL		Crown	Orkney	Drown.	10 Dec 1697	Castletoun
William	WADDEL		Crown	Orkney	Survived	10 Dec 1697	Monklands
James	WADDEL		Crown	Orkney	Drown.	10 Dec 1697	Monklands
Walter	WADDEL		Crown	Orkney	Drown.	10 Dec 1697	Sprouston
John	WADDELL	GF					Shotts
John	WADDELL			Magus Moor	Exec.	18 Nov 1679	New Monkland
Alleaxander	WALANCE	DU				20 May 1685	
Pat	WALKER	DU				20 May 1685	
Elizabeth	WALKER	DU				20 May 1685	
Patrick	WALKER	ET,DU					
George	WALKER			Wigtown	Hung	1685	Penninghame
Alexander	WALKER		Crown	Orkney	Drown.	10 Dec 1697	Shotts
Patrick	WALKER		H&F				
Robert	WALLACE	GF					Phunuch
Francis	WALLACE	GF					Whytehill
John	WALLACE	GT, DU				20 May 1685	
Robert	WALLACE		Crown	Orkney	Survived	10 Dec 1697	Fenwick
John	WALLACE			Lochenkit	Shot	2 Mar 1685	Rosehill
	Dumfries						
Andrew	WALLET		Crown	Orkney	Drown.	10 Dec 1697	Irongray
John	WALLETT	DU				20 May 1685	

Halbert	WALLS	CT, DU				20 May 1685	
James	WARDROPE		H&F	at sea			
Archibald	Johnston WARISTON, Lord			Edinburgh	Exec.	22 Jul 1663	
William	WATERSTONE	GT, DU				20 May 1685	
James	WATSON	DU		Dunnottar	in escape	20 May 1685	
John	WATSON		Crown	Orkney	Drown.	10 Dec 1697	Evandale
Thomas	WATSON			Ayrsmoss	Battle	22 Jul 1680	
John	WATT	ET, DU				20 May 1685	
John	WATT			Edinburgh	Exec.	24 Nov 1684	Kilbride
Patrick	WATT		Crown	Orkney	Survived	10 Dec 1697	Kilmarnock
John	WATT		H&F				
John	WEDDALL	GF		Magus Moor		18 Nov 1679	Llidesdale
George	WEIR	GF					Carmichaell
Thomas	WEIR			Drumclog	Wounds1 Jun 1679		Lesmahagow
Andrew	WELCH		Crown	Orkney	Drown.	10 Dec 1697	Ochiltree
John	WELCH			Blackness			
William	WELSH			Dumfries	Hung	2 Jan 1667	Kirkpatrick
John	WELWOOD			Perth		Apr 1679	Dron
John	WHARRY			Glasgow	Exec.	14 Jun 1683	Lesmahagow
James	WHITE			Little Blackwood	Shot	Apr 1685	Fenwick
John	WHITE		Crown	Orkney	Drown.	10 Dec 1697	Kirkoswald
John	WHITE			Dunnottar	in escape	20 May 1685	
John	WHITELAW			Edinburgh	Exec.	30 Nov 1683	New Monkland
Elizabeth	WHITELAW		H&F				
Elizabeth	WHITLAW	DU				20 May 1685	Dumfries
John	WHYTE	GT, DU		Dunnottar	in escape	20 May1685	Paisley

George	WIER		Crown	Orkney	Drown.	10 Dec 1697	Lesmahagow
Robert	WIER		Crown	Orkney	Drown.	10 Dec 1697	Lesmahagow
James	WILKINSON			Edinburgh	Exec.	12 Aug 1685	
John	WILLIAMSON	DU				20 May 1685	Dalry
Thomas	WILLIAMSON	GF					Nether
Cranstoun							
Thomas	WILLIAMSON	GF					Over Cranstoun
Thomas	WILLIAMSON	GF					Over Waristoun
Thomas	WILLIAMSON		Crown	Orkney	Drown.	10 Dec 1697	Cranstoun
John	WILLIAMSONE	GF					Douglas
Robert	WILLSON	GF					Douglass
William	WILSON	CT, DU				20 May 1685	
James	WILSON	GF					Balgeddie
Patrick	WILSON	GF					Lewingstoun
John	WILSON			Edinburgh	Exec.	22 Dec 1666	Kilmaurs
John	WILSON			Edinburgh	Exec.	16 May 1683	Lanark
John Capt.	WILSON			Edinburgh	Exec.	17 Apr 1683	Lanark
Patrick	WILSON		Crown	Orkney	Drown.	10 Dec 1697	Livingstoun
Margaret	WILSON			Wigtown	Exec.	11 May 1685	Penningham
Thomas	WILSON		Crown	Orkney	Drown.	10 Dec 1697	Quathquhan
Joseph	WILSON			Corsegellioch Hill	Shot	Apr 1685	
William	WILSON		H&F				
James	WINNING			Glasgow	Exec.	19 Mar 1684	Glasgow
George	WISHART			St Andrews	Burnt	1 Mar 1546	
Grizel	WITHERSPOON			H&F			
John	WODROW			Edinburgh	Hung	22 Dec 1666	Glasgow

Francis WODROW		Crown	Orkney	Drown.	10 Dec 1697	Glasgow
James WOOD	GF					Lanark
Thomas WOOD			Edinburgh	Hung	15 Aug 1684	Kirkmichael
James WOOD			Magus Moor	Exec.	18 Nov 1679	Newmilns
George WOOD			Tinkhorn Hill	Shot	Jun 1688	Sorn
Thomas WOOD			Edinburgh	Exec.	9 Dec 1684	
Alexander WOOD			Glasgow	Exec.	24 Oct 1684	
George WODBURN			Midland	Shot	Nov 1685	Fenwick
Grisell WOTHERSPOON	DU				20 May 1685	
Thomas WYLIE	GF					Loudon
John WYLIE		Crown	Orkney	Drown.	10 Dec 1697	Fenwick
Thomas WYLIE		Crown	Orkney	Drown.	10 Dec 1697	Loudon
Thomas WYLIE		Crown	Orkney	Drown.	10 Dec 1697	Stewarton
Andrew WYLIE		Crown	Orkney	Drown.	10 Dec 1697	Stewarton
Robert WYLIE		Crown	Orkney	Drown.	10 Dec 1697	Stewartonr
John WYNET		Crown	Orkney	Drown.	10 Dec 1697	Monklands
William YOUNG	GF					Evandale
Robert YOUNG	GF					Gallosheills
William YOUNG	GF					Seamore
Robert YOUNG	GT, DU				20 May 1685	Alloway
Robert YOUNG	GT, DU				20 May 1685	
Robert YOUNG	GT, DU				20 May 1685	
Andrew YOUNG		Crown	Orkney	Drown.	10 Dec 1697	Airth
James YOUNG		Crown	Orkney	Survived	10 Dec 1697	Cavers
Richard YOUNG		Crown	Orkney	Drown.	10 Dec 1697	Caverse
Robert YOUNG		Crown	Orkney	Drown.	10 Dec 1697	Gallshiels

James	YOUNG		Crown	Orkney	Drown.	10 Dec 1697	Galstonr
William	YOUNG						Eaglesham
John	YOUNG		Crown	Orkney	Drown.	10 Dec 1697	Melross
William	YOUNG			Edinburgh	Hung	27 Aug 1684	Strathaven
Thomas	YOUNG			Mauchline	Hung	6 May 1685	
Andrew	YOUNG			In custody	Illness		
James	YOUNG			Orkney	Drown.	10 Dec 1679	
Robert	YOUNG	H&F					
William	YOUNGER	GF					Bathgate
William	YOUNGER	GF					
William	YOUNGER		Crown	Orkney	Drown.	10 Dec 1697	Livingstoun

CT	Canongate Tolbooth
Crown	ship aka Crown of London dep Leith 27 November 1679. Sank 10 Dec 1679 Deerness, Orkney.
DU	Dunnottar Castle
ET	Edinburgh Tollbooth
GF	Greyfriars Kirk Yard
GT	Glasgow Tollbooth
H&F	ship Henry & Francis dep. Leith 5 Sep 1685. Arrived Perth Amboy, N.J. mid December 1685.
LT	Leith Tollbooth

Appendix 8

Scottish Settlers on The Montgomery Estates ca 1607 Granted Denization in 1617

Cited in the Montgomery Manuscripts by Rev. Geo Hill (1869) from the Calendar of Patent Rolls, James I

John Wyly of Ballyhay. Nynnan Bracklie, Newton of Donghadie; Robert Boyle of Drumfad; John Montgomery of Ballymacrosse; Robert Harper of Provostoun; William Caderwood of Ballyfrenzeis; John Barkley of Ballyrolly; Hector Moore of Donan; William Hunter of Donan, William Moore of Milntowne; John Thompson of Blackabbey; Charles Domelston of; Walter Logane of Proveston; Thomas Nevin of Ballicopland; William Wymis of Newtowne; William Crawford of Cuningburn; Andrew Agnewe of Carnie; Gilbert Adare of Ardehine; Robert Wilson of Newtowne; James Williamson of Clay; Claud.Conyngham of Donoghdie; James Cathcart of Ballirogane; Patrick Montgomerie of Ballycreboy; William Cuninghame of Donoghdie; Robert Montgomery of Donoghdie;William Montgomery of Donoghdie; John Peacocke of Ballidonan; John Cuningham of Rinchrivie; Hugh Cunyngham of Castlespick; David Cunyngham of Drumfad; Patrick Shaw of Balliwalter; Hugh Montgomery of Granshaghe; John Maxwell of Ballihalbert; John Montgomery of the Redene; Michael Craig of the Redene; James Cowper of Ballichosta; Thomas Agnew, Grayabbey; Quintene Moore of Aughneill; Thomas Boyde of Crownerston; John Mowlen of Crownerston; Patrick Allan of Ballydonane; John Harper, John

Fraser, John Moore, James McMakene, and John Aickin, all of Donaghdie; John Harper of Ballyhay; James Maxwell of Gransho; David Boyde of Glasroche; Uthred M'Dowgall of Ballimaconnell; Thomas Kelso of Ballyhacamore; David M`Illveyne of Ballelogan; William Moore, preacher at Newton; Thomas Harvie of Newton; William Shaw of Ballykilconan; Andrew Sempill of Ballygrenie; David Anderson of Castlecanvarie; David Kennedy of Gortivillan; Allen Wilson of Newton; Mattbew Montgomery of Donoghdie; John Marten of Dunnevilly; Alexander Speire of Gray Abbey.

Appendix 9

Early Scots Settlers on the Montgomery Estates

Cited in the Montgomery Manuscripts
by Rev. Geo. Hill (1869)

It is to be regretted that no list of these original settlers can now be found. Among them, were several named Orr, who appear to have originally settled in the townlands of Ballyblack and Ballykeel, and were the Progenitors of a numerous connexion of this surname throughout the Ards

The earliest recorded deaths in this connexion, after their settlement in the Ards, were those of James Orr of Ballyblack, who died in the year 1627, and Janet M'Clement, his wife, who died in 1636. The descendants, male and female, of this worthy couple were very numerous, and as their intermarriages have been carefully recorded, we have thus, fortunately, a sort of index to the names of many other families of Scottish settlers in the Ards and Castlereagh.

Orr in the male line married with the families of:

Abernethy	Hanna	M'Quoid
Agnew	Harris	Miller
Barr	Irvine	Milling
Boyd	Jackson	Minnis
Bryson	Johnson	Moorehead

Busby
Cally
Campbell
Carr
Carson
Catherwood
Chalmers
Clark
Cleland
Corbet
Coulter
Cregg
Creighton
Cumming
Dunlop
Frame
Ferguson
Gamble
Gray
Hamilton
Kennedy
King
Lamont
Lindsay
Malcolm
Maxwell
Malcomson
M'Birney
M'Caw
M'Cleary
M'Connell
M'Creary
M'Cullough
M'Garock
M'Gowan.
M'Kee
M'Kibbin
M'Munn
M'Roberts
M'Whirter
Neilson
Patty
Patterson
Pollok
Porter
Rea
Reid
Rodgers
Shannon
Smith
Smyth
Stevenson
Stewart
Taylor
Todd
Wallace
Walker
Wilson
Winter

Orrs who married wives of the same surname and resided in:

Ballyalloly
Ballygowan
Ballybeen
Ballyblack
Ballycloughan
Ballykeel
Ballyknockan
Ballymisca
Bangor
Castleaveriey
Clontinacall
Conlig
Dundonald
Gilnahirk
Gortgrib
Granshaw
Killaghey
Killinether
Lisleen
Moneyrea
Munlough
Newtownards
Tullyhubbert

The descendants in the female line from James Orr and Janet McClement of Ballyblack married with the families of:

Appleton of Conlig
Barr of Bangor
Barr of Lisleen
M'Munn of Lisleen.
M'Quoid of Braniel
M'Quoid of Donaghadee

Black of Gortrib
Blakely of Madyroe
Boden of Craigantlet

Burgess of Madtroe
Burns of Cahard
Campbell
Clark of Clontinacally
Crawford of Carrickmadyroe
Davidson
Davidson of Clontinacally
Dickson of Tullygirvan
Dinwoody of Carrickmadyroe
Dunbar of Slatady
Dunwoody of Madyroe
Erskine of Woodburn
Frame of Munlough
Garret of Ballyknockan
Gerrit of Ballyknockan
Gregg
Hamilton of Ballykee
Hanna of Conlig
Hanna of Clontinacally
Harris of Ballymelady
Harrison of Holywood
Henderson of Ballyhaskin
Hill of Gilnahirk
Huddlestone of Moneyrea
Hunter of Clontinacally
and Ravara
Irvine of Crossnacreevy
Jamieson of Killaghy
Killaglicy
Jennings

Johnson of Rathfriland
Kennedy of Comber

Kennedy of Tullygirvan
Kilpatrick
Lewis

M'Kee of Lisleen
M'Kibbin of Haw
M'Kibbin of
Knocknasham
M'Kinning Lisnasharock
M'Kittrick of Lisleen
M'Lean of Ballykeel
MacWilliam of Ednaslate
Malcolm of Bootan
Malcolm of Moat
Martin of Ballycloughan
Martin of Gilnahirk
Martin of Killynure
Mathews
Miller of Conlig
Morrow of Belfast
Moore of Drummon
Murdock of Comber
Murdock of Gortrib
Neilson of Ravara
Orr of Ballybeen
Orr of Ballygowan
Orr of Ballykeel
Orr of Ballyknockan
Orr of Bangor
Orr of Castlereagh
Orr of Clontinacally
Orr of Florida
Orr of Iisleen

Orr of Munlough
Patterson of Moneyrea

Patterson of Moneyrea
and Lisbane
Patterson of Tonachmore
Pettigrew of
Ballyknockan
Piper of Comber
Piper of Moneyrea
Porter of Ballyristle

Lowry of Ballymacashan
M'Bratney of Raferey
M'Burney
M'Calla of Lisdoonan
M'Clure of Clontinacally
M'Cormick of Ballybeen
M'Creary
M'Creary of Bangor
M'Connell of Ballyhenry
M'Coughtrey of Ballyknockan
M'Cullock of Ballyhanwood
M'Culloch of Moneyrea
M'Fadden of Clontinacally
M'Gee of Todstown
M'Gown of Crossnacreevy
M'Kean
Porter of Beechhill
Reid of Ballygowan
Riddle of Comber
Shaw
Shaw of Clontinacally
Steel of Magherascouse
Stevenson of Ballyrush
Stewart of Clontinacally
Stewart of Clontinacally and Malone
Strain of Newtownards
Thomason of N'townards
Todd of Ballykeel
Watson of Carryduff
White
Wright of Craigantlet
Yates

Appendix 10

A List of the Scots to be Transplanted from the Counties if Antrim and Down Carrickfergus 23 May 1653

Extracted from the Pinkerton MSS. Cited in "Old Belfast" by R M Young (1896)

BELFAST AND MALONE QUARTERS

Lt. Thomas Cranston
Corp. Thomas M'Cormack
Hugh Doke
Robert Clugston
George Martin
Alexander Lockard
Robert King
Quintine Caterwood

WEST QUARTERS OF CARRICKFERGUS

John Murrey
John Russell
John Reade
Thomas Young, of Ballynehery
John Donelson
John Hanna
James Reade
James Patterson
William Biggard
George Russell
Archibald Crafford
George Gibson
Robert Dickie
John Clarke, Sr
Patrick Martine
Richard Cambell
Andrew Reade, Jr
John Homes
Robert Archball
Andrew Wilson
Alexander Miller

BROAD ISLAND AND EAST QUARTER OF CARRICKFERGUS

Hugh Donellson
Capt. Edmonstone
Ensign David Macley
Robert Gardner
David Harper
William Miller
John McKergor
John Dowgell
Matthew Logan

ISLAND MAGEE, MAGHERAMORNE, AND BALLYNURE

Capt. Robert Kinkede
James Browne
Ensign William Stephenson
Capt. James M'Cullogh
John Blare
William Agnew
John Agnew

SIX-MILE WATER QUARTERS

Capt. George Welch
Thomas Wyneam
Capt. Ferguson
Lt. Hewston
Lt. Robert Ferguson
Alexander Pingle
Andrew Taggart
Quintine Kenedy
James Cuthberd
John Cowtard
Robert Gragham
John Cowan
Thomas Rea

EARL OF ARDES' QUARTERS

Lord of Ardes
Capt. James Cambell
Capt. William Buchannon
Teige O'Monney
William Crafford
John Crafford
Brice Crafford
John Crafford
Mr. Francis Shaw
Gilbert McNeile
William Sloane
George Young
John Wilson
Peter Young
Mr. Arthur Upton

ANTRIM QUARTERS

Capt. Henry Sibbalds
John Davison
John Wagh, merchant
Robert Shannon

Capt. John Williams
Capt. John Fisher
Capt. James Collvill
Quar.Mst Mitchell
Major Clotworthy
Ensign John M'Cormett
Quar.Mst Ferguson
John Whyte
Capt. John McBride
David Mitchell
Lt. James Lynsey
Lt. James McAddams
Gilbert Eikles

SHANE'S CASTLE, LARGEE, AND TOOME QUARTERS

Lt. Col. Walter Stewart
Lt. Andrew Adayre
Henry Vernor
William McCullough
Lt. James Dobbins
Ensign John Bryen
Thomas Bollock
Ensign Robert Cunningham
Captain Robert Hewston
Lt. Robert Carr
Lt. James Pont
Lt. Hamill
Lt. Greenshields
Ensign Dobbin
Lt. Alex Cunningharn
Lt. Martine
Matthew Hamele, Leard of Raughwood

BRAID AND KEART AND CLENOGHORTI QUARTERS

Thomas Adair
Corporal James M'Cullogh
William Hamilton
John Sprule
Lt. Paul Cunningham
Capt. William Hewston
Capt. Thorn Fawebarne
Capt. David Johnston
James Ewart
Nimion Dunbare
Halbert Gledstone
Lt. Arthur Aghmuti
Lt. William Johnstone
Maj. Alexander Adaire
Cornet James Browne
Cornet John Stewart
Adam Johnstone

KILLELOGH AND KILMACKUETT QUARTERS

David Kenedy
Lt. Hugh Cambell
William Norris
Lt. Erwine
Lt. Mcllroy
Lt. Anthony Ellis
William Cunningham
George Cambell
George (if not John) Gordon, of Bowskeagh
Capt. Hercules Longford

GLENARM BARONY

Mr. James Shaw
Capt. John Shaw
Mr. Donnelson
Capt. John Agnew
William Greige
Randall Bushell
James Donellson
Capt. Lt. John Hume
James Fenton
John Mount Gomery
John Shaw
James Crumy
Francis Agnew

ROOTE QUARTERS

Major John Stewart
Lt. Col. Robert Kenedy
Capt. Alexander Stewart
Fergus McDougall
John Boyle
John Getty
Alexander Stewart, Sr
James Maxwell
Capt. Marrnaduke Shawe
John Henery
Cornet Robert Knole
William Hutchin
Alexander Scott
Donnel M'Cay
Lt. James Moncricoe
Robert Harvey
Maj. Hugh Mount Gomery
Thomas Boyd
Samuel Dunbarr
Alexander Dunlapp
Adam Dunlap
Patrick Glen
William Spherling
Andrew Rowan
Angus Cambell
Cornet John Gordon
Captain John Hewston
Lt. Col. Cunningham
John Kidd
Lt. Arch. Cambell
Mr. John Peebles
Mr. Cartaret
Capt. John Robbinson
Quar.Mst Robert Stewart

COLERAINE QUARTERS

John Johnstone
Thomas Abernethy
James Carr, of Arteslone
James Johnston
David Wilson
Robert Fulton
Andrew White

CASTLEREAGH, KILIORHNI, AND LISNEGARVY QUARTERS

Corporal Gilbert Matthew
John Streane
John Cowtard
James Gragham
John Cowan
Thomas Rea

LORD OF ARDES' QUARTERS

Lord of Ardes
Capt. James Cambell
Capt. Willtn. Buchannon
Lt. Hugh Dundas
Capt. John Keath
John Mountgomery, of Movill
James Mowell
Lt. McDowell, of Comber
William Catterwood
Mr. William Shaw
Fergus Kenedy
Capt. Hugh McGomery
Hugh Mountgomery
Lt. John Wilson
Lt. Andrew Cunningham
James McConchy

LITTLE ARDES, GRAY ABBEY, AND LISBOROUGH QUARTERS

Capt. Magill
Gilbert Harran
Robert Rosse
John Parke
Lt. John Mumpeny
James Maxwell

LORD CLANEBOYE'S QUARTERS

Lord Claneboye
Lt. Gawen Hamilton
Capt. John Bayly
Lt. Hugh Wallas
James Ross, Sr
Wm. Hamilton, of the Rowe
Mr. George Rosse
Patrick Allen
James Rosse, Jr
Gawen Hamilton
Capt. Alexander Stewart
Wm. Hamilton, Jr
Quar.Mst Edward McKee
James Hamilton, of Ballymegonnan
John Steephenson
Nimion Pate
Lt. Edward Baylye
Francis Purdy
Capt. John Stephenson
John Barkley
Ensign James Cooper
Lt. Robert Cunningham
Lt. Carre
Capt. Mathew Hamilton
Capt. Collin Maxwell
David Williamson

LECALE QUARTERS

Lt. Hugh Mountgomery	James Stewart
Lt. Launcelot Greere	John Dunbarr
Lt. Thomas Lynsey	John Tennent
Lt. Wodney	James Porter
Lt. John Reynolds	Stephen Major
Capt. John Wool	John McDowell

A List of the persons delivered by the Scottish Agents for the Counties of Down and Antrim, and desired to be dispensed with for their removing [appeal against removal]

BELFAST QUARTERS

Quintine Caterwood	Alexander Lockard

BROAD ISLAND QUARTERS

John McKergor	David McLay

SIX-MILE WATER QUARTERS

Capt. George Welch	Lt. Hewston

ANTRIM QUARTERS

Capt. John Williams	Ensign McCormack
Capt. John McBride	John Wagh

SHANE'S CASTLE QUARTERS

Capt. Robert Hewston

KILLELEAGH AND KILMAKEWET QUARTERS

David Kennedy	John Gordon
Lt. Cambell	

GLENARM QUARTERS

John Shaw

ROOT QUARTERS

John Boyle
John Getty
Alexander Scott
Anthony Kennedy
Andrew Kenan
Mr. Carcart

LORD OF ARDES' QUARTERS

James McConchy
John Montgomery
Capt. William Buchanan
Lt. Hugh Dundas
Lt. George Nowell
Lt. Andrew Cunningham

LITTLE ARDES QUARTERS

Gilbert Haron
Robert Maxwell
Lt. John Mompeny
Lt. John Wilson

LORD CLANEBOYE'S QUARTERS

Lt. Gawin Hamilton
Lt. Hugh Wallace
Quar.Mst McKee
Capt. Mathew Hamilton
David Williamson
Lt. Andrew Carre
Lt. Robert Cunningham

LECALE QUARTER

Lt. Thomas Lyndsay

Appendix 11

Presbyterian Ministers in Ireland. Salaries Paid 1655 - 1661

Extracted from A History of the Irish Presbyterians by W. T. Latimer (1902)

Name	Church	Notes
James Abernethy	Moneymore	Tithes 1660
James Blair	Dunbo	Tithes Dec 1658
Thomas Boyd	Aghadoey	Tithes1660
Wlliam Brown	Bellaghy	Tithes 1660
Robert Craighead	Donaghmore, Co. Donegal	Tithes Dec 1658
Archibald Hamilton	Benburb	Tithes 1660
John Hamilton	Donaghedie, Co.Tyrone	Tithes Dec 1658
John Law	Desert-oghill & Errigill	Tithes
Robert Rowan	Magheragh, Co Derry	Tithes 1658
Robert Wilson	Termon M'Gurk	Tithes 1658

Name	Church	Salary
Patrick Adair	Cairncastle	100
William Aldrich	Clones	80
John Ayton	Tynan	100
Dr William Baile		100 Pension
John Bames	Drumcree,Loughgall & Tandragee	100
James Baxter		20 Pension
Mungo Bennett	Loughgilly	

Eber Birch	Belturbet	80
Michael Bruce	Killinchie	100
Anthony Buckworth	Magheralyn	60 Tithes
David Buttle	Ballymenagh	100
William Caldwell	Mullabrack	
James Campbell	Loughbrickland	100
Andrew Carleton	Maghery-Kilmony, Fermanagh	100
George Creighton	Glenawly	60
Gabriel Cornwall	Balliwoolen	100
Thomas Craford	Donagore	60 - 80
Robert Cunningham	Broadisland	100
Ralph Davenport	Loghgaule	100
Robert Dewar	Connor	100
Essex Digby	Belfast	120
Willam Dix	Belfast	120 to Denyaghy
John Douglas	Braid	100
John Drisdale	Portaferry	100
Joseph Dunbar	Aghalee & Aghagallon	80
Patrick Duncan	Hillsborough	80 to Drumgollen
Robert Echlin	Strangford	80
Dr Jonathan Edwards	Drumgoone	120 to Navan
David Fearfull	Drumcade	50
James Fleming	Glenarme	100
John Fleming	Bailee	100
William Fullerton	Derrykeighan	80,100 1657
William Gillice	Killdallon	60
James Gordon	Comber	100
Hugh Graffan	Magheradoyle	25 Raised to 50
Thomas Gowan	Donnagh,Glasslough	Tithes
John Gregg	Newtown, Co Down	100
Thomas Hall	Lame	100
George Hamilton	1)evenish	80
Robert Hamilton	Killead	100 Tithes
David Hardy	Ballinderry	80 Died 1658
Cuthbert Harrison	Shankhill cum Lurgan	
Robert Hogsyeard	Ballyrashane	100
Edward How	Chademont	60 to Monaghan

Robert Huitson	Rathfriland	120
Alexander Hutchison	Tannaghneve (Saintfield)	60
William Jack	Aghadowey	100 to Longford
James Johnston	Lisnaske	60
Thomas Johnson	Dromore	100
John Jones	Segoe	80
James Kerr	Ballimoney	120
John Kerr	Monaghan	100
Patrick Ker	Dartry	100
Alexander Kieth	Newtown,Co Fermanagh	Tithes
Anthony Kennedy	Templepatrick	100
James Lang	Killeshandra	60
Andrew Law	Dundrum	
Dr Henry Leslie	Bishop of Down & Connor	120 Pension
Dr John Leslie	Bishop of Raphoe	160 Pension
Henry Livingston	Drumbo	100
Jeremiah Marsden	Armagh	150 to Carlow
Clinton Maund	Antrim	100 Tithes
Dr Robert Maxwell	Bishop of Kilmore	120 Pension
William Milne	Isle Magee	100
Andrew M'Cormick	Magheraly	100
Daniel M'Neill	Ballycastle	80 - 100
William Moore	Knockbredah	50
Jeremy O'Quinn	Billy	100 d 1658
Thomas Peebles	Kirkdonnell	100
Mr Pettard	Loughgall	Tithes
Gilbert Ramsay	Bangor, Co Down	100
Francis Reddington	Upper lveagh	100
William Richardson	Killyleagh	100
Donald Pichmond	Hollywood	
Anthony Shaw	Ballywalter	100
James Shaw	Carnmoney	100
John Shaw	Magherichohell (Ahoghill)	100
Robert Sheydon	Emiskillen	60
Hope Sherwood	Down	150 to Armagh

Gilbert Simpson	Ballyclare	100
Thomas Skelton	Newry	100
Andrew Stewart	Donaghadee	100
William Swaiden	Carlingford	100
Philip Tandy	Lisnegarvey	60 tithes
Timothy Taylor	Carrickfergus	200
James Threlfall	Kilmore, Co Armagh	60-100
Hugh Vanse	Route	100
John Wallwood	Glenavy	40 tithes to Co.Cavan
James Watson		50-80
Bamham West	Kilwarlin	120
David Wier	Carricknacross	80
Andrew Wike	Lisnegarvey Changed to Donacloney & Tullylish	100

Appendix 12

Ministers to whom Queen Anne Paid the Royal Bounty, Christmas 1712

Extracted from A History of the Irish Presbyterians
by W. T. Latimer (1902)

Co. Down		Co. Antrim	
Name	**Church**	**Name**	**Church**
William Biggar	Bangor	John Abemethy	Antnin
James Blair	Moyra	Patrick Adair	Carrickfergus
James Bruce	Killyleagh	Alexander Brown	Dunagore
Michael Bruce	Holywood	John Campbell	Carncastle
Alexander Colville	Dromore	James Cobham	Broad Island
Archibald Dixon	Tannaghnieve	Andrew Crawford	Carnmony
Robert Gordon	Rathfriland	James Creighton	Glenarm
John Goudy	Ballywalter	John Freeland	Killead
Thomas Gowan	Drumbo	Thomas Futt	Ballyclare
Henry Hamilton	Donaghadee	Robert Haltridge	Finvoy
James Johnson	Donaghmore	James Kirkpattick	Belfast
Robert Kemedy	Donoghcloney	Wiliam Leech	Ballymenagh
George Lang	Loughbrickland	Wm.Levington	Templepatnck
John Maires	Newtown	John Major	Ramoan
James Moore	Ballyrony	John Malcom	Dunmurry
Thomas Neven	Downpatrick	Charles Masterton	Connor
Thomas Orr	Comber	Robert Nelson	Kilraghts
Robert	Newry	Alexander Orr	Clogh
Hugh Ramsay	Drumca (Clouth)	Staford Petigrew	Ballyeastoun
James Reid	Killinchy	Thomas Shaw	Ahoghill
Thomas Seaton	Anahilt	Robert Sinclair	Isle Magee

Samuel Shannon	Portaferry	Thomas Sterling	Derrykeighan
William Smith	Ballee	James Stewart	Cushindall
James Stewart	Kirkdonald	William Taylor	Drummaul
Charles Wallace	Morne	Fulk White	Braid
Samuel Young	Magherally	Thomas Wilson	Ballyclare

Co. Londonderry		**Co. Donegal**	
Archibald Boyd	Maghera	John Ball	Lifford
William Boyd	Mcosquin	Robert Campbell	Raymochie
Mathew C lark	Kilrea	Seth Drummond	Tullyauchnish
Henry Crooks	Moneymore	John Dunlop	Donegal
John Harvey	Glendermott	Samuel Dunlop	Letterkenny
Robert Higinbotham	Coleraine	David Fairly	Raphoe
WilliamHouston	Ballywillin	Andrew Ferguson	Burt
Jarnes M'Gregor	Aghadowie	Neal Gray	Taughboine
Henry Neil	Ballyrashane	William Gray	Taughboine
John Sterling	Baliykelly	Thomas Harvey	Donagh
Hans Stewart	Bovelie	Francis Laird	Donaghmore
John Thomb	Dawson Bridge	Charles Lynd	Clandevaddogh
David Wilson	Drumacose		Robert
Wilson	Stranorlar		
James Woodside	Drumbo		

Co. Tyrone		**Co. Armagh**	
Wm. Ambrose	Kinaird	Moses Cherry	Clare
Baptist Boyd	Aghalow	James Flening	Lurgan
Robert Clothart	Golan	John Hutcheson	Armagh
Josias Cornwall	Aghalurcher	Archibald M'Clane	Markethill
Wm.Comwall	Clogher	William M'Kay	Vinecash
Thos Craighead	Castlederg	Thomas Millikan	Kedy
Samuel Haliday	Ardstraw	Hugh Wallace	Loughgall
Wm Holmes Sr	Strabane	Wm Holmes Jr	Urny
Thos Kenedy Sn	Donoghmore		

Co. Monaghan			
Thos Kenedy Jr	Ballyclog	Richard Darrock	Monaghan
James Maxwell	Omagh	Alexder Fleming	Stone Bridge
John M'Clave	Cookstown	Samuel Maghain	Drum
Alex. M'Crackan	Badony	Humphrey	
		Thompson	Tullycorbet
Thos Wensley	Donaghedy		

Co. Cavan		**Co. Fermanagh**	
James Teate	Killeshandry	John M'Gaughin	Enniskillen

Appendix 13

Presbyterian Ministers from the Northern Presbytery, Ejected January 1661

Extracted from A History of the Irish Presbyterians
By W. T. Latimer (1902)

Jeremy Taylor, Bishop of Down and Connor was to the fore in pursuing Presbyterian ministers for non conformity. In 1661 he and his colleagues caused some 80 non conformist ministers to give up their livings rather than conform to the prelates. The Presbyterians were:

John Abernethy	Desertlyn (Moneymore)
Patrick Adair	Cairncastle
John Adamson	Leckpatrick
Robert Auld	Magheracross (Fermanagh)
James Blair	Dunboe
Thomas Boyd	Aghadoey
Michael Bruce	Killinchy
David Buttle	Ballymena
James Campbell	Loughbrickland
John Cathcart	Randalstown
Ganriel Cornwall	Ballywillan
Robert Craghead	Donaghmore
William Crooke	Ballykelly
John Crookshanks	Raphoe
Thomas Crawford	Donegore

William Cumming	Kilraughts
Hugh Cunningham	Ray
James Cunningham	Antrim
Robert Cunningham	Broadisland
Robert Dewart	Connor
John Douglas	Broughshane
Thomas Drummond	Ramelton
John Drysdale	Portaferry
James Fleming	Glenarm
John Fleming	Ballee
Thomas Fulton	Drumachose
James Gordon	Comber
Thomas Gowan	Glasslough
John Greg	Newtownards
Thomas Hall	Larne
Archibald Hamilton	Clonfeacle (Benburb)
John Hamilton	Donagheady
Robert Hamilton	Killead
John Heart	Taughboyne
Robert Hogsyeard	Ballyshrane
Henry Hunter	Dromore
Alexander Hutchinson	Saintfield
William Jacque	Clongish (Co. Longford).
James Johnson	Lisnaskea
James Ker	Ballymoney
George Keith	Dungannon
Anthony Kennedy	Templepatrick
Thomas Kennedy	Donaghmore
William Keyes	Belfast
John Law	Garvagh
Henry Livingstone	Drumbo
Andrew McCormick	Magherally
William Moorcraft	Ardstraw & Badoney
Alexander Osborne	Ballyclog (Brigh)
Hugh Peebles	Aghalow
Thomas Peebles	Dundonald
William Reid	Ballywalter
William Richardson	Killileagh
Gilbert Ramsay	Bangor
William Semple	Letterkenny
James Shaw	Carnmoney

John Shaw	Ahoghill
Gilbert Simpson	Ballyclare
Andrew Stewart	Donaghadee
James Wallace	Urney
Adam White	Fannet
Hugh Wilson	Castlereagh
Robert Wilson	Camus (Strabane)
John Wool	Clondermot

Ten ministers are known to have conformed:

Mungo Bennett
William Brown
William Caldwell
Alexander Dunlop (probationer)
James Fleming
William Milne
Andrew Nesbitt (probationer)
Andrew Rowan
Robert Rowan
George Wallace

Appendix 14

THE DECLARATION OF BREDA, 1660

CHARLES, by the grace of God, King of England, Scotland, France, and Ireland, defender of the faith, &c.

To all our loving subjects of what degree or quality soever, greeting. If the general distraction and confusion which is spread over the whole kingdom doth not awaken all men to a desire and longing that those wounds which have so many years together been kept bleeding may be bound up, all we can say will be to no purpose. However, after this long silence, we have thought it our duty to declare how much we desire to contribute thereunto; and that, as we can never give over the hope in good time to obtain the possession of that right which God and nature hath made our due, so we do make it our daily suit to the divine Providence, that he will, in compassion to us and our subjects, after so long misery and sufferings, remit, and put us into a quiet and peaceable possession of that our right, with as little blood and damage to our people as is possible: nor do we desire more to enjoy what is ours, than that all our subjects may enjoy what by law is theirs, by a full and entire administration of justice throughout the land, and by extending our mercy where it is wanted and deserved. And to the end that the fear of punishment may not engage any conscious to themselves of what is past to a perseverance in guilt for the future, by opposing the quiet and happiness of their country in the restoration both of king, peers, and people to their just, ancient, and fundamental rights, we do by these presents declare, that we do grant a free and general pardon, which we are ready upon demand, to pass under our great seal of England, to all our subjects, of what degree or quality soever, who within forty days after the publishing hereof shall lay hold upon this our grace and favour, and shall by any public act declare their doing so, and that they return to the loyalty and obedience of good subjects; excepting only such persons as shall hereafter be excepted by Parliament. Those only excepted, let all our subjects, how faulty soever, rely upon the word of a king, solemnly given by this present Declaration, that no crime whatsoever committed against us or our royal father, before the publication of this, shall ever rise in judgement, or be brought in question, against any of them to the least endamagement of them, either in their lives, liberties, or estates, or (as far forth as lies in our power) so much as to the prejudice of their reputations, by any reproach, or term of distinction from the rest of our best subjects; we desiring and ordaining, that henceforward all notes of discord, separation, and difference of parties, be utterly abolished among all our subjects; whom we invite and conjure to a perfect union among themselves, under our protection, for the resettlement of our just rights and theirs, in a free parliament; by which, upon the word of a king, we will be advised. And because the passion and uncharitableness of the times have produced several opinions in religion, by which men are engaged in parties and animosities against each other; which, when they shall hereafter unite in a freedom of conversation will be composed, or better understood; we do declare a liberty to tender consciences; and that no man shall be disquieted, or called in question, for differences of opinion in matters of religion which do not disturb the peace of the kingdom; and that we shall be ready to consent to such an act of parliament, as, upon mature deliberation, shall be offered to us, for the full granting that indulgence. And because in the continued distractions of so many years, and so many and great revolutions, many grants and purchases of estates have been made to and by many officers, soldiers, and others, who are now possessed of the same, and who may be liable to actions at law, upon several titles; we are likewise willing that all such differences, and all things relating to such grants, sales, and purchases, shall be determined in parliament; which can best provide for the just satisfaction of all men who are concerned. And we do farther declare, that we will be ready to consent to any act or acts of parliament to the purposes aforesaid, and for the full satisfaction of all arrears due to the officers and soldiers of the army under the command of General Monk; and that they shall be received into our service upon as good pay and conditions as they now enjoy.

Given under our sign manual, and privy signet, at our court at Breda, the 4/14th day of April 1660, in the twelfth year of our reign.

Appendix 15

Covenanter Grave sites - map references.

Most listed below are accessible but there are others which may be reached only by experienced hill walkers

Ref	Place Name	MapRef
1	Dunnottar	NO8884
2	Dunscore	NX9383
3	Ayr	NS3422
4	Ayrsmoss	NS6425
5	Balmaclellan	NX6579
6	Barr	NX2794
7	Barrhill	NX2382
8	Blackwood	NS7843
9	Carsgailoch Hill	NS5515
10	Colmonell	NX1485
11	Cumnock	NS5720
12	Fenwick	NS4643
13	Galston	NS5637
14	Irvine	NS3239
15	Kilmarnock	NS4237
16	Kirkmichael	NS3408
17	Lochgoin	NS5347
18	Loudon	NS4938
19	Mauchline	NS4927
20	Muirkirk	NS7028
21	Newmilns	NS5437
22	Priesthill	NS7332
23	Sorn	NS5526
24	Straiton	NS3804
25	Tarbolton	NS4327
26	Waistland	NS6613
27	Stonehouse	NS7547
28	Stonepark	NS5920
29	Blagannoch	NS7818
30	Craighaugh	NY2599
31	Dalgarnock	NX8894
32	Dalveen	NS8907
33	Dumfries	NX9776
34	Durisdeer	NS8904
35	Friarminnin	NS7419
36	Glencair	NX8191
37	Ingliston	NX7890
38	Moniaive	NX7791
39	Sanquhar	NS7910
40	Troqueer	NX9675
41	Tynron	NX8093
42	Wanlockhead	NS8712
43	Bass Rock	NT6087
44	North Berwick	NT5585
45	Claremont	NO4615
46	Cupar	NO3613
47	Magus Moor	NO5615
48	St Andrews	NO5116
49	Cambusnethan	NS7754
50	Campsie	NS6180
51	Anwoth	NX5856
52	Auchencloy	NX6071
53	Balmaghie	NX7163
54	Caldons Wood	NX4079
55	Crossmichael	NX7366
56	Girthon	NX6053
57	Irongray	NX9179
58	Kells	NX6379
59	Kirconnel Moor	NX6760
60	Kirkandrew	NX6048
61	Kirkcudbright	NX6851
62	St Johns Dalry	NX6281
63	Twynholm	NX6654
64	Wellwood	NS6726
65	BrigBothwell	NS7758
66	Drumclog	NS6340
67	Glasgow	NS5965
68	Glassford	NS7347
69	Hamilton	NS7755
70	Inchbelly	NS6775
71	Kirk of Shotts	NS8463
72	Lanark	NS8843
73	Lesmahagow	NS8139
74	Lochenkit	NX8175
75	Logan House	NS7435
76	Medwynhead	NT0852
77	Strathaven	NS7444
78	Bathgate	NS9769
79	Edinburgh	NT2773
80	Rullion Green	NT2263
81	Deerness	HY5708
82	Tweedsmuir	NT1024
83	Dron	NO1415
84	Ecclesmagirdle	NO1116
85	Forgandenny	NO0818
86	Cathcart	NS5860
87	Eaglesham	NS5752
88	Paisley	NS4863
89	Craigmoddie	NX2473
90	Wigtown	NX4355

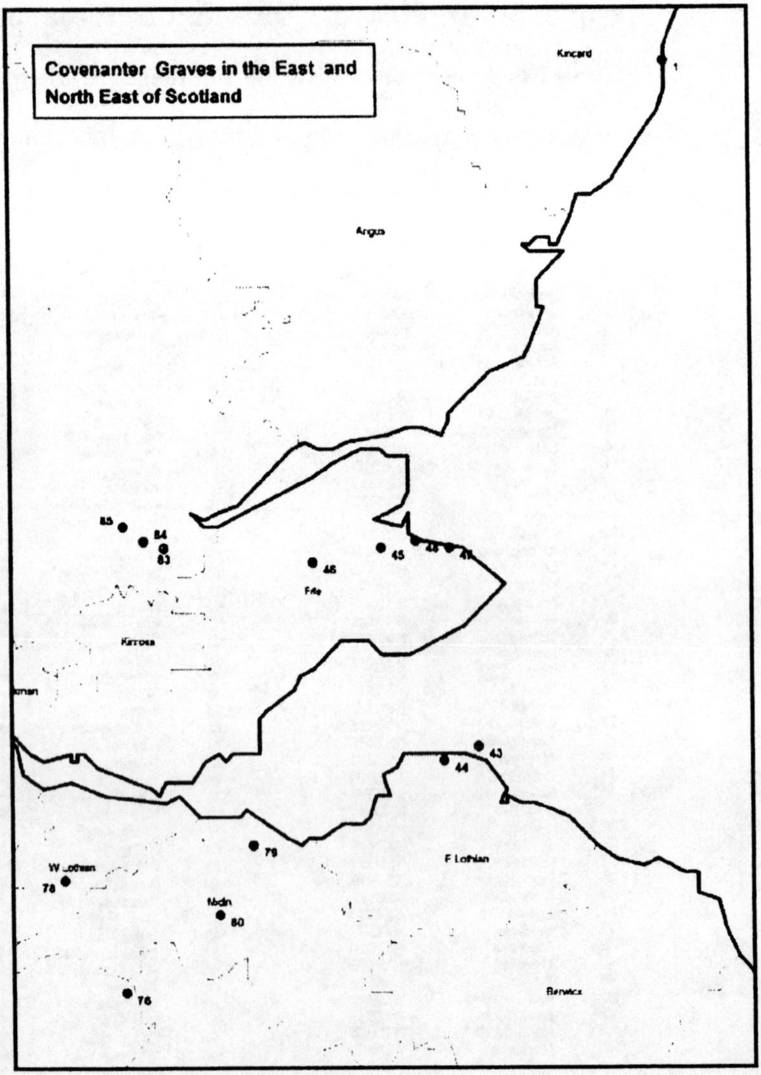
Covenanter Graves in the East and North East of Scotland
Angus
1
85
84
83
46
45
79
78
80
76
44
43

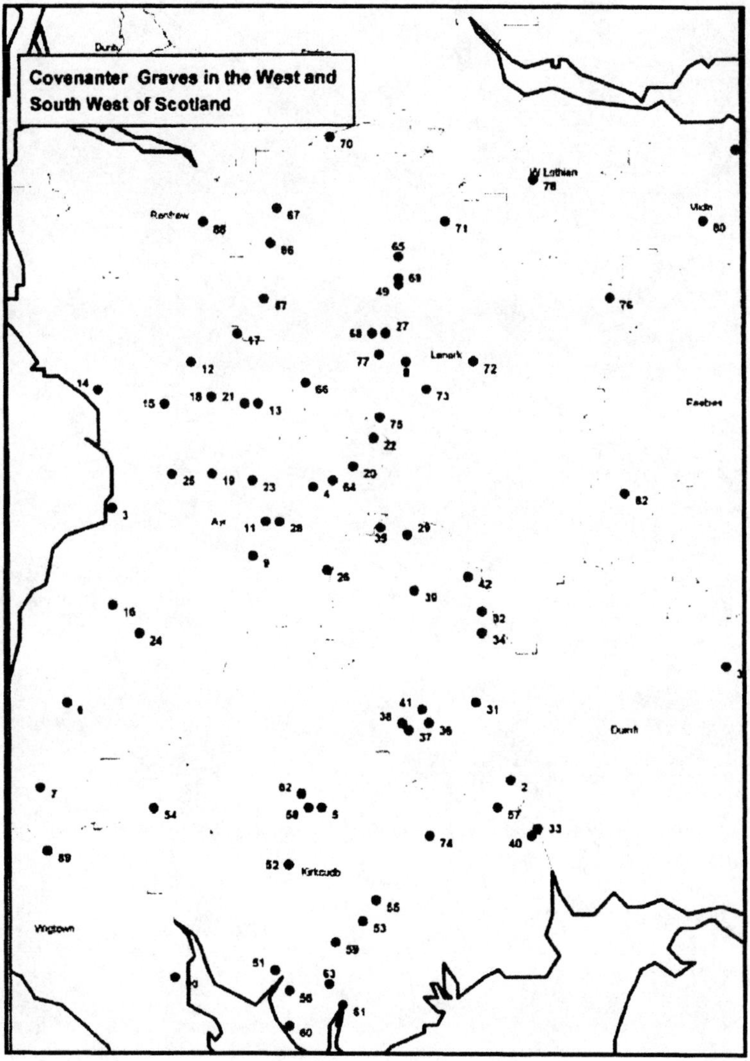
Covenanter Graves in the West and
South West of Scotland
Renfrew
W Lothian
Lanark
Kirkcudb
Wigtown

Bibliography

For those readers who can use the facilities the obvious resources are the National Archives, the Edinburgh Public Library and the National Library of Scotland. The on line catalogue of the National Library is especially helpful in identifying sources and may be accessed on the Internet at www. nls.uk. Local libraries and Family History associations in the south west of Scotland also hold publications of interest.

The bibliography below is in four broad categories and offered as a source of further reading. Some books may well be out of print but available from antiquarian booksellers and companies specialising in re prints. It is always worthwhile to enquire of your local library about a book which may be available through an inter library loan service.

Covenanter specific:

Anderson, Rev. James. *The Ladies of the Covenant.* New York, Redfield. (1851).

Balmaghie Kirk Session. *The Kirk above Dee Water.* .Balmaghie, Scotland. Undated.

Calderwood, David, Ed. Rev. Thos. Thomson. *The History of the Kirk of Scotland.* Edinburgh. Wodrow Society. (1842)

Cameron, Thomas. *Peden the Prophet* Edinburgh. Blue Banner Productions. (1998)

Campbell, Thorbjorn. *Standing Witnesses*. Edinburgh, Saltire Society. (1996)

Carslaw, Rev. W H. *The Life and Letters of James Renwick the Last Scottish Martyr*. Helensburgh, Oliphant, Anderson & Ferrier. (1893).

Cook, Faith. *Samuel Rutherford and his Friends*. Edinburgh, Banner of Truth Trust. (1992)

Daviot, Gordon. *Claverhouse*, Collins, London. (1937)

Furgol, Edward M. *A Regimental History of the Covenanting Armies 1639 – 1651*. Edinburgh, John Donald Publishers Ltd. (1990)

Howie, John of Lochgoin. *The Scots Worthies*. Revised W. H. Carslaw, Banner of Truth Trust, Edinburgh Reprint (1995)

Johnston, John C. *Alexander Peden, The Prophet of the Covenant*. Ireland, Mourne Missionary Trust Reprint. (1988)

Johnston, Rev. John C. *Treasury of the Scottish Covenant*. Edinburgh, Andrew Elliott. (1887).

M'Crie, Rev. Thomas. *Life of John Knox*. Edmonton,Canada. Still Waters Revival Books, Reprint. (1996)

M'Crie, Rev. Thomas. *Life of Andrew Melville*. Edmonton, Canada. Still Waters Revival Books, Reprint. (1996)

M'Crie, Rev. Thomas. *Sketches of Church History*. Edinburgh, John Johnstone. (1846)

McGregor, A. A. *The Buried Barony*. London, Robert Hale Ltd. (1949)

Moir, W Bryce. *The Flodden Wall. The Covenanters Prison on Greyfriars Yard Edinburgh*. Edinburgh, T & A Constable. (1910)

Pollok, Robert. *Ralph Gemmell, a story of Covenanting times.* Scotland, John Ritchie. Undated.

Roy, David. *The Covenanters.* Scotland, The Covenanter Theological Institute, Reprint. (2000)

Rutherford, Rev. Samuel. *Lex, Rex or The Law and the Prince.* Harrisonburg,VA, Sprinkle Publications, Reprint of 1644 edition. (1982)

Rutherford, Rev. Samuel. *Letters of Samuel Rutherford.* Edinburgh, Banner of Truth Trust, Reprint of letters published in 1644. (1996)

Sawyer, Beatrice Mair. *Seven Men of the Kirk.* Edinburgh, Church of Scotland Youth Committee. (1959)

Simpson, Rev. Robert. *Traditions of the Covenanters.* Edinburgh, Gall & Inglis. (1867)

Smellie, Rev. A. *Men of the Covenant.* London, A Melrose. (1903)

Spottiswoode, John. *History of the Church of Scotland*, London, Mernston Scolar Press, Reprint 1655 edn. (1972) National Library of Scotland.

Stewartry District Council. *Covenanting Sites in the Stewartry of Kirkcudbright.* Scotland, Stewartry Museum Service. (1995)

Thomson, John H. *A Cloud of Witnesses for the Royal Prerogative of Jesus Christ.* Virginia, Sprinkle Publications, Reprint. (1989)

Thompson, Rev. J. H. *The Martyr Graves of Scotland.* Edinburgh, Johnstone, Hunter & Co. (1877) National Library of Scotland.

Vos, Johnannes G. *The Scottish Covenanters.* Edinburgh, Blue Banner Productions, Reprint. (1998)

Wylie, James A. *Story of the Covenant.* Edinburgh, Blue Banner Productions. (1998)

Historical:

Dick, Rev. C. H. *Highways & Byways in Galloway & Carrick.* London, MacMillan & Co Ltd. (1927)

Durisdeer, Ian. *More Stewartry Sketches.* Scotland, The Forward Press. Undated.

Kenyon, Ed. & Ohlmeyer. *The Civil Wars, A military History of England, Scotland and Ireland 1638 – 1660.* Oxford, University Press. (1998)

Maclean, Colin. *Going to Church.* Edinburgh, National Museum of Scotland. (1997)

Prothero, G. W. *Select Statutes and other Constitutional Documents of the reign of Elizabeth I and James I.* London, Oxford University Press, Reprint. (1946)

Robertson, Sir Charles Grant. *Select Statutes Cases and Documents.* London, Methuen & Co Ltd. (1904)

Shapiro, Hyman. *Scotland in the days of James VI.* London, Longman Group Ltd. (1970)

Smout, T. C. *A History of the Scottish People 1560-1830.* London, Fontana Press. (1985)

Terry, C. Stanford. *A History of Scotland from the Roman evacuation to the Disruption. 1843.* Cambridge, University Press. (1920)

Wilkinson, John T. *1662 and After, Three Centuries of English Nonconformity.* London, Epworth Press. (1962)

Ireland:

Many churches in Ulster have produced publications about their history.

Black, J. S. P. *Speaking Yet. Limavady Presbyterians.* Ireland, North West Books. (1986)

Carson, John T. *Presbyterian and proud of it.* Belfast, The Sabbath School Society for Ireland. (1948)

Corish, Patrick J. Ed. *A History of Irish Catholicism.* Dublin, Gill & MacMillan. (1971).

Curl, James S. *The Londonderry Plantation 1609-1914.* England, Phillimore & Co Ltd. (1986)

Dickson, R. J. *Ulster Emigration to Colonial America 1718-1775.* Belfast, Ulster Historical Foundation. (1966)

Houston, C. J. & W. J. Smyth. *Irish Emigration and Canadian Settlement.* Toronto, University of Toronto Press. (1991)

Hamilton, Rev. Thomas. *History of Presbyterianism in Ireland.* N. Ireland, Ambassador Productions Ltd. (1992)

Hamilton, Rev. T. *History of the Irish Presbyterian Church.* Edinburgh, T & T Clark. Undated.

Latimer, Rev. W. T. *A History of the Irish Presbyterians.* Belfast, James Cleland. (1902)

Larne Kirk Session. *Historical Sketch of the First Presbyterian Congregation of Larne.* Belfast, M'Caw, Stevenson & Orr Ltd. (1889)

Lecky, W. E. H. *A History of Ireland in the Eighteenth Century.* London, Longmans Green & Co, Reprint. (1913)

Lockington, John W. *Robert Blair of Bangor.* Belfast, Presbyterian Historical Society. (1996)

Long, S. E. *The Emergence of Presbyterianism in Post Plantation Ulster*. Belfast, Education Committee, Grand Orange Lodge of Ireland. Undated.

Loughridge, Adam. *The Covenanters in Ireland.* Belfast, Cameron Press. (1984)

MacCuarta, Brian Ed. *Ulster 1641, Aspects of the Rising.* Belfast, Queens University Institute of Irish Studies. (1993)

Maitland, W H. *History of Magherafelt.* Londonderry, Moyola Books, Reprint. (1988)

McCartney, D. J. *Nor Principalities Nor Powers, The First Presbyterian Church, Carrickfergus (1621-1991).* Belfast, McCartney. (1991)

Moore, Tom. *A History of the First Presbyterian Church Belfast 1644-1983.* Belfast, The Kirk Session. (1983).

Perceval-Maxwell, M. *The Scottish Migration to Ulster in the Reign of James I.* London, Routledge & Kegan Paul. (1973)

Reilly, Tom. *Oliver Cromwell, An Honourable Enemey.* Ireland, Brandon. (1999)

Robinson, Philip. *The Plantation of Ulster.* Belfast, Ulster Historical Foundation. (1984)

Stevenson, John. *Two Centuries of Life in Down 1600-1800.* Belfast, McCaw, Stevenson & Orr Ltd. (1920)

Wilson, William. *1623-1973, 350th Anniversary of First Bangor Presbyterian Church.* Bangor, N. Ireland, Kirk Session. (1973)

<u>*Antiquarian sources:*</u>

Hewison, James King. *The Covenanters. A History of the Church in Scotland from the Reformation to the Revolution.* Edmonton, Canada, Still Waters Revival Books, Reprint of 1908 version. (1996)

Hill, Rev. George. *The Montgomery Manuscripts*. Belfast, James Cleland. (1869)

Hill, Rev. George. *The MacDonnells of Antrim*. Belfast, Archer & Sons. (1873)

Lowry, T. K. Ed. *The Hamilton Manuscripts*. Belfast, Archer & Sons. (1867)

Morley, Henry Ed. *Ireland under Elizabeth and James the First.* London, George Routledge & Sons Ltd. (1890)

Shields, Rev. Alexander. *A Hind Let Loose*. Edmonton, Canada, Still Waters Revival Books, Reprint of 1797 version. (1996).

Walker, Rev. Patrick. Ed. Hay Fleming. *Six Saints of the Covenant,* London, Hodder & Stoughton. (1901)

Wodrow, Rev. Robert. *History of the Sufferings of the Church of Scotland*. Glasgow, Blackie & Son, Reprint. (1836) National Library of Scotland.

Young, R. Ed. *Old Belfast*.Belfast. Marcus Ward & Co. (1896)

Index

About the Author

Brian Orr is the eldest son of an Ulster Scot from Belfast whose ancestry stretches back to the early Scottish settlers of the Counties Down and Antrim ca1607. A career civil servant in the UK he took early retirement in 1995 and renewed research into his direct family line first begun nearly thirty years ago. On being confronted by the genealogist's "brick wall" with his Ulster researches he began to look into the origins of the family and the historical setting in which they lived. A member of the Scottish Genealogy Society and the Ulster Genealogical and Historical Guild as well as several regional societies, he joined the Guild of One Name Studies in 1998, registering the Orr name for worldwide research, since then he has accumulated a very substantial international database.

With the early origins of the family traced to the west and southwest of Scotland it was inevitable that extensive research of the Ulster Plantation led him to explore the reasons for migration. From this flowed a wider interest in the history of Ulster and Scotland in the 17th and 18th centuries, the persecution of the early Presbyterian kirk and the Covenanters. Although he has had a range of articles about Scotland published on web sites this is his first book. Married with two daughters and two grandsons he lives in Formby in the North West of England where he considers himself fortunate to be able to visit Scotland regularly on research trips and for holidays.